The Good Study Guide

ANDREW NORTHEDGE

Author: Andrew Northedge
Project Managers: Penny Bennett, Susan Lowe
Course Manager: Corinne De Souza
Course Co-ordinator: Maureen Richards
Production Team:
    Composition: Diane Hopwood
    Editor: Kathleen Calder
    Design: Vicki McCulloch, Glen Darby
    Graphics: Jon Owen
    Production Assistants: Elizabeth Rowell-Tinsley, Kathryn Smith, Linda Cambourne-Paynter
    Open University Worldwide

This publication forms part of an Open University course K100 Understanding Health and Social Care. Details of this and other Open University courses can be obtained from the Student Registration and Enquiry Service, PO Box 625, Milton Keynes, MK7 6YG, United Kingdom: tel. +44 (0)1908 653231, e-mail general-enquiries@open.ac.uk

Alternatively, you may visit the Open University website at http://www.open.ac.uk where you can learn more about the wide range of courses and packs offered at all levels by The Open University.

To purchase a selection of Open University course materials visit www.ouw.co.uk, or contact Open University Worldwide, Michael Young Building, Walton Hall, Milton Keynes MK7 6AA, United Kingdom for a brochure. tel. +44 (0)1908 858785; fax +44 (0)1908 858787; e-mail ouwenq@open.ac.uk

The Open University
Walton Hall, Milton Keynes
MK7 6AA

First published 2005. Reprinted 2005, 2007

Edited and designed by The Open University.

Typeset in Europe by the Alden Group, Oxford.

Printed and bound in Malta by Gutenberg Press.

ISBN 0 7492 5974 4

2.3

The paper used for this book is FSC-certified and totally chlorine-free. FSC (the Forest Stewardship Council) is an international network to promote responsible management of the world's forests.

CONTENTS

PREFACE

This second edition of *The Good Study Guide* is much more than an update of the original. The whole book has been rethought and substantially rewritten. Piecemeal updating was never an option, given the book's use of integrated examples and the critical importance of coherence in the advice. Since nothing less than a complete overhaul was feasible, I have taken the opportunity not only to bring the book up to date, fifteen years on, but to strengthen it and widen its relevance.

Purpose

The Good Study Guide retains its primary purpose as a guide for students with a serious interest in long-term development of their learning and study skills. It is not a source of quick fixes and instant remedies. It assumes a willingness to invest time in working on exercises and reflecting on them. It is a thoughtful, theoretically grounded, exploration of the nature of studying and, at the same time, a practical guide to reflective experimentation with techniques, drawing as it does on many years of exploring skills with students.

Changes

The first edition of *The Good Study Guide* reached an audience far broader than the part-time, adult, distance-learning students for whom it was written. Consequently, this new edition has been recast to address the needs of *all students* aspiring to study beyond school-level. It has also been restructured to reflect the *sweeping changes in university study* over a decade and a half. Thus it now has *five more chapters* than before and has been organised into *two parts*. So, with the updating of *case material* and consequent reworking of all the study exercises, this is a long way towards being a new book. However, the basic strategy and underlying assumptions about the nature of learning remain.

Part 1: Studying intelligently

The first part of *The Good Study Guide* addresses the broad strategic aspects of successful study and consists of four new chapters. Three of these address one of the key changes of the past decade, the *relocating of study skills* from their former status on the periphery as 'remedial' activities for beginners, *to the mainstream* under the new marque 'learning skills'. Developing skills as a learner is now recognised as essential preparation for life in the twenty-first century. This is reflected in the title of Chapter 1: 'Investing in yourself'. These skills are not simply practical, but also strategic, requiring a capacity for self-management; hence Chapter 2: 'Taking control of your studies'. They are also 'reflective' skills, which depend on self-knowledge, self-analysis and an understanding of the learning process; thus

Chapter 4: 'Understanding how you learn'. This chapter includes an introduction to the principles of critical-analytical reading and writing, reflecting growing recognition of the importance of supported entry into academic discourse for an increasingly diverse student body.

The other key change of recent times is the revolution in study practices brought about by *computing* and *the internet*. This is addressed in Chapter 3: 'Using a computer to study'. Students are often aware of only a few of the many ways they could use a computer to support their studies. This chapter, influenced by my own experiences of designing and teaching online courses, encourages students to explore and experiment. Meanwhile, the rest of the book has been reworked to reflect changes to basic study activities brought about by word-processing, global access to online information, electronic information storage, and the like. And *The Good Study Guide* is now accompanied by a website to which students are directed for resources.

Part 2: The essential skills

The second part gets down to the practical business of developing skills in the core activities of studying. As in the original edition, readers are asked to undertake genuine study activities, most of them based around a single text. Though the former article on the growth of shopping centres remains remarkably relevant, it has been replaced by a new one: 'The Secrets of Happiness' by Richard Layard (2003). Generally the content of the original chapters remains, however, 'Making notes' has been separated off from 'Reading', to give it wider relevance and to allow exploration of electronic note making. Also, the chapter formerly titled 'Other modes of learning' has been recast under the title 'Learning through talk', with extensive new material on group discussions and making presentations. In 'Working with numbers and charts', as well as updating the data, students are introduced to online data sources. Then there is a new chapter, 'Researching online', introducing the basics of searching for online resources.

The two chapters on writing remain the longest and perhaps the most important, since the acquisition of an academic writing voice and the ability to assemble material and present it in the form of an argument is in many ways the culmination of the transition into competent academic practice. Retitled, as 'Writing the way 'they' want' and 'Managing the writing process', they retain the same broad division into the 'what' and 'how' of academic writing. However, the first has been completely reorganised to make the treatment more transparent and accessible. Both take advantage of resources on the Good Study Guide website (www.goodstudyguide.co.uk), to simplify exercises that were previously rather cumbersome. The final chapter, 'Preparing for an exam', is the least changed, though again there is re-working.

Notes

Level

I have assumed that many readers will be starting studies at post-school level. However, students in the later years of schooling may find the book useful preparation for the switch to higher level studies. Equally students who have progressed beyond the entry stages of a degree will find much to reflect on. I can say that, many years on from student days, working on the book has reminded me of skills I needed to hone.

Assumptions about computing

I have assumed that all readers will have at least some access to a computer and to the internet. Many will already be using a computer for routine study tasks, while others will be looking for advice on ways in which they might profitably switch to computer-based working.

The Good Study Guide website

This book has an accompanying website (www.goodstudyguide.co.uk). This is intended to be used as a kind of service centre. At various points in the book, readers are prompted to download resources in order to work on them in activities.

Updating of references

The internet has made the task of keeping references up to date much more challenging. We will post an annually updated list of references on the website.

Terms used

Because the original *Good Study Guide* was used in schools, colleges and campus universities, I have dropped the use of specific Open University terminology and adopted more general terms. However, one or two are somewhat awkward. For example, I have avoided the term 'lecturer', on account of its narrow connotations, even though it is the typical descriptor of a teacher's post. And I have used 'tutor' only in the context of discussion groups, because its usage varies institutionally. Instead, I have used 'teacher' throughout – echoing usage in, for example, The Institute for Learning and *Teaching* in Higher Education.

Personal acknowledgements

The original edition of this book benefited enormously from the comments of Open University colleagues and students, and now the same is true all over again of the new edition. So, it is important that I include all those acknowledged in the original addition, before adding the recent ones.

First edition

For support with the original book, I must thank all the members of the D103 Foundation Course Team, who read drafts and gave detailed advice: in particular Marilyn Ricci, James Anderson, David Coates and Elaine Storkey. Then there were the members of the 'tutor panels', who undertook heroic assignments of rapid reading and commentary: Lyn Brennan, Alan Brown, Ian Crosher, Donna Dickinson, Norma Sherratt, Jan Vance, Mona Clark, Phil Markey and Brian Graham. Also, thanks to Chris Wooldridge, who as editor gave painstaking attention to the all-important details. Finally, Ellie Chambers of the Open University's Institute of Educational Technology who not only read and appraised every word of every draft, but as my partner made family life bearable for all of us.

Second edition

For this new edition I am indebted to the production team for their unflagging support over a long period: Mick Jones, Corinne De Souza, Maureen Richards, Deb Bywater, Sara Mills, Elizabeth Rowell-Tinsley and Linda Camborne-Paynter. And again I received invaluable advice from colleagues who read draft chapters and provided detailed commentaries: Ann Allen, Chris Baker, Sally Baker, Liz Burton-Pye, Terry di Paolo, Paula Faller, Lynne Fisher, Ingrid Jefferys, Wendy Martin, Karen Miller, Gill Needham, Jo Parker, Jenny Pearce, Lucy Rai, Pam Read, Katie Sainsbury, Kate Stilliard, Ravina Talbot, and especially Fiona Harkes, who not only read and commented on everything but also provided extensive consultation by telephone. Kathleen Calder as editor worked tirelessly to achieve clarity, consistency and accessibility, and once again Ellie Chambers read and advised on every word, as well as providing support in every other way.

I am also grateful to students of the Birmingham Reachout project at Northfield and Newtown, who read the Richard Layard article and gave me their reaction; in particular those at Northfield who also wrote essays for me to use in the book and whose names are in the list below. Thanks too to Marion Bowl and Peta Wymer for making this possible. And thanks to the students who completed my questionnaire asking for their reflections on the learning process and to those who agreed to let me quote their online messages. (Note that names which appear in the book itself are fictional.) The following students of various institutions contributed in one way or another: Billy Anderson, Lorna Archibald, Shirley Bain, Gillian Brewin, Shona Brydson, Jacqui Campbell, Janice Clerk, Jo Chandler, Roseann Cooper, Lesley Dickinson, Ceri Edwards, Ceri Evans, Suzie Eaton, Carol Ferguson, Nicky Gane, Julie Gibbins, Gwyneth Girling, Simon Harris-Dack, Melanie Harvey, Hayley Hill, Gillian Howie, Patricia Jordan, Matthew Lane, Nicola Lloyd, Pauline Knox, Tracy Mogridge, Shirley Moody, Sophie Nichol, Charlotte Northedge, Laura Northedge, Shona Paterson, Tracy Reynolds, Angela Parker, Jan Reis, Janie Richter, Chris Robinson, Kelda Sinclair, Tina Smith, David Shortall, Diane Sloey, Peter Staffell, Ann-Marie Stewart, Deirdre Stewart, Mandy Sutch, Stella Taylor, Matthew Thompson, Jennie Tomlinson,

Laura Ward, Ruth Webb, Gail White, Julie Williams, Pepe Wilson and Correne Witchard.

Finally, I am grateful to Richard Layard for permission to use his article as a basis for study exercises.

Andrew Northedge

STUDENT VOICES

You will see quotations from students scattered about the book. These are largely taken from Open University internet chat areas, with the permission of the students. They are intended to offer informal reflection and light relief – a kind of background chorus of those up to their arms in the toils and triumphs of study. They are simply dropped in where relevant and signalled by italics. The names of contributors are acknowledged above.

PART 1 STUDYING INTELLIGENTLY

CHAPTER 1 INVESTING IN YOURSELF

Welcome to *The Good Study Guide*! This is a book of advice, tips and practical exercises to help you develop your study skills and get the most you can from your studies: better results, a greater sense of personal achievement and more enjoyment.

1.1 Who this book is for

If you are starting out on higher level studies, or part way through a degree and looking to boost your performance, this book is for you. It will be equally helpful whether you are studying:

- full time, or part time
- on campus, or by distance learning
- having recently left school, or after a long break away from study.

It will be particularly helpful if you are studying the kind of course that involves a good deal of reading and essay writing.

But do you need a study skills book at all?

Activity 1.1 Should you read this book?

Do any of the following thoughts hover in your mind?

Tick any boxes that apply

1 With so much to study already, I doubt I can spare the time ☐ for a book like this.

2 I'm not sure I need to bother about study skills. I've come ☐ through years of schooling. Why start now?

3 I already have my own ways of studying and I don't ☐ particularly enjoy being told what to do.

4 I think I need a few hints and tips, not a whole book. ☐

5 I find it easier to get advice from people than from books. ☐

---

1 I doubt I can spare the time for a book like this ...

A fair point. It is a chunky book and there always seems to be more to study than you have time for. But you will certainly waste a lot of time if you don't study effectively. Reading this book will actually save time, by helping you make better use of it. You don't need to drop everything right now and read the book from cover to cover. Skills take time to develop. Just set yourself to read a chapter every three or four weeks, squeezed in amongst your other studies.

2 I'm not sure I need to bother about study skills ...

Perhaps you think study skills are for beginners, but studying never becomes easy. There are always new challenges and your skills can always be improved. Successful students recognise the importance of continuing to develop and refine their skills.

3 I already have my own ways of studying ...

A good thought. It is right to feel ownership of your ways of doing things. Your study techniques express who you are. Be proud of them. Be confident. But don't commit yourself to remaining forever locked into the same ways of doing things. Try out and take ownership of new approaches. This book will not *tell* you what to do. It will *help* you to review what you already do and weigh up alternative strategies. You will remain in control.

4 I think I need a few hints and tips, not a whole book

Hints and tips are very helpful, and there are plenty in this book, but they are not enough. If you really want to get ahead through your studies you need insight into the way your mind learns, together with flexible strategies for getting the most from all kinds of learning opportunities. To achieve this you need to invest small chunks of 'quality time' over a fairly long period. You will not understand your own learning overnight. That is where this book will help. It offers exercises and discussion within a coherent overall approach to thinking about study. The exercises will help you work out ways of meeting immediate challenges, but the understanding you develop will help you take control of your learning throughout your life.

5 I find it easier to get advice from people than from books

Advice from teachers and other students is excellent for building up your confidence and giving you new ideas to try out, but studying at a higher level is often a solitary activity. Working on your own with a study skills book helps build up your capacity for this independent learning.

Key points

Why read this book?

- It will help you make better use of your study time.

- It offers much more than handy hints and tips; it will help you to understand how you learn and build up your capacity for independent study.

■ Whether you are an experienced student or a beginner, this book will build on your existing skills and insights.

1.2 How this book works

This book has two parts. Part 1 considers studying as a whole and how to think your way into it. Part 2 then focuses on how to develop your skills in specific study tasks.

Part 1: Studying intelligently

To be a successful student you must use your intelligence. You must approach studying strategically and systematically. Chapter 1 is about recognising the value of investing significant time and effort in developing your study skills. Chapter 2 'Taking control of your studies' then discusses how to get yourself organised so that you can manage your studies effectively. Chapter 3 'Using a computer to study' outlines different ways to enhance your studies through the use of a computer. Finally, Chapter 4 'Understanding how you learn' explores the nature of learning at university level, to help you better understand what it is you are trying to achieve when you study.

Part 2: The essential skills

Courses in many subject areas involve a lot of reading and essay writing. Part 2 explores the essential skills needed to study successfully in such subjects. These skills include:

■ Reading articles and books (Chapter 5)

■ Making notes to help you understand and remember (Chapter 6)

■ Listening to talks and lectures (Chapter 7)

■ Talking in seminars and workshops (Chapter 7)

■ Working with numbers and charts (Chapter 8)

■ Finding information on the internet (Chapter 9)

■ Writing essays (Chapters 10 and 11)

■ Preparing for exams (Chapter 12)

1.2.1 Ways of using this book

This is not a book to read from cover to cover in a single sweep. You should dip into it and select what you need. Begin it now, but keep coming back as your studies continue. The book is designed to be used in a variety of ways:

- If you want to work seriously on developing skills in a particular study area, then set aside an hour or two to work carefully through a chapter, doing all the activities in full.

- If you want to review a particular skill area (say, note taking or preparing an essay) skim through the relevant chapter to get a general overview from the headings and pick up ideas from the boxes and key points lists.

- If you need advice on a specific point, such as avoiding plagiarism, or preparing slides for a presentation, look it up in the index and read just a paragraph or two.

This book is intended to be easy to use whichever way you choose, with a detailed contents list at the beginning, a comprehensive index at the end, and topic boxes and key points lists throughout.

1.2.2 Making an investment in yourself

If you *only* 'dip in' for tips, however, you will miss the best of this book. Tips often sound like little more than common sense, whereas the difficult part is putting principles into practice. By far the best way to learn study skills is to start from practice, then think about the principles. For this reason, the chapters in Part 2 are based on *real study tasks* and *detailed practical activities*. You are invited to immerse yourself in these, then reflect and consider what wider conclusions you can draw. The approach is relatively time consuming, but it produces significant benefits. Think of it as an investment in yourself and in your future as an independent learner.

The activities in three of the chapters in Part 2 are based on a short article, 'The Secrets of Happiness' by Richard Layard (2003), which you will find at the end of this book. You are invited to study this article in Chapter 5, to make notes on it in Chapter 6, and to read some short essays about it in Chapter 10. *To get the full benefit of these key chapters you will need to invest an hour or so in reading the article and doing the accompanying activities.*

Once you have invested time in getting to know this book, you will be able to keep returning to it over the years, like a favourite cookery book. Some ideas will make sense right away, because of the study tasks you are currently engaged in. Others will acquire greater force as you become a more accomplished student. And some are basic truths about learning, which you may need to return to periodically throughout your studies, to understand again at a new level.

Key points

- When you face an immediate study challenge skim through the book to find the advice you need.

- Invest an hour or so in yourself from time to time by working seriously on one of the chapters.

- Expect to take several months to work your way through the whole book.

- Occasionally return to chapters you have read, to remind yourself of what you learned and to rethink your strategies.

1.3 Investing in your own development

In the past education was associated with childhood. Most people expected to leave studying behind when they entered adult life. Now, however, in a rapidly changing world, none of us can afford to assume we have finished with learning. Employers too must keep educating and training their workforces. We are all expected to be lifelong learners, continually adapting to change by acquiring new skills and new ways of thinking. A daunting prospect, but also exciting.

From this perspective, your present studies are just one phase within a lifelong project of maintaining your competence as an educated person in the twenty-first century. By taking a course, you are investing time and money in your future. But it is important to get a good return; you cannot afford to stumble into your studies hoping for the best. You need a clear eye on *what* you are trying to achieve and *how*. In short, you need well-developed learning skills.

BOX 1.1 KEY SKILLS

The UK government has, in collaboration with employers, identified six sets of 'key skills' which all of us are said to need:

1 Communication

2 Application of number

3 Information technology

4 Working with others

5 Problem solving

6 Improving own learning and performance

" Key skills are a range of essential skills that underpin success in education, employment, lifelong learning and personal development.

(Department for Education and Skills (DFES), 2004) "

In a world that requires people to respond to and anticipate change, these skills are essential to remaining employable.

(Qualifications and Curriculum Authority (QCA), 2000)

This book offers plenty of support with *communication* skills – in Chapter 5, on reading, Chapter 6, on note taking, Chapter 7, on discussing and listening and Chapters 10 and 11, on writing.

Application of number is addressed in Chapter 8 and *information technology* in Chapters 3 and 9.

Improving own learning, meanwhile, is what this whole book is about.

So, deciding to read a book like this is not an idle whim. By investing time in working your way through it, you will acquire essential skills for 'education, employment, lifelong learning and personal development' (DFES, 2004).

Key points

Investing in your study skills

In a world where you need to keep learning throughout your life, developing your study skills is one of the most valuable investments that you can make. The time spent on this book will be at least as valuable to you as the time spent on your course work.

1.4 The challenge of studying

Why so much fuss about study skills? Surely studying is a fairly straightforward activity – you read books, attend classes and then write essays. Where is the problem? Well, perhaps it isn't so simple ...

 Zahra looked up again and saw it was 7.20 pm – nearly an hour since she'd started and still she was only on page two. Another hour and she'd have to collect Mark from his class – and would she ever get started again after that?

Early start tomorrow morning – so can't afford to work late tonight. And it's the detective serial at nine o'clock – last episode – can't miss this one. Wonder if the accountant is running the drug ring – but then what's the link with the police chief?... No! Must get back to the book – perhaps a cup of coffee would help me concentrate – not that the last one did – and that was only twenty minutes ago.

She looked at her note-pad. The book title and chapter heading were written across the top, but the page below was blank.

They said to make notes as we read – but notes of what? No point copying the book out. "Sum up the key points." How?... What is there to sum up? Is it totally obvious, or have I missed the point? ... apart from those brain-busting long words, which don't make sense even when you look them up in the dictionary.

Why am I bored? I thought studying would be interesting. The book title looked fascinating, but I can't even get through a few pages. There are so many words in the sentences. The first few I think, "OK – I get you", but by the sentence end I've lost it. Why can't they say it simply. Is it just a big con – blinding us with complexity? ... Just remembered, I meant to sort out my desk ... .

The phone rang. It was Holly ...

Zahra brought back another cup of coffee and sat down again.

Only half an hour left. Must concentrate. Let's go back to the top of page two. On second thoughts, I may as well go right back to the start, since I can't remember a word. I'll try to get some notes down ... . Yuk! It still seems like a foreign language. Oh forget it!... It's too late to get anywhere now. I might as well get tidied up before fetching Mark. Perhaps I'll give it another go, after the serial ... .

Meanwhile, in another room a few streets away ...

Nathan stared blankly at the computer screen. What now? He'd made half a dozen starts and hadn't yet reached the middle of a page before deleting the words and starting again.

How can I be stuck when I've hardly started? How long is this thing going to take? Will I ever finish it? ... "Can happiness be a goal of social policy?" How do you start on a subject like that? How am I supposed to know what happiness is? Even the book doesn't seem to be able to make up its mind. And what do they mean by social policy? What if I wrote, "Yes and no, depending on your point of view"? ... or perhaps I could just pick out a few sentences from the textbook and change the words around a bit. At least they wouldn't be able to say I'd got it wrong. But then the tutor said to write in your own words ... .

As his mind slipped back to the classroom he winced. Why hadn't he kept quiet? He knew he didn't really understand what the others were going on about – but the tutor was so keen for everyone to speak. He'd finally wound himself up to say something, but it was so long to the next gap in the discussion that the subject had changed. Then the tutor looked straight at him, so he blurted his point out so fast that no one understood what he was saying. Of course, they pretended to agree as they carried on the discussion, but he knew he'd made an idiot of himself. How could he face going back again?

> Anyway, I didn't come away with that much – no notes. In fact I can hardly remember a thing that was said. Why not give it a miss this week? Would the tutor be offended? Perhaps I'll get marked down?... Oh well, think about that later. Must get back to this rubbish essay. Should I re-read what I've written so far? No, can't bear to read a word. How about looking up "happiness" in the dictionary and starting from there? I'm sure I wrote down some ideas for this essay when I was reading. Where did I put them? Brain's turning to water ... . Why am I doing this to myself?

Is studying really as bad as this? Well, not all the time. But there are times when things look pretty bleak. Although Zahra and Nathan are fictitious, their problems are very common – and not just among new students, or 'weak' students. They are general problems which all students face – problems of struggling to *understand*, of struggling to *write*, of managing *time*, of *completing a task*, and of keeping up your *morale*.

- Zahra has a problem with *making time* for study between her social commitments, her work commitments, and her leisure interests.

- Both have problems *using time* effectively.

- Both are confused about *what* exactly they should be doing and *how long* it should take.

- Both are *stuck* and cannot see a way forward.

- Zahra is repeatedly *distracted* – by a phone call, by her own thoughts, by making coffee, by tidying her desk, and most of all by the boredom she experiences when reading the text.

- Nathan is inhibited by his sense of revulsion when he reads his own words and by his general *feelings of inadequacy* as a student. He thinks of himself as a weak student and feels overawed by the tutor and the other students. He is approaching his essay in such a diffident way that he cannot take hold of the subject and express his own ideas. Instead, he sits, hypnotised by the title, casting around in desperation.

■ Both have *lost* the surge of *enthusiasm* they felt at the start of their studies. They are in danger of giving up and wasting all those good intentions.

They need help. Yet they may be doing better than they think. Studying often feels like a struggle, however good you are at it. In fact it is in the process of struggling that important learning starts to happen. We looked in on Zahra and Nathan when they happened to be at a particularly low ebb, but we can easily join them again when things are looking up ...

Nathan squeezed between the plastic chairs crowding the coffee bar and put his cup on the table. Had to phone to check the kids are OK. What are you all talking about?

Zahra grinned. Megan's going off on one. She's discovered the secret of happiness.

Well it's just that we all know money doesn't make us happy – and basically I've got everything I need – but still it gets to me that my younger brother earns twice as much as me. What a crazy society. Why do we compete with each other to earn more and more, when happiness is really what we want?

Swap with me Megan, said Adam. You can be happy on the dole, and I'll be happy on half your brother's income.

Megan doesn't want to pollute us with her wealth and make us unhappy – do you? said Nathan.

Look, I'm not rich. I'm just saying my lifestyle's OK. But we all chase each other's tails to have holidays and flash cars, instead of putting money into the community, where it would really make a difference, you know, make people happier.

But then, said Nathan they'd just get habituated to it in a few years, so what's the point?

Ooh – habituated – hark at him, Vikram chipped in. Been memorising your dictionary again Nathan?

I've found myself using words like that, joined in Emma. Norms – nuclear family – now my friends laugh at me.

Yeah – I have to be careful at work, or I sound like a prat, said Zahra.

But isn't it amazing how much more you understand on TV, said Vikram. I'm watching a programme and I'm thinking – yeah, I know that, but what about the other point of view – you know, give us some evidence, don't just tell us your opinion.

Yes, said Megan. My Joe is starting to feel the pressure. Says he'll be forced to start studying himself. But I can't help getting stuck in.

You hear such rubbish on TV. I'm so into it now – I want to phone in and tell them where they're wrong....

Later, as they stood at the bus-stop, Zahra said Nice bunch of people.

Amazing mixture, replied Nathan. I thought they were all school teachers and managers the first week. I didn't want to open my mouth in case I made a fool of myself.

Never thought I'd be sitting chatting about theories. I didn't even think I'd make it through a whole chapter of the book, I took so long on that first one. I still don't know how I stuck with it to the end.

Well you should have seen me struggling with that first essay. Nearly drove everyone in the house mad – not just me. I still find writing the worst. But at least I seem to be improving … . Don't fancy the look of that next piece of reading, though, do you?

Oh, I don't know – could be quite interesting. Look out, here's your bus – see you next week – take care!

And so they disappear into a rosy sunset and we see that studying can be wonderful after all. Well, I just wanted to show that although it is frustrating and tough, studying is also very rewarding. Like climbing mountains, there is a lot of hard slog on the way up, and sometimes you wonder why you bother; but when you reach the peak you remember how fulfilling it is. Many students say that studying not only gives them greater knowledge and understanding of the subjects they study, but also more *confidence, broader interests*, and more *purpose* in life; that it helps them to achieve more in areas of their lives not directly connected with study. This is another reason why it is worth studying this book. As you develop as a student you will strengthen your capabilities all round.

1.5 What does it take to be a skilful student?

No magic tricks, or quick fixes, will make you a skilful student overnight. Study skills improve gradually through picking up practical know-how, swapping ideas with other students, being creative in trying out new approaches and taking time to think about how your studies are going.

1 Accumulating practical know-how

You pick up practical know-how from day-to-day study experience. For example, with more experience Nathan would have recognised the importance of filing, and would have kept important documents, such as notes for an assignment, together in a folder. Developing an effective filing system is not a difficult skill. It does not require great insight, or hours of practice, just application and a little thought. Other kinds of practical know-how include knowing:

- where to get information about what your course expects from you (e.g. timetables, booklists and past exam papers)

- how much time to allow for different tasks (e.g. researching for an assignment, then planning and drafting it), and

- who to go to for help and support.

You accumulate this knowledge by reading information sheets, asking questions and working out your own solutions.

2 Mastering the core study tasks

As well as general know-how, you need to develop insights and techniques for tackling the core tasks which take up most of your study time. The chapters in Part 2 of this book offer practical examples and guidance to help you develop a broad repertoire of strategies and skills that you will be able to apply to a wide range of study tasks.

3 Knowing how to keep your spirits up

There is nothing more damaging to your studies than low morale. You saw how little progress Zahra and Nathan made when filled with doubt and despair – starting one thing, then another – frittering away time and achieving little. Managing your morale is a key topic of Chapter 2.

4 Taking control

To be successful as a student you must be determined to take control of your studies. It is easy to let a course just 'happen to you' – lurching along from one day to the next, without an overall plan. Instead, you should strive to make the most of the time and money you are investing in the course. You can't afford to be half-hearted. Nobody will be impressed if you blame the course, or your circumstances. You have to take responsibility for your own learning. This too is a key theme of Chapter 2.

5 Becoming an independent learner

You also need to take responsibility for the big questions:

- What do you want to achieve from your studies?

- How much of yourself and your time are you prepared to invest?

- Where do your studies stand in relation to other priorities in your life?

The higher you go in the education system, the more accountable you are for your own progress. In school, teachers shouldered much of the responsibility for what you learned and how. At higher levels, you have to decide your own priorities, set your own targets and work out your own strategies for achieving them. *You* decide what subjects you are interested in, what points of view you agree with, what evidence you accept and what opinions you will express.

It takes a while to adjust to this autonomy, especially if you are returning to study after a long break. Nevertheless, your target is to become an independent learner. Ultimately, you want to be able to find your own way, without the support of teachers, around any subject you become interested in. Then you have the freedom to find out whatever you want to know. The purpose of this book to support you in achieving that independence as a learner.

1.6 Being a reflective learner

To become an *independent* learner you need to be a *reflective* learner. By reflecting on your study experiences, you develop insight into the ways you learn. Then gradually, as your insight grows, you become able to take control of your studies. The process of learning through reflection on experience is illustrated in Figure 1.1 (an adaptation of David Kolb's diagram of the experiential learning cycle).

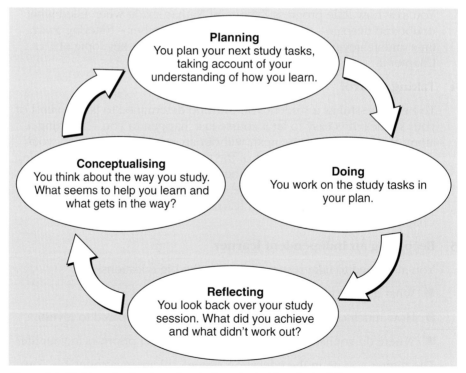

Figure 1.1 Kolb's reflective learning cycle, adapted for study skills

(Source: Kolb, 1984)

1 Planning

You look ahead to the course work you have been set and the deadlines for completing it. You also think about what is going on in your life, the time available for study and any difficulties you have to circumnavigate. Then you think strategically about how to manage the work: Which parts of the work present the toughest challenge? Which parts are most important to complete? In what sequence will you tackle the various tasks? What targets will you set yourself? How will you keep on learning well? How will you maintain your morale? Will you try out any new ways of doing things?

Having thought about such questions, you then sketch out a plan in the form of a task list.

2 Doing

Then you work at your studies, following your plan as best you can.

3 Reflecting

At a suitable point, you pause to reflect on how your spell of study has gone. (It could be at the end of the day, the end of the week, or at a point during your studies when things have ground to a halt.) What have you achieved? You tick off items on your list. What did you not complete? What events intervened? Did you feel you were learning well? What parts were tough going? What parts did you enjoy? Did anything go differently from previous sessions? Perhaps you make a few notes of your answers to these questions.

4 Conceptualising

Then you try to make sense of what you have observed. What seems to help you learn? What seems to interfere with learning? Where did your strategy work best? Where did it go wrong? Did you misjudge some of the tasks, or the time required? How does this all fit in with your ideas about the way you learn? What changes in your approach to study might help you to learn better?

See Chapter 4 Section 4.1, Developing ideas about learning

5 Continuing round the cycle

This brings you back to the planning process, as you look ahead to the next set of tasks. However, now, as a result of the reflective process, you have more insight than last time. You can make better plans, which you then test out further by 'doing', 'reflecting' and 'conceptualising'. In this way, as you continue your studies, circling round and round the reflective cycle, your understanding steadily deepens and you become more skilful in your learning.

In reality, of course, the process of reflective learning is much more messy than Kolb's diagram suggests. The four stages are not neatly separated off from each other. You might well 'reflect' on learning, or revise your 'plan' in the middle of 'doing' some study, or you might 'make sense' in a new way whilst you are 'planning'. And mostly you are not aware of the four stages because it feels like a single coherent process.

However, the purpose of the diagram is not to propose a strict sequence of steps to carry out. Its value lies in helping you to think about the nature of reflective learning – what it involves and what it delivers. The essential point is to keep your approach to study under continual review. You think ahead about what you want to achieve and take note of what you actually achieve. And you ponder over your successes and your failures, so that you bring increasingly subtle insight to your studies.

BOX 1.2   KEY SKILL: IMPROVING YOUR OWN LEARNING AND PERFORMANCE

'Improving own learning and performance' is one of the six key skills identified by the UK Government and employers. Reflective learning is the central theme. You are expected to show that you can:

Develop a strategy for improving your own learning

- review your current capabilities as a learner
- identify what you hope to achieve in order to be a better learner
- set realistic targets
- plan how to reach your targets.

Monitor your progress as a learner

- seek and use feedback
- monitor what you are learning and how you are learning it
- reflect on what you are learning and how you are learning it
- adapt your strategy to improve your performance.

Evaluate your strategy and present outcomes

- assess the effectiveness of your strategy
- identify ways of further improving your learning
- organise supporting evidence of your achievements.

(Source: QCA, 2004)

---

6   Keeping a study diary

One way to take a reflective approach is to keep a diary of your studies. If you write a page each week about what you have achieved and how you feel about it, this will trigger ideas about why you study in particular ways. Use headings such as 'Main achievements', 'Main setbacks',

'Feelings about study', 'Lessons learned', 'Major tasks ahead', 'Ideas for tackling next tasks'. It can be an informal, loose-leaf diary – just sheets kept together in a folder.

As you look back over your notes, you will see patterns in your experiences of study. These will help you to think strategically about whether you are achieving as much as you could. Even keeping a study diary for a fairly short spell will stimulate valuable reflective and strategic thinking. Some courses may ask you to keep a diary, but you don't have to wait to be asked.

1.7 Thinking about how you learn

In order to set about your studies intelligently, you need some kind of notion of how your mind learns. It does not have to be a complicated theory, just a workable, practical understanding – enough to enable you to make choices between different study strategies and to evaluate the outcomes of your choices.

1.7.1 Drawing insight from other people

As the Kolb cycle suggests, you can develop an understanding of your own learning through reflecting on your experiences. But this is only part of the story. You can develop a fuller understanding of your own learning by talking with other people about *their* experiences of learning. Talking with other students is a powerful way of 'thinking aloud'. You make sense collectively of the way the learning process seems to work. Teachers offer insights too, both in class and through their comments on your assignments. And, of course, you can read what other people have to say about the learning process in books like this one. You will pick up many insights about how you learn as you work through the chapters in this book.

See Chapter 4, Understanding how you learn

1.7.2 What kind of learner are you?

While there are general truths about learning which apply to everyone, it is also clear that people differ in the ways that they learn. Since this book tends to focus on the general truths, you may want to look up other sources to explore your personal characteristics as a learner. Educational researchers have developed various schemes that distinguish between different types of learners.

Serialist *vs* holist

One scheme divides students into:

■ serialists – who tend to work in a sequential way through study tasks, starting at the beginning and proceeding step by step until they reach the end; and

■ holists – who tend to approach a task as a whole and hop about from one part of it to another, trying all the time to keep the overall picture in view.

For example, a serialist is said to be more likely to start a book on page one and read on to the end, while a holist might read the contents list and the conclusion, skim through some of the illustrations and then dip into selected sections to build up a picture of what it is about. Either strategy can work, but some people have a clear preference for one or the other (Pask, 1988).

Controlled *vs* impulsive

Some people study in a steady and systematic way. Others are inclined to put in bursts of intensive study, learning a lot quickly before shifting to something else. Again, both approaches work.

Deep learning *vs* surface learning

Some students tend to search for the underlying meaning of a text as they read (deep learning), while others are more inclined to treat a text as information to be remembered (surface learning). Deep learning is seen as a much more appropriate strategy for most university level study (Marton et al., 1997).

Verbal *vs* numerical *vs* spatial

Some people read text relatively quickly, but struggle with diagrams and tables. Others find it easy to read tables of numbers and enjoy working with information organised diagramatically, but get bogged down in long passages of text. Indeed, it has been argued that that there are seven or eight different kinds of 'intelligence' and that these affect the way we study (Gardner, 1993).

However, there is a disagreement about how useful it is to make distinctions between learning styles and about which distinctions are most meaningful and practical. New classification schemes and new versions of old schemes continue to emerge. If you want to explore the topic of 'learning styles' you can follow it up for yourself by searching the internet. Type 'learning styles' in the search box and you will find plenty. You may even find questionnaires you can fill in to see what style of learner you are said to be. Whether some of these schemes are more 'correct' than others is not necessarily important. You can simply make use of them to stimulate thinking about your learning preferences. Try them out and borrow whatever ideas seem useful.

1.7.3 Becoming your own psychologist

Ultimately you need to piece together your own 'picture' of yourself as a learner, not rely on questionnaire scores. For this, you need to become a practised observer of yourself. In effect, you become your own psychologist, tracking how your mind learns and develops, and comparing your experiences with those of other students and with what you read about learning. Then you can work out what kind of a learner *you* think you are and develop your study strategies accordingly.

1.7.4 A lifelong process

Understanding how you learn is a lifelong process. At every stage you can discover more. And, it is not always a matter of learning something 'new'. There are many basic truths you can revisit and understand again at a new level. Some sections of this book will be just as revealing if you return to them in future years, when you have much more experience of studying.

Key points

Study skills are not a set of 'tricks' that you learn once and apply forever. Becoming a skilled student involves:

- accumulating practical know-how, on things you have to do as a student and how to do them

- mastering the essential skills in your area of study

- knowing how to keep your spirits up

- being determined to take control of your studies in a practical and realistic way

- becoming an independent learner by taking broad responsibility for your own studies and making your own judgments about your priorities and your progress

- taking a reflective approach to your studies, so that you learn from experience and continually refine your skills

- developing an understanding of what learning is and how it happens, so that you can plan and monitor your own learning.

With this approach, your study skills will continue to develop throughout your life.

Studying with full concentration and deep thought expands your mind. It enables you to participate in new realms of ideas. It extends your powers of expression and helps you to engage with the world with new confidence. But none of this is guaranteed. If you cannot connect effectively with your studies, if your time dribbles away on patchy, half-focused activity, then studying leads to frustration, disappointment and low self-esteem. That is why developing your study skills is one of the best investments you can make in yourself. It is an investment which will bear fruit throughout your life, enabling you to keep abreast of a rapidly changing world. This book assumes that you are intelligent enough to give serious thought to why and how you study, and determined enough to invest significant time in improving your skills.

References

Department for Education and Skills (2004) *What are key skills?*, www.dfes.gov.uk/keyskills/what.shtml (accessed 23 April 2004).

Gardner, H. (1993) *Multiple Intelligences: The Theory in Practice*, New York, Basic Books.

Kolb, D.A. (1984) *Experiential Learning: Experience as the source of learning and development*, Englewood Cliffs, NJ, Prentice Hall.

Layard, R. (2003) 'The secrets of happiness', *New Statesman*, 3 March 2003, p. 25.

Marton, F., Hounsell, D. and Entwistle, N. (1997) *The Experience of Learning: implications for teaching and studying in higher education*, Edinburgh, Scottish Academic Press.

Pask, G. (1988) 'Learning strategies, teaching strategies, and conceptual or learning style' in Schmeck R.R. (ed.) *Learning strategies and learning styles*, New York, Plenum Press.

Qualifications and Curriculum Authority (2000) *Key skills units: Levels 4 and 5*, London, QCA Publications.

Qualifications and Curriculum Authority (2004) *Improving own Learning and Performance*, www.qca.org.uk/qualifications/types/2764.html (accessed January 2004).

CHAPTER 2 TAKING CONTROL OF YOUR STUDIES

Studying at higher level is always a tough challenge, yet you can make it one of the most satisfying experiences of your life by rising to the challenge and taking control of your studies. But to do that you need to understand the nature of university study.

2.1 Taking responsibility for your own learning

University is a world of its own, with customs and values you encounter nowhere else, and extraordinary freedom to do, think and speak as you please. Faced for the first time with this openness, it is natural to feel confused. Here is an account of two campus-based students. Ryan, a full-time student, is a recent school-leaver. Tracy is a mature student with a young family and a part-time job.

Ryan looked around the coffee bar, soaking up the atmosphere. It was his first week at university. Round the other side of the table he could hear Tracy telling a friend that she was really determined to try for a good degree, in spite of her family and work commitments. She was saying that she'd worked out a plan for setting aside 25 hours a week for study and she was hoping this would be enough. Ryan listened sceptically. He was anticipating a far more intensive study routine. At the departmental freshers' talk he'd been inspired to remodel himself as a serious student. He wasn't sure how, but he imagined himself working round the clock if necessary. Tracy, he guessed, was heading for disappointment.

Activity 2.1

This account is based on real people. Can you guess which of the two was the more successful in their studies?

Back to the story ...

Three years on, Tracy achieved an excellent degree, while Ryan struggled to more modest achievements. As Ryan discovered during the semester when he was studying the same course, Tracy produced her work very consistently. She said she had only a few 'windows of opportunity' between her shifts and looking after her children, so she had to be disciplined and use them to the full. In spite of crises when children were ill or child-minding arrangements broke down, she had mostly been able to find 25 hours, or thereabouts. Looking back, Ryan realised that Tracy had seemed as much on top of the work as any of them. By sticking to a well-defined and realistic plan, she had achieved what she intended. She also visibly enjoyed her studies.

Activity 2.2

Think of some reasons why Ryan was less successful. Jot down a few ideas.

Tracy said that studying in short bursts suited her, as she found it difficult to keep her mind focused intensively for more than a couple of hours at a time. However, Ryan, with no job or family commitments, aimed higher, vaguely committing whole weeks to intensive study. Yet, he found himself easily distracted. Stretches of a day would slip away and, feeling guilty, he blotted his studies out of his mind by sneaking off to play pool or cards. He comforted himself with the thought of all the potentially virtuous days that lay ahead.

At school, Ryan's work had been timetabled. Teachers made sure he fitted all that was required into the school year. Now he was at sea. At university, time came in vast undifferentiated swathes. What to do with it all? With 112 hours in a week (allowing eight a night for sleeping) how many was it reasonable to spend on study? And working out what to do with the hours was just as hard. Take the booklists. How many books should he try to read? How long should a book take? It took him so long to read just a few pages, he felt defeated looking at the lists. And should he take notes as he read? If so, how long should that take?

He would sit in the library for hours, dipping into one book after another, stopping frequently to gaze around at other students, or out of the window. What was he trying to achieve? How would he know when he had achieved it? By comparison, he went to lectures gratefully. It was clear when they started and finished and what he was supposed to be doing. At the end, his lecture notes were scrappy, but at least he felt he had met a target.

Eventually, during his final year, Ryan discovered that he could learn a lot from close reading of just selected sections of text and that taking notes could sometimes be very satisfying, while at other times it was not necessary. The trick was to take control, to decide what he wanted to find out and then work at it until he had absorbed enough to think about for the time being. It was a shame that he had not talked to Tracy about these matters in the first year. In the end, like most students, he stumbled his way towards an adequate strategy for coping with the work, but he could have got there much quicker, learned a lot more and avoided a lot of anguish on the way.

"

The most significant difference between Ryan and Tracy was that from the outset Tracy knew that she had to take responsibility for her studies. The teacher on her pre-degree access course had impressed this upon her and had emphasised the value of intensely focused, high-quality study, compared with bitty time-filling. Ryan, by contrast, just had good intentions. He thought big, but did not know how to deliver. Nobody had told him what university would be like and he had given little thought to how he would cope. Here are some aspects of university study that took him by surprise:

2.1.1 Independent study

Ryan expected to be learning mostly in a familiar group of students, as at school, with a teacher shepherding them along together. But, though he attended several lectures and seminars each week, he was surprised to have little personal contact with staff and little guidance; and he was often amongst students he knew only by sight. He had no idea that he would be spending so much time studying under his own steam.

2.1.2 Absence of work schedules

Nor had it struck Ryan that organising his time was now his own responsibility. If little work was set for a particular day, then he generally did little. He never thought to follow Tracy's lead and write out a schedule of tasks for himself. He just hoped for the best. He assumed that success was mainly to do with how clever you were. He had yet to appreciate how central is time management to achievement in adult life.

2.1.3 Breadth of courses

He was also completely taken aback by the broad sweep of the courses, with more topics and suggested texts than were possible to cover. He had expected to be told what to study when. And he assumed that teachers would help to pull the courses together from time to time to make sure everyone was keeping up. Instead, they just moved on to new topics. Some topics were not even covered in class. He had not realised he was expected to make decisions about where to focus his efforts.

2.1.4 Long time horizons

Ryan had never worked to assignment deadlines so many weeks ahead. He did not think to plan his assignments across a semester, fitting them in alongside other study commitments. He assumed there would be time later. He felt he had enough to worry about with the reading and that, anyway, he would be better able to tackle the assignments later on, when he had learned more. He did not realise that working on assignments would help him understand the reading, nor that spacing them out would help him build up his skills and confidence. He got into particular difficulties with the dissertation, the deadline for which lay more than a year ahead. In spite of secret hopes of carrying out an impressively penetrating study, he ended up cobbling the thing together in a last-minute panic and consequently learned little from the experience.

2.1.5 Responsibility for seeking help

Unfortunately, even when Ryan began to recognise that he was not coping, he did not think of seeking support. He kept his feelings of inadequacy to himself and sank into a cycle of avoidance and denial. Though he knew about the counselling service, it never occurred to him that it was for people like him. He did not realise how common his experiences were, nor how quickly the support services could have helped him transform his studies. He did not even talk things over with friends, such as Tracy. Instead, he took the long slow route of bitter experience.

In summary, Ryan was completely unprepared for taking responsibility for his own studies. He felt that courses 'happened' to him, rather than *he* taking advantage of *them*. For a long time he felt adrift, until eventually it dawned on him that he had to seize control.

Key points

It is vital to take responsibility for your own learning at university because:

- You spend a lot of time in private study.

- You are responsible for your own day-to-day work schedule.

- The scope of courses tends to be broad, touching on many more topics and texts than you can cover, so you have to decide where to focus your efforts.

- You often have distant deadlines and have to work out your own strategy for meeting them.

- You are expected to seek out support when you need it, not wait for it to come to you.

2.2 Managing the work

Taking responsibility involves managing your own progress through the coursework. You are studying for your own reasons and under your own particular circumstances, with your own background in the subject, so it is up to you to work out where you need to direct your efforts. You may have particular difficulties with parts of the subject, or with finding time, or accessing books, and it is for you to develop a strategy that addresses these challenges. That strategy might include seeking advice and support, but *you* remain the person in charge.

2.2.1 Sketching the big picture

To take control of your work, you need to begin with the 'big picture'. What are the main components of the course? What work do you have to hand in – and when? Are there other assessed elements? Which are compulsory and which are optional? Is there an exam? Is the course divided into topics? Are there key books that the course works with? All this information should be available on printed sheets, or on a departmental website. Make sure you have tracked down the relevant sources, then take time to go through them carefully with highlighter pens, or write down your own notes of the key things you have to do.

Identify priorities

Use different coloured highlighter pens, or double and treble underlining, or star ratings, to indicate the importance of different course components. What is absolutely essential? What looks particularly challenging? What will need to be planned well in advance? What is optional?

'Own' the course

Take ownership of the course information by putting your markings all over it. It is easy to feel overwhelmed by 'official' documentation, so assert yourself. You are the one doing the course, not 'them'. Build up your *own* picture of the course. Having reviewed the big picture, pick out some of the first tasks and begin to think about how to tackle them.

2.2.2 Breaking big tasks into smaller tasks

A key principle in keeping on top of your studies is to break big tasks into small, bite-sized tasks.

> I set myself just one or two small, manageable tasks. I find if I can achieve these it's so much better than setting myself a full working day and then not getting round to much at all. I often feel so virtuous at having achieved the little tasks that I go on and do more. I get a kick out of ticking things off my list.

The trouble with big tasks is that their shape and scope is hard to comprehend. You can't see where to start, so, like Ryan, you keep putting things off. And if you do get started, it is very hard to tell how much progress you are making. Bite-sized tasks give you much more control.

Make tasks specific

It helps to turn vague, abstract tasks, such as 'make progress with the book', into specific, concrete tasks, such as 'read the next ten pages'. You then know where to start and what to do. You can set yourself a time allowance and check your progress as you go. And when you complete the task, you can pat yourself on the back.

2.2.3 Making a To Do list

An excellent way to begin to engage with your work is to create a To Do list. This is a simple device, but very effective (particularly if you use a computer, which makes it very easy to update). The example in Figure 2.1

shows tasks arranged in the order they are to be tackled. Each item has some stars indicating its importance, and an estimate, in brackets, of the number of hours it will take. Tasks 3 and 5 have been broken down into sub-tasks.

To Do list: 5 March 2005

1   Read chapter 3 of textbook ★★★★ [2]

2   Sort out and file last week's notes ★★ [1]

3   Essay ★★★★★ [due 12th]

    3.1   Phone Lucy: compare notes on last essay [½]

    3.2   Plan essay [½]

    3.3   Gathering together material for essay [2]

    3.4   Organise, sketch outline [1½]

    3.5   First draft [4]

    3.6   Final draft [3]

4   Read the two set articles ★★★ [3]

5   Presentation for seminar (on 9th)★★★★★

    5.1   Prepare [2–3]

    5.2   Get set up, then give presentation [1½]

6   Look in library for articles on new topic: do photocopying ★★★ [1½]

7   Search on the internet for next topic ★★ [1]

8   Fill in course choice forms for next year ★★★★ [1]

Figure 2.1   **Example of a To Do list**

Activity 2.3

You may already have a To Do list. If not, make yourself one. List your study tasks for the week ahead using either pen and paper or your word-processor. Use coloured paper if you have any, then the list will be easy to find amongst other papers.

If you use a word processor, number the items in your list. Try moving list items around: put the cursor on an item, hold down the Shift and Alt keys and use the arrow keys ↓↑. This should move the item up and down the list.

Try the right arrow for 'demoting' a task to a sub-task and the left arrow for 'promoting' it back. If these moves don't work with your word-processor, try the Help menu. When your list is done, save it and print it off.

Using your To Do list

As you complete your tasks, cross them off your list. When other tasks arise, write them in, using arrows to show where they fit into the sequence. If you made the list on your computer, go back to the saved list to delete completed tasks and add in the new ones; then rearrange the sequence as appropriate, save the updated version and print it off. In this way the uncompleted tasks will gradually move up your list. Nothing gets forgotten, and you don't have to keep writing a new list.

A To Do list is a guide to action. It turns a shapeless mound of work into a sequence of tasks you can tackle. It tells you where to start and enables you to track your progress. You may find yourself working on tasks out of sequence, but that's fine. Your To Do list is a creative tool, not a straightjacket. With it in front of you, you can think intelligently about modifying your plans when things have not worked out. You remain in control.

Key points

To manage your work effectively you need to:

■ Review course information, marking up the important features, so that you can build up the 'big picture' of what you have to do.

■ Break big tasks into smaller 'bite sized' tasks.

■ Make a To Do list to help you steer your way through the work.

2.3 Managing time

Having got the work into perspective, you need to think about how to manage your time.

2.3.1 How much time should you spend on your studies?

The official view

University courses in the UK are measured in credits and each credit is notionally ten hours of learning activity. So a 60 credit course, for example, is seen as involving around 600 hours of work. Spread over a 30-week year, this translates to twenty hours of study per week. In other words, you multiply credit points by ten to get the overall number of hours for a course; then you divide by the number of weeks, to get a figure for hours per week.

Most full-time students study 120 credits per year, which works out at around 40 hours a week – equivalent to a working week in many jobs. Meanwhile, a part-time student might study 60 credits per year, equating to a twenty-hour week. (This covers *everything*, including time spent getting things sorted out at the beginning of the course, searching the internet, managing your notes, talking with your teacher, preparing for exams and so on.)

However, the link between credits and hours is intended only as a rough rule of thumb. The UK Quality Assurance Agency for Higher Education stresses that credit is awarded for achievement not for 'time served' (QAA, 1999).

The reality

But what about real life? Are you in a position to set aside the number of study hours implied? If you're not, don't just give up on the idea of studying. A lot depends on the quality of your learning. If you are very focused, like Tracy, you can achieve a lot in under the recommended hours. A part-time student with a full-time job will do very well to find twelve good hours a week for intensive study. But with lighter tasks squeezed into any other spare moments, this can be enough.

Be aware of the 'official' number of hours your course expects, but be realistic about the number of hours you can actually spare for your studies. If you find yourself having to manage with less, be assured that plenty of other students are in the same position. In the end what counts is how well you use your study hours rather than the sheer number of them.

A major review of learning and teaching in North American universities observed that:

 many of our students [are] trying to balance significant demands of families, jobs, and careers [...] many of today's students seem unable to devote sufficient time to their studies. Students need help balancing these demands, and [making] the most of the time that they have available [...]. There is no magic number of hours that students should study in order to maximise learning [...] the amount of time isn't the issue. It's how that time is spent.

(Vorkink, 1995 p.70)

2.3.2 Creating time

How, then, do you find the hours you need? When studying comes into your life it generally means that something else has to go. However it's important to strike a balance which allows you to carry on with the important things in your life, including relaxation and entertainment. As the saying goes: 'all work and no play makes Jack a dull boy' and studying should never make you dull. Effective studying requires a lot of time in reasonably good-sized chunks. You have to become an expert at creating usable time. One way to set about this is to draw up a study week chart (see Figure 2.2) showing time spent on your 'typical' week's activities and see where there is room for manoeuvre.

	Monday	Tuesday	Wednesday	Thursday	Friday	Saturday	Sunday
Morning							
Afternoon							
Evening							
Total hrs							

Figure 2.2 **Study week chart for working out time spent on a 'typical' week's activities**

Activity 2.4

Make yourself a study week chart like the one in Figure 2.2. Either draw it by hand, or, quicker for future updates, use a word-processor. Then, once you have saved the chart, you can keep making new copies whenever you want to re-plan your time. Use the table creating facility (look in Help if you don't know how). When you have created your chart, fill in the hours spent on your main non-study activities for each day (work, family commitments, travel, leisure, etc.)

How many study hours per week will you aim for? Write in a target number of study hours for each day in the 'Total hrs' row, trying to make them add up to your target number of hours per week. Then start marking in possible study slots, to see if you can achieve your daily totals. What will you cut back on? Where might clashes arise? Can you achieve something close to your target number of study hours per week?

To find time for study in a busy life, you need to review the way in which your time is normally taken up. Identify the most likely opportunities for making time – whether first thing in the morning, or after putting children to bed, or at weekends, or during lunch hours, or on your journey to work.

Don't panic if you found this activity extremely difficult. Life is messy. Indeed, having struggled to draw up a study week chart, life will intervene to make it hard to stick to. But sticking to it is not necessarily the point. Even if you constantly have to change your chart it is *still* worth the effort of making it. Deciding to change it makes you think about your priorities. Planning helps you to think *strategically* instead of just drifting.

Key points

The first steps in managing study time are to:

■ estimate how much time your course requires

■ work out how you can release an adequate amount of study time within your 'typical' week.

2.3.3 Using time strategically

Having identified your best 'time windows' for study, it is important to think strategically about how to use this precious time.

High- and low-quality study time

Not all your available time will be of the same quality. It will range between:

■ *high-quality study time* – when you are alert, able to concentrate and can work undisturbed for a decent chunk of time

■ *low-quality study time* – when you are tired, your concentration is poor, there are distractions around you and you do not have long enough to get deeply involved.

I'm an early bird. I think and write much better straight after I get up.

My best time to study is in the morning after 11 am, when the kids are at school.

I concentrate best after 9 o'clock at night, when I've got everything from the day sorted out.

You need to manage your studies so that you use your best quality time for the tasks that most need it.

Activity 2.5

When are your best times for study? When do you concentrate best? When do you have fewest distractions? When can you find decent chunks of time? Note down your thoughts.

Now get your chart and use a highlighter pen to mark in your best quality study time. How much high-quality time do you have in a week? Is it enough? If not, are there ways you might reorganise your activities to give yourself more high-quality time. Could a friend or partner help you create more quality time by sharing some of your other responsibilities?

Now look at your To Do list. Which items do you think need the high-quality time? Which could you do in lower quality time?

Give your highest quality time to demanding tasks such as reading a difficult passage of text or drafting an essay. These are only worth starting when your mind is alert and you have a good stretch of time ahead of you.

There are plenty of other tasks, such as organising notes, or reading through a draft essay, or talking things over with another student, which can be squeezed into odd moments, when you are less alert. Experiment to find which times of day are best for different kinds of task.

Mapping the course weeks

Now you are ready to get down to specifics. What do you actually need to achieve within the time that's ahead of you? Again it is useful to start with the big picture. For how many weeks does the course last, and how can the coursework be mapped across them? What you need is a course calendar. If your course provides one, use highlighter pens to mark the key milestones, such as dates when assignments are due; then stick it on a wall in a prominent place.

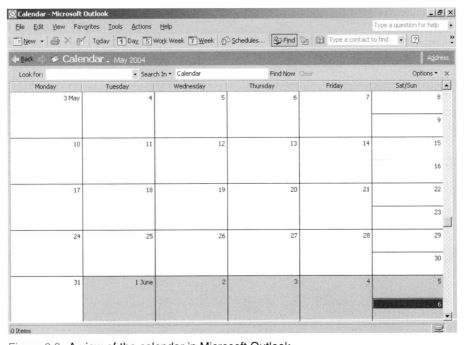

Figure 2.3 A view of the calendar in Microsoft Outlook

If your course does not supply a calendar, make your own. You could buy a year planner for your wall, or just find a calendar feature on your computer and use that (see Figure 2.3.) You can print off calendars for the next month or two and fill in the details by hand, or you can type in key course information before printing. If you like working on a computer, it is worth investing a little time exploring whatever calendar program you have, it can probably be used in a variety of interesting ways.

Planning the week ahead

■ Your course calendar provides an overall map of the course weeks.

■ Your study week chart tells you where to find time in a typical week.

■ Your To Do list shows you the tasks immediately ahead of you.

Now you need to work out how to fit the tasks into the actual week ahead of you, in order to keep abreast of the targets on the calendar. So, sketch out a study plan. Figure 2.4 shows a study plan for someone working shifts while studying part-time.

	Mon 6	Tue 7	Wed 8	Thu 9	Fri 10	Sat 11	Sun 12
AM	10-12: read chap 3	morning shift	morning shift	morning shift	10-12: finish 2 articles	day off	11-1: gather stuff
PM	afternoon shift	finish shift 2:30-3:30: file notes 4:00: pick up kids	finish shift 2:30-3:30: phone Lucy plan essay 4:00: kids	finish shift 2:30-3:30: start to read 2 articles 4:00: kids	afternoon shift	day off	2-4 prepare presentation for Tue – do next week's plan
Eve	evening shift	7-9: go to class	evening out	7-9: go to class	evening shift	day off	evening off
Total (15)	2	3	1	3	2	0	4

Figure 2.4 Example of a completed study plan

Activity 2.6

Sketch out a study plan by copying the tasks from your To Do list into:

■ your diary, or

■ a fresh copy of the blank study week chart you made for Activity 2.4, or

■ your printed-off calendar for the month ahead (if you made one).

(Or you could do the whole thing on your computer using a calendar planning feature.)

With your study plan and your To Do list you have the means to stay in control of your coursework. When things go wrong, as they will, you can readjust intelligently. You can consult your study plan to see where there is room for manoeuvre in your schedule. And, if time is running out, your To Do list will tell you which activities to prioritise.

2.3.4 Using time well

It is one thing to plan your time strategically, and quite another to stick to your plans.

Why, oh why, when I find three hours of peace and quiet, and all I want to do is write my essay, do I suddenly become hungry? I make myself tip the remains of last night's wine down the sink, then I make that urgent phone call to a friend who was having a downer yesterday. Then I remember some birthdays I mustn't forget ... Off to the loo, as I'm now on my third cup of coffee. The cat has peed in the bath because I forgot to let him out. I might as well clean the loo while I'm at it, and yes the sink, and the dust round the skirting board. Better put some washing in the machine too. 'What's for tea mum? I'm starving.' Pile of coats and bags in the hall, as daughter and friends arrive giggling about whether gorgeous Jack Scott really did follow them home from school. Now what was that essay topic?

BOX 2.1   WHY IS IT SO EASY TO BE DISTRACTED WHEN YOU ARE STUDYING?

The feeling of drifting in a sea of uncertainty makes you grasp at straws of distraction. When you don't understand the text and you're not really sure what you're trying to do, you feel restless and uneasy. Distractions provide relief. They offer the chance to focus on familiar and meaningful aspects of your life and escape from the uncertainties of studying. Routine, orderly tasks are particularly appealing. You reassure yourself that you can control your domestic world, even if your studies feel chaotic. The urge to avoid uncertainty is very strong. That is why it's important to set yourself specific tasks which help to give shape and meaning to your work.

Keeping up your concentration

To keep up your concentration, work out ways to keep actively engaged as you study. For example:

- When you read, use a highlighter pen to mark useful passages in the text. The choices you make about which words to highlight keep your mind in gear and so reading feels less passive. It is not just the writer who is running this show. You are in there making judgements of the writer's words. Make notes in the margin too, when you agree or disagree.

- Check your progress. Are you going to reach your target? Do you need to change strategy to finish in time? Set yourself an interim target to achieve before your next break.

- Sit somewhere else for a while. Switch to a task you find more interesting. Take a short break. Do something physically active.

- Focus on what you find interesting. Play to your strengths. Approach your studies creatively. Don't let the course dominate you. Stay in control.

Time vs task

Try to balance *time management* against *task management*. If you become too obsessed with *time*, you tend to think in terms of 'hours put in' rather than what you have achieved, then you find yourself 'filling up' time with relatively unimportant tasks. To avoid this, you need to set out with the goal of completing specific tasks (even if you don't always succeed). On the other hand, if you focus too much on completing a *task* you can let it drag on for too long and it will stop you attending to something else just as important. You need to switch your attention between task management and time management to achieve a balance.

> ### *Key points*
>
> In order to manage your time strategically, you should:
>
> - identify your high-quality study times and use them for the tasks which require most concentration
>
> - mark up a course calendar to keep key targets clearly in view
>
> - create a study plan for the week ahead by mapping your To Do list onto the study times you have identified in your study week chart
>
> - keep yourself actively engaged with the ideas in the course
>
> - stay in control of your study strategy, switching tasks from time to time, to give yourself a new angle
>
> - balance time management against task management.

2.4 Managing your study circumstances

Your studies will, inevitably, be affected by your circumstances. But whatever those circumstances are, there's a lot you can do to make the best of them.

2.4.1 Setting up a place to study

Activity 2.7

Where are you reading this book? Are you able to concentrate without disturbance?

- Are you comfortable? Have you enough space to work in?

- Do you have all the equipment you need close at hand?

- Do you have space to keep books and files?

Do your answers to these questions suggest that you should make changes to your study environment?

If you try to study at the kitchen table, with other people milling around and the TV on, the odds are stacked against you. To study you need to be able to concentrate intently. If you can set up a regular study area it helps get you into the habit of switching off from everything else. You may prefer different places for different activities – for reading, for jotting notes, for writing assignments. For some activities you need a surface on which to spread books and papers. For some you need access to a computer. You also need storage space and easy access to your files, and you need adequate light and heat. You may not be able to set up the ideal study environment, but it's important to get as close as you can. Concentrating on study is hard enough, without struggling against your surroundings.

Figure 2.5 **A typical 'study kit'**

2.4.2 Equipping yourself

It's much easier to study efficiently if you have the right equipment:

- pens and highlighter pens
- A4 note-pads and printer paper
- paper clips and a stapler
- cardboard pocket files, filing boxes and sticky labels
- pads of coloured Post-it notes
- a box of index cards
- a good dictionary (unless you use online dictionaries)
- shelf space for books and filing boxes.

See Chapter 3 Section 3.2.1, What equipment do you need?

You may also need access to a computer with an internet connection and a printer.

2.4.3 Maintaining a filing system

An important aspect of your study environment is entirely of your own making: the degree of confusion you allow to develop, as course paperwork accumulates – notes, handouts, printed material, and completed assignments. If you never know where things are, your efficiency is significantly reduced. You find yourself deciding against using that excellent quote for your essay because it would take you so long to find it; and, anyway, you doubt that you kept a note of the reference. In studying, much can be achieved simply by being able to organise information effectively. The sooner you start the better, as you can quickly become overwhelmed.

See Chapter 3 Section 3.4, Organising files

Treat your filing system as work in progress. Have to hand a good supply of wallet folders and labels, or spring clip files and dividers. Keep adding new folders, or file sections, whenever you think you need them, and take the trouble to label them straight away. You can always stick on new labels as you work out better ways of organising your system. The time you spend on the upkeep of your filing will pay big dividends later. If your files are a mess, you rarely go back to them. But if you can find things quickly, your past work remains a permanent asset. In the end, what counts is not so much what you can remember, as *what you can lay your hands on when you need it.*

2.4.4 Taking advantage of amenities

Studying is enough of a challenge to make it worth taking advantage of every support available to you; yet students often don't.

In his first weeks at university Ryan felt overwhelmed by information, so he left all the leaflets and handouts in a pile to 'look at later'. Consequently, he remained unaware of the many services and amenities available to him. He missed the library tour and the introductory session at the computer centre. And he didn't think to explore the university website carefully. He just waited for the initial confusion to subside and hoped he would hear about things when he needed them. Generally he didn't. He simply missed out.

Don't let uncertainty and inertia prevent you from taking advantage of all that is on offer.

Websites

Your university's website is a good place to start looking. Set aside time to explore it thoroughly. There will be services and facilities designed specially for students like you. It is also worth looking at the websites of other universities. There is often excellent advice on a wide range of study issues.

Be sure to visit your university library's website, to find out about access to online resources. Look for guidance on how to use the library system, there may be online introductory tours, or workshops you can attend. It is vital to invest time in familiarising yourself with the resources available to you and in how to access them. Don't rely on picking up this knowledge as you go along.

Bookshops and libraries

Visit bookshops and libraries in your area to find out what they have on your subject. It can be rather awe inspiring to walk into a large library or bookshop, not knowing how to locate the section you need, especially if you are not sure what the section is called – but assistants will help if you take the plunge and ask them. You may be pleasantly surprised at how much relevant material is on hand. Or you may be disappointed and have to learn how to order books and articles through the library, or join book-exchange schemes with other students.

2.4.5 Social arrangements

It is difficult enough to make sense of subjects which are new to you without being constantly interrupted. Unless you can arrange to be left alone while you study, you are in for a very hard time. The people in your life may not realise just how hard you need to concentrate when you are studying. Or in some cases, they may be quite dependent on your support and feel they have a right of instant access to you at all times. They may even secretly hope you will drop out, so that they can 'have you back'. These are issues that need to be talked about. Your studies are very important to you. You may need to discuss your right to have space in your life to pursue your own goals. Whatever the case, you need to negotiate boundaries around your time, so that you can work undisturbed for fairly lengthy spells. You need to make sure those around you understand your study needs and know when to leave you alone.

Key points

To make the best of your study circumstances you need to:

- fix up a suitable place to study
- get supplies of basic equipment, so that you are not held up when you need things
- set up and maintain an effective filing system
- find out about all available services and facilities
- explore and learn to use the available routes to academic information
- make arrangements with family and friends to leave you in peace.

2.5 Managing your morale

Nothing drives learning forward more effectively than enthusiasm, and nothing damages progress more than low morale. Yet study is intrinsically unsettling and frequently affects your mood. You may be competent and confident in the rest of your life, but study sets you back in the role of 'beginner'. You find yourself dependent on teachers, whose approval makes your spirits rise and whose disapproval hurts. You experience the excitement of new insights, but dislodge old, comfortable ways of thinking. 'Truths' you took to be obvious become uncertain, yet new half-formed knowledge slips frustratingly from your grasp. Often it seems you know less than you did – that your studies keep revealing new incompetencies.

The uncertainties of the student role can bring big mood swings: from inspiration to despair, from pride in achievement, to a collapse of confidence. It is important to be ready for these highs and lows, and to understand them, so that you don't get blown off course. Here is a list of common 'lows', to help you think about them and put them in perspective. Then follows a list of 'highs' to help you in seeking out the uplifting side of study.

2.5.1 What lowers morale?

Initial shock

- **Disruption to your daily life** So much study to fit in, creating pressures on family commitments, social commitments and leisure interests.

- **Information overload** Too much to take in: timetables, tasks, deadlines, books to buy, new names and faces, places to find, course descriptions, regulations, special services, student societies.

- **Culture shock** New ways of talking and thinking, new ways of relating to teachers and other students, new environments, new assumptions about the world and what is important: a whole new identity as a student.

Personal pressures

- **Loss of confidence in your own abilities** Apparent lack of progress, and doubts that you will make it to the end of the course.

- **Lack of structure in your life** Feeling disorganised and not in control of events.

- **Alienation** Feeling set apart from university ideas, language, people, attitudes, ways of talking, ways of relating; doubting that you will ever 'belong'.

- **Dislocation** Feeling that your studies are distancing you from your family, friends and community.

 My family wanted to know, 'What are you trying to prove?' I fought and fought. Now they don't bother me because they know I'm studying.

Everyday crises

- **Feeling overwhelmed by the work** Too many challenging and complicated tasks and little idea where to start.

- **Struggling to make sense** Feeling adrift in a sea of meaninglessness.

- **Writing assignments** Not being able to get started, not finding the books you need, struggling to achieve a plan, feeling that you will never finish, hating what you've written, feeling inarticulate.

- **Bad days at the office** You leave your notes on the bus, the library is closed when you get there, your internet connection breaks down, your printer runs out of ink.

- **Disagreeable course elements** A tiresome book, an irritating teacher, a dreary seminar group.

- **Disappointing results** A presentation goes badly, an assignment grade is worse than you expected, your teacher seems only to find fault.

- **Obsession with grades** Irrational concern over why you lost five marks on your last essay, or why your tutor made that criticism, when actually you are doing just fine.

- **Mid term blues** Your interest in the subject flags, you don't seem to be making progress, it's sunny outside and you can't remember why the course seemed a good idea.

- **Exam anxiety** The exam looms like a distant black cloud casting a shadow over your enjoyment of the course.

These are typical low points. If you experience them you are no different from countless others. The important thing is to know how to rise above them.

2.5.2 What lifts morale?

Achievement

- **Completed tasks** You finish a difficult chapter, make good notes, submit your assignment; you feel capable and effective.

- **Good results** A better than expected assignment grade, nice things written on it.

Creating structure

- **Tidying up** You label some folders and get that growing pile of notes sorted out.

- **Admin** You complete the forms you were sent, choose your next courses, arrange to see your teacher, or pay your rent.

- **Planning** You update your To Do list and plan the week ahead; you feel organised and on top of things.

Knowledge

- **Understanding** You get really interested in an article, have a flash of insight during a lecture, say something that everyone discusses in the seminar; you feel your mind shifting up a gear.

- **Using knowledge** You find yourself taking sides in a TV debate; you chat to someone and hear yourself bringing new knowledge into play; you find yourself approaching life differently.

Personal growth

- **Expressing yourself** You speak in seminars, or join in online conferences; your writing style opens out, you feel yourself putting thoughts into words.

- **Accepting new challenges** You volunteer for a turn as discussion chair, choose the tough assignment option.

- **Self esteem** You notice how many things you have achieved which you once doubted you could do; you find yourself thinking, 'If they can do it, so can I.'

Belonging

- **Enjoying your student group** You look forward to meeting other students; they ask about your life, make you laugh, help when you need support and care whether you do well.

- **Feeling valued by your teacher** Your teacher shows interest in your assignments, asks your opinion in class, is sympathetic during a difficult patch, gives thoughtful advice when you ask.

- **Speaking your mind** You don't worry about saying what you think in class, you don't mind being out on a limb with your views; you enjoy the cut and thrust of debate.

- **Feeling comfortable as a student** You don't feel like an outsider in the university setting, you know where to find the resources you want; you feel you have a right to all the amenities.

Sharing

- **Peer support** You talk about study problems with other students and share tips for coping; you realise that your struggles are quite normal and that, with mutual support, everyone can make it in the end.

- **Staff support** You talk with your teacher about struggles with your essay; you ask the counsellor about problems with sleeping; you feel that university staff are on your side and want you to succeed – it isn't you against them.

- **Home support** You talk with family and friends about your study experiences.

2.5.3 Managing your morale

Studying makes everyone feel inadequate at times. That is why talking with other students is so helpful. It puts things in perspective and keeps your spirits up. What matters is not what you have failed to do, but the progress you have made. When your spirits sag, remind yourself of your achievements. Focus on the parts of the course you enjoy. Remember, *it is your course.* It is your time and money going into it. Make sure you enjoy it and get what you want out of it. If you don't enjoy the course you won't learn much. You may not even stay with it to the end. Thinking positively is not an indulgence, it is essential.

Key points

When study gets you down:

- Focus on aspects of study that you enjoy and do well.

- Make a list of what you have achieved. Forget the plans you didn't fulfil. Ignore the abilities and achievements of other students – it isn't a race.

- Do some organising, to show yourself that you are in charge. Tidy your workspace, set yourself some bite-sized tasks. Update your To Do list.

- Talk to other students. Talk to your teacher. Remind yourself that you are a normal person, experiencing normal challenges.

- Remember that you are doing this for *you*.

2.6 Being a successful self-manager

To be a successful student you have to become your own manager guiding yourself through your studies. Here are the essentials.

Be active As a student, you are not a passenger. You are the driver. You have to take the initiative in finding out what needs to be done, drawing up plans and implementing them. You don't wait to be told. You act.

Be strategic Assess your situation. What needs to be done? What difficulties present themselves? How can you best achieve your goals? Develop plans which take these factors into account, but modify them as appropriate. For example, when you recognise that your powers of concentration have dipped, take the strategic decision to switch to a less demanding task. Don't stumble ahead. Weigh things up and work out how to achieve the best you can, under the circumstances.

Be systematic Take time to gather information and organise it. Maintain your filing system, work out detailed plans. For example, the study plan in Activity 2.6 required you to find out deadlines, create a To Do list and then map out your week's study. By developing such a plan systematically you will have a much clearer picture of what has to be achieved and of how to manage your progress flexibly and intelligently.

Be analytical Analyse complex issues into more manageable components. For example, in updating your To Do list, you break big tasks into subtasks.

You then shift items up and down the list, thinking about the consequences of different sequences of tasks.

Be reflective Learn from experience, (see Figure 1.1 'Kolb's reflective learning cycle'). Review your study activities regularly and consider whether your strategies are working well.

See Chapter 1 Section 1.6, Being a reflective learner

Give yourself incentives Remind yourself of your goals, long- and short-term, and keep track of your progress towards them. Set yourself targets and give yourself rewards for achieving them. Encourage yourself, by taking satisfaction in your achievements.

Manage your morale Keep your spirits up by playing to your strengths and focusing on what you enjoy. Give yourself bite-sized tasks with clear outcomes. Keep your To Do list, your files and your workspace well organised, so that you feel on top of your studies. Keep in touch with other students. And keep reminding yourself that this is all for you.

Key points

The theme of this chapter is that to enjoy studying and achieve success you have to take control. To do this you have to:

- Take on responsibility for your own learning, no longer relying on being told what to study, when and how.

- Review the work set by the course and break it into sequences of specific, manageable tasks.

- Find ways of creating study time, then plan how to use it to best effect.

- Make efforts to create the best circumstances for study that you can.

- Work at keeping your morale up.

- Take an active and intelligent approach to managing yourself.

References

Quality Assurance Agency for Higher Education (1999) *A consultative paper on Higher Education qualifications frameworks for England, Wales, and Northern Ireland and for Scotland*, www.qaa.ac.uk/crntwork/nqf/consultation/contents.htm (accessed 31 January 2004).

Vorkink, S. (1995) 'Time on Task' in Rickey Hatfield, S. (ed.) *The Seven Principles in Action*, Bolton, MA, Anker Publishing Company Inc., pp. 67–78.

Computer uses discussed in this chapter

Here in Chapter 3 we explore some of the other excellent ways you can use a computer to help with your studies:

See Section 3.3, Useful things you can do with a word-processor

Word-processing A word-processor can take a lot of the drudgery out of writing and enable you to produce neat, legible assignments. Many courses require your assignments to be word-processed.

See Section 3.4, Organising files

Storing information Computers are excellent for storing information. With a well-designed filing system you can find items in seconds.

See Section 3.5, 'Talking' online

Talking online Computer chat rooms and conferences enable you to enjoy the human contact side of learning, wherever you are and whatever the time of day.

See Section 3.6, eLearning

eLearning Computers can bring powerful new learning experiences straight to your desk, such as interactive videos, digital simulations, and online tutorials.

BOX 3.3   VARIETIES OF SOFTWARE

In this chapter (and others), I explore how to use your computer as a study aid. However, every brand of software has its own particular way of presenting things and its own 'look and feel'; and new versions keep coming out. So, in describing how to use software, it's impossible to take into account all of the brands and versions. Yet, in practice, the various word-processors, spreadsheets etc., work in similar ways. For simplicity's sake, I am going to use the terms favoured by Microsoft in the XP version of its widely used Office suite. My examples will give you a general idea of what to look for and how things work, but if your computer has different software, you may need to do a little exploring, using Help, to find equivalent functions.

Working with your computer

It will help to read this chapter sitting alongside a computer. Then, you can work with the relevant software as it is discussed and you will learn a lot more. If you come to anything you don't understand then look it up in the Help menu.

Key points

- Nowadays it can be difficult to study effectively without access to a computer and the internet.

- If you don't have your own computer, look for other ways of getting access to one.

3.2 Getting started

We begin with a summary of the equipment you need and the skills you will need to develop if you are new to using computers.

3.2.1 What equipment do you need?

To use a computer for studying, the basic things you need are:

- **A computer** Preferably one not much more than three years old (technology moves on quickly). Cheap entry-level computers are usually fine for study purposes, unless you are told otherwise by your university. If a computer comes with a software 'bundle', make sure that it meets your needs (see software, below).

- **A printer** Printers are generally cheap; it's the cost of replacing ink, or toner, that counts. Laser printers may be more expensive than ink-jets but for black and white printing they can work out cheaper per thousand pages.

- **An internet connection** To use the internet you need to have an account with an internet service provider (ISP). If you can already send emails and view websites with your computer then you have an ISP. For advice on choosing an ISP ask at a computer shop, your university's computer centre, or someone you know who uses the internet.

- **Software** Check with your university to find out what software is required for your course, they may even supply you with it. You will need a word-processor and possibly a presentation package, a spreadsheet and a database. The most convenient way to buy these is as a software suite (e.g. Microsoft Office); there are usually good discounts for students. If you are considering a cut-down package, seek advice at your university before buying as it may not cover all your needs.

3.2.2 Developing your computer skills

Students have very different levels of ICT skills. Some have grown up using computers as part of daily life, while others have picked up the bare minimum needed to get by, or even avoided computers altogether.

 I've used a computer at work, but only as a glorified typewriter.

Whatever level you start at it is well worth setting aside regular chunks of time to work on your skills. Developing ICT skills has a lot to do with confidence. Give yourself time to play with software. And don't be shy about asking for help from friends, family, other students and your university advisers.

Other students often supply the answer you are looking for, as they had the same problem a few days earlier. You can always go back and do it again, and again, if necessary. This is a good way to build up confidence and gain experience.

ICT skills are nowhere near as daunting as the name suggests and as you progress they get easier. The secret is to take them slowly – don't try to rush.

What skills do you need?

Getting set up

If you are a complete beginner, it is best to get someone you know who is familiar with computers to show you the basics. It is much easier to learn 'hands on', by watching, imitating and experimenting; you will soon pick up the gist of it. You need to know how to:

- open the software you want to work with

- use a mouse, the arrow keys and the 'return' key

- use an internet browser (such as Internet Explorer or Netscape)

- send and read email messages

- use a printer

- look for information in your software's Help facility.

Once you can do these basic things, you may be able to get along fine on your own, developing new skills as you need them using on-screen tutorials and manuals supplied with your computer and software. Alternatively there are many guidebooks for beginners. An excellent way to get to know your software is to spend time playing around, trying things out and browsing the Help facility.

Communications

If your studies involve using email and online conferencing, you will need to invest time in learning:

- how to set up a connection to your university's internet server (following all supplied instructions very carefully)

- how to use the appropriate communications software, taking advantage of any manuals, built-in tutorials, online training, or campus workshops

- where to go for help when connections go wrong or you need advice on using the software.

With online communications, there is always an intense burst of initial learning and perhaps some tension if you run into difficulties establishing internet connections. But when messages start to flow, it becomes easy.

> Work at your own speed and don't ever presume that someone else is right and you are wrong. Read the instructions (I printed out everything, this for me was a necessity) and if at first you don't succeed, then try again. What was initially daunting has now become second nature.

Taking precautions

A computer will occasionally behave oddly, but the consequences are seldom disastrous. There is no need to be anxious, thinking that at any moment something you do might cause a disaster, there is usually a way of rescuing the situation. However, you do need to take a few precautions:

- Develop the habit of regularly saving and labelling work.

- Find out how to 'back up' the documents on your hard drive then do it regularly.

- Seek advice about virus protection, from your university or your computer supplier.

See Chapter 3 Section 3.3.2, Taking control of your documents

---

BOX 3.4   DO YOU NEED TO BE ABLE TO TYPE?

Many people get by with two-finger typing. But, you won't enjoy the full benefits of word-processing until you can make words appear on-screen at a reasonable speed. The good news is that your computer can help you. There are excellent typing tutor programs available (enquire through your university, or search online). A few weeks of regular 20-minute sessions will have you touch-typing faster than you can write.

Learning to touch-type does take a substantial time investment. There is no shortcut to avoid an initial period of regular practice, which can be frustrating and tiring. However, with several years of study ahead, your investment will repay itself many times over. And, of course, you can use typing and word-processing skills in many other areas of life.

The wider value of ICT skills

The skills you develop will be of value far beyond your course both at work and in your life generally.

BOX 3.5   KEY SKILLS: INFORMATION TECHNOLOGY

The UK government has placed IT skills at the heart of its Key Skills strategy (alongside communication skills and number skills). The core elements involve being able to:

- search for and select information

- explore, develop and exchange information

- derive new information

- present information, including text, images and numbers.

These skills are seen as essential to modern life and work and are to be incorporated into education at all levels. Four levels of IT skill are defined, and as you progress through the levels the focus shifts from using IT in specific situations to applying IT skills to general work demands over an extended period of time. For more information see the Qualification and Curriculum Authority's 'Key Skills' publications (QCA 2002a–d).

ICT accreditation

As your ICT skills develop through your studies, you may want to acquire a certificate as proof of your achievement. Your current course of study may provide ICT skills accreditation. If not, and you are looking for a widely recognised certificate, you could work towards a European Computer Driving Licence (ECDL).

BOX 3.6   THE EUROPEAN COMPUTER DRIVING LICENCE

The ECDL consists of seven modules:

1   Concepts of Information Technology

2   Using the Computer and Managing Files

3   Word-processing

4   Spreadsheets

5   Database

6   Presentation

7   Information and Communication.

For more information visit the ECDL website at www.ecdl.com/main/index.php

---

Key points

- **Use the Help facilities** When you run into difficulties check the software's own Help resources first. You will often be able to sort things out for yourself.

- **Ask others** If you are still stuck, ask for help from family, friends, other students, or your university advisers.

- **Get a guidebook** Consider borrowing or buying a guidebook for your software package.

- **Keep exploring** Don't feel you have to learn everything at once. Set time aside occasionally to find out about a new feature.

- **Watch the clock** A computer helps you do many things very efficiently, but it also has a tendency to eat up time. Keep an eye on how long you spend on the computer, and maintain a balance with other study activities.

- **Don't strain yourself** Working long hours on a computer can cause serious strain to your eyes, hands, wrists, neck and back. Position your computer and chair properly (your university should be able to advise you on this) and take regular breaks away from the screen.

- **Learn to touch-type** A big investment of your time, but very worthwhile.

3.3 Useful things you can do with a word-processor

A word-processor is a tremendously flexible, multi-purpose tool which you can use in many aspects of your studies. If you have never used one you can learn the basics in about an hour. Equally you can continue for years finding out new and amazingly useful things it can do. Simply jump in and get started, then make time now and again to explore another feature when you have reason to use it.

3.3.1 The basics

One of the things you are most likely to use a word-processor for is writing essays. Figure 3.1 shows an example:

Your university should provide you with guidelines about how to lay out the pages of an essay (Figure 3.1 is fairly typical). If you are new to word-processing there are a few basic things you need to find out how to do in order to be able to achieve the required effects:

- Create a new document, give it a file name and save it.

- Move the cursor around text using the mouse or the arrow keys.

- Move the page up, down, left and right in the document window, using the scroll bars, mouse-wheel or keyboard.

■ Select text and move it around by clicking and dragging, or by cutting and pasting.

■ Change the appearance of selected text, using Bold, Italic, Underline and the font formatting menus.

■ Use the toolbars and menus at the top of the screen to find the functions you need.

■ Print what you have written.

■ Save and close your document, then find and open it again.

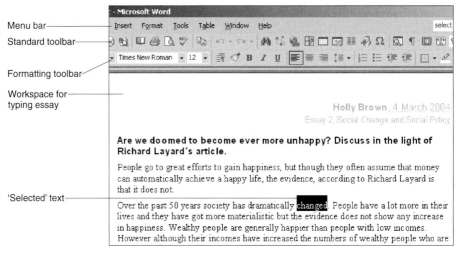

Figure 3.1 **An essay typed using a word-processor**

One of the great benefits of word-processing is being able to change what you have typed to improve the way it reads and looks. This gives you the freedom to write things down just as they come to you then try out different ways of shifting them around until you are satisfied.

3.3.2 Taking control of your documents

It's great to be able to put printed words on paper but you also need to feel in control of your on-screen documents.

Multi-tasking

You need to feel confident about working on two or three documents at the same time. If you have your essay notes in one document, your essay-plan in a second and the essay itself in a third, then it's very useful to be able to switch freely from one to another, perhaps to copy and paste sections of text. This is very easy if you have an up-to-date operating system: open documents will show as icons on the 'Taskbar' at the bottom (or side) of your screen – if they don't, look up 'Taskbar' in Help to find out how to switch this feature on. You switch between documents by clicking on the icons.

Protecting your work

It is easy to overwrite your work accidentally but you can develop a few habits to protect it.

Routine saving

As soon as you start a new document, save it and give it a name. As you work, your word-processor should save your work automatically at regular intervals (if not, look up in Help how to switch this feature on). However, these saves are temporary; if you switch off without clicking 'Save' they will be lost. Remember that every time you click 'Save' you over-write the previously saved version of the document.

Saving different versions

You may want to retain copies of earlier versions, just in case you change your mind and want to go back to them. If so, save the document with a new name (e.g. you might add '2' to the end of the old name). This creates a second version to work on, leaving the original one intact. You probably have plenty of space on your computer's hard disk, so create new versions of documents whenever you feel inclined. Name and number them systematically – you can always delete old versions later, when you are sure you won't need them.

BOX 3.7 PEACE OF MIND AS YOU EDIT

When you are trimming non-essential bits from an essay, it can be helpful to create a new document called 'Dump'. Then if you are unsure about making a cut, you can paste the material into Dump so that if you change your mind you can retrieve it. I find this makes cutting much easier. I hardly ever do retrieve cut material, but I feel much more relaxed about making cuts.

Undoing and redoing

A reassuring feature of most word-processors is the ability to go back a few steps. If you delete a chunk of text by accident, or spoil its appearance, you can simply click the 'Undo' button as many times as it takes to get back to where you were. If you subsequently decide your changes were right after all, then you can click 'Redo'.

Labelling your work

As you write notes and assignments it becomes increasingly important to be able to keep track of your work. Whenever you start a new document use the *header* or *footer* to put your name, the date and the course on the pages, as shown at the top right of the page in Figure 3.1. Also make sure that *page numbering* is turned on.

Controlling the look of your documents

With word-processors you can make text look just the way you want it, so play around with different features to find out how to use them. Here are some to explore:

- Set the view to *Print Layout* so that you can see how your pages will look when printed.

- Find out how to use the page set-up to reset page margins or turn the page on its side (landscape orientation).

- Learn how to use the different styles, especially the headings, in the styles list.

BOX 3.8 FORMAT FRENZY

When you see large, bold, purple, gothic lettering on a marble background, you know someone has discovered the joys of formatting. However, if you look around at books, newspapers and magazines, what formats do you see? Plain, black fonts on a white background are generally easier to read (and more attractive). Play around with special effects by all means, but when it comes to submitting work, take your lead from professional publishers and keep it simple.

3.3.3 Getting help with your writing skills

As well as helping you put words on paper, your word-processor can support you in developing your spelling, grammar and vocabulary.

Improving your spelling

You can use your word-processor's spell-checker to improve your spelling by paying attention to the mistakes it picks out. Every time you see an underlined word, take the trouble to find the correct spelling and take note of where you went wrong. You could keep a note-pad next to your computer with columns headed 'Wrong' and 'Right'. Then, write down the first five words you get wrong and put the correct spelling against each. Underline where the mistake is and at the end of the session go over the words to remind yourself of the correct spelling. Just five words per session will gradually make you a more confident speller. Don't let your spell-checker take over responsibility so that you stop thinking about spelling. Your spelling will deteriorate as you pay it less attention.

See Chapter 9 Section 9.2.1, A quick search

BOX 3.9   DOES A SPELL-CHECKER REPLACE DICTIONARIES?

Clever though it is, your spell-checker has limitations. It can't spot a mistake if it's actually another word, for example if you write 'their' when you should have written 'there'. Also, it may suggest a word which is not the one you want, so think before accepting suggestions. It may mark as wrong a specialist word it does not recognise, in which case you need to check in a textbook or dictionary, then instruct the spell-checker to add the word to its list. Anyway, a spell-checker tells you nothing about the meanings of words, so you will still need to use dictionaries.

Improving your grammar

You can also work constructively with your word-processor's grammar checker by checking that you understand the changes it suggests and thinking about whether you agree with them. I often don't agree with the grammar suggestions offered by my word-processor. In fact I prefer to work with the grammar checker switched off, as it can be quite distracting. Its usefulness depends on how confident you are about your grammar.

Extending your vocabulary

If you sometimes struggle to find the word you need, a thesaurus can be useful. If your word-processor has a thesaurus you can use it to help you to develop the range of your vocabulary, but beware of relying on it too much; your writing can become very stilted if you use lots of words that are not part of your normal vocabulary. As you continue to read about your subject and get more experience in writing, your vocabulary will extend naturally. Words tend to be of more value to you if you let them come to you when you are ready, rather than trying to use them before they really match your thoughts.

Counting words

An important aspect of writing an assignment is to be able to achieve the appropriate number of words, so find out how to use the word-count facility.

3.3.4 Using shortcuts

You can increase your word-processing efficiency by learning a few shortcuts. It takes practice to build them into your repertoire, but they soon become second nature and save a lot of time. Here are just a few (based on the default settings for Microsoft Word):

Selecting text

- To select a word, double click on it.

- To select a paragraph, treble click anywhere in it.

- To select a sentence, hold down the 'Ctrl' key while clicking anywhere in the sentence.

- To select a long passage of text, place the cursor at the start, hold down the 'Shift' key, then click at the end.

Cutting and pasting

- To cut, hold down 'Ctrl' and press X.

- To paste, hold down 'Ctrl' and press V.

- To copy, hold down 'Ctrl' and press C.

- To undo what you have just done, hold down 'Ctrl' and press Z.

- To delete a whole word at a time, hold down 'Ctrl' and press 'Delete'.

Moving quickly with the arrow keys

- To move the cursor to the start of a word, hold down 'Ctrl' and press the left or right arrow key.

- To move the cursor to the start of a paragraph, hold down 'Ctrl' and press the up or down arrow key.

- To delete text a word at a time, rapidly and accurately, hold down 'Ctrl' and press 'Delete'.

3.3.5 Exploring further

Many people stick to word-processing at a very basic level, but there are many marvellous facilities that you can find by exploring the main menus and looking things up in the Help facility. Here are some other features you may find useful:

See Chapter 6, Making notes

Tables You can create tables quickly and easily for all kinds of purposes.

Heading styles If you are writing a document which contains sections with headings, such as a report, using heading styles gives you access to some powerful features, including:

- automatic creation of a table of contents with correct page numbers

- viewing the structure of your document and navigating around it using the *Document Map* or the *Outline* screen view.

Footnotes and endnotes If you want to use footnotes or endnotes in your document your word-processor can manage them for you automatically.

Graphics It is easy to insert charts and graphs into your document and you can draw your own diagrams using drawing tools.

Customise your toolbars When you find yourself using a feature of your word-processor very regularly, you can put a button on a toolbar to give yourself instant access to it.

BOX 3.10 AUTOMATING YOUR REFERENCES

You will be spending a lot of time working with references – noting them down, filing them and citing them in your essays, so think seriously about using referencing software. Seek advice from your university library about which software to consider and whether you can get a price discount. You will find plenty of packages on offer if you search on the internet for 'reference and citation software' or 'bibliographic software'.

Word-processing makes writing a more relaxed and creative process. You can begin as informally as you like, just typing in ideas and starting a new line whenever another thought comes to you. Then, when you feel ready, you can switch to shaping the bits and pieces into something more coherent. Finally, you print your work out and it looks wonderfully neat and stylish when compared with your best handwriting.

But smartness will not cover up poor ideas, weak organisation and hasty writing. Writing remains primarily a thinking process, word-processing just helps with the production side. It does not replace jotting ideas down on a note-pad, or printing out a draft to get a proper look at it and scribble any changes. Make full use of your word-processor, but don't be a slave to it.

Key points

- With a little help you can produce a word-processed document in your very first session.

- After that you need to learn a few techniques for increasing your control over your documents.

- Then, over the months, you can keep adding useful new techniques to your repertoire. Just play with the software and consult Help.

3.4 Organising files

Computers are superb for storing immense quantities of information which you can find again in seconds, and the beauty of it is that once you have set up a filing system it is almost effortless to manage. Each time you work on a document the computer reminds you to save it, then files it in a folder of your choice. You can save all kinds of information: scraps of notes, completed essays, charts, photographs, articles downloaded from the internet – whatever is available in digital form. No more pulling out folders from boxes on shelves and sifting through papers. What is more, you can reorganise your folders or their contents in moments. And when you want to find something you have superb file search tools at your fingertips. In the past, information buried in paper-based filing systems often stayed buried. It simply wasn't worth the effort of digging it out. Now you can store and access information at will.

3.4.1 Setting up a filing system

To set up a filing system use your operating system's file organiser (for example Windows Explorer or Mac Finder). Figure 3.2 shows an example of a filing system set up by a student we'll call Wayne.

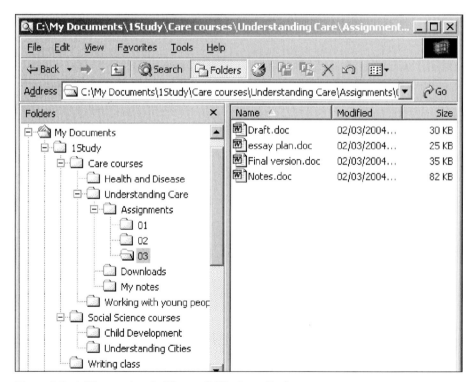

Figure 3.2 **A filing system in Microsoft Windows Explorer**

Activity 3.1

Does Wayne's filing system make sense to you?

1   From what you can see, how many courses has he studied?

2   One of the folders in the left panel is open. What has Wayne filed in it?

3   What name has Wayne given to the main folder in which he keeps all his study files?

4   How will he file documents for his fourth assignment for the *Understanding Care* course?

Here's how Wayne appears to organise his files:

1   Wayne has studied six courses: three relating directly to care, two social science courses and a writing class.

2   The open folder is where Wayne filed four documents relating to his third assignment for the *Understanding Care* course. The right-hand panel shows the contents of this folder.

3   Wayne keeps all his study folders in a folder named '1Study'. (He put '1' in front of 'Study' so that it would appear at the top of the list of folders in 'My Documents'.)

4   When he begins work on the fourth assignment of the *Understanding Care* course Wayne will create a new folder in the 'Assignments' folder and label it '04'.

Wayne has set up his filing system as a hierarchical structure, with folders inside other folders. It's a simple, clear system. He knows exactly where to put new documents and where to look for old ones.

Developing a filing system like this is quick and simple. And you can keep reorganising and improving it as you go along. You can create a new folder whenever it seems a good idea, you can re-label or delete folders, and you can move files and folders around by clicking and dragging them to other folders.

From time to time, you need to tidy up your filing system as it's much less use to you if it becomes a mess. If a folder begins to get cluttered, create a new folder label 'Old' or 'Archive' and drag the old files into it.

It is worth investing time in setting up a filing system on your computer at the start of your studies. Aim for a simple system with a structure that makes obvious sense to you. Just jump in and get started. It is very easy to move things around later, if you decide to reorganise the system. Play around with the settings to get your file organiser looking the way you want it. Finally, check whether it has a search facility and, if so, practise using it to find documents. Even with an excellent filing system you may sometimes forget where you put something.

Key points

- You can store many files on your computer and find them again quickly if you develop a hierarchical filing system.

- Use your file organiser to set up a filing system as soon as you can. Otherwise, you will accumulate a confusing jumble of files and won't be able to find the things you need.

3.5 'Talking' online

When you are studying, a group of friends makes all the difference. Instead of battling away alone, wondering whether you have the ability and willpower to cope, you can talk about whatever is bothering you and quickly confirm that everyone else is having the same thoughts. When you share worries and exchange strategies, everything starts to look more manageable. Remember Nathan in Chapter 1, deep in gloom as he struggled with his essay? How much easier it might have seemed if he had dropped in on the following online discussion:

Sophie: Hi – Still on the 2nd paragraph with ideas floating around now. Essay writing is a skill we acquire at school. Perhaps in a couple of essays it will become like riding a bike – you never really forget! For now I think I've got the stabilisers on!

Gita: Hi all – I really hope that I have answered the question because I was absolutely hopeless at writing essays in school. So I am on the tricycle never mind the bike with the stabilisers! lol Oops just remembered I can't ride a bike!!!!!!!!!!!!!!

Leah: Well I sent my essay in. I found it hard as I'm not good with big words to describe things. So mine is written with basic words.

Aisha: Leah I think having no big words, just your own, makes it clearer that you have understood the thing you are writing about without using technical jargon or trying to spout from dictionaries!!

Joe: What a good image of writing essays. Problem is I keep falling off the bike..!

Mehmet: What bike ???!!! LOL.

Aisha: As this is my first essay in 30 years, I keep looking at the question to make sure I'm not veering off course. Think it's going to take a lot of practice.

Cerys: Hi all – Getting my head around essays is hard for me. To keep myself focused I write out the question in a bold pen on A4 paper and then put it on the wall in front of me.

- put key points on a mind map (I'm not good at these but every bit helps)
- spread out the key headings on another A4 piece of paper on which I
add my notes.
After this I rub my eyes a lot and get a drink.

Liam: Hi Guys – When you are writing an essay that has discuss in
the title, what do you do if you cannot find a good argument for AND
against. For example in the essay we're doing I can find loads of
arguments that agree with the statement, but none that positively
disagree. How can I say this in the essay? PS Found the advice in
the past very useful. Usually stops me banging my head on that
brick wall!!

This dialogue was extracted from an online conference where a group of
students were 'talking' together by leaving messages in a common area.

3.5.1 Online conferencing

There are various types of conferencing systems; the students
talking previously were using 'FirstClass', as are the group shown in
Figure 3.3:

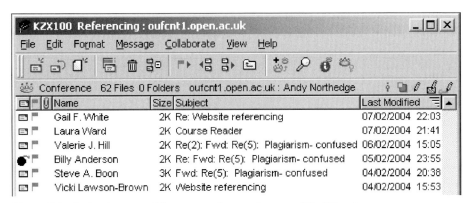

Figure 3.3 **A short segment from an online conference (FirstClass)**

Essentially, a conference is a string of messages. On the right-hand side of
Figure 3.3, in the 'Last Modified' column, you can see that messages were
posted by conference members over several days, at times of day ranging
from mid-afternoon to midnight. It is like a slow-moving conversation in
which you can participate at any time, dropping in for twenty minutes, say,
to read the latest messages and leave your own. In the 'Subject' column you
can see that the top message is a response to a message left three days
earlier. There is also a run of three messages on the same topic: plagiarism.
Meanwhile, a new topic has been opened concerning the Course Reader.
This is typical, with different themes being pursued alongside each other
within the conference.

Although conferencing works through viewing text rather than listening to speech, it can have the flavour of conversation amongst friends; a sense of the spontaneous sharing of ideas and experiences, and of human contact. A short visit can spark new ideas, making you feel less isolated and more confident.

> I love this conference. If it wasn't available I wouldn't be enjoying the course as much. Its great to know that everyone is feeling the same — nervous, uncertain, etc. The tips and advice are great. Knowing that someone out there will have a few ideas for you to try whenever you get stuck, or give you a boost whenever it's all getting too much, is brilliant.

Online conferencing does not, however, have to take place over several days. In chat rooms you can have free-flowing, real-time dialogue, with people dropping in and out:

> Abbie has joined the chat.
>
> Zekia: I've just finished reading chapter 14 I found that really interesting not as hard going as 13
>
> Abbie: Hi all
>
> Jamil: hi Abbie
>
> Hannah has joined the chat.
>
> Hannah: blimey is there room to sit down? Hi all
>
> Zekia: hi Abbie
>
> Jamil: hi Hannah there's a seat at the front
>
> Hannah: ok thanks
>
> Zekia: How far have you got Helen?
>
> Jamil: i think if the reading is difficult you have to concentrate more
>
> Abbie: If the reading is about something familiar it's ok, I enjoyed the childbirth chapter and understood it, I'm finding it harder to get to grips with the new chapter.
>
> Paul has joined the chat.
>
> Hannah: same here....
>
> Paul: Hi all
>
> Ella: If you can get your head around some part of an article the harder sections do seem to 'slot' in eventually after re-reading a few times — I agree with Abbie's last comment
>
> Will: we all seem to be in the same boat
>
> Rena: shame its the boat with a hole!!

> ## BOX 3.11   SYNCHRONOUS AND ASYNCHRONOUS CONFERENCING
>
> A live web-chat is said to be 'synchronous', because everyone is online at the same time. But conferences can also be 'asynchronous', with each person participating at a time of their choosing.

If more than three or four people are participating, live chat tends to be frenetic and chaotic, but fun. An hour can be exhausting as you try to type fast enough to keep up with the flow. You have little time to compose messages carefully, because the topic keeps moving on as new messages arrive. Chat rooms are more interactive than asynchronous conferencing forums and the spontaneity makes them feel sociable, but the quality of the content is more variable. In an asynchronous conference you can go back and remind yourself of what was said previously; but in a synchronous chat you may only see the messages that have arrived while you were online.

Your course may provide facilities for online conferencing. Alternatively you could look for links to student chat rooms or message boards on your university website. Or you might link up with students of all subjects and all ages from around the world, by visiting student conferences via portals such as Yahoo (www.yahoo.co.uk), or Microsoft Network (www.MSN.co.uk).

Tutorials

If one member of a conference is the teacher, the dialogue can be structured in the form of a tutorial. The teacher posts a message which poses a question or suggests an activity, and says how long the tutorial will run (for example, one week). Students then visit the conference to give their responses to the question or activity, and to each other's responses. From time to time the teacher revisits to respond to students, to summarise, and perhaps to move the discussion along with new questions. Students visit several times to see how the discussion develops and at the end of the tutorial period the teacher draws the discussion to a close.

The tutorial tasks made me think more about the texts I had been studying. So did the comments other students wrote. I found this a good way to be involved in group study.

Group projects

A conference environment can also be used for group project work. If the project is well structured and students participate wholeheartedly, online teamwork can be a very rewarding experience.

> Hello All. I think it's brilliant that the project has got us all 'chatting' and having read the other team's report – I am equally impressed and think they have done a great job. This project has achieved a lot. I hope it continues into our next courses. It doesn't matter how skilled you are at computing – once you get over the fear of 'I can't' anything is possible!

3.5.2 Pitfalls of online conferencing

The conferencing environment can be intimidating at first; it looks complicated and formal until you get used to it. There are no signals as to what is supposed to be going on and no visual clues as to what other participants are thinking, so it is quite a challenge to leave your first message, to be read by strangers. Who are they? What do they think of your messages, and of you? Even when you become acclimatised to online conferencing, the experience can sometimes disappoint.

- Conferences are not always lively - they depend on active, motivated participants.

- Conferences are not always friendly - people can easily misread each other and fall out rapidly in the exchange of a few heated messages.

- Conferences which are not well focused and well managed can become confusing and tedious.

- Conferences can be overwhelming if they are so active that there are always dozens of new messages to read every time you visit.

- Conferences can also be addictive, distracting you from other study activities.

Used well, however, they can be very supportive to your studies.

3.5.3 Making online conferencing work

Online conferences have the potential to be open, democratic and friendly environments. However, as in any social forum, some rules and conventions are required.

BOX 3.12   NETIQUETTE

The good manners of conferencing and chatting on the internet are known as 'netiquette'. An online conference is a kind of virtual social space, communally shared by a group of people. Unlike most social spaces it is unaffected by people's physical attributes (their appearance, manner, confidence, gestures, or accent). However, like any other social space, it has to develop its own culture, so that people can understand each other and get along together (see Alexander, 2000).

Conferencing is a team effort. Members have to be ready to contribute and support each other.

> The more you put into conferencing, the more you get out. One of the most important things is to answer someone when they speak, even if just to agree or disagree. Help bring other people into the conversation just by giving them a mention. There is nothing worse than being in company and no-one hears you. If no reply appears, you're worried that your original message was inappropriate! You find yourself logging on constantly to see if anyone has answered or even acknowledged that you are there. When I started to get people mentioning my name I was so chuffed with myself.

Online conferencing generally works best when everyone feels relaxed about what they say in messages – not worrying about spelling and grammar, or getting their thoughts completely sorted out before they write. Since you are communicating through the formal, structured medium of writing rather than the fluid medium of speech, there is a danger of losing the humanity and sociability of face-to-face conversation. It is best to be spontaneous and natural in your messages, dashing them off before the thought evaporates, not waiting until you have something 'important' to say. Conferences become involving and entertaining when everyone lets their personality show. For more on this topic, read 'How students can make conferencing work' by Ben Plumpton (2003).

Key points

- Online conferencing is a way of making study more sociable. It can give you the stimulation and support of sharing ideas and study experiences with like-minded students.

- It may be an integral part of your course, particularly if you are studying by distance education; or it may be an option you can explore for yourself by checking out the websites of your university, your course, your student union, or the wider web.

3.6 eLearning

We have looked at ways you can use a computer to enhance conventional text-based studies; but computers can also be used to deliver the content of the course, bringing learning experiences and resources right to your desk, from a website or on a CD-ROM or DVD.

3.6.1 eLearning materials

Electronic learning materials allow you to learn interactively. Instead of being told things in a sequence devised by your teacher or a text's author, you make your own selection of learning activities, work at your own pace, and participate directly in the teaching and learning process.

English grammar, for example, is notoriously difficult to learn from a teacher. It often sounds unnecessarily complicated when explained and can quickly become boring if not targeted specifically at your needs. It is also hard to tell whether you have understood the principles until you try them out. Software such as that shown in Figure 3.4 allows you to choose which particular aspect of writing skills to focus on. If you want to work on using commas, you read a few lines explaining the principles, then plunge in to punctuate some sentences. Two commas are supplied in the box to the right. You are invited to drag them to the appropriate places in the sentence, then click for feedback (one has been placed, the other is still waiting).

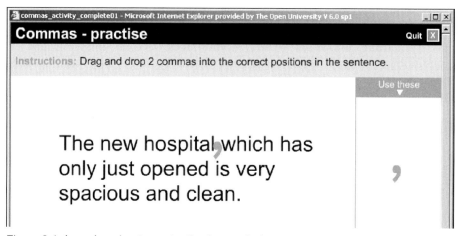

Figure 3.4 **Learning about punctuation interactively**

(Source: The Open University, 2003)

Some elearning materials incorporate a range of high-quality resources designed to work together. The example in Figure 3.5 shows video material used alongside text resources.

Figure 3.5 is taken from a course on managing care. The menu on the left of the screen presents a sequence of scenarios, with instructions, tools and activities. This engages students in working with a range of resources, such as video sequences of a manager in action. The video can be paused and replayed using the control bar underneath. Meanwhile, students can work with a transcript of the video dialogue, to help focus their thoughts. Combining resources in this way provides a rich learning experience.

Figure 3.5 **Learning management skills through the interactive use of video**

(Source: The Open University, 2004a)

Another way electronic materials can provide a unique learning experience is by 'modelling' a complex dynamic process, such as the growth of a city, the spread of a disease, the impact of services on population growth, or budget cuts. You can watch the process as it evolves, stopping it to explore details, and replaying key moments. Or you can go back and rerun it, with changes to some of the conditions, to see how the process is affected.

3.6.2 eTuition

A growing number of courses provide all tuition online. You don't meet your teacher directly, instead you participate in online tutorials then email your assignments to your teacher.

The electronic assignment system was fantastic and saved the worry of – 'has my tutor actually received it?' You knew straight away it was delivered safely.

eTuition delivers many benefits, though not the same benefits as face-to-face tuition. There are issues you can explore face to face which become tedious or confusing when pursued through written messages in conferences. On the other hand, you have instant and ongoing access to friendly group support, without the expense and time involved in attending classroom-based tutorials.

> *I'm a bit worried about doing a conventional course next year, as this online course was my first experience of study and I think it's great.*

3.6.3 Virtual learning environments

A virtual learning environment (VLE) gives access to a wide range of resources and services, as well as to course materials, at the click of a button. These vary enormously, but here is one example – of an Open University student homepage:

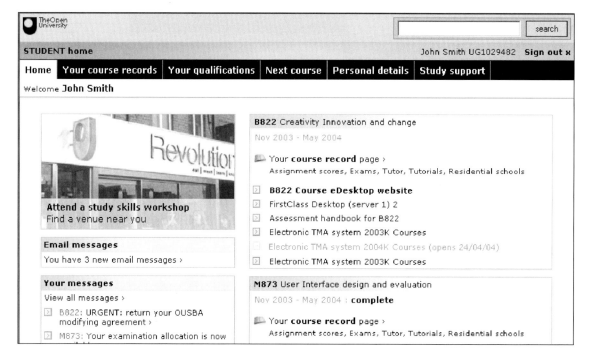

Figure 3.6 A student homepage, providing instant access to online resources

(Source: The Open University, 2004b)

Key points

- eLearning has the potential to bring an immense wealth of resources right to your desktop.

- It also allows you to customise your learning experience to match your interests and needs, studying when you like and focusing on whatever you choose.

- In effect, your desktop travels with you wherever you have access to a computer and an internet connection.

BOX 3.13 INTERNATIONAL ACCESS

Education has always transcended national boundaries through its international community of scholars. Now eLearning is taking internationalism into a new dimension as it enables students from different parts of the world to enrol on the same courses, and also allows students whose lives take them around the world to continue their studies, regardless of where they happen to be.

3.7 Conclusion

You don't have to be an ICT expert to gain a tremendous amount from using a computer; whether for routine tasks such as word-processing assignments and filing documents, web searching and online conferencing, or using interactive learning materials. A computer can bring you learning opportunities undreamt of in previous generations, though it does not displace conventional university teaching and learning. There is, however, an initial hurdle to overcome – you have to be prepared to invest time and effort in familiarising yourself with the software and facilities relevant to your studies. In the first weeks the experience can be quite irritating, as computers have a way of doing the inexplicable at times. But if you have the confidence to drive on through setbacks and a willingness to seek help when stuck, there does come a time when all seems perfectly straightforward and natural, and using a computer becomes seamlessly integrated into your study experience.

References

Alexander, G. (2000) *Extract from a Communications Guide, prepared by Gary Alexander for use on various Open University courses*, The Open University, http://sustainability.open.ac.uk/gary/papers/netique.htm (accessed 1 April 2004).

Office for National Statistics (2002) 'Living in Britain – 2001, Table 4.21', National Statistics, www.statistics.gov.uk/lib2001/index.html (accessed 1 April 2004).

Office for National Statistics (2003) *Internet Access: Individuals and households*, Omnibus Survey press release 16 December 2003, National Statistics, www.statistics.gov.uk/pdfdir/intc1203.pdf (accessed 1 April 2004).

The Open University (2003) 'Practice using the tools of writing', *K100 Learning Skills*, The Open University, www3.open.ac.uk/learners-guide/K100eue/flash/commas_activity_complete01.htm (accessed 1 April 2004).

The Open University (2004a) K303 *Managing care*, www.open.ac.uk/shsw/courses/K303taster/index.htm# (accessed 1 April 2004).

The Open University (2004b) *OU StudentHome*, https://msds.open.ac.uk/students/index.aspx (accessed 1 April 2004).

Plumpton, B. (2003) *How students can make conferencing work*, The Open University, http://oufcnt2.open.ac.uk/~ben_plumpton/tu170/ (accessed 1 April 2004).

QCA (2002a) *Key Skills: Information Technology: Level 1*, London, Qualifications and Curriculum Authority.

QCA (2002b) *Key Skills: Information Technology: Level 2*, London, Qualifications and Curriculum Authority.

QCA (2002c) *Key Skills: Information Technology: Level 3*, London, Qualifications and Curriculum Authority.

QCA (2002d) *Key Skills: Information Technology: Level 4*, QCA/99/455, London, Qualifications and Curriculum Authority.

CHAPTER 4 UNDERSTANDING HOW YOU LEARN

Most of this book takes a practical approach to studying. It focuses on specific tasks explored through real examples. This chapter, however, is concerned with how you make *sense* of your experiences of learning so that you can *think* about your approach to your studies.

4.1 Developing ideas about learning

See Chapter 1 Section 1.6, Being a reflective learner

In order to think, you need ideas. You will develop many ideas about learning through your own experiences of studying – this is the 'conceptualising' stage of Kolb's reflective learning cycle shown in Figure 1.1, Chapter 1. As you experiment with different ways of studying, you will form concepts such as 'studying actively' and 'using time effectively'. But you will acquire concepts about learning from other sources too. You will develop them as you talk with other students about their study experiences, and as you pick up advice from teachers. Reading this chapter offers further help with conceptualising. It will help you to think about the steps you can take to make yourself learn well.

4.1.1 Different kinds of learning

We learn all the time. Daily experience continually shapes how we think and act. This learning is very visible in young children; however, in adult life we tend not to think of routine everyday adaptation to our surroundings as learning. Rather, we associate learning with those times when we have to make a conscious effort to accumulate new knowledge and skills – such as starting a new job, finding our way around a strange town, or learning to drive.

Practical learning

A lot of this learning is achieved by 'doing' – by trying things out, watching others, asking for advice, reflecting on experience, practising, and simply 'being there' as part of the action, so that we gradually become familiar with the surroundings and how to act within them.

Abstract learning

However, you can't learn history, or economic modelling, or the functioning of the brain simply by 'doing'. You can't 'do' the Middle Ages as direct experience. Our knowledge of the past is the product of historians gathering information, debating what it means and writing accounts. Similarly, models of the economy and theories of brain function are products of human thought and debate. They are abstract ideas, not something you can learn about by direct experience.

So how do we learn ideas? That is the subject of this chapter. I will *not* be discussing the various ways we learn by *doing*, important though these are. Instead, my focus will be on the type of learning most associated with the word 'study' – the learning of *abstract knowledge*, achieved through reading, listening, discussing and writing.

Using this chapter

Read this chapter when you feel ready to think more about the learning process. It covers a lot of ground, some of it quite challenging, so you may want to read a section at a time rather than tackle the whole thing in one go.

■ Section 4.2 'What does learning mean?' explores the way that learning happens in the background while you are busy getting on with your study activities.

■ Section 4.3 'Why do they write that way?' is about the very distinctive way academic subjects are discussed and written about. This will help you to follow arguments when you are reading and listening. It will also help you to write better essays. You may want to leave reading this section until you have written an essay or two.

■ Section 4.4 'Reading, listening, speaking and writing' looks in detail at the advantages and the challenges of studying through different modes of dialogue. It will help you to reflect on your experiences after you have been studying for a while.

4.2 What does learning mean?

As a student you spend hours learning a subject, but what is the nature of the learning you are trying to achieve and how do you make it happen?

Activity 4.1

Think about some studying you have done and jot down a few thoughts in answer to these questions:

1   How do you know that you have learned something you have studied?

2   What is learning?

3   What do you have to do to learn something?

These are difficult questions to answer. I put them to some students who were part-way through their degree studies to find out what conclusions they had drawn from their experience. In the following sections you can compare some of their answers with your own. Don't worry if your answers are different – just treat any differences as food for thought.

4.2.1 How do you know that you have learned something?

Have you reached the end of a chapter and wondered whether any of it would still be in your head in a few days' time? Have you been asked about a lecture or talk you recently attended and found yourself unable to say anything much about it? I am sure most people would answer 'yes' to both these questions. But do experiences such as these mean that you have learned nothing – that your study time was wasted? Ought you to be able to give a detailed summary of what you have read or heard? The answer to both these questions is 'no'. Your mind does not work like a photocopier, making exact copies of what you read or hear, to store as files in your head. The learning of ideas is a much more subtle process than that. Evidence of what you have learned does not emerge from your head as a well-formed replica of what went in. It can show up unexpectedly in fragments while you are working on other things. Here is how one student put it:

When you are in lectures, or talking with mates, and some piece of information enters your head, then you know you've learnt it; also when you get interested and start analysing an idea in your head.

So, ideas and information that you have learned begin to appear in your thoughts and words as you are listening and talking. They become part of your mental equipment. Also, when you find yourself 'interested' in a new idea and turning it over in your mind, this too is evidence that the learning process is under way. Another student had a similar view:

I can tell I have learned something when I am able to rephrase an argument in my own terms and link it to other arguments – often comparing the points they make. I also know when I have learned about a whole topic when I can organise an overall picture in my head of how all the different points relate to each other. For example, I found it very satisfying to be able to piece together an overall picture of the progression of post-war European cinema, and the different movements in various countries.

So, being able to turn over new ideas in your head is another sign that you have begun to learn them, being able to put them into your own words and organise them, so that they fit together to create an overall picture. As you take ownership of new ideas you begin to be able to use them to say things of your own. Another student noted that:

You know something must have begun to sink in when you eventually find the confidence to start thinking about your approach to the next essay – you begin to feel you might have the knowledge to hack it.

Another student interestingly observes that one sign of having learned a new idea is that you are able to carry on and learn more:

When you find you can understand new aspects of the subject, then you know you learned what you read before.

Knowledge does not sit like a rack of neatly organised CDs in your head which you can take out and play whenever you want. Instead, what you learn becomes embedded in the way that you think. It isn't easy to say 'look, this is what I have just learned', yet evidence of your learning does emerge in subtle ways.

Key points: Evidence of learning from study

Learning through study doesn't create a detailed replica of knowledge in your head, rather, it develops the way you think. Indirect evidence of what you have learned will appear in a number of ways:

- New ideas and information pop up in your thoughts as you are chatting, reading, listening and thinking.

- You find yourself becoming interested in a new idea and thinking it over.

- You can put an argument into your own words.

- You can create your own summary of the topic.

- You are able to think your way into an essay.

- You are able to move on to learn something else.

These are signs that learning has happened, but what exactly is 'learning'?

4.2.2 What is learning?

 I think learning is mainly understanding what you have read or heard. If you understand it, then it is easy to remember without actually having to memorise. The other main part of learning is being able to fit what you learn together with what you already know.

This student suggests that there are two key aspects to learning:

- making an effort to understand as you read and listen

- connecting this understanding with what you already know.

Here is another student who takes a similar view:

 At one level learning is about taking in other people's ideas, and also, facts. At another level it's about analysing and working on these ideas and combining them with your own thoughts to create a viewpoint. For example, I took in ideas and data about people's perceptions of nature and re-worked them to link with another topic, conservation, to produce new ideas. And I retained the original information in the process.

Both of these students recognise that you have to take in new ideas and information and that you have to do some work to weave them in with what you already know. Another student points to a third aspect – being able to express new knowledge.

 Learning is gaining knowledge and the ability to express it in the way that is expected.

For knowledge to be useful, you have to be able to speak and write it. So, learning is not simply about getting ideas and information *into* your head, it is also about being able to *communicate* what is in your head to other people, and being able to do this in the accepted ways.

Key points

We have identified three aspects to learning through study:

- **Taking in new ideas** by making the effort to understand what you read and hear.

- **Working on new ideas** by fitting them in alongside what you already know.

- **Expressing new ideas** by using them to say things of your own.

What are the practical implications of learning in this way?

4.2.3 What do you have to do to learn something?

These aspects of learning are rather like stages in a dialogue that you have with the subject you are studying. You listen or read, then you think, then you speak or write. In the process of participating in this dialogue, your mind adapts to the way the subject works. This adaptation is the essence of higher level learning.

I find learning normally just happens — I dive in, take bits at a time, write notes, and then maybe go over them another time — it's a gradual process. Writing essays is an important part of learning for my courses.

Notice that, for this student, although learning 'just happens', he actually takes a very active approach — diving in, taking bits, writing notes and going over. So he is doing a lot, but it does not feel to him like 'learning' as a deliberate activity. It is more like finding out and thinking about things, and working out what he wants to say about them.

Notice too that writing plays an important part. Making notes is a key way of working on new ideas. In the process of deciding what to note down you begin to 'own' the ideas you have heard or read. Then as you start expressing new ideas in an assignment your ownership increases. That is why written assignments are a key part of learning.

Here is how another student said she learned:

Most things I learn come originally from my reading, which I take notes from, and we sometimes discuss in seminars. Often the things I learn most about are essay topics, because the process of structuring and writing an essay helps me to understand the main points of the argument.

She too puts reading and note taking at the heart of learning, but adds discussing in class. This is another way of pursuing your dialogue with the subject. Like the first student, she sees essay writing as central, but she emphasises the process of planning – the thinking required before writing.

These students do not see learning as being achieved by a single action. You work at it in stages, and you approach it as an active effort to make sense of the subject, by organising your thoughts, working out what you want to understand and looking for answers.

> I have realised that in order to feel happy about understanding a topic in my head I have to organise it. I try to plot things out on paper as I learn them. I also plan essays quite thoroughly, as this helps me to learn my notes. My note taking has changed because I don't just write down everything I read now. I work out what I want to get from an article before I read it.

Key points

Studying is like having a dialogue with the subject. Your mind adapts to the way ideas are used within the subject – this adaptation is the 'learning'. So, learning involves:

- making an effort to understand as you read course texts and listen to lectures

- making notes selectively and creatively

- thinking about what you are learning and organising it in your head, or on paper

- listening closely to and joining in with discussions in class

- reworking your notes, especially in preparation for assignments

- treating writing as a key learning experience.

You might like to look back now to Activity 4.1 and the notes you made. Would you give the same answers now? What do you think you have learned from this section of the chapter? Has your dialogue with it altered the way you think about learning?

4.3 Why do they write that way?

Reading study texts is a tough challenge. It isn't like reading a newspaper, or a novel. You have to concentrate much harder. So why do they write in that difficult way? In this section we consider who 'they' are and explore the key features of the writing.

Activity 4.2

What do *you* think makes academic writing challenging to read? Here are two sentences taken from the opening of a public lecture given by Richard Layard under the title 'Happiness: Has social science a clue?'.

In the eighteenth century Bentham and others proposed that the object of public policy should be to maximise the sum of happiness in society. So economics evolved as the study of utility or happiness, which was assumed in principle to be measurable and comparable across people.

(Layard, 2003a)

Do you find it easy to 'get into' this kind of writing? Jot down your thoughts about what makes this passage tougher to read than a newspaper or a novel.

These are the challenges I picked out

Unfamiliar wording The word 'utility' is used here in an unusual way. In everyday speech it refers to a cheap, no-frills product, such as utility furniture; here it means 'usefulness'. Also words such as 'sum', 'measurable' and 'comparable' may not be ones you use every day. However it does not seem to me that the words themselves present the most difficult challenge in this passage, rather, it is the way they are used.

Abstractness This passage is about abstract ideas: 'public policy', 'the sum of happiness', 'society', 'economics', 'utility', 'measurability' and 'comparability'. There is no story to follow and there are no events to visualise in your mind. You have to hold these abstract ideas in your head and try to follow how they are meant to link together, so it is easy to lose the thread of what is being said.

Style The writing is very compact. A lot is squeezed into a few words; there is no attempt to be 'chatty'. The main business is to set out an argument and nothing interferes with that. If you are not ready mentally for Layard's argument there are no support rails to help you along.

Assumptions Layard assumes that readers know that the eighteenth century was a very important period for new ideas in Europe (a time known as The Enlightenment), that Bentham was a major figure in debates about the proper organisation of society, and that utility and happiness were key ideas in his writing. The writer also assumes that we are interested in economics and public policy and are aware of the importance in these subjects of being able to measure human activities and experience and to make valid comparisons.

4.3.1 Accessing academic knowledge

See Chapter 4
Section 4.3.2, Key
features of
academic
discourse

The specialised use of words and the abstractness and compactness of style in the quotation in Activity 4.2 are typical of the language associated with academies (universities, colleges and research institutes). This way of writing is called 'academic discourse'.

Engaging with academic discourse

If you want to acquire academic knowledge you have to learn how to engage with academic discourse. As with learning a language, it is a long process, but you certainly don't need to wait until you are fluent before you join in. The aim of this section of the chapter is to help you understand the way academic discourse works so that you can read and listen to it more easily and gradually bring elements of the academic style into your own writing.

Note that if you are taking a work-related, practice-based course, you may not be involved much with academic discourse. If the reading and writing you do is essentially based on the language of the work environment, and if the set work has a practical focus, you may prefer to skip the rest of this section.

Academic disciplines

Although it is a public lecture, Richard Layard seems to assume his core audience to be members of the academic community of social scientists, or more specifically, the communities of economists and social policy experts.

Members of a discipline community 'meet' through debates in journals and at conferences. And when they speak or write in these debates they assume a certain amount of background knowledge amongst other members of the discipline. For example, they make reference to earlier debates which they assume discipline members will be familiar with and they try to anticipate objections that discipline members might make to their arguments. They are also aware of the research standards expected within the discipline. In effect, the discipline functions as a self-regulating community, with a common interest in maintaining high standards of debate and research within the subject area.

Academic values

The members of an academic discipline are held together by the goals and values they share. These include commitment to:

- a perpetual search for better understanding within their subject area
- high-quality research
- open debate (in which all members have the right to participate)
- logical argument
- fairness and impartiality

■ free exchange of information and ideas, in order to promote the advance of knowledge within the community (on the assumption that members will not take unfair advantage).

Individual members may disagree strongly with each other's ideas, but, through their commitment to these values they can participate together in the community's core work of advancing knowledge and understanding. Recognising the importance of these values will help you to understand the way they write and speak.

Getting to know your discipline

The subjects you study may fall within a single discipline or across several (say, sociology, psychology and health studies). In either case you will find that, alongside mainstream information and ideas, you are learning about the history of your discipline(s). Gradually as you build up a picture of influential past writers and key debates you see why particular issues came to be treated as important. This is extremely valuable because, as we have seen, what is said in academic discourse often takes such background knowledge for granted. Eventually, you find the meaning of texts in your discipline(s) much more transparent, because you know 'where they are coming from'. You discover that you are becoming a member of the community, able to join in debates and understand what is going on.

Key points

■ Academic knowledge does not come in handy, off-the-shelf packages. You have to seek it out by engaging in academic discourse.

■ It is easier to understand academic discourse if you are aware of the value placed on a perpetual search for truth through logical reasoning, research and open debate.

■ Understanding becomes easier as you get to know some of the background to your discipline(s) and become more aware of what is generally taken for granted.

4.3.2 Key features of academic discourse

We have talked of the values underpinning the search for knowledge within academic disciplines. Now we explore in more detail the way those values shape academic discourse. This will help you to understand what is going on as you read and listen. It will also help you in learning to write in the academic way *but do bear in mind that it takes practice to become skilled in this way of writing*. You will pick it up a little at a time as you continue your studies.

Here then are eight key features of academic discourse, which make it powerful, but at the same time challenging to read and to write.

1 Debate

Debate lies at the heart of academic discourse. Discipline members advance knowledge by taking up opposing positions and trying to defeat each other's case. Ideas emerge from these debates either strengthened or else damaged and in need of re-working. Any academic text you read is likely to have been written as an argument against someone else's position. For example, in his three lectures, Richard Layard argues that because economists have assumed that happiness cannot be measured satisfactorily, they have paid too little attention to how people's happiness might be increased. So, he sets out to show that happiness can and must be measured because it is too important to ignore. He begins his argument by claiming that, in the early days of economics, happiness *was* a central concern. Layard's three lectures only make proper sense if you recognise that this debate with fellow members of his discipline is a key theme.

As a newcomer, it is easy to miss the point of something you have read because you are not aware of the debate that it is responding to. Learning about major debates in the history of your discipline is an important part of becoming competent in your subject. You also have to get into the mindset of valuing debate. In essays, for example, you are expected to compare different points of view and present each one fairly, before weighing them up against each other. And you write from the point of view that readers will be 'debating with you' as they read.

2 Scholarship

See Chapter 10 Section 10.7.1, How academic debate works

Academic writers are expected to maintain standards of scholarship by keeping abreast of debates within their discipline. You presume that a writer will have researched recent publications relevant to their subject – this is known as a 'literature search'. When in the quote Richard Layard claims that economics 'evolved as the study of utility or happiness' you expect him to have read relevant sources and to be able, if asked, to explain how he drew this conclusion.

Because academic arguments build on what has been written before, writers are expected to supply details. *References* are scattered throughout academic texts to indicate who contributed to the debate, and when – for example, '(Layard, 2003)'. A list of references at the end of the text gives full details of all the references used. Learning to put references in your assignments is one of the most visible steps towards adopting an academic writing style.

See Chapter 10 Section 10.6.2, Plagiarism

Free exchange of knowledge within a discipline rests on the assumption that members will play fair and give due credit when they use other people's ideas, arguments and research. Not to do so is seen as a major breach of faith. If you go further and pass off another person's work as your own this is 'plagiarism' and it will seriously damage your reputation.

3 Argument

In academic discourse what you say should unfold as logical argument. An argument starts from a clearly established issue for debate then presents a sequence of points, each logically connected to what has gone before. This sequence is arranged so as to lead up to a conclusion. You have already seen the first manoeuvres in launching an argument in the earlier extract from Richard Layard's lecture. Activity 4.3 contains another example, this time from the opening of his article 'The secrets of happiness' (which is at the end of this book):

Activity 4.3

 There is a paradox at the heart of our civilisation. Individuals want more income. Yet as society has got richer, people have not become happier. Over the past 50 years we have got better homes, more clothes, longer holidays and, above all, better health. Yet surveys show clearly that happiness has not increased in the US, Japan, Continental Europe or Britain.

(Layard, 2003b)

Can you see how Richard Layard sets up his argument? Look at each sentence in turn and jot down what you think it does for the argument.

- The article begins with three short sentences. The first sentence signals that the article will focus on a key paradox (or contradiction) in our kind of society. The second and third sentences each present one side of the paradox.

- The fourth sentence elaborates on the third sentence by giving a time scale and examples of what is meant by 'richer'.

- The final sentence indicates the evidence that can be used to support the second part of the third sentence, as well as indicating the geographical sweep.

Every word is part of the setting up of Layard's argument, which he then goes on to develop in the rest of his article.

When you read Layard's article in full for the activities in Chapter 5, you will see that everything in it has a direct bearing on what is said in this opening. In an academic text you assume that every part contributes in some way to the author's argument. As you read you should be trying to pick out this argument. Similarly, when you write an essay you should plan it as an argument, leading from the title to the conclusion. Anything which does not contribute to your argument you should leave out.

See Chapter 10 Section 10.7.1, How academic debate works

4 Criticism

In academic discourse as well as presenting your own arguments you criticise other people's. In this context, to criticise means to discuss bad *and* good aspects of an argument. Knowledge advances through examining arguments carefully and judging their strengths and weaknesses. In everyday life it may seem impolite or boring to keep picking holes in what someone says, but in academic discourse it is a duty. You are expected to be constantly on the look out.

5 Analysis

Analysis means taking things apart to see what they are made of and how they work. You might analyse the power struggles in a period of history, the way words are used in a poem, or the processes of change in an organisation. Layard offers some analysis of what getting richer means by listing aspects of our increasing wealth. In academic discourse you analyse arguments to see how the logic flows from one step to the next. This is what *you* did in Activity 4.3, when you examined Layard's opening argument by taking it apart sentence by sentence.

Analysis and criticism go together. You take ideas and arguments apart in order to probe for weaknesses and identify strengths. This is called *critical analysis*. The critical–analytical approach is, perhaps, the most distinctive characteristic of academic discourse.

6 Evidence

You do not accept what you have read simply because it is written by a respectable person, or because it is written with style and conviction. You expect to be offered the evidence to back up the arguments. It may be evidence which the writer has found from personal research, or evidence quoted from other sources. Here is another extract from Layard's article 'The secrets of happiness', where he is quoting evidence from another source:

> We [...] know that clinical depression, assessed professionally through population surveys, has risen in most countries. A survey from London University's Institute of Education, out this month, shows that as many as 29 per cent of women aged 30 in 2000 reported suffering trouble with nerves or feeling low, depressed or sad.
>
> *(Layard, 2003b)*

7 Objectivity

Arguments are expected to be presented objectively, or neutrally. They are judged on the quality of their logic, scholarship and evidence, not who they are presented by nor how enthusiastically, stylishly, or entertainingly. As a writer you set your own beliefs and feelings to one side and adopt an objective stance – detached and unemotional. You leave readers to analyse, criticise and come to their own conclusions. Richard Layard, for example, does not suggest that people are greedy for wanting more income, or that not being happier serves them right. We don't know what he thinks about affluent lifestyles. He doesn't try to whip up alarm. He simply presents us with logical analysis, argument and evidence.

8 Precision

Finally, academic discourse strives to be precise. You try to say exactly what you mean and no more. You avoid sweeping generalisations. You avoid overstating your case. You leave out whatever does not make a direct contribution to your argument. There are no frills – no pleasantries, diplomacy, anecdotes, or human interest. It is a task-oriented discourse and that task is to seek truth through reasoning. All else is irrelevant.

Key points

Academic discourse is the tool-kit of the academic trade. The basic tools are:

- **Debate** Setting ideas and viewpoints up against each other in order to test them out.

- **Scholarship** Showing how your arguments link to the literature of the discipline.

- **Argument** Presenting logically connected sequences of points that lead to conclusions.

- **Critical analysis** Taking ideas and arguments apart to evaluate their strengths and weaknesses.

- **Evidence** Presenting the evidence to back up your arguments.

- **Objectivity** Writing in a detached, unemotional way, leaving your arguments to stand on their own merits.

- **Precision** Saying what needs to be said to present your argument and no more.

You need to be aware of these tools at the outset, so that you have an idea of what you are aiming towards. Your skill in using them will develop as you continue your dialogue with the subject.

4.4 Reading, listening, speaking and writing

In Section 4.2.3 I suggested that studying is like having a dialogue with your chosen subject. You 'take in' new ideas and information, then you 'reply', putting the ideas and information to use. The four basic ways of engaging in this dialogue are reading, listening, speaking and writing. Two use the written word and two the spoken word.

The principal challenges of reading are:

- **Getting started** Getting a sense of what the text is about and what it is trying to say (establishing a frame of reference) so that you can get a flow of meaning going in your mind.

- **Keeping going** Maintaining the flow of meaning when you encounter unfamiliar words and ideas.

- **Coping with blocks** Developing strategies to kick-start your reading when the flow of meaning stalls.

4.4.2 Listening

There are various ways in which you can learn by listening – lectures, seminar discussions, the radio, TV or recorded material. What all these have in common is that the speaker drives the flow of meaning. You still have to work at making sense of what you hear, but you get carried along by the momentum of the speaker's words.

Advantages of learning by listening

Framing When people speak they usually recognise, at some level, the need to let listeners know what they are talking about. Good lecturers set out a clear frame of reference for what they are going to say.

Last week I outlined the main features of the Beveridge Report and the circumstances under which the post-war Labour government set out to implement its recommendations. This week I'm going to look at how and why the initial principles were modified by both Labour and Conservative governments over the next thirty years.

As you will remember, Beveridge had set out to slay the five giants: Want, Disease, Ignorance, Squalor and Idleness [...]

Even if the speaker doesn't frame the topic as explicitly as this, there are usually other indirect clues. Unlike reading, where you have to get a frame up and running for yourself, when you listen the framing is done for you. This is especially valuable with unfamiliar topics which you have little experience of framing.

Pacing The speaker drives the meaning forward. You don't have to work at sustaining the momentum. Even when you hear unfamiliar words and ideas that don't make much sense, you can carry on listening, pick up clues and tune into the meaning once again.

Multi-channel communication Speakers invest words with meaning through the way they are spoken and through facial expressions, hand gestures and body posture. They may use visual aids such as slides, or handouts showing the structure of the ideas they are presenting. Consequently, the flow of meaning is supported by much more than just spoken words.

Hearing an expert Hearing the language and ideas of the discipline spoken by an expert gives you first-hand experience of how the ideas of the discipline are used to make sense of the world. You hear how arguments are linked to the big debates, how criticism works, how conclusions are drawn. The speaker models how academic discourse is spoken, providing valuable support in developing your own ability to speak it.

BOX 4.3 TAKING IN NEW IDEAS THROUGH LISTENING

You know the old conundrum about which came first, the chicken or the egg? Working with new ideas involves a similar puzzle. The members of an academic discipline share many assumptions about the questions they are trying to answer. When you try to join a discussion, it can be hard to make sense of what is being talked about, because you don't know these underlying assumptions. The only way you can begin to grasp these assumptions is through participating in discussions within the discipline. But participating is what you are having difficulty with because you don't share the assumptions. So which comes first?

To get into a new topic you have to circle around for a while, picking up the gist as best you can, until ideas and underlying assumptions start to come together for you. The problem is particularly acute when you are reading, because you are on your own, whereas when you hear someone speak you get a sense of how the meaning is intended to flow. Even if you don't understand fully you pick up clues about the kind of ideas in play, where the argument starts from, how it draws on evidence and where it ends up. These clues give you much more to work with next time you are reading and thinking about the discussion on your own.

Ironically, when new ideas eventually 'click', it's hard to remember what was so difficult. Because the ideas and your assumptions now 'fit' together the meaning seems obvious.

Challenges of listening

Of course, the advantages outlined above depend on a reasonably good speaker, and lecturers can be rather variable. But even with a good speaker, listening is demanding:

See Chapter 7 Section 7.4, Listening to talk

- **Keeping pace** A speaker has to guess the pace at which 'average' audience members are able to absorb the flow of ideas – too fast and listeners are left floundering, too slow and attention wanders. The speaker's guess may not be right for you.

- **Maintaining concentration** Even when the pace is manageable, it is easy to lose the thread after a period of close concentration. You may become distracted because you are learning a lot, which is making you think, and the next thing you notice you've lost track.

- **Taking notes** It is hard to stay in touch with a speaker's flow of information and make high-quality notes at the same time.

- **Summarising and recalling** Even when you follow a talk closely, it is difficult to pull together everything you have heard. Since the speaker is in control, you have to go with the flow and it can be hard to keep the 'big picture' in mind.

We have looked at reading and listening, the 'taking in' modes of dialogue. Now we turn to speaking and writing, the 'expressive' modes through which you learn to put new ideas to use. This is where you gain control over your new knowledge.

4.4.3 Speaking

Opportunities to learn through speaking generally arise in group work of some kind: seminars, tutorials, workshops and team projects; though you can also learn from informal chats outside of the classroom.

Advantages of learning through speaking

Spontaneity By joining in with a discussion you experience new ideas in action. This helps you gain hands-on knowledge of how to develop arguments. You don't have time to stop and worry about what to say. You seize the moment and make sense as best you can. Whereas reading and writing give a sense of dealing with ideas at arms length, in discussion you are in there amongst them.

Momentum In the flow of a discussion the supports for making meaning are all around you. No staring at a blank page. You simply ride on the framing and momentum generated by the group.

Dialogue In a discussion you participate in a two-way exchange. Questions can be asked and answered, understandings can be shared. As you explain a point to someone else, you find you understand it better yourself. Much of your student experience is one-way; either you are taking in arguments from a writer or speaker, or you are giving out your arguments in an assignment. In dialogue you can share in shaping an argument and experience being part of a community of thinkers, making meaning together.

Instant feedback Discussion helps you learn how to use the language of your subject. You try out ways of saying things and find out instantly whether you have been understood. This live practice is also very helpful in improving your written fluency.

Social context Discussion helps you to feel that you are part of the discipline community and this in turn helps you develop an academic voice. Over a sequence of discussions you start out with your everyday voice and gradually find yourself using a more analytical voice.

BOX 4.4 FINDING YOUR ACADEMIC VOICE

One of the challenges of writing about academic ideas is to develop a suitable 'voice' in which to discuss them. Discussing ideas can help you find the calm, detached voice of critical analysis, objectivity and precision, rather than using the persuasive, personal voice of everyday conversation.

Challenges of speaking

- **Awkwardness** Classroom discussion can sometimes be strained and intimidating, with awkward silences and nobody venturing to say much. If you are new to the subject matter the risks of appearing foolish can seem to loom large.

See Chapter 7, Learning through talk

- **Finding an opening** In a large class and with an evolving debate, it can be difficult to find the right moment to join in, unless the teacher breaks the class into smaller groups.

- **Keeping track** The focus of discussion shifts with each new speaker, so it can be difficult to keep track of what is being talked about. This can also make it hard to work out what to say.

4.4.4 Writing

Writing enables precise expression and detailed criticism. Once you capture an idea in words you can examine its logic. You can move words around or substitute other words to see if the idea can be expressed more clearly and accurately. You can come back to the idea as many times as you like, and, because it is fixed on the page, you can build on it. You can create a sequence of clearly connected points – a precisely stated argument, and offer it to others for criticism. This is why academic knowledge is strongly associated with the written word. It is also why writing is a key mode of learning. It draws your attention to the structure of arguments, to the assembling of evidence and to coherent presentation.

Assignments offer the most compelling opportunity to learn through writing. For many students this is the most demanding of study activities but, as the students in Section 4.2 of this chapter observed, it also leads to the most profound learning. If you are tempted to think of assignments primarily as a means to achieving grades, don't. They play a key role in your learning.

Advantages of learning through writing

Putting knowledge to use Writing gives you the incentive to pull together the knowledge you have gained through studying and to work out how to put it to use. This helps you to take 'ownership' of knowledge so that it becomes part of your thinking apparatus.

Taking control Whereas it can be difficult to organise a coherent argument when you speak, you can build arguments carefully in writing. You can sketch out plans and alter what you have written to make your argument more convincing. It is your best opportunity to learn how to argue effectively.

Using your own words You can use the language of the discipline to say things in ways that make sense to you. This is vital in your becoming competent in using the ideas and arguments of your subject.

Expert feedback Assignments provide your best opportunity to receive coaching in how to present arguments using the language of the discipline. Your relationship with your teacher through your writing plays a key part in developing your identity as a member of your academic discipline.

BOX 4.5   DEVELOPING A DISCIPLINE IDENTITY

Who are you speaking as when you write? What is your relationship to the knowledge you are presenting? Is it in any sense *your* knowledge, or are you just going through the motions? To argue convincingly you need to develop a sense of identity as a member of the academic community which discusses this knowledge. Though initially you are an apprentice member, you still share ownership of the community's knowledge. Developing this sense of identity as a student of your subject is part of finding an academic 'voice'.

In a sense, your student years are a period of apprenticeship to your subject discipline. As you learn the language and culture of your discipline, you gradually secure a more established identity, which will allow you to participate with increasing effectiveness.

Challenges of writing

See Chapter 10, Writing the way 'they' want and Chapter 11, Managing the writing process

Because writing advances your learning significantly it calls on all your resources.

- **Deciding what to say** Working out the assignment task and making a selection from the many issues you could discuss.

- **Presenting an argument** Working out an argument and how to support it and present it.

■ **Speaking to your reader** Writing in a way that makes sense to someone else; creating a flow of meaning and keeping the reader in touch with it.

■ **Keeping up morale** Surviving the long slog and crises of writing.

Table 4.2	Advantages and challenges of different modes of discourse	
	Advantages	**Challenges**
Reading	you can search, focus, analyse, revisit, take detailed notes and reflect	getting to grips with the meaning, keeping it flowing, coping with blocks
Listening	meaning is framed and driven along for you, and you hear the discourse spoken by an expert	maintaining concentration, thinking while listening, trying to summarise and recall
Writing	you can put ideas to use, learn to argue using the language of the subject and develop your voice and identity	deciding what to say, structuring an argument, supporting it, creating a flow, finding a voice
Speaking	you can ride on the framing and momentum generated by others and develop your discourse skills	feeling confused and exposed, expressing unfamiliar ideas, competing for 'air time', losing the thread

4.5 Becoming knowledgeable

In this chapter we have seen that learning at higher levels is primarily about understanding ideas. You make these ideas your own by engaging in debates through reading, listening, speaking and writing. You also learn the skills of academic discourse, which enable you to construct powerful arguments backed by scholarship and evidence. The outcome of all this is considerably more valuable than a 'pile of information' in your head. You become an actively knowledgeable person – able to follow what experts are talking about, able to question what you read, able to ask probing questions and criticise arguments, and able to find things out and present arguments of your own.

If any of this sounds rather overwhelming, as you take your early steps in studying, remember the people you met in earlier chapters, such as Zahra, Nathan, Ryan and the students quoted from chat-rooms. Everyone struggles to begin with. Everyone doubts their abilities and their determination. It's a long route with many twists and turns, but it is also a very interesting journey, full of insights and moments of achievement. You don't have to spend every minute thinking about the big issues discussed in this chapter; you just get stuck into next week's work and enjoy the learning. What you have read here is for those moments when you are puzzled about why you are not making progress or when you want to understand more about what it is you are striving to achieve.

I hope that the ideas in this chapter have provided a helpful background for the more practically-focused chapters in Part 2 of the book. And I hope that Part 1, by taking a broad view of the study enterprise will, as its title claims, help you to study intelligently.

References

Layard, R. (2003a) 'Happiness: Has social science a clue?', *Lionel Robbins Memorial Lectures 2002/3*, London School of Economics 3-5 March 2003, http://cep.lse.ac.uk/events/lectures/layard/RL030303.pdf (accessed 1 April 2004).

Layard, R. (2003b) 'The secrets of happiness', *New Statesman*, 3 March 2003, p. 25.

PART 2 THE ESSENTIAL SKILLS

CHAPTER 5 READING

5.1 Reading is easy, isn't it?

On any ordinary day without even noticing, you read shop signs, newspaper headlines, TV listings, a magazine, or a chapter of a paperback. So why would a message like this one appear in an online student chat room in the early weeks of a course?

> Is there any one out there feeling overwhelmed by the reading, or is it just me? Starting to think about giving up – bit pathetic I know, but just wondering if any of it is going in! Feeling bogged down – not sure whether to keep going, or try to recap or what. Any suggestions gratefully received.

Clearly, reading for higher level study is quite different from everyday reading. The most obvious differences are:

- **Quantity** As a student you can find yourself reading for many more hours a week than usual.

- **Difficulty** Instead of the message slipping easily into your mind, as when you read a newspaper or a paperback, you find yourself having to concentrate to grasp it.

But there are also more subtle differences:

- **Purpose** Instead of reading to pick up information, or to be entertained, with studying your aim is to introduce yourself to *new ideas* and *ways of thinking*, which will enable you to understand the world differently.

- **Active engagement** Studying involves actively working with new ideas, not just racing through the words. You have to look for the *meaning* as you read, asking yourself '*what is the author trying to say?*'

Research into how students read (see, for example, Entwistle 1997, p.19) has shown that to be successful you need to understand these more hidden aspects of the reading process.

5.2 The experience of reading

The best way to develop your understanding of the reading process is to follow the principles of the Kolb learning cycle, by *doing* some reading and then *reflecting* on your experience. To this end, Activity 5.1 asks you to read an extract from an article by Richard Layard (2003) titled 'The secrets of happiness' which appeared in the *New Statesman* and which we reproduce in the Appendix. To keep the task manageable I have reduced the article to

See Chapter 1 Section 1.6, Being a reflective learner

half its original length and, for ease of reference, paragraph numbers have been added.

It is important that you read the article as a lot of discussion in this and later chapters assumes you have done so.

BOX 5.1 MAKING COPIES OF RICHARD LAYARD'S ARTICLE

You will find Richard Layard's article in Appendix 1, at the end of this book. As you will be coming back to it several times to work on it in different ways, it could end up looking a mess. A better option is to download it from the *Good Study Guide* website at www.goodstudyguide.co.uk, print off a few copies and work on them without inhibition.

Activity 5.1

First note down the time you start, then read the article 'The secrets of happiness' by Richard Layard. As you read, jot down a few thoughts on the first five questions below. Don't skip this note taking, it will help you to reflect on your reading afterwards.

1 What are your feelings about reading the article?

2 Are you experiencing any difficulties as you read?

3 Are there parts of the article you find unclear?

4 Does the article seem interesting? Does it seem worth the time you are spending on it?

5 Where and at what time of day are you doing the reading?

When you have finished reading the article, jot down your answers to these final questions:

6 How long did you take to read it?

7 Did you make any markings on the article as you read it (using a highlighter pen, ballpoint, or pencil), or write notes?

8 In a sentence, what is the article about? (Don't look back, work from memory.)

9 What can you remember from the article? Write down two or three points that stood out for you.

10 Do you think you will be able to remember what was in the article this time next week?

Below you will see the responses to Activity 5.1 given by four students: Salim, Erin, Lewis and Kate. Like you, they were busy with other coursework. Compare your notes with theirs and reflect on the reasons for any differences.

1 What are your feelings about reading the article?

Salim: It's interesting, but a bit of a struggle to finish.

Erin: It's widening my knowledge of how different people think.

Lewis: I first turn the pages and think – two and a half pages – groan.

Kate: Visually, it looks difficult to read. I feel it will be a 'drudge'.

Notice that Lewis and Kate seem to have approached the article as 'work', something to 'get through'. Neither looks forward to reading it. (Lewis explained later that he receives support for dyslexia and feels daunted when confronted with several pages to read.) Salim and Erin, on the other hand, focus on what the article is *about*, rather than what the pages look like. They take an interest in what it has to offer, though Salim is flagging towards the end.

2 Are you experiencing any difficulties as you read?

Salim: Paragraph 6, I'm losing a bit of concentration. There's a lot to keep thinking about.

Erin: I am finding some parts hard to grasp. Not easy reading. I wouldn't be able to read it if there were distractions. Don't know what 'marginal tax' is.

Lewis: Just that it's the morning after the night before.

Kate: Put off by the word 'paradox'. Too many facts and figures. Too much to learn.

They all seem to agree that the article is demanding. Salim and Erin feel that they are being made to think hard. Lewis is wondering whether he is just having a bad morning. Kate, meanwhile, is already recoiling by the fourth word. She doesn't sound very keen to immerse herself in what the article is about.

3 Are there parts of the article you find unclear?

Salim: Don't really get paragraphs 13 and 14 about tax rates.

Erin: Yes – several parts.

Lewis: Paragraph 6 seems a bit of a jumble to me, reading straight through the article and not going over it again.

Kate: The article doesn't flow well. It seems to jump about. Richard Layard doesn't seem to be getting across what he wants to say.

Salim, Erin and Lewis have all got stuck at particular points, while Kate says she finds the whole article unclear.

4 Does the article seem interesting? Does it seem worth the time?

Salim: I found the article interesting, worth the time I spent on it.

Erin: It does seem worthwhile and makes me want more information on the subject.

Lewis: Interesting but goes on a bit. Can relate to some of it. The Harvard survey seems interesting.

Kate: The subject is interesting, but Richard Layard's article isn't.

In spite of the challenges the article presented, Salim and Erin seem to have found it stimulating. Lewis has a more mixed response and Kate, once again, expresses hostility.

5   Where and at what time of day are you doing the reading?

Salim: At home, 8.22 pm.

Erin: 6 pm – It is a nice day, Jamie is asleep so I am sitting outside.

Lewis: Sunday 9.47 am, in front room, quiet.

Kate: Morning. It is quiet and I'm at my best.

The four have found the opportunity to do the reading at very different times of day. Clearly there is no 'correct' time for reading. It depends on you and the patterns of your life.

6   How long did you take to read it?

Salim: 30 minutes

Erin: 16 minutes

Lewis: 20 minutes

Kate: 10 minutes

Since the article was not 'coursework', the students did not have an incentive to spend much time on it. However, Salim spent three times as long on it as Kate. Both Salim and Erin, in later answers, indicate that they would have spent further time re-reading the article, if they needed to remember what was in it.

7   Did you make any markings on the article, or write notes?

Salim: Yes, I used a highlighter.

Erin: I made a few notes separately.

Lewis: No.

Kate: No.

Salim and Erin worked actively as they read. Lewis and Kate didn't.

8   In a sentence, what is the article about?

Salim: It's about happiness and how if one person has more money, especially someone in your family, you will feel down about this.

Erin: It is about money and how different people become happy.

Lewis: How happiness is increased or decreased from the effects of people themselves, or other people's wages.

Kate: We are a lot unhappier now, even though we have more money.

Salim and Lewis show a grasp of one of the key themes of the article. Erin's answer is a bit vague. Kate's is accurate, but could be taken from the first paragraph alone.

9   What two or three points stood out for you?

Salim: Having more money makes people want still more; when we earn more, other people are less happy; we have a better life style, nice homes and holidays and good health but we are no happier.

Erin: It is not always being the wealthiest which makes you happy; comparing wages to families i.e. husband and wife. Keeping up with the Joneses.

Lewis: The Harvard survey; how east Germans compare their wages to west Germans.

Kate: Harvard students are stupid; Denmark and Germany were somewhere in there.

Salim has captured some of the central points. So has Erin to a lesser degree. Lewis has focused in on specific elements in the article which he found interesting. Kate's response is flippant and suggests she didn't approach the article very seriously.

10 Will you be able to remember the article next week?

Salim: I would have to read things over and discuss them to start remembering what was in the article. I might remember a bit.

Erin: Yes some parts, but would need to read it again.

Lewis: Some aspects.

Kate: Yes, the main points.

Interestingly, Salim and Erin, who both seem to have engaged quite effectively with the article, suggest that they would need to do more work on the article to remember it. Kate thinks she will remember the main points, though her responses don't indicate having grasped much beyond the opening paragraph.

A pattern seems to emerge here. Salim and Erin appear to have worked actively on the article and tried to understand its main themes. In the process, they found the article interesting, could remember it better and wanted to continue with further reading. Lewis was feeling somewhat the worse for wear and tended to focus on particular parts of the article that interested him, but he nevertheless gained a reasonable grasp of what it was about. Meanwhile Kate seems to have taken against the article from the outset, spent little time on it, read fairly superficially and learned little. It would be a mistake to draw firm conclusions from just these brief notes, however, in Chapter 10 you can read extracts from essays these students wrote and consider whether the impressions we have gleaned here are reflected in the quality of their writing.

How did your responses compare with those of Salim, Erin, Lewis and Kate? Did reading their responses cast light on your own approach to reading the article?

Key points

Reading for study purposes is a demanding activity. You will learn best if you:

- take an interest in what the text is about

- make a determined effort to understand the main arguments

- work actively on the text as you read.

5.3 Getting round obstacles

Salim, Erin, Lewis and Kate all mentioned various difficulties encountered as they read the Layard article. Perhaps your experience was similar. If so, how did you respond? Was your progress held up, or did you manage to keep going? With lots of reading to do, it is important to have ways of finding your way round the obstacles you encounter.

5.3.1 Unfamiliar words

Kate was put off by the word 'paradox' and Erin did not know what 'marginal tax' meant. I, too, noted down 'real income', 'norm', 'habituation' and 'non-monetary benefits', as terms not common in everyday speech. Were there words *you* were not familiar with? If so, what did you do about them?

Should you stop reading to look words up?

It depends. Looking up words slows you down, and you may be able to make reasonable sense of their context without having to. For example, I found it fairly easy to guess the meaning of 'habituation' in paragraph 8, from the way it was discussed. However, I looked it up on the internet anyway, as I happened to have my computer on (this search is described in Chapter 9). I also looked up 'real income' and 'marginal tax' and found useful clarification of their meanings.

See Chapter 9 Section 9.2, Finding information

You have to decide how important a word seems to be. Do you feel you are missing something by not knowing it? Does it keep appearing? If you just carry on reading, the word may become clearer as you experience it being used (after all, that's how we get to know the meaning of most words).

Sometimes it's not one particular word that's difficult, but a string of them. For example, when I read 'clinical depression, assessed professionally through population surveys', I had to slow down. Having taken in the meaning, it seemed to me that 'depression' was the main word I needed to pay attention to, so I underlined it.

See Chapter 5 Section 5.5, Reading actively

BOX 5.2   FRUSTRATION WITH SPECIALIST TERMS

It's easy to feel put-off by unfamiliar terms, or by words used in unfamiliar ways. You feel excluded from the in-crowd and it's annoying having to struggle to squeeze meaning out of every sentence. But specialist language is not used deliberately to annoy. Developing new ideas and fitting new terms to them is part of the process of creating knowledge. In the end, you have to accept that grappling with specialist terms is part of the learning process.

Dictionaries

One way to tackle the challenge of unfamiliar words is to use a dictionary. You could use a traditional printed dictionary, or an online dictionary, or both. A printed dictionary is easy to keep beside you wherever you happen to be reading. But an online dictionary holds the advantage when it comes looking up words quickly as you can look up a word in three or four online dictionaries simultaneously, to compare the definitions they offer.

You also have a choice between using a *general* dictionary, or a *specialist* dictionary for the subject that you are studying. How helpful you find either will depend on your subject, so it is worth doing a little exploring to find out. Note down a few 'difficult' words from one of your main textbooks. Then visit a bookshop, or go online and find a few dictionaries. Look your words up to see if they are included and whether the definitions make sense to you.

See Chapter 9 Section 9.2, Finding information

Dictionaries are an invaluable resource but don't expect them to be infallible. A general dictionary will often not include key words from your subject area, or will give a definition which is misleading because the nuances of meaning are not right for your subject. On the other hand, specialist dictionary definitions can be difficult to understand.

Concept cards

Another way to tackle unfamiliar words is to start a 'concept card' system, using index cards. When you meet a word which seems important, take a new card and write the word at the top, followed by any useful information you have found. File the cards alphabetically and add details as you come across new information. (It is worth getting an index card box anyway, then you can try out various ways of using it to organise your studies.)

> Real Income
>
> Income of indiv., org., or country, after taking into account effect of inflatn. on purchasing power. (Also: real wages) http://www.investorwords.com
>
> Layard: New Statesman. 3 Mar 2003: real incomes have risen hugely → no change in patterns of happiness

Figure 5.1 **Sample of a 'concept card'**

If, on the other hand, you prefer to use your computer, you could search online for index card software. Try www.download.com, which reviews free software and provides download links. Just type 'index card' into the Search box. The example in Figure 5.2 is from PS CardFile Pegasus.

Of course, making concept cards is time consuming. You need to weigh up, as you go along, how much benefit you are getting and how much time is worth investing.

5.3.2 The 'academic' style

You might also be put off by the 'academic' style of writing. In everyday life, what you read is usually written to grab your attention and get a message across quickly before you 'switch channels'. By contrast, academic texts often raise broad, abstract questions and are unconcerned about arriving at quick answers. For example, where a newspaper headline might say:

VOTERS READY FOR TAX & SPEND CLAIMS GURU

Layard actually says:

... taxation is one of the most important institutions we have for preserving a sensible balance between work and leisure [...] I suspect that, in some almost unconscious way, the electorate now understands that the scramble to spend more is partially self-defeating and that this explains why people are more favourable to public expenditure. But the time is ripe to make the argument explicit.

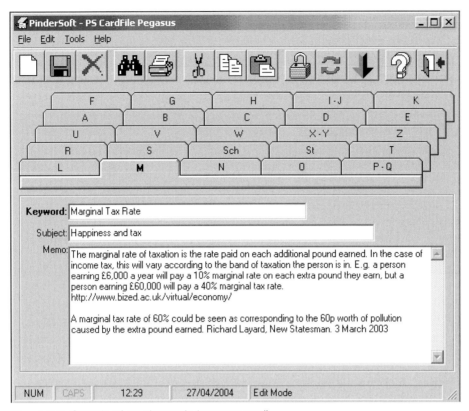

Figure 5.2 **Sample of an electronic 'concept card'**

(Source: PinderSoft, 2004)

The headline makes its point quickly, but it says far less. It presents little basis for analysis and debate. You can agree or disagree, but you can't easily discuss the proposition. Layard carefully teases out a variety of issues, but the headline simplifies everything down to a well-established formula: free markets or public spending – which side are you on? Unlike general public debate, academic debate advances through finely tuned language and disciplined methods of argument. The Layard paragraph may be a lot longer than the headline, but it is not 'wordy' for the sake of it. It is very precisely argued; it would be quite difficult to cut out words without altering the meaning.

BOX 5.3 ACADEMIC WRITING

Academic writers use cautious, considered language in an effort to be as *exact* as they can in their analysis. They try to say *only* what they mean and what they think can be *justified*. In daily life we cheerfully use language as a blunt instrument, to cudgel our way through the discussions that spring up around us. By contrast, academic writing uses language as a scalpel, to cut precisely between closely related

See Chapter 4 Section 4.3, Why do they write that way?

arguments, so that they can be prised apart and analysed in detail. Learning how to read, think and write in this way is a central part of learning at degree level.

5.3.3 Coping with difficult parts

Salim and Lewis mentioned that they found some sections of Layard's article difficult. So did I; for example, anyone without a background in economics would have difficulty grasping the arguments in paragraphs 13 and 14.

So what should you do when you can't make sense of what you read? Should you search online to find out about taxation theory? For my own satisfaction I searched for a definition of 'marginal rate of taxation' just to get the gist of it. I also tried to write down the main steps of the argument in paragraphs 13 and 14 in my own words; however, I soon felt I wasn't doing much more than copying out the original words, without getting any closer to the nub of it. So, I decided to move on; but first I made a stab at summarising what I had read. This is what I wrote:

Top levels of tax should be higher, to discourage people from 'polluting' the happiness of others → then more can go into public expenditure. Europeans seem to accept 60% as top tax rate (including indirect tax).

As the article is about 'happiness' not 'tax', it did not seem worth investing any more time in these two paragraphs. I felt I understood enough to follow the general gist of Layard's argument. You don't have to understand fully to benefit from reading when you study but you do have to constantly keep weighing up:

- *why* you are reading that particular text,

- what you need to *get out* of it, and

- whether you are making enough *progress* to justify the time it is taking.

How long did *you* spend on paragraphs 13 and 14? Did you feel you were able to understand enough for the purposes of getting through this article? Or did you just skip ahead to the last paragraph? If you weren't 'getting it', that was a good decision. It's important not to let the tough bits beat you. They often make more sense when you come back another time.

BOX 5.4   GLIMPSES OF UNDERSTANDING

When you are new to a subject, your ideas keep being shaken up and reshaped. A thought comes briefly into focus then dissolves into confusion again. It is rare to feel you understand something fully. Instead you learn to get by on glimpses of insight.

5.3.4 Disagreeing with the author

It is clear from Kate's responses that from the outset she felt hostile to Layard's article and to Layard himself. As she later explained in a seminar, she felt that he looked down on people with low incomes, such as herself. She felt she was being told that she wasn't happy with her life and that she envied people with lots of possessions. In her philosophy, she said, happiness had nothing to do with wealth. She was just as capable of being happy as the richest people in the country. Because of her hostile feelings she read quickly, writing sarcastic ripostes on to the text.

Reacting to what you read is good; it gets you thinking. It can be very helpful to write 'dead right', or 'rubbish', or 'what about the effect of ...?' in the margins of a text. However, Kate did not, in reality, react to Layard's arguments, she reacted to what she *expected* him to say. Kate was so convinced that Layard knew nothing of what he was writing about, and that his evidence was biased, that she took in very little of what he actually did say.

Yet, on the face of it, her position was not so different from Layard's. They both agree that wealth does not bring happiness and both favour redistribution to the less well-off. Although Kate referred to him as a privileged 'fat cat', with nothing useful to say about her world, his expertise is in policies to improve the prospects of unemployed people such as herself. Kate had important points to make about the way research can belittle the lives of 'ordinary people', by reducing the richness of their experience to tables of numbers. But the strength of her commitment to this point of view seemed to exclude her from participating in *any* discussion about the issues Layard raises.

We are, of course, all entitled to our own views. However, if you want to access a body of knowledge, you have to be ready to enter into the ways of thinking in that discipline. To benefit from reading a text you have to be prepared to get alongside the writer and think their thoughts *with* them. You have to be ready to try out the writer's point of view in order to understand what they are saying (see Box 4.1 'How reading works'). *Then* you can pause to reflect and react.

Many ideas seem unappealing when you first meet them, but if you only read what you already agree with, you won't learn much. Part of the skill of studying is learning to cope with not feeling happy with what an author is saying, *distancing yourself* from your hostile feelings, so that you can read on. It isn't easy, because reading is like a conversation with a very talkative person, who leaves no breaks for you to speak. If you disagree with the writer, this can feel very oppressive. However, to participate in academic debate you have to be able to think on all sides of an argument.

See Chapter 4 Section 4.4.1, Reading

BOX 5.5   A DETACHED STANCE

Logic is supposed to work best when it is not distorted by emotions. When you read academic texts you are supposed to be able to detach your thoughts from your feelings. You are expected to put your personal bias to one side and judge arguments on their soundness. However, you cannot be completely detached, or you wouldn't have a position from which to think about what you read. So *first* you have to get 'inside' the author's point of view, *then* stand back and compare it with other points of view. You can learn a lot by thinking and arguing from points of view that you don't actually hold.

5.3.5 Poor environment

Were you held back at all in your reading by the environment you were reading in? Were you reading in bed, in the bath, sitting at a desk, on the bus, or in the park? Any of these *could* be a good time and place, but did it actually work for you?

 I regularly leave some reading material close at hand in the bathroom.

Were you able to maintain your concentration for a good long spell? Did you have all the materials you needed to hand, such as pen, paper and dictionary? Did you need a surface to write on as you read? Do you read best in a regular spot, or do you need to keep moving to different places? Don't just take your reading environment for granted. Think about whether you are giving yourself a reasonable chance of success. You may not be able to arrange a 'perfect' reading environment, but there are often significant things you can do to improve the one you have.

Key points

To get through large amounts of reading you have to be ready to cope with obstacles. You need:

■ strategies for coping with difficult words and with passages you can't understand

■ patience with the academic style of writing

■ an ability to detach yourself from disagreements with the author's views

■ a well set-up reading environment.

5.4 How quickly should you read?

Did you read the Layard article quickly enough, or perhaps too quickly? Reading speed is a persistent worry when you study. There always seems to be much more to read than you have time for, so you feel a tremendous pressure to read faster. But then, if you go too fast, you don't learn much. So what is the 'right' speed? The answer is – it depends on what you are trying to achieve.

5.4.1 Skimming

It's surprising how much you can pick up if you push on quickly through a few pages.

BOX 5.6   SKIMMING FIRST SENTENCES

You can get a rough idea of what a piece is about by skimming quickly through the first sentence or so of every paragraph, looking for key words. Doing this for the first nine paragraphs of the Layard article, I came up with:

society richer – people not happier

happiness – enjoying life

rich people happier

depression risen

evidence from different countries

why – income norm rising

two things drive up norm

habituation – adjust to good and bad

keeping up with Joneses.

This gives me a sense of what this section of text is *about*, but it doesn't convey what Layard's arguments are. It certainly doesn't save me the job of reading the article, however skimming in this way is useful in:

- helping me to decide whether to read the article 'properly'

- putting me in a frame of mind able to understand the article

- reminding me afterwards of what the article was about.

There will be many times in your studies when you need to look through texts quickly, scanning through lots of pages to get the gist of the issues, or to find specific information. It is very useful when you pick a book off a shelf, for example, to be able to review it quickly so that you can decide whether or not to read it. You just skim through the contents list, glance at details about the author, look for familiar names in the reference list, scan the preface and dip into a chapter or two.

Similarly, when you are about to start reading an article or a book, you can prepare your mind by skimming through chapter headings, contents lists, introductions, summaries and conclusions. This helps you construct a framework within which to make sense of what you read. It also helps you think strategically about how to tackle the reading: whether to read the whole thing or just sections, how long to allow yourself, and whether to take notes. Rather than simply wading in you prepare yourself so that you can work intelligently on the text.

It is important to be clear however that this rapid scanning of texts is not *reading*. Skimming can tell you *about* a text, but you will not *learn* what is *in* it.

5.4.2 Reading to learn

In order to learn you need to *follow the argument* as you read. With an important text, *you should slow right down* and take it bit by bit. Here is a student describing how he tackled a particularly challenging chapter:

I found the reading very hard. Twice I sat down, got through a few lines and threw the towel in. Then I set myself an hour to read with highlighter, notebook and pen. I read a few lines, wrote on my notepad and in the margin what it meant to me, in plain English, and highlighted what I thought were important phrases. Then I moved on to the next few lines. I even ended up with small diagrams of how some things impacted on others – what they led to, etc. It took me over an hour to read the six pages, but when I look at them now I just read my own words and the bits I highlighted. It's far easier to digest than the wording in the book. I find when I look at my notes that I can recall parts of it quite easily, and it made the whole complex discussion far more understandable. It takes time to go through so carefully, and you do need peace and patience, but it is worth it if you make the chapter into something you can think about in your own language.

This intensive kind of reading is at the opposite end of the scale to skim reading. It plays an important part in getting you to the heart of the subject.

See Chapter 4 Section 4.2, What does learning mean?

BOX 5.7   THE PURPOSE OF READING

When you are studying the underlying purpose of reading is to *develop your thoughts* – to weave *new ideas* and *information* into the understanding you already have and to develop *new points of view*. If you try to bypass this *thinking*, you are not really *learning* as you read.

5.4.3 Choosing a reading speed

As a student you cannot afford to read at just whatever speed comes naturally. If you are trying to keep abreast of a course, you have to push yourself. However, reading speeds range from a lightning skim through a whole book to intense concentration on a difficult paragraph. You need to become skilled at working at speeds right across the range. How quickly you need to read will depend on:

■ what you already know about the subject,

■ how difficult the text is, and

■ how thoroughly you need to understand it.

Kate said she spent ten minutes on the Layard article, while Salim said he spent three times as long. Lewis, though slowed by dyslexia, spent twenty minutes. How long did you spend?

If, like Erin, you spent fifteen minutes on the article, you may have picked up as much as you wanted. On the other hand if you stopped to think you could easily have spent more than Salim's half hour. If you were also taking notes perhaps you took an hour. And if you read the article more than once, you could have spent an hour and a half.

Because of my special interest in the article for the purposes of this book, I have spent *several hours* on it. The longer I worked on it the more interesting I found it, and the more clearly I grasped its arguments. This shows that there is no 'correct' amount of time to spend. It depends what you are trying to achieve. You might find the target reading speeds in Table 5.1 helpful as a rough rule-of-thumb.

Table 5.1 Reading speeds		
Text type	**Words per minute**	**Pages per hour**
Easy, familiar subject matter	100 or more	12 or more
Moderate, fairly familiar subject which you want to follow reasonably closely	70	8
Difficult, unfamiliar subject matter which you want to understand in depth	40 or fewer	5 or fewer

For the Layard article these three speeds translate into reading times of 15 minutes, 20 minutes, and 35 minutes (roughly the times taken by Erin, Lewis and Salim; Kate being faster). As all four were new to the subject and the ideas quite challenging, this was a difficult text. I would suggest that Salim came closest to the speed required for picking up the main arguments, and he said he would re-read the article if he wanted to remember it.

BOX 5.8 TIME INVESTMENT

In choosing to study, you have decided to *invest time* in developing your intellectual powers. Sometimes you will get a good return by investing in a very detailed reading of a small section of important text. At other times you will get a good return by dipping into several texts and skim reading in order to broaden your ideas. You have to weigh up the tasks ahead of you, then *distribute your time* in a way that gives you a good overall return. A key test is to ask yourself, 'Is this making me *think*?' If the answer is 'No', then your investment is being wasted. You need to switch to a new activity.

5.4.4 Time chunks

Apart from sheer speed, there is the question of how to parcel out your study time. With a two-page article you would assume a single study session, but a chapter of a book might be spread over several sessions, depending on the content and on your own time constraints.

> Hi, can anyone advise on how much to read at once? Housework done, kids at school ... day free for study. I've just spent 3 hours reading 2 chapter sections — made notes, read some bits twice, did the exercises, listened to the cassette ... then just sat thinking about what I've read. Started reading next section ... couldn't get into it, so have come away ... but feel guilty as I still have a couple of hours free. I don't think I can absorb any more today, but I'm worried my pace may be too slow for the course.

This is a message from a student to her online tutorial group in the second week of a course. Three hours is a substantial chunk of serious reading and it seems that she has taken in as much as she can for the time being. She might as well stop worrying and switch to something else, such as planning her assignment, or sorting her notes. Or she could take a complete break and come back to the chapter later in the day. I would guess that this student's studies went well – firstly, because she is actively engaging with the study materials, and secondly, because she is thinking about her study strategy and her use of time.

It is important to recognise that your span of concentration is limited. You can't learn intensively hour after hour, so it is better to divide your reading time into several shorter sessions than a few longer ones. However if your reading sessions are *too* short, you don't get properly into the frame of thinking before breaking off again. You might find two hours a reasonable span for a study session after a day of work. Or you might find that after an hour of intensive concentration you need to take a short break, or switch to another task.

Reading habits are very personal, take time to reflect on your own. Practise setting targets of various numbers of pages to see what works best for you within the contours of your life.

Key points

There is no ideal reading speed. Skill in reading slowly is just as important as skill in reading quickly. To manage your reading effectively you need to:

- pitch your reading *speed* according to your purpose and the degree of challenge presented by the text

- set yourself *targets* (number of pages per session)

- *monitor* your progress and keep adjusting your strategy.

5.5 Reading actively

To be able to *make* sense of what you are reading, you need to read actively. One method that can help is to use a pen:

5.5.1 Underlining and highlighting

Activity 5.2

Did you underline or highlight any words as you read the Layard article? If not, go back over the first three paragraphs and use a biro or a highlighter pen to mark important words. Try not to mark too many words; pick out just enough, so that you still get the main points if you read *only* those words.

My selection

I chose to underline rather than highlight. You can see my underlining for paragraph 3 in Box 5.9. Does it look anything like yours? Why do you think I used double underlining in several places?

BOX 5.9   TEXT UNDERLINED WHILE READING PARAGRAPH 3 OF LAYARD

It is true that, within any particular society at any particular moment, rich people are on average happier than poorer ones. For example, 41 per cent of people in the top quarter of incomes are 'very happy', compared with only 26 per cent of those in the bottom quarter of incomes. The problem is that, over the years, the proportions in each group who are very happy have not changed at all although the real incomes in each group have risen hugely. This is true of all the main western countries.

There is no 'correct' way to underline. You may have had excellent reasons for marking quite different words. It depends what your mind focuses on as you read.

To me it seemed that the first sentence was telling me that the paragraph was about happiness in a *society,* rather than the happiness of *individuals,* so I double-underlined 'within' and 'society'. The focus of the paragraph then stood out clearly. I also underlined 'any' to remind me that we were not just talking about the UK. I then tried to pick out words that I would be able to read more or less as abbreviated sentences. Here are all the words I underlined in Box 5.9:

Within any society – rich happier than poorer – 41 per cent top quarter very happy – 26 per cent bottom. Over years proportions not changed – though real incomes risen hugely – all western countries.

On reaching the end of the paragraph I decided that the main point was about the proportions of happy people not having changed, so I double-underlined those words.

Now when I look at the paragraph, its meaning seems to come out to meet me halfway. The thinking I did while reading is visible to me in the underlining, and I quickly connect back to those thoughts when I read the underlined words. If that doesn't work, I can go back to the original words.

I often use underlining rather than highlighting because of its flexibility. I can accurately target specific words, double or treble underline, put an asterisk in the margin to emphasise an important point, put numbers against points, or write brief notes. If a text is particularly important, or I'm gathering material for writing purposes, then I might go through again with a highlighter, picking out a few key passages.

We all work differently. Some people prefer to highlight rather than underline, because they feel it looks nicer and has a less intrusive effect. Experiment with different approaches to find out what works for you.

Too much underlining and highlighting

The challenge, especially when you are new to a subject, is to avoid underlining or highlighting everything. Everything seems important, so how do you know what to leave out?

Will I be able to find what I'm looking for in a sea of yellow!? Hmm ... perhaps a change of colour is in order. Or will I then just have a multicoloured mess?

If you make too many markings, you defeat your purpose; nothing stands out. The trick is to highlight or underline sparingly. See how few words you can mark and still be able to find the markings helpful. Aim to pick out key words, not whole sentences; don't worry about capturing *everything.* You can always go back to the original words if you need to.

Some passages of text need more marking than others. You might have a couple of heavily marked pages followed by several with very little at all. Sometimes underlining slows you down, or makes reading boring; it depends on the type of text and why you are reading it. You have to work all this out by trial and error. Experiment with different amounts of marking, then go back later and weigh up what seems to have worked best for you. Reflect on your experience.

After a period of regular reading I find I adapt to it and can pick out relevant points more easily. When you start it's natural to highlight everything, especially in a new field of study.

5.5.2 Notes in the margins

I regularly notice that I've just read something and not a single thing has entered my head. The only option is to reread it and make small notes in the margins.

It is easy, with underlining or highlighting, to find that you have switched to autopilot without noticing. The process becomes too passive and you follow the flow of the text without asking enough questions. Writing comments or questions in the margins is a way to keep yourself more actively engaged.

I like to write ideas down in the margin as I am reading. It makes the reading more interesting. If later I think it's rubbish, I can always scrub it.

5.5.3 Does writing on a book seem wrong?

My mum always told me never to mistreat books. I find it really hard to take a highlighter to a new page.

In new books I underline anything important in pencil lightly so then if I'm not going to need the book any more I can sell it on.

I have that same guilt about 'defacing' nice new books. To get around it I use yellow stickies stuck to the edge of the page, with a relevant phrase hanging off the edge of the page. This works like a bookmark, but also points me to the important section.

Obviously you have to take into account whether you own the text you are studying and, if so, whether you intend to keep it. Does it seem extravagant to write on a book and make it unfit for selling on? How important to you is selling it? Is it really a saving? If a book is important, why not assume you will keep it anyway? Then you can think of writing in it as an investment;

you invest significant amounts of your time and mental energy in studying the book, in any case. If writing in it means you can quickly reconnect with the ideas and information you have studied, that investment is greatly enhanced. The marked-up book becomes an item in your personal system of knowledge. Part of this system is in your head and part on your bookshelf. Within the overall cost of studying, creating your own personalised versions of significant books can represent excellent value.

I think of books as part of my student work kit, to be used in ways that help me learn. Art students use up canvas – I use up books.

Key points

Underlining or highlighting words as you read is a powerful study technique:

- it focuses your *attention* on the text

- it forces you to *think* about what the key concepts and issues are

- it leaves a *record* on the page of the meaning you found in the words as you read them.

When you return to a marked text you can quickly tune back in to those earlier thoughts – especially if you have written occasional comments in the margin.

5.5.4 Questioning what you read

Another way to keep your mind active while you read is to ask yourself questions about what you are reading.

Engaging with the content

For example, when I read in paragraph 3 of Layard's article that '41 per cent of people in the top quarter of incomes are 'very happy'' I asked myself:

- Why is 'very happy' in quotation marks?

- Is 41 per cent about what I'd expect?

- What is this telling me?

As soon as I thought about it, I realised that 'very happy' could be a response that people had ticked on a questionnaire. Perhaps they had been asked a question such as: 'Thinking about your life in general, how happy are you? – (1) very unhappy, (2) unhappy, (3) middling, (4) happy, (5) very happy'. I wondered which of these answers I would tick, if asked, and which might be ticked by other people who I know. It then struck me that 41 per cent is quite a high figure for *very* happy – that's four people in every ten, right up at the top of the scale. This made me wonder how large the proportions were for 'happy' or 'middling', and whether many people would answer 'very unhappy'. (In the next paragraph I got more information on this when I read that almost three in ten young women were reported to be depressed.)

Then I noticed the 26 per cent figure for people in the lowest quarter of incomes. I thought to myself, 'That's a quarter of the *least* well-off saying they are *very* happy. That *does* seem surprising'. Obviously, happiness doesn't directly depend on wealth. I tried to think of the least and most wealthy people I know and how happy they might say they were; this reminded me of all the other things in life that contribute to happiness and sadness. I also thought about how people *want* to feel that they are happy, and concluded that perhaps the high proportions saying they were very happy weren't so surprising after all.

These thoughts helped me to get a general sense of scale of the figures in paragraph 3. It's not important to remember the actual figures 41 per cent and 26 per cent, I can always look them up again if I need them. The important thing is to get the general picture. I wouldn't pause to ponder over *every* number, if I felt I was slowing down too much, but these seemed to be significant to the argument.

When I came to the third sentence of paragraph 3, I found myself challenged. 'The proportions in each group who are very happy' is quite an abstract idea to hold on to; but then I also had to think about these proportions *not* changing and about 'real incomes in each group' *rising*. It was too much for me. When I asked myself 'What is this really saying?', I couldn't answer. As this was clearly an important part of the argument, I decided to try to write it down in my own words:

– Huge rise in real incomes for all groups

– But no change in % very happy in each group

– So society getting much richer but not happier

This helped me feel that I had grasped the point. But I still found it difficult to hold this idea in mind at the same time as the point about richer people being on average happier than poorer people, so I wrote down:

– On average richer are happier – yet getting richer hasn't made us happier.

I felt I needed to think more about this to take it in properly. Later, as I read about habituation and keeping up with the Joneses, it all began to make more sense. In fact, I found myself getting very interested in this later discussion about rivalry over incomes in families and organisations. I found myself thinking about rivalry within my own family and in organisations for which I have worked. The more you can make what you are reading 'real', by linking it to what you know and care about, the more your mind enters into working with the new ideas you are encountering.

I have tried to illustrate here how reading can trigger questioning and thinking. Reading for study purposes is an argumentative dialogue in your head. No doubt *you* would ask quite different questions. The specific questions are not important – it's the process of questioning that is.

Key points

Questions are what make reading interesting and challenging. They give a sense of a 'quest' to find answers. They help you to engage with what you are reading about.

You need to ask questions of the kind:

- What is this telling me?

- What do I think of this? (Am I surprised; How does this relate to me and my life; Does this help to make sense of the world as I know it?)

- How does this fit in with what I already know?

5.5.3 When you get stuck

Sometimes as you read you will get stuck. When this happens, don't sit staring at the page; find a way to tackle the problem.

See Chapter 4 Box 4.1, How reading works

Reading requires you to 'project' meaning onto the words on the page. When you are stuck it means that you have lost track of the argument and can no longer see what meaning to project. So, you have to find ways to reconstruct the argument in your mind. One way is *to cast around for clues* by looking elsewhere in the text.

You might look *back* to the earlier parts:

- Check the title, the contents list and the introduction to remind yourself what the writer set out to discuss.

- Re-read some of what you have already covered to firm up the arguments.

Or you might look *ahead*:

- Skim a few pages to see what is coming up.

- Turn to the conclusion to see where the argument eventually leads.

Another tactic is to use your pen:

- Write down the main issues you think the text is addressing.

- Try to summarise what you have read so far, particularly the part just before you got stuck.

- Underline words that seem important in the section you don't understand.

■ Try to summarise the underlined words.

If you are still stuck:

■ Search for clues on the internet.

■ Look in other books on the subject.

■ Scan through your lecture notes.

■ Contact other students by phone, email or internet chat room.

Whether or not what you write is 'correct', the process of writing notes helps you get into the text. It makes you take hold of ideas and put them in your own terms. It helps you force meanings on to the subject matter and construct a base from which you can launch another assault on the text.

And if all this doesn't help, just skip ahead and try to pick up the thread somewhere else in the text; or leave it altogether and start on another piece of work. It may all seem clearer another day. In any case, there is no point in sitting achieving nothing.

Key points

When you are stuck:

■ Make an active attack on the problem.

■ Look for clues in earlier or later parts of the text.

■ Make detailed notes on the bit you are stuck on and on the preceding section.

■ Cast around for ideas from other sources.

5.6 Reading critically

As well as making sense of what you read, you have to think about whether or not you are convinced by the arguments being presented. At degree level, you don't simply accept what you read – you read 'critically', weighing up the strengths and weaknesses of the case the author makes. This means asking another set of questions, such as the ones discussed here.

5.6.1 Critical questions

How much trust can I put in this text?

You would generally assume that the set texts for your course are trustworthy. But when you find a text through your own research you need to run a few checks to assess the soundness of its content.

Who is the publisher?

See Chapter 9
Section 9.3.1, The
PROMPT checklist

If an article is from an academic journal, you can assume that its quality has been vetted by the journal's editors. Also if a book is published by a major academic publishing house, you would expect it to be 'respectable'. And if it's a book from an academic series, you would expect the series editor to have vetted the quality. However, in other cases you need to run a few checks. Richard Layard's article is published in a weekly magazine. This does not guarantee academic soundness, so I need to consider other information.

Who is the author?

At the end of Layard's article, a note says that he is Co-Director of the Centre for Economic Performance at the London School of Economics. This gave me confidence in the quality of his scholarship. I did a little further research on the internet and found out that he is an advisor to the government, particularly with respect to its New Deal for the unemployed, and that he has been made a Lord.

In what context was the text published?

See Chapter 10
Section 10.7.1,
How academic
debate works

This amounts to asking, *when* was it written and for what *audience*. Academic texts are written to make a contribution to the debates going on within the field. To understand where an author is coming from and why arguments are being presented in a particular way, you need to be able to place the text in context. Layard's article was published in 2003 in the UK, and was drawn from a prestigious series of public lectures. So the context is a major statement by a prominent academic to colleagues and policy leaders, during the sixth year of a New Labour government, after nearly 25 years of growing incomes inequality.

Does the argument follow logically?

As I was making sense of paragraph 3, I did pause to consider whether it was logically possible to say that on average richer people are happier, yet getting richer has not made us happier. Later, when I read that women in the US were less happy since their incomes had come closer to men's, it occurred to me that they would be unlikely to volunteer to revert to previous levels of inequality. This made me question what happiness really means, if it is not necessarily a state that a person would opt for. I then wondered whether the measures of happiness that Layard was quoting were as straightforward as they might seem. That did not stop me from taking a strong interest in his arguments, it just made me a bit more cautious about accepting them. Generally, though, I found Layard's logic stood up very well to the questions I posed.

What evidence is offered?

Layard frequently offers evidence for his main points. I had the impression that this was just a sample from a wide range of relevant evidence that he had reviewed. Because of the prestigious context, I tended to assume that the evidence would be reliable and that Layard's interpretations would be pretty watertight. Nothing in the evidence seemed to conflict with my existing knowledge. However, if I were studying the subject more thoroughly, I would go back to the lectures from which his article was taken, as published on the internet, so that I could look more closely at the kind of evidence being quoted and how it was gathered.

Is there an alternative school of thought?

I guessed that plenty of economists would disagree with Layard's point of view, if he is right that they have *not* used measures of happiness and have treated rises in real incomes as an unquestioned 'good thing'. If I were studying this topic seriously, I would search for an article which tackled Layard's arguments from another perspective. When you encounter new ideas, it is useful to get more that one perspective on them, so that you can weigh one against the other.

Are the conclusions justified?

Though I was interested in the idea of treating high incomes as 'pollution', I did wonder whether taxing people to pay for the pollution caused by their rising incomes would work. In general though I was reasonably convinced by the conclusions Layard drew. On the other hand, if I was studying the subject more seriously, I might find that wider reading and further thought would make some of the conclusions seem less convincing.

See Chapter 4 Section 4.3.2 Key features of academic discourse

5.6.2 Thinking for yourself

These are the kinds of questions you need to ask in order to read critically. As a higher-level student, you don't read simply to 'find out facts'. It is assumed that you will think for yourself and question what you read and hear. The 'truth' is taken to be uncertain, so you weigh up ideas and arguments as you read about them. According to Marton and Säljö (1997, p. 49) research shows that successful students read as if they are constantly asking themselves questions of the kind: 'How do the various parts of the text relate to each other? [...] Is the argument consistent or are there any logical gaps? [...] How does this relate to what I already know?'.

Critical reading lies at the heart of good learning.

> ### *Key points*
>
> At degree level you are expected to read critically; you don't simply accept what you read. Ask yourself:
>
> ■ Can I trust what I'm being told here?
>
> ■ In what context was this published?

- Do the arguments follow logically?
- What evidence is offered?
- What do those on the other side argue?
- Are the conclusions justified?

This questioning approach will help you become a more effective and enthusiastic student.

5.7 Are you a good reader?

If you ever worry about:

- your rate of progress as you read
- how much you understand
- how much you will remember later

then join the club. Here is one student offering support to another who expressed self-doubt in an online chat room:

> You are not alone in these feelings. We all feel overwhelmed at times. Don't worry about recapping at the moment. Read at your own pace. If you get behind it doesn't matter. Nor does it matter if you don't understand everything first time. Don't sit there endlessly going over it again and again, move onto the next section. Some parts will 'click' eventually and some might never 'click' in the way they should, but it doesn't mean you won't successfully complete the course. Sometimes I read sections in more detail and at others I'm pushed for time and skim read things and don't really feel I've taken it all in. That's the way it is.

5.7.1 What is a 'good' reader?

Some approaches to reading are better than others, of course. Research has found that less successful students take a 'surface' approach to reading, while more successful students take a 'deep' approach.

Surface approach

'Students who did not get 'the point' failed to do so simply because they were not looking for it'.

'Instead they concentrated on trying to learn discrete bits of information'.

Deep approach

Successful students were 'more concerned [...] to make sense of the article as a whole. [They] focused [...] on what the text was about: the author's intention, the main point, the conclusion to be drawn'. Entwistle (1997, p.18)

Instead of worrying about whether you are naturally a good reader, it is far more useful to work at making yourself the best reader you can be. The secret is to search for meaning as you read, taking the active, questioning approach described in this chapter.

5.7.2 Specific difficulties

Some students contend with physical difficulties in reading. Here is one:

> I find it almost impossible to read from the textbooks for any length of time before pain limits me. I'm having a super-duper all-singing all-dancing chair delivered any time soon (hah!), and hope to be able to spend more time with the books.

And here is another being offered advice by a friend:

> I have ME and find reading and writing notes too exhausting and get overwhelmed.
>
> Have you thought about speaking notes into a tape recorder?
>
> No I hadn't. That sounds good. Thanks.

Other students, like Lewis in Section 5.2, experience dyslexia. Some face the challenge of studying in a second language, or in a different dialect from the one they speak in everyday life. Many students who experience difficulties with reading are able to get support. If you think you might benefit similarly, contact your university support services without delay – support arrangements often take time to set up. You could also look for support on the internet; for example, if you search for 'dyslexia' you will find several websites offering a wide range of advice and support.

5.8 Conclusion

Reading is a core activity in most courses of study. The purpose of it is to enable you to *learn*. But learning is not a *passive* process, you don't just let ideas wash over you. You have to *make* sense of them as you read and then *use* them to *think* with.

> ## Key points
>
> Reading for study purposes is not merely a matter of passing your eyes over hundreds of words. It is a *set of practices* which enable you to *engage* with the *ideas* in a text, including:
>
> - setting targets
> - *underlining or highlighting* as you read

- asking *questions* to make yourself think about what you read

- *stopping* to look ahead or look back when you lose the thread

- reading *critically*

- *monitoring* your progress from time to time, and

- *changing* tack when things are not going well.

You need to *experiment* with different ways of doing things, in order to develop a robust, flexible, all-round style.

References

Entwistle, N. (1997) 'Contrasting perspectives on learning' in Marton, F., Hounsell, D. and Entwistle, N. (eds) *The Experience of Learning: Implications for teaching and studying in Higher Education*, Edinburgh, Scottish Academic Press Limited.

Marton, F. and R. Säljö (1997) 'Approaches to learning' in Marton, F., Hounsell, D. and Entwistle, N. (eds) *The Experience of Learning: Implications for teaching and studying in Higher Education*, Edinburgh, Scottish Academic Press Limited.

Layard, R. (2003) 'The secrets of happiness', *New Statesman*, 3 March 2003, p. 25.

PinderSoft (2004) *Software*, www.pindersoft.com/Software.htm (accessed 1 June 2004).

Useful links

www.download.com

CHAPTER 6 MAKING NOTES

6.1 Thinking on paper

Making notes is a significant study activity. It helps you to engage purposefully and creatively with the many challenges of learning: keeping your mind active and bridging the gap between your own thoughts and the subject matter of your course. One of the clearest signs of becoming a capable student is having a range of effective and flexible note making strategies.

When you make notes, you are operating on the borders between the bubbling, indistinct inner world of your mind and the outer world with its bustling trade in ideas and information.

■ As new ideas pass *into* your mind, making notes helps you to translate and organise them so that they mesh with your current thought processes.

■ As you prepare to put ideas *out* into the external world, making notes helps you to get your thoughts into sufficient order to be shared with others.

Ideas and knowledge arise out of dialogue, and note making is essentially a dialogue with yourself. Consequently, as you make informal jottings you frequently find you have expressed thoughts that you had not been aware of. In effect, you 'discover' your own ideas through the unassuming activity of writing untidy scribbles.

Note making is 'thinking on paper' (or 'thinking onscreen'). It ought to be a satisfying process of engaging with a topic and creating meaning for yourself. If you find it a chore, you should reflect on whether you are doing it right. Note making is *not* note *taking,* in the sense of passively writing down an accurate record of what is said. It is much more constructive and personalised than that.

Note making is valuable in a variety of contexts and for various purposes. This chapter divides these into 'capturing knowledge', 'organising knowledge', 'supporting creativity' and 'making notes strategically'. More space is given to the first of these, but the other three are equally important. There is also a section on 'supporting your memory' through the way you make notes.

BOX 6.1   RECOMMENDED PREPARATION

To get the full benefit from reading this chapter, you should first work through Chapter 5 Section 5.2 'The experience of reading'. This guides you through reading the article by Richard Layard reproduced in the Appendix. Having read the article you will gain much more from the examples in this chapter because you will know what is being summarised and be better able to reflect on your own note making strategies.

6.2 Capturing knowledge

As you work to stay abreast of the relentless flow of knowledge presented by a course, it seems that ideas and information are only fleetingly in your grasp before you have to let go and turn your attention to something else. It's unnerving. You don't know whether to consolidate what you have already covered, or to keep driving onward. You wonder how much you are actually learning.

- Will the lecture you are struggling to understand evaporate from your mind over the coming days?

- Will the time you are investing in reading a book be wasted?

At one level the answer to these questions is 'No'. As new ideas pass through your thoughts they influence and reshape them. So, even if you can't remember the specifics, a trace is left. When you are asked questions later, your answers are influenced by such traces. This is seldom enough, however. You want to feel that you have captured at least some of the knowledge and brought it under your control. For this you need notes.

6.2.1 Notes from reading

In Chapter 5 we looked at ways of highlighting text and making notes in margins. Sometimes these markings are sufficient because you have understood the subject well enough. At other times you need to make additional notes to help pull your thoughts together and clarify them; for example, when it is a key text or one that you will not be keeping, or when you are getting ideas together for an essay.

There are many ways to make notes, ranging from a few jotted lines, to elaborate diagrams. To explore these we will look at some examples. But first try making a few notes of your own.

Activity 6.1

From your reading of Layard's article, how much of it do you think you will be able to remember in future? What notes would you need in order to 'capture' the essence of it, so that it doesn't slip away from you?

Go back to the article and make about half a page of notes.

How did you set about making the notes?

The type of notes you need depends on:

- the kind of text you are reading

- what you want to use the notes for

- how your mind works

- the amount of time you think it is reasonable to invest.

A 'summary card'

If you want very brief notes, you could restrict yourself to an index card. Just go back through your highlighted or underlined text, looking out for anything you marked extra heavily, then pull out a selection of the points that seem most important. A card like the one in Figure 6.1 might provide all the notes you need.

Layard R. <u>Secrets of happiness</u> (N. Statesmn, 3/3/03)
<u>Rich socs</u> – <u>increasingly rich</u> – but <u>people not happier</u>
• At diff income levels – proportns happy have stayed same
• Depressn risen – most countries
• Countries w avg inc > £10K – avg happiness unrel to avg inc
<u>Why↑ wealth not →↑ happiness?</u>
• <u>Habituation</u>: get used to what you've got
• <u>Keep up w. Joneses</u>: adjust to ref gp
  eg E. Germans, US women
  (NB rivalry re inc in families & workplace = pollution)
<u>Implications for society</u>
• <u>Raise tax</u> on higher incomes →↑ public expenditure
  wealthy no less happy + poor happier = ↑ happiness
Importance of <u>scientific study</u> of happiness

Figure 6.1 **Summary card showing key points**

I could make these notes even shorter by leaving out the first three bullet points and the very last line. This still leaves the essence of the argument. It depends on what I need the notes for and how significant Layard's article is within the course reading.

(Don't worry if your notes from Activity 6.1 look different; there are many ways to summarise this article. In any case, I allowed myself plenty of time to get down to this version because it was for publication. My first version wouldn't have made any sense to you.)

Abbreviations and symbols

Were you able to make sense of my abbreviations and symbols?

■ I shortened some words (e.g. statesman, societies, proportions, depression, with, average, income, unrelated, reference, group).

■ I sometimes left words out and wrote a dash instead.

■ I used arrows: ↑ to mean 'rising', → to mean 'leads to' (or in this case 'not →' to mean 'does not lead to').

■ I used '>' to mean 'greater than' and 'K' for '1,000'.

■ I didn't bother with full stops.

Some of these are standard abbreviations. Others I made up. All helped me to write quickly without losing track of the meaning. It's important to develop your own system of abbreviations and symbols. This makes your notes both quicker to write and quicker to read (for you, if not others).

Layout

Notice, too, the way I laid out the notes on the card and how I used underlining and bullets. Why do you think I did it this way? For me, it's a way of making the structure of the argument stand out: three main themes (underlined), each with bulleted subpoints.

Writing for yourself

By combining abbreviated writing with effective layout, you can capture a lot of information very economically. Your compressed notes work for *you* because the ideas have already passed through your mind, so you don't need to explain them to yourself. You write just enough to reawaken the understanding you achieved as you were reading.

BOX 6.2   GETTING TO THE 'BONES' OF AN ARGUMENT

Any text has a few central ideas running through it. However if the writer stated these baldly, in the fewest possible words, then you wouldn't be able to understand them or see their significance.
A writer has to put 'flesh' on the bare bones, giving examples and evidence, and talking you through the ideas so that you can see how they work.

Once you have understood the ideas, you don't need the flesh. Like the writer all you need in your mind are the bones. Making notes is a way of making yourself seek out the bones, so that you end up with a clear, simple outline of the underlying skeleton of the argument.

Outline notes

I will admit that I didn't arrive at the summary card in Figure 6.1 straight from reading Layard's article. I began by making notes using the outlining facility on my word-processor (in Microsoft Word this is the 'Outline' view). You can see the beginnings of these notes in Figure 6.2.

Outliners are superb tools for studying and for writing because they help you to organise content hierarchically. As you can see I have put key themes to the left (level 1) then arranged my notes below into sub-themes (level 2), main points (level 3), subpoints (level 4) and so on. Using an outliner it's very easy to move text around, promoting it to the left, demoting it to the right, or moving sections up or down the page. (In MS Word click on the button at the start of a line of text then drag it to where you want it, or use the buttons on the Outline view toolbar.)

See Chapter 5 Section 5.5.1, Underlining and highlighting

I selected the Outline view in my word-processor then went back through the points I'd underlined in Layard's article (see Box 5.9). If a point still seemed important, I typed it into my notes, using the different levels to try to show the relationship between them. For example, I used level 4 for

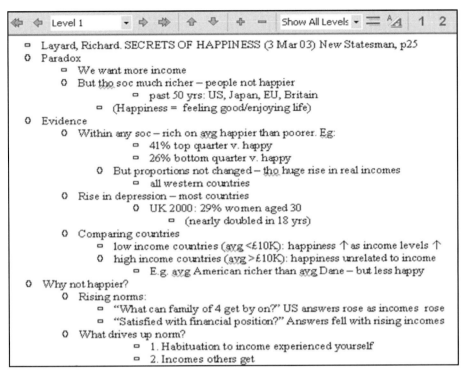

| ⇦ ⇦ Level 1 | ▾ ⇨ ⇛ | ⇧ ⇩ | ⊕ — | Show All Levels ▾ ≡ ᴬ𝐴 | 1 2 |

- ▫ Layard, Richard. SECRETS OF HAPPINESS (3 Mar 03) New Statesman, p25
- ◊ Paradox
  - ▫ We want more income
  - ◊ But tho soc much richer – people not happier
    - ▫ past 50 yrs: US, Japan, EU, Britain
  - ▫ (Happiness = feeling good/enjoying life)
- ◊ Evidence
  - ◊ Within any soc – rich on avg happier than poorer. Eg:
    - ▫ 41% top quarter v. happy
    - ▫ 26% bottom quarter v. happy
  - ◊ But proportions not changed – tho huge rise in real incomes
    - ▫ all western countries
  - ◊ Rise in depression – most countries
    - ◊ UK 2000: 29% women aged 30
      - ▫ (nearly doubled in 18 yrs)
  - ◊ Comparing countries
    - ▫ low income countries (avg <£10K): happiness ↑ as income levels ↑
    - ◊ high income countries (avg >£10K): happiness unrelated to income
      - ▫ E.g. avg American richer than avg Dane – but less happy
- ◊ Why not happier?
  - ◊ Rising norms:
    - ▫ "What can family of 4 get by on?" US answers rose as incomes rose
    - ▫ "Satisfied with financial position?" Answers fell with rising incomes
  - ◊ What drives up norm?
    - ▫ 1. Habituation to income experienced yourself
    - ▫ 2. Incomes others get

Figure 6.2 Notes made in Microsoft Word's Outline view

examples, cases and evidence. However I didn't spend a lot of time thinking about this, I just put things wherever they seemed to fit. As I worked I tried to detect the structure of Layard's argument, and occasionally saw a better way to group points, so I moved things around. I was typing *Layard's words* in the main, but I was *organising* them to make sense to *me*. Doing this helped me to understand better what it was he was saying.

Most word-processors have an outlining facility. Use your word-processor's Help menu to find out how to use yours and print out the relevant pages to have beside you the first time you work with it. Just type in a few lines of nonsense and move the text around. If everything appears as large headings, find the button that hides the formatting so that you can work with ordinary text. You will soon get the hang of it. Alternatively, you could try out a specialised outliner program. You will soon find one if you do a web search for 'outliner'.

If you have never used an outliner, it is worth trying one out. I find mine indispensable. One of the great advantages of making electronic notes is that it's very easy to file them on your computer where you can find them quickly. You can also run searches for particular names or words, so when you are looking for a quotation for your essay, you can locate it in moments.

See Chapter 3 Section 3.4, Organising files

A comprehensive overview

On the other hand, you may prefer to write notes by hand. You might, for example, try to capture the bones of Layard's article on a single page as in

Figure 6.3, laying the whole thing out so that you can take it in at a single sweep. You will seldom want to invest time in making such a detailed summary, but I offer this example to show how, in principle, you can extract the entire skeleton of an argument in a way that lets you see the structure and follow the logical links.

Activity 6.2

Read carefully through the notes I've made in Figure 6.3.

You will see that I have placed the points in clusters and picked out the key words by underlining them. I also have arrows: those pointing up and down are my shorthand for 'increases' and 'decreases', while others show which points follow on from other points. You can make notes that will be meaningful to yourself in all kinds of creative ways.

How much detail should you include?

Although there is a lot of information in Figure 6.3, I also left out a lot. So what did I choose to include? I began by writing full details of author, title, date and publisher at the top of the page. This information is vital as it will enable me to find the article again if I need to, and I have all the reference details if I want to quote from it.

From Layard's article I included:

- **Key concepts** Rising norms, habituation, reference groups
- **Useful numbers** 'High' income means greater than £10,000 p.a. (converted from $15,000)
- **Examples** East Germans, Americans and Japanese
- **Research studies** Study of depression in young women

In a different article I might also include names of researchers and writers, Acts of Parliament, theories – basically the things I most expect to want to use again in the future. I didn't attempt to make detailed notes of the tough paragraphs, 13 and 14, as it would have taken too long to work out how to summarise them. If I ever need to grasp those points properly, I would revisit the article to work on them.

> ### BOX 6.3 HEALTH WARNING: MAKING VERY DETAILED NOTES CAN DAMAGE YOUR MORALE
>
> The notes in Figure 6.3 may be more than you need. You don't want to slow yourself down too much, or undermine your interest in the subject. If making detailed notes makes you feel more confident in your grasp of the subject, then fine, but don't let note making become a burden.

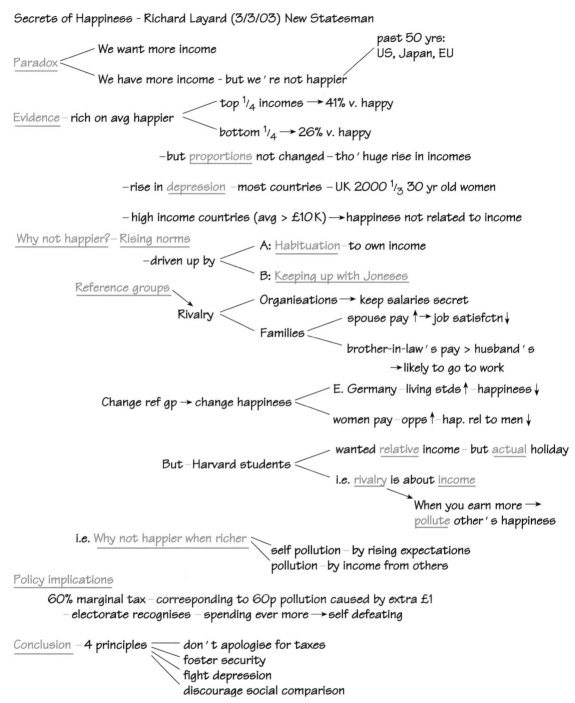

Figure 6.3 Comprehensive notes on Layard's article

Why make separate notes?

If you have already highlighted or underlined a text, why would you bother making separate notes? Firstly, it helps you to see the bones of what the text is about, so that it's then much easier to work the ideas into an essay or a presentation, or draw them together in preparing for an exam. Secondly, note making forces you to *think* as you decide what to write down and how to organise it on the page. Regardless of whether your notes are 'good', the act of writing them takes you much further into the meaning of the text. And thirdly, without notes, no matter how good your memory, ideas will gradually drift away from you.

So, although note making is demanding and time consuming, it is an investment which adds much to the value of reading. When a text is thought-provoking and full of ideas that you can use in future assignments, the investment pays handsomely.

> I write the next essay topic on a sheet. Then, when I find a point I think is relevant, I write it on to the sheet, and include the reference so I can find it again. Post-it notes can be handy too. And I use index cards for key points. It doesn't seem a lot of work because it pays off when it comes to the essay. I know I've already got enough info to get started.

There are many ways you might make notes on Layard's article, and I expect your notes were different from my examples. It's very useful to experiment with different styles. Your notes on an important and challenging text that you have read in depth will be quite different from the single line you might write on an article you happen to dip into. What you need is a range of note making styles from which you can select according to the circumstances.

Key points

- Making separate notes is an additional investment which can add a lot to the value of reading a text. However, it is not necessary for everything you read.

- There are many ways of making notes, according to the nature of the text and your reasons for studying it.

- Notes should never be simply an abbreviated copy of the original text; they should be an attempt to pick out the *bones* of the text.

6.2.2 Lecture notes

When you make notes while reading, the book sits there at your mercy; you are in control. Making lecture notes however is much more challenging as you have to listen and write at the same time. Lectures can also be quite variable, so you have to be able to adjust your strategy according to the context.

Context

The kind of notes you need will depend on several factors:

■ Is the lecture your only source of information on the topic? Do you risk losing important ideas and information if you don't write things down? Or are there texts to back up what the lecturer says? In this case your notes can be less detailed and more reflective.

■ Is yours a subject with a lot of detailed information to remember? Is it a broad theoretical subject in which your main aim is to follow arguments and understand how ideas work? Or is it a professional subject where understanding practical implications is what counts?

■ Does your lecturer use slide presentations or an overhead projector to show the main points and structure of the lecture? Are there handouts which provide a framework for your notes? Does your lecturer post an outline on the internet?

■ Do you expect to use your notes for writing an essay, for guiding further reading, or in revising for an exam in a few months' time?

Sometimes you find these things out after a lecture has started; so note making is an unpredictable activity. You need to be well organised in advance, ready to swing into action with a technique to suit the situation.

Cornell notes

One widely used approach is the Cornell system developed by Walter Pauk (Pauk, 2001, pp. 236–46). It involves dividing your note paper into four sections as shown in Figure 6.4.

To use the Cornell system:

1   Fill in the top (section 1) before the lecture.

2   Make notes in the main area (section 2) during the lecture.

3   Soon after the lecture, while it's fresh in your mind, read through your notes picking out key concepts and write them in the left margin (section 3). Better still, write down questions to which your notes provide answers as I have done in Figure 6.5. Working out the questions helps you to think about the meaning of your notes.

4   Cover up section 2 and test yourself by looking at the cues in section 3 and saying out loud whatever you can remember. As you work down the page, uncover the answers to see what you remembered and what you forgot. Vocalising the ideas helps you into the language and thinking of the subject. You start to take ownership of new knowledge by making yourself a speaker of it. You also remember better.

5   Finally, reflect on the contents of the page, asking yourself such questions as: How does this fit with what I already know? How can

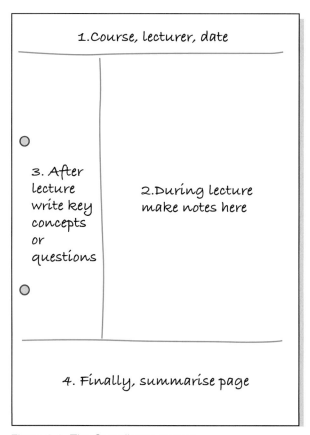

Figure 6.4 **The Cornell note system**

I apply it? How significant is it? Then, in section 4, write a brief summary in your own words. This helps you to think about what it all means.

Making lecture notes in this way is much more than capturing a *record* on paper. You become actively engaged with the lecture and internalise what you hear. A systematic approach like this helps you to cope with the unpredictability of lectures, by providing an off-the-peg strategy for taking control.

See Chapter 6 Section 6.4.2, Making connections

The Cornell system is not the only way to make lecture notes. For example, some people prefer to make notes in the form of 'mind maps': putting the topic of the lecture in the centre of the page, with sub-topics branching out. However, the Cornell system provides a useful starting point if you are new to making lecture notes.

Tips on making lecture notes

What to avoid

- Don't try to take *verbatim* notes, copying down the lecturer's every word; you won't be able to listen properly. You need to involve your mind as you make notes.

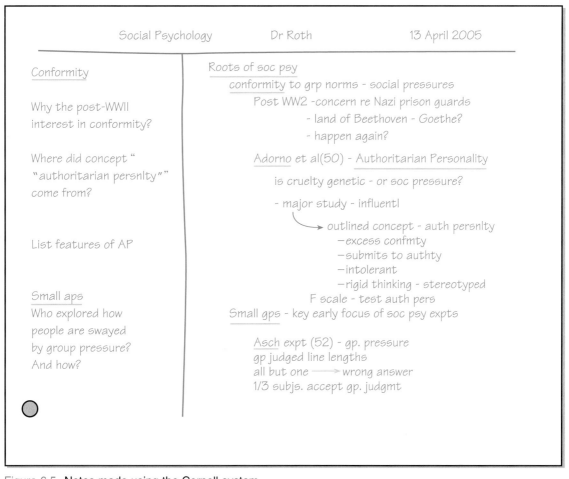

Social Psychology   Dr Roth   13 April 2005

Conformity	Roots of soc psy
	conformity to grp norms - social pressures
Why the post-WWII	Post WW2 -concern re Nazi prison guards
interest in conformity?	- land of Beethoven - Goethe?
	- happen again?
Where did concept "	Adorno et al(50) - Authoritarian Personality
"authoritarian persnlty""	is cruelty genetic - or soc pressure?
come from?	- major study - influentl
	→ outlined concept - auth persnlty
	−excess confmty
List features of AP	−submits to authty
	−intolerant
	−rigid thinking - stereotyped
	F scale - test auth pers
Small aps	Small gps - key early focus of soc psy expts
Who explored how	
people are swayed	Asch expt (52) - gp. pressure
by group pressure?	gp judged line lengths
And how?	all but one → wrong answer
	1/3 subjs. accept gp. judgmt

Figure 6.5 Notes made using the Cornell system

- Don't produce reams of notes as this just creates a reading burden later. The lecturer will speak several thousand words. You want at most a few hundred.

- Don't use a cassette recorder. To extract the main points you'll have to listen to the whole lecture again and then make notes, which is a very inefficient use of your time. You may as well make the notes the first time around.

Equip yourself properly

- It's a good idea to use A4 notepaper with holes ready punched, and keep your notes in a ring binder with dividers to organise them. Your notes will be easier to work with later if you write on just one side of the paper.

Listen out for the structure of the lecture

- A lecturer usually has a few main points to get across. The rest is explanation, much of which you don't need to record.

■ Listen out for phrases such as 'The main issues are', 'Another important factor', or 'So why is this?'. These signal that key points are about to be made. Take note of pauses, changes in tone of voice and body language, indicating that points are about to be summarised or new themes started. And pay particular attention at the beginning and end of the lecture when clues to structure are most likely to be given.

■ Include examples given by the lecturer, not just concepts and facts (e.g. the Nazi guards and the Asch experiment). Examples are very helpful in reminding you what the ideas in the lecture are about.

Use the lecturer's words

■ Although you are trying to pick out just the key points from what the lecturer says, don't try to translate into your own words. You haven't the time and it will interfere with your listening. In any case, one of the key benefits of a lecture is to hear how the specialist discourse of the subject is spoken. By selecting from the lecturer's own words, you'll be better able to follow the flow of ideas and pick up the way the knowledge is put to work.

Make notes meaningful

■ Don't take down single words. You have to be able to make sense of the notes when your mind has moved on to other things. The meaning of words arises from the context in which they are used.

■ It generally helps to write fragments of sentences, leaving gaps that your mind can easily fill in later when you read the notes. The notes in Figure 6.5 are meant to work like this.

Abbreviate

Don't write things out in full; use your own abbreviations. For example, a lecturer might say something like:

We've all experienced pressure to 'go along with the crowd'. But most of us think, if the crunch came, we'd stand up for what's right. But would you? Would you be prepared to go against everyone else around you if you knew you were right? In 1952 Solomon Asch reported a series of experiments in which he explored whether people could be influenced by group pressure to go against their own judgement. He put people in groups of eight. The group members were asked to say which of three lines on a card was the same length as a line on another card. This was repeated for several cards. But, seven of the group had been briefed in advance and at a secret signal they all picked a wrong line, to see what the other person – the subject of the experiment – would do. Asch found that some subjects stuck to their guns whatever. However, about a third of subjects were prepared to agree with the group, against the evidence of their own eyes.

I've summarised this in Figure 6.6, representing nearly 200 words in under 20 words. In my shorthand 'expt' stands for 'experiment', 'gp' for 'group', 'subjs' for 'experimental subjects', and so on. These notes are enough to remind me of the key features of Asch's experiment. Should I have any trouble recalling it, I know Asch's name and the report year, so I can easily look it up on the internet.

Solomon Asch expt. (52) - gp. pressure

    gp judged line lengths

    all but one ⟶ wrong answer

    1/3 subjs. accept gp. judgmt

Figure 6.6 **Abbreviated lecture notes**

Don't use 'proper' shorthand

■ If you happen to know a phonetic shorthand system such as Pitman's, it might seem ideal for lecture notes. But in practice to make the notes useful you'd have to translate from the symbols. As you write and read your notes, you need to pay attention to meanings, not sounds.

Organise your points on the page

■ Don't be stingy with paper. Spread your notes across the page and use lines, arrows, brackets, boxes, and so on to emphasise divisions and links in the material. A general principle is to set things out hierarchically with main headings on the left and subpoints indented, as shown in Figure 6.5.

■ Work out a way to add comments and questions so that you can distinguish them from your main notes, for example you could put them in square brackets.

Take advantage of handouts

■ If your lecturer provides you with a handout *before* a lecture, you can write your own notes directly onto it. These become more like a commentary than a basic record of the lecture.

■ If you get a handout at the *end* of the lecture, it may be worth transcribing key points from your own notes onto it so that you can build on the lecturer's way of structuring the main ideas and information.

■ If your lecturer doesn't provide handouts but puts notes up on a screen or whiteboard, then take advantage of this when structuring your own notes.

Keep an open mind

■ If you find yourself disagreeing with what the lecturer says, write down your objections and queries, but don't let this interfere with making notes of the lecturer's arguments. Try to be open minded; you may see things differently as you get further into the subject.

Tidy up afterwards

■ It's tempting to put your notes away straight after a lecture, thinking you will come back to them another day. However that day seldom comes, and it's extremely valuable to spend a few minutes tidying up the notes while the lecture is still fresh in your mind. You'll be able to fill in blank spaces and make illegible words legible. If you don't do it then, your notes may be unintelligible later when your thoughts have moved on.

Note making strategy

Reflect regularly on whether you are getting what you need from your lecture notes. Ask other students what they do. Think of making notes as one element within your overall strategy. As the Cornell system emphasises, the way you make notes is tied in with:

■ preparing yourself before a lecture (by reading and annotating set texts and by reviewing your notes from the previous lecture)

■ focusing your attention during the lecture

■ consolidating your learning after the lecture (by tidying up, reviewing and summarising your notes).

You need to enter lectures armed with more than just good intentions. You need a clear sense of purpose and a workable technique – that is the value of starting with a systematic approach such as the Cornell system. As you get to know the subject and exchange ideas with other students you can then go on to develop an approach of your own.

Key points

■ Aim to make lecture notes concise and organised.

■ Try to map the main topics; don't try to record everything.

■ Use the space on the page to structure your notes.

6.3 Supporting your memory

Making notes from reading and from lectures is a way of supporting your memory. But how important *is* memory when you study? Were you trying to remember particular things as you read Layard's article? If so, what?

6.3.1 What should you be able to remember?

Activity 6.3

Which of the following points from Layard's article do you think it would be useful to remember?

Yes No

1   Rising levels of wealth in rich societies have not brought rising levels of happiness.

2   Questions about happiness in surveys get 99% response rates.

3   Clinical depression has increased in the richer countries over recent decades.

4   On average, Icelanders are happier than Americans.

5   People adjust expectations of income according to their reference groups.

6   David Beckham was mentioned.

7   Harvard students said they would settle for earning less, so long as it meant that they were earning more than other people were.

8   The amounts of money mentioned in the Harvard study were: $50,000, $25,000, $100,000 and $250,000.

It would be foolish to say that anything was definitely not worth remembering, but some things are more important than others and you can't remember everything. My answers for Activity 6.3 would be:

'Yes' for questions 1, 3, 5 and 7.

'No' for questions 2, 4, 6 and 8.

Although points 1, 3, 5 and 7 might seem worth remembering, they are not points you would set out to 'memorise'. You just 'know' them if you have made sense of the article as you read it. The act of understanding puts thoughts in your head which then become part of what you are generally aware of. Memory is not a particularly helpful concept here; 'understanding' is more significant.

It would not be particularly useful to remember points 2, 4, 6 and 8 on the other hand. Point 2 is just one that Layard makes in passing, to support Layard's view that we should take happiness surveys seriously. The specific figure, 99 per cent, is not significant, it indicates 'virtually everyone'. In the case of point 4 it might be useful to have the example of Icelanders in your head but it seems that they are a randomly chosen example, along with the Danes, of people with lower income but greater happiness than Americans. Similarly with point 6 you may find David Beckham's inclusion easy to remember simply because his name is familiar, but it could have been the name of anyone who is famously rich. Finally, in point 8, the specific sums of money quoted in the Harvard study are unimportant; they are there to give you a general sense of the choices being presented to the students. The importance of the Harvard study is summarised in point 7.

> ## BOX 6.4   FACTS, FIGURES AND NAMES
>
> Should you try to remember facts, figures and names? As you can see from Activity 6.3 it depends on your purpose. Often the answer is 'No' because you only need to get the general gist of the information. However if you *do* think particular details would be useful to hang on to, then *write them down* in your notes. *Don't try to memorise them.*

It is *not* the purpose of reading to be able to store the whole text in your mind. Even authors, on re-reading their own texts, find ideas they had forgotten they'd had. If authors are not able to recall in detail what they have written, why should *you* need to? What you want is to be able to *think* with the ideas that the author has presented.

You know you have retained some of what you have read when you can re-read a piece more easily the second time around, or read another text on the subject more easily. You will also find that ideas which you have encountered begin to appear in your conversation and your writing. This shows that your mind is gradually accommodating to new ways of thinking.

In other words, a lot of learning is not directly to do with *memory* as it is conventionally understood, in the sense of being able to produce rapid answers to quiz-type questions, but rather with getting new ideas embedded into your thought processes. However, to the extent that memory plays a part it is worth recognising some of its key features.

6.3.2 How memory works

In most courses there will be *some* things you need to commit to memory. If you are studying medicine or biology, for example, you need to remember the names of human body parts. So how can you use your memory to your best advantage? A good place to begin is to explore your memory's powers.

Activity 6.4

Find a clock or watch that displays seconds. Spend one minute trying to memorise the items listed below. Then get a piece of paper and without looking back at this page write down as many of the items as you can remember.

lemon tart	cabbage	sparkling water	ham
Beverages	corn flakes	*Sweets*	yoghurt
apple juice	*Starters*	turkey breast	rib steak
cheese	<u>Dinner</u>	*Side dishes*	broccoli
cucumber	beer	rice	<u>Supper</u>

How well did you do? There are twenty items. Did you remember eight or more? If so, you did well. Seven items from a list is as many as most people can remember, unless there is some kind of pattern to latch on to. Did you use a strategy of any kind? You would be exceptional if you did, with so little time and very little to help you.

Activity 6.5

Now try a test that offers more support. Here are another twenty items, this time organised in a menu format. Again, give yourself one minute to memorise them, then see how many you can write down.

Breakfast   Lunch

muesli   *Main course*   *Dessert*
grapefruit juice   lamb chop   ice cream
bacon   roast beef   apple pie
eggs
tomato   *Vegetables*   *Drinks*
                             potatoes   mineral water
                             carrots   wine
                             spinach

Did you do better? You should have been able to remember more items this time because there are four important principles working in your favour: grouping, nesting, visual structure and links to existing knowledge. These are ways that your mind copes with large amounts of information by organising and structuring it. Structured information is more easily remembered.

Structuring information

Grouping

In Activity 6.4 the items are presented as four lists, but there is nothing meaningful about the grouping. Although some items are underlined or italicised, you had very little time to work out how to make use of these features. For your mind, this was not much different from one long list.

In Activity 6.5 the items are laid out as groups under two main headings (Breakfast and Lunch), and the italicised words are subheadings that have a meaningful relationship to other words. Now you have just six headings to remember along with whatever sticks in your memory from the lists. Information is much more memorable when it is grouped meaningfully.

Nesting

Another feature of Activity 6.5 is that some groups of items are 'nested' within other groups. There is a broad grouping into breakfast or lunch. Then nested within Lunch are subgroups: Main course, Dessert, Vegetables and Drinks. Nesting is a powerful principle. It is the essence of what an outliner does. Look at Figure 6.2 with its main categories, sub-categories and sub-sub-categories. Instead of knowledge being a formless mass, you can organise it into categories within other categories. In this way your mind can store and then access enormous amounts of information. You can use this principle to great effect in revising for an exam.

Visual structure

The use of grouping and nesting in Activity 6.5 is emphasised by the way in which the words are laid out on the page. Also the underlining and italicisation highlight the principles underlying the structure. Indeed the headings no longer seem like words to be memorised. Instead of being part of the problem, they become part of the solution.

Linking to existing knowledge

Finally, Activity 6.5 takes advantage of your existing knowledge about meals and food. The Breakfast items are commonly seen together and the Lunch items are grouped as you might see them on a menu. When you read the items in Activity 6.4, you couldn't predict what might come next, but in Activity 6.5 the items are quite predictable. This allows your mind to group them into well-established categories where you will be able to find them again. Because the knowledge in your mind is already elaborately structured, new information can be organised to take advantage of this structuring.

Other memory techniques

You can explore other memory techniques by searching the internet. Two of the most commonly used are:

Visualisation Imagine a scene, then place the items that you have to remember into that scene. You might have done this with the food items in Activity 6.5 by visualising a plate with meat and vegetables on it, or visualising a table with the breakfast items sitting there. To remember the items, you bring the picture back to mind and 'see' what is there. Our minds are good at storing images of complex visual scenes. Finding ways to organise information visually, particularly if you can make use of scenes and actions, adds great power to your memory.

Mnemonics Make up a rhyme or a nonsense phrase to help you remember something which has no obvious meaning that you can latch onto. For example, I was taught 'Richard of York gave battle in vain' as a mnemonic for remembering that red, orange, yellow, green, blue, indigo and violet are the colours of the rainbow. And there is the famous 'Doh Re Mi' song in the film *The Sound of Music*, for remembering the names of the notes: doh, reh, mi, fah, so, la, ti, doh. Mnemonic techniques have a very long history stemming from the days when knowledge was held in people's minds and transmitted orally.

Memory 'tricks' are generally useful only when information is fundamentally lacking in meaning, or for special circumstances, such as last-minute preparations for an exam, when you need to load up on information quickly then dump it to make way for the next exam. Rather than put your energies into creating *artificial* meanings and structures, it is generally much more valuable to develop *real* understanding and *genuine* long-term structuring of knowledge in your mind.

6.3.3 Worries about memory

Age and memory

Older students often worry that their memory might let them down. In terms of raw speed and 'processing power', everyone's memory does gradually decline, however, in practical terms, this is balanced out by the fact that you accumulate better organising structures in your mind for 'filing' information and ideas. As you get older, you will have a much more effective memory for certain things because you can make better sense of them, and you have developed more sophisticated mental organisation. As long as you keep *using* your mind to *think* about and *organise* new information, your studies are unlikely to be affected by declining memory until very late in life.

Putting memory in its place

Perhaps you worry that your memory may let you down in your studies, but memory is less important than you might think. As you progress to higher levels of study, the focus is increasingly on understanding and putting ideas to use. On most higher-level courses there is little need to spend time 'memorising' in the sense of learning lists of words by rote. Instead, you can concentrate on the much more interesting challenge of learning to think in new ways.

Key points

■ Pure memory plays a relatively small role in higher-level studies; it's what you understand that counts.

■ If you need to remember things, just write them down in your notes.

■ You can help your memory by applying the principles of grouping, nesting, visual structure and linking to existing knowledge when you are making notes.

- When you have a specific need to remember information, there are various techniques you can call on, such as visualisation, mnemonic rhymes and word associations.

- Don't worry about the effect of age on your memory; greater knowledge and efficiency generally outweigh any physical changes.

6.4 Organising knowledge

One way to make new knowledge memorable is to impose structure upon it. You might do this as you go along, making notes that summarise readings and lectures. You might do it as you gather together material for an essay or prepare for an exam. Or you might just do it periodically, to clear your head and make yourself feel more on top of things. When you've been reading books or listening to lectures and are feeling swamped by new ideas and information, it can be helpful and morale-boosting to do some reviewing and organising.

6.4.1 Getting things straight

There are various ways in which you can set about organising knowledge. One simple but powerful technique is to draw a grid or table and arrange ideas and information in the cells under different headings. Figure 6.7 is an example of a grid which I used to organise my thoughts about how we learn through reading, writing, listening and speaking.

Written word		Spoken word	
Reading		Listening	
Advantages	Challenges	Advantages	Challenges
Writing		Speaking	
Advantages	Challenges	Advantages	Challenges

Figure 6.7 Engaging with ideas and information: an example of an empty grid ready for ideas

Making this grid encouraged me to think *analytically* by reflecting on the key differences between learning through the spoken and the written word. It also made me realise that while learning is most obviously done through reading and listening, I must also think about what to put in the 'Writing' and 'Speaking' boxes. As I wrote ideas in these, I found myself questioning whether they were really different from what I'd written in the boxes above, and if so, how? The grid headings also reminded me to pay attention to both the advantages and challenges of all four modes of learning.

In other words, the grid encouraged me to think systematically by helping me to dig out and examine ideas which I had not formulated properly. By setting ideas alongside each other, it helped me to examine their coherence and consistency. I played around with what was already in my mind, getting things clearer and more organised, and eventually this stimulated me to do some more reading to check things out and develop my analysis. So, working with the grid pulled together my existing knowledge and ideas and set me up to move forward again.

You can make similar use of grids to pull together knowledge and ideas from your course. For example if you were studying the growth of care services in the UK, you might find it useful to put together some of the key developments you have come across and organise them chronologically as in Figure 6.8. This would give you an overall picture of what has happened in different decades and of how developments in law were linked to the creation of new organisations and to action on the ground.

	Legislation	Organisations	Implementation
1950s	Rent Act (1957) Mental Health Act (1959)	National Council for Civil Liberties (1951)	NCCL campaign for patients
1960s	National Assistance Act (62) Children & Young Persons Act (63, 69) Rent Act (65)	Cncl f. Profs Sup. to Medicine (60) Housing Corporation (64) Nat. Cncl f. Single Woman (65)	Register of profs sup to m. (60) Policy to end mental hospitals (61) Enforcement of fair rents (65)
1970s	NHS Reorganisation Act (74) Children Act (75) Homeless Persons Act (77)	CCETSW & BASW (71) Regional Health Authorities (74)	Loc Auth homes for older p. (70-75) Invalid care allowances (75) Definition of homelessness (77)
1980s	...	...	...

Figure 6.8 Using a grid to organise information

If you were studying parenting you might draw up a grid like the one in Figure 6.9 to help you compare psychological theories, giving a column to each type of theory and a row to each different parenting issue dealt with in the course. This would help embed in your mind the key differences between the theories.

	Behaviourist	Socio-cultural	Psychoanalytic
Young child tantrums	Consistent pattern or rewards for non-conflict behaviour	Participation in family activities Role playing games	Acting out Oedipus & Electra crises
Teenager-parent conflict	Earn privilege points for calm behaviour	Dialogue to renegotiate roles and power relations	Support in resolving identity crisis
Drug issues	etc ...	etc ...	etc

Figure 6.9 Using a grid to compare theoretic approaches

In Microsoft Word you just click on the Table and drag out a table with the number of columns and rows you want. Grids are particularly easy to use if you are working on a computer, taking advantage of your word-processor's table creating facility. Having created a grid and given headings to columns and rows, you can either work with it onscreen or print it off and write on it by hand. Alternatively, you can just create columns with headings.

 I have four columns headed Key themes, Key words, Key writers, Key examples. As I work through a topic I add things to the lists, so that at the end I have organised information to hold on to.

6.4.2 Making connections

A grid offers the power of schematic structure. However there are other ways to organise knowledge that encourage you to make creative links between ideas. 'Mind mapping' is one such technique. Figure 6.10 shows a mind map for Layard's article.

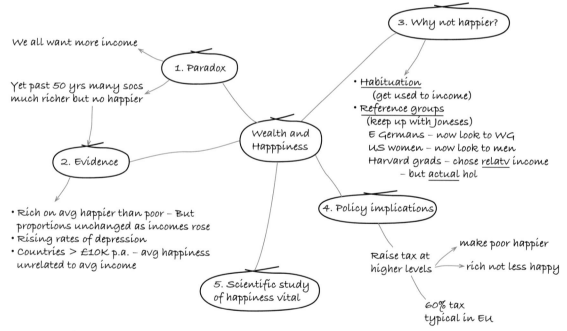

Figure 6.10 **A mind map for Layard's article**

The bubble in the middle of Figure 6.10 states the topic. Then the numbered bubbles around it contain main themes, each being linked to the main topic. Some of the main themes have notes linked to them. Notice that the note for '4. Policy Implications: Raise tax at higher levels' has further notes of its own. An arrow links the note for '1. Paradox': 'Yet past 50 yrs: ... ', to '2. Evidence', to show the relationship between them. You can mark in as many connections between elements of a diagram as you find useful.

Activity 6.6

1   Explore Figure 6.10 and consider why I have used arrows in certain places.

2   Does the diagram work for you? Does it represent the bones of the whole article?

3   Look back at Figures 6.1, 6.2 and 6.3 and compare them with Figure 6.10. Which of the four ways of summarising Layard's article is most helpful to you?

4   Which summary method do you think would take longest to create? In what situations might each be used?

There are no right answers to these questions. It depends on how your mind works, what you want to do with your notes, and how much time you are prepared to invest in note making.

I made the mind map in Figure 6.10 by going through my underlining of Layard's article, picking out what seemed important, and fitting it into the diagram where it made sense to me. I did it with pen and paper, but I could have used my computer. You can use the drawing feature of your word-processor or obtain mind mapping software. You can get an idea of what's available by searching the internet for 'mind mapping' or looking on a site such as www.download.com.

 What a nifty little mind map program! Thanks for the tip. I just used it to sort out a presentation I'm due to give.

Creating a diagram is an additional time investment, but visualisation can help a lot in clarifying your thoughts. It is worth playing around with techniques such as mind mapping to find out whether the gain in understanding and remembering is worth the time and effort.

6.4.3 Pulling things together

Some people use mind maps when revising for exams. They encourage you to *group* things together and to make links, both of which help to structure your memory. Figure 6.11 shows a mind map of a topic in a course on care for children and young people. It is a very thorough piece of work prepared for students by a teacher. It gives an idea of what level of detail can be achieved, but you'll probably find that less detailed and orderly mind maps work fine for you.

 I find doing mind maps for revision really helps. It gives you confidence that you do actually remember something.

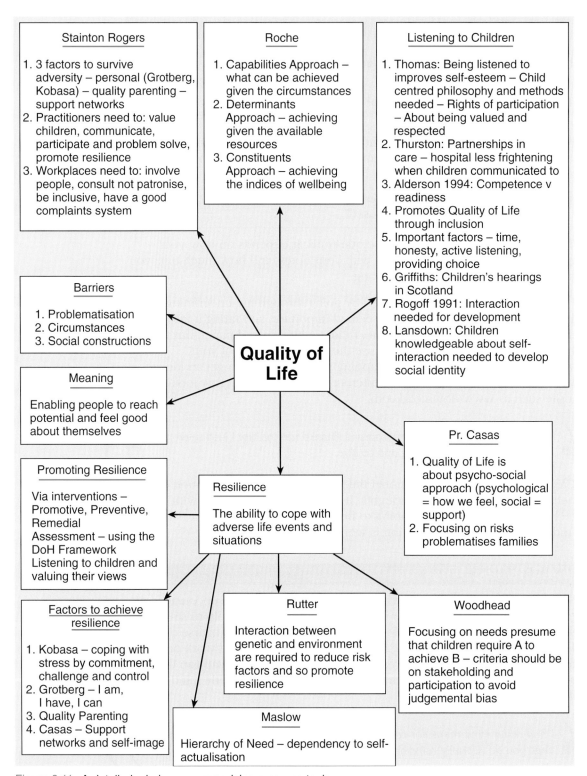

Stainton Rogers

1. 3 factors to survive adversity – personal (Grotberg, Kobasa) – quality parenting – support networks
2. Practitioners need to: value children, communicate, participate and problem solve, promote resilience
3. Workplaces need to: involve people, consult not patronise, be inclusive, have a good complaints system

Roche

1. Capabilities Approach – what can be achieved given the circumstances
2. Determinants Approach – achieving given the available resources
3. Constituents Approach – achieving the indices of wellbeing

Listening to Children

1. Thomas: Being listened to improves self-esteem – Child centred philosophy and methods needed – Rights of participation – About being valued and respected
2. Thurston: Partnerships in care – hospital less frightening when children communicated to
3. Alderson 1994: Competence v readiness
4. Promotes Quality of Life through inclusion
5. Important factors – time, honesty, active listening, providing choice
6. Griffiths: Children's hearings in Scotland
7. Rogoff 1991: Interaction needed for development
8. Lansdown: Children knowledgeable about self-interaction needed to develop social identity

Barriers

1. Problematisation
2. Circumstances
3. Social constructions

Meaning

Enabling people to reach potential and feel good about themselves

Quality of Life

Pr. Casas

1. Quality of Life is about psycho-social approach (psychological = how we feel, social = support)
2. Focusing on risks problematises families

Promoting Resilience

Via interventions – Promotive, Preventive, Remedial
Assessment – using the DoH Framework
Listening to children and valuing their views

Resilience

The ability to cope with adverse life events and situations

Factors to achieve resilience

1. Kobasa – coping with stress by commitment, challenge and control
2. Grotberg – I am, I have, I can
3. Quality Parenting
4. Casas – Support networks and self-image

Rutter

Interaction between genetic and environment are required to reduce risk factors and so promote resilience

Woodhead

Focusing on needs presume that children require A to achieve B – criteria should be on stakeholding and participation to avoid judgemental bias

Maslow

Hierarchy of Need – dependency to self-actualisation

Figure 6.11 A detailed mind map summarising a course topic

> **Key points**
>
> - Grids and mind maps enable you to bring together and summarise a lot of information so that you can get a structured overview.
>
> - Setting out ideas or information in a grid helps you to organise your knowledge and encourages systematic analysis of similarities and differences.
>
> - Making a mind map lets you work more creatively and helps you to see how different aspects of a topic link together.

6.5 Supporting creativity

We have explored how valuable notes can be for capturing and organising knowledge, but perhaps the most valuable use of all is in helping you work up ideas for a *presentation* or an *essay*.

6.5.1 Capturing thoughts

Notes help you to capture your thoughts as they float by, whether you are doing course work, reading a newspaper, sitting on a train, or watching TV. At the time, your thoughts may seem obvious and not particularly important, yet these scraps become the seeds of your creativity. Ideas don't conveniently flow into your mind the moment you sit down to write. To achieve originality in your speaking and writing, you have to trap thoughts as they come to you. Keep a note-pad or a wad of 'stickies' (e.g. Post-it notes) handy. If you are working at your computer, you could create a document called 'Essay Notes' and work in outline view. Then, when a thought strikes, type in a new line. You can move things around later to get your ideas straight. Or you could use electronic stickies to keep track of ideas (see Figure 6.12). Search for 'stickies' on the internet or go to www.download.com.

I use virtual 'stickies'. They are incredibly useful, just like real Post-its, you can have them 'on top' or hidden, and are dead easy to use. I use mine for referencing websites – when I visit a website, I just put the address, the data, and the date I accessed it on a sticky, then when I write the essay I've got the reference info all to hand. It's free too!

These things are great. I have sent one to 'sleep' so it will appear in the middle of March to remind me to start work on the project.

6.5.2 Shaping ideas

When you have written down enough scraps of ideas, you can gather them together and play around with organising them to make an effective line of

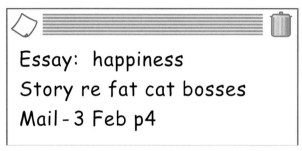

Figure 6.12 An electronic 'sticky'

argument. Start with the most promising ideas and set aside those you have lost interest in. Then try different ways of grouping and sequencing them to make the logic flow.

You can do these informal jottings on the back of the proverbial envelope, or you could sketch out a mind map. Alternatively this is where your outliner comes into its own. Having typed in various ideas you can rearrange them effortlessly. Expanding and collapsing an outline allows you to examine the flow of your argument at different levels of detail. Figure 6.13 shows the same outline as Figure 6.2 but with only two heading levels showing. You can switch back and forth between the big picture and fine detail whenever you want to check on how things are shaping up.

```
┌─────────────────────────────────────────────────────────────┐
│ □ ═══════════════ Good_Study_Guidef06.13 ═══════════════ 昌 │
├─────────────────────────────────────────────────────────────┤
│ ⇦ ⇐  Level 2         ▾ ⇨ ⇛ ⇧ ⇩ ⊹ −  ᴬ⁄A 1 [2] 3 4 All │
├─────────────────────────────────────────────────────────────┤
│   ⇧  Central paradox                                         │
│         ▫  People want more income                           │
│         ⇧  Soc now much richer –                             │
│   ⇧  Evidence: Happiness & rising incomes                    │
│         ⇧  Within soc – rich  happier than poorer (on avg)   │
│         ⇧  Depression risen – most countries                 │
│         ⇧  Diffs betw countries                              │
│   ⇧  Why doesn't rising wealth bring rising happiness?       │
│         ⇧  Norms:                                            │
│         ⇧  What drives up norms?                             │
└─────────────────────────────────────────────────────────────┘
```

Figure 6.13 Outline with two levels of heading in view

6.5.3 Sketching what you might say

Another kind of creative note making is sketching out possible sentences and paragraphs for your essay. Many of your jottings will be thrown away, but the point is that by working first in note form, you create an informal space where you can let your mind 'speak' without the pressure of having to get it right.

See Chapter 11, Managing the writing process

> ### Key points
>
> Your notepad is a private, low-key space where the pressure is off and you can be creative. Here you can:
>
> - trap thoughts as they pass
> - shape ideas into convincing arguments
> - sketch out ways of putting arguments into words.

6.6 Making notes strategically

Note making is not a single skill but a range of activities whose common feature is that you *write for yourself,* rather than for an audience, so that you don't have to worry about explaining yourself. Making good notes involves:

- **Taking an active, enquiring approach to study** Asking yourself questions such as 'What is this about?', 'What do I want to remember?' and 'What do I want to say?' and writing down the answers.

- **Flexibility** Making sketched notes or detailed notes according to circumstances and need.

- **Reflection** Looking at your notes and asking yourself 'Are they doing the job I want?' and 'Could I be using my time more effectively?'

How many notes do you need?

I seem to be writing so many notes. Reading, highlighting, then making own notes. Am I doing too much? My time is limited. Can someone reassure please?

That sounds pretty much like me. I've been writing notes, highlighting, and typing up the key points. I'm hoping that as we get more confident we'll know what notes we should be aiming to have.

Note making can help your studies in many different ways, but it is not a panacea. If you make too many, then studying becomes tedious. You have to weigh up *when* to make notes, what *kind* of notes to make, and what level of *detail* suits your needs.

What will you do with your notes?

See Chapter 2
Section 2.4.3,
Maintaining a filing
system and
Chapter 3
Section 3.4,
Organising files

The time you invest in *making* notes is wasted if you don't also invest in maintaining an effective *filing* system. But having stored your notes, will you use them? Will you sit down one day and read carefully through them all? If your notes are lengthy, unstructured and disorganised, you probably won't *ever* make use of them. Going back over old notes is seldom as urgent or appealing as moving on to something new; the exceptions are when you are looking for material for an essay, or pulling together ideas for an exam. It doesn't *matter* if you only go back to your notes occasionally, however, the process of writing them is valuable in itself.

Key points

Benefits of note making:

- It keeps you *actively focused* on studying.

- It's good for your *morale* because it's a creative task with a visible product; you can *see* that you have been studying.

- It makes you look for *meaning* in what you read and hear; and it helps to translate that meaning into your own words, turning knowledge 'out there' into *your* knowledge.

- Notes serve as an *extension of your memory*; they give you access to a far wider range of knowledge than memory alone can provide.

- Working in note form helps make *writing* a creative activity.

- Making notes which *pull together* the course is a key part of preparing for an exam.

Note-making strategy:

- You need to find the right balance, don't turn studying into a chore. Note making should be a creative process which makes study more satisfying.

- If your notes are to be useful in future, you need to make them succinct, intelligible, well-organised and effectively filed.

- Experiment with different ways of making notes and reflect on their effectiveness so that you develop a repertoire of robust, flexible techniques.

Reference

Pauk, W. (2001) *How to Study in College*, Boston, Houghton Mifflin Company.

Useful links

www.download.com

CHAPTER 7 LEARNING THROUGH TALK

7.1 Talk in higher learning

From birth most people learn about life through speaking and by hearing other people talk, so talking and listening seem 'natural' ways of learning about things. Certainly talk is the main means of learning in school. At higher levels of learning however the balance shifts to reading and writing, yet talk retains a significant role, with lectures, seminars, tutorials, presentations, workshops and field trips, featuring prominently on the curriculum of most courses.

However, it's important to qualify this. Talk does not play a prominent role in everyone's life. If you experience communication difficulties you will be highly skilled in using alternatives to speech to achieve the same ends. Meanwhile, distance education offers the possibility of gaining a degree without direct use of the spoken word. So, although this chapter explores the benefits of learning through talk, it is important to bear in mind that these benefits can be sought in other ways, the online dialogues in Section 3.5 of Chapter 3 being a prime example.

7.1.1 The dynamics of dialogue

Talk has the capacity to sweep your thoughts along. Compared with words sitting on a page, awaiting your efforts to invest them with meaning, the dynamics of speech can be very compelling and direct. And talking also offers you opportunities to try out ideas for yourself, in direct dialogue with other people. Instead of composing careful written sentences, you pitch in and try to explain your thoughts as they come to you.

Developing ideas through dialogue is important in daily life. It is not enough just to 'understand' ideas and be able to write about them with books open around you. You need to be able to take part in intensive, disciplined discussions, where ideas are put to use in the world. Being able to grasp the significance of what others are saying and make a well argued contribution of your own is part of what it means to be knowledgeable in your subject.

> **BOX 7.1 KEY SKILLS: COMMUNICATION**
>
> Communication is one of six 'key skills' identified by the UK government and business community as essential to successful participation in a modern society. To demonstrate the key skills of communication you are expected to be able to:

- **Listen closely** 'balancing a number of points simultaneously, while evaluating the relative importance of each'.

- **Discuss** 'be sensitive to the contributions of others, develop points and ideas and actively encourage others to participate'.

- **Make presentations** 'demonstrate a clear sense of purpose and be able to engage [an] audience's attention'.

(Source: QCA, 2002, p. 21.)

There is a fuller discussion of learning through the spoken word in Section 4.4.3 of Chapter 4.

Skills of learning through talk

Section 7.2 of this chapter explores the many facets of learning through *discussion* in groups. Section 7.3 then discusses how to make effective *presentations*. Finally, Section 7.4 looks at various ways of learning by *listening*.

Key points

- Although university learning emphasises the written word, talk has traditionally played an important role.

- The dynamism and fluidity of talk are very helpful in grappling with the meaning of new concepts and ideas.

- Moreover, being able to 'speak' your knowledge in real life situations is an important skill in itself.

7.2 Learning through group discussion

Discussion groups of various kinds are a common feature of degree level courses. Indeed, on many courses attendance at group sessions is compulsory and on some participation in sessions is assessed. The key feature of this form of study is that it allows *dialogue*. Most of your study time is spent in one-way communication. Either you are at the receiving end, or you are writing to an absent reader. Whereas, in a discussion, ideas can be traded back and forth between teacher and students and amongst students themselves. Such sessions go by a variety of names and the nature of the dialogue can vary enormously, but all are intended to be *interactive*. Instead of ideas and arguments being neatly packaged and put on show, they emerge in action, rough and ready, to be put to use in making sense of the world.

7.2.1 Different types of learning group

The terms *seminar, tutorial, discussion group, class* and *workshop* are all used to refer to sessions involving a tutor and a group of students. However, different institutions, and sometimes different subject areas, use the terms differently. In fact, for our purposes here, it is not important which term is used. The significant factor is that you are expected to learn through group interaction. I will mainly use the general term *discussion group*, but the issues discussed will be relevant to your own group learning situations, whatever they may be called. I will also use the term '*tutor*' for the group leader.

Whatever the label, there are several key factors which give a discussion group its character.

Group size

A discussion group can involve anything from two students to more than fifty.

- **Small groups** (six students or fewer): All group members can participate intensively. They can talk informally, say what they think, interrupt each other, and still expect to reach a workable consensus on issues.

- **Medium-sized groups** (seven to sixteen students): Although everyone should be able to speak at some point, there is more of a need for turn-taking and waiting for appropriate opportunities to speak. Some form of 'chairing' is required, whether by the tutor or one or more students, to manage the progress of the group. Usually a pattern emerges in that a few students contribute more actively and others contribute more occasionally.

- **Large groups** (seventeen students or more): In the full group a few students can contribute, but many, necessarily, can only listen. (Some large groups are divided into small groups for part of the time.)

Degree of tutor control

In some groups the tutor takes very close control of all that happens: setting the agenda, doing most of the talking, directing questions to individual students and commenting on their answers. At the other end of the scale, students take turns to lead sessions, while all group members contribute freely and comment on each other's contributions; meanwhile, the tutor stays in the background, coming in only when asked. Between these two extremes lie many alternatives which share control between the tutor and the students to differing degrees.

Structured or open-ended

Some group sessions are run to very carefully structured plans, for example, with pre-designed tasks and students breaking into smaller groups, then reporting back according to prescribed guidelines. Others simply start with

159

a broad topic, then pursue whatever themes and issues arise during discussion. Again there are many points between these extremes.

Theoretical focus or practical

Some groups address tough theoretical issues to help students engage with abstract analysis and criticism. Others encourage students to apply new knowledge to the world around them using case material drawn from real life and focusing on finding practical solutions to problems.

Topic-centred or student-centred

In some groups the agenda is driven by the current course topic and the concepts and theories connected with it. In others students are encouraged to bring their own course-related concerns into the group for discussion – perhaps a problem with a forthcoming assignment, or concerns about coping with workload and exam preparations.

Whatever the label used for group sessions on your course what they offer will depend on your tutor's approach and on the culture and traditions of your subject, your department and your university. The only reliable way to find out about them is to attend.

Key points

- Discussion-based learning sessions are given various names including *seminars, tutorials, group discussions, classes* and *workshops.*

- The dynamics of the discussion is significantly affected by the *size* of group. In small groups all students can participate fully, while in large groups most participate primarily through listening to dialogue between the tutor and just a few students.

- The character of a group is also affected by the degree of *control* exerted by the *tutor,* the extent to which sessions are *structured,* the balance between *theory* and *practice* and the degree of emphasis on *student needs* as opposed to the *topic.*

7.2.2 How groups help you learn

Group discussion is an unpredictable process and it isn't easy to pin down exactly what you learn from it. After a group session you may have few notes and only a hazy memory of what has been talked about. Yet important learning processes can be stimulated within the flow of a discussion.

Bringing ideas to your level

In group sessions you can pull the discussion to a level that makes sense to you. If concepts are very abstract, or theories obscure, you can try to apply them to examples you understand. If you are confused you can ask for clarification, and ideas can be made more personally relevant by applying them to your own life. Meanwhile, your tutor can listen out for where difficulties seem to be arising and try to explain in ways that make more sense to you.

Collective thinking

In a discussion you take your understanding forward alongside other students. As one gropes to express a thought another may contribute from a slightly different angle while a third then tries to clarify what is being said. The group progresses by pooling its thinking resources. Within the shared understanding generated by the group you find yourself able to use ideas which you cannot yet grasp independently. When you are reading, writing, or thinking on your own, it's easy to get stuck. Discussion is a way of playing flexibly with language and ideas and negotiating meanings in a supportive environment.

Making connections and recognising implications

Discussion helps you to explore how ideas link to each other. You suddenly see that a concept has wider meanings than you had realised and you begin to appreciate your new knowledge as not just a set of separate items, but as a working body of interconnected ideas.

Applying ideas to practical situations

Many concepts and theories which you think you understand turn out to be more fuzzy and ambiguous than you realised when you try to apply them to real examples. For example it's all very well to have a neat diagram of the workings of the human body, but to view a live operation and identify what you can see is another matter. Working collectively helps with mapping ideas onto reality. Other students' guesses and approximations help you in making your own. Together you share in interpreting situations, matching concepts to cases and making judgements about the relevance of particular explanations.

Practising skills

Group sessions also provide an environment where you can develop skills. You might be provided with problem sheets to work on, given a role-playing situation to act out, documents to analyse and draw conclusions from, or a sample essay to mark and discuss. This type of session is often described as a 'workshop'. It is an opportunity for a tutor to provide feedback and support – coaching you in skills relevant to your subject area.

Learning the language of the subject

Meanwhile, as you participate in discussions, a subtle form of learning goes on in the background. Gradually, you become more comfortable and confident with the language of your subject area. Specialist terms which previously seemed to be unnecessary 'jargon' start to become meaningful. They slip unnoticed into your own vocabulary.

Picking up the 'academic' way of thinking and arguing

Also going on behind the scenes is a general shift in your approach to the subject. Discussions helps to 'initiate' you into the culture and ways of thinking of experts in your field of study. You begin to 'internalise' the criteria against which arguments and evidence are judged and to acquire the 'voice' in which your subject is discussed. You get a feel for how the debates work – how to position yourself and how to present an argument. And as you share in discussion you begin to develop an identity as a member of that community of experts. You begin to get the feeling that 'this is the way *I* talk – I'm a psychologist, an economist, a social worker. I belong. This is *my* field of knowledge'.

Boosting morale

Most important of all learning with a group keeps your spirits up. You make friends and feel valued within the group. Soon you find out that everyone is experiencing the same difficulties as you, and as you exchange study tips, you stop feeling that it's just you against the texts. Knowing that other people are working alongside you, the subject matter starts to seem more relevant and accessible

Key points

- Discussion is a communal mode of learning which allows you to share the burden of understanding new ideas.

- Discussion helps to develop your thinking skills as you follow the cut and thrust of argument and try out your grasp of concepts and theories.

- Meanwhile you pick up the language of your subject and internalise the culture, values and general orientation of those who study your field.

- Group study lifts your morale as you discover that you are not alone in your struggles and share study tips with other students.

7.2.3 The variability of group work

Group discussions vary enormously from one group to another and from session to session. Energy surges, then slumps. Deadlock is followed by rapid progress; students get irritated with each other, then come to terms. Even for tutors this variation is baffling.

> What's puzzling is that sometimes it seems to go pretty well, then the next time it falls flat and I can't really tell why. Anyway, the students keep coming back, so they must think they're getting something.

However some of the variability is not so baffling.

Different kinds of students

If students are knowledgeable, enthusiastic about the subject and eager to debate, a very different discussion develops than where students are unprepared, uninspired and reluctant to join in. A lot depends on how experienced students are, both in discussion environments and in life. Mature students are often noticeably readier to speak and to draw on their own life experience than students recently out of school.

Social and cultural diversity

Social and cultural backgrounds are also important. Some students feel disadvantaged by their schooling and lack of resources. Some are used to a cooperative classroom culture, others assume competition and point scoring. Some are from cultures which expect vigorous, egalitarian participation in groups, others are used to deference towards seniority – particularly towards a teacher. And some have different expectations of participation for men and for women.

Different tutoring styles

Tutors also differ in their styles of teaching. Some like to keep discussion under tight control while others prefer to guide students in exploring ideas for themselves.

> Yeah, he won't tell you the answer, he makes you think for yourself, but he sort of prompts you along the lines. I mean he won't come out and say what the answer is.

Some tutors like to make sure that students understand the subject 'correctly'. Others try to guide students towards arriving at their own judgements.

> they don't say you're wrong, but they can sort of work it round so that you realise that you were wrong.

(Anderson, 1997, pp. 185–198)

Changes over time

The nature of discussion changes markedly as you progress through your studies. You begin in groups where students are relatively nervous, unprepared and unsure of what is expected. But gradually everyone becomes familiar with group working and more confident in their subject knowledge. Discussions become less awkward, better informed and more challenging.

Group discussions depend on 'group chemistry'. Particular combinations of people, circumstances and events produce very different flavours of group experience. Sometimes group work is the highlight of a course, leading to profound learning, personal commitment to the subject, and valuable friendships. In other cases it plods along at a more mundane level or even becomes quite uncomfortable.

Key points

- Groups vary enormously depending on the subject you are studying, the kinds of students on your course and the expectations and experience they bring.

- They are also very much affected by the personal style and approach of your tutor.

- Group study changes as you progress through your studies and you and your peers become more knowledgeable and confident.

7.2.4 The experience of group learning

Being in a discussion group can produce strong feelings. You may find yourself stimulated, amused and appreciated, or bored, frustrated and alienated.

Good experiences

Here is a collection of the kinds of things students say about discussion groups they enjoy:

The discussions are really interesting. You don't think of it as study – you know like – 'work'. It makes me glad I chose politics. Sitting there hearing such important ideas going back and forth, I kind of feel proud to be a student of it.

It's such a relief to find that everyone else has the same struggles with the books and essays. You feel you've got friends to ask if you're in difficulties. Some of them are very interesting people, who cope with so much in their lives.

The tutor's always ready to talk about things and never patronises us. It makes the subject come to life to be able to discuss with someone who knows so much.

Now and then you get a flash of insight and wish you'd known all this years ago. I hear myself joining in discussions and think – I'm a real student now.

It's great to be able to ask questions and get things sorted out, instead of just reading all the time. You suddenly get the point of the concepts and theories. You feel that you're getting closer to the heart of the subject.

I just wish my family and friends at work could take a course like this – then we could have some decent discussions, like in the tutorials, instead of all that prejudiced stuff from the tabloids.

When discussion groups go well they help you to understand your subject in depth and keep you motivated and working well. Take full advantage while you can.

Difficult experiences

If your experiences in discussion groups are less happy, you need to think what to do about them.

Activity 7.1

Read each of the scenarios below and write down what you think the problem is and what, if anything, the student should do?

1 Daniel

I wish I knew what they're talking about. Sometime I think I get it, but then I lose it again. I've no idea what those jargon words mean. If anyone asks me a question I'll be totally lost. Better keep my eyes down. If I make some notes it'll look as though I'm following. Maybe I'll be able to make some sense of it all when I read them later.

2 Caitlin

Should I just say what I think? Or does she only want to hear from the ones who know the answers? I didn't finish all the reading – perhaps I'm meant to keep quiet. Or do we get marks for the number of times we speak? Am I allowed to ask a question even if I don't really know what I'm asking? I thought Ella took us off the point – should I say so?

3 Harry

It's so hard to join in I really want to speak, but every time I work out something to say other people are talking and then the topic moves on. Then when the tutor actually asks what I think my mind goes blank and I say something useless. And when I do jump in, I can't explain my point, so they all just pretend to understand and carry on what they are saying.

4 Maya

I shouldn't be here. Everyone's so studious and clever and confident, with all their A levels. They breeze through those books and articles which I have to struggle over just to get through a few paragraphs. And when the tutor made me speak, someone else disagreed straight off. So I obviously don't get it. Why make a fool of myself. I should just stay home and stick to the books.

5 Jessica

If Kelly goes on about her kids any more I'm going to scream. Why do some students think their lives are so fascinating and relevant to the course? Does she think we've never been in families? Why doesn't Paul shut her up and get us back to the topic? Why is it always just one or two going on about whatever's on their minds, while the rest say nothing?

6 Amir

Why doesn't Gina take more control? We drift around all over the place and never get back on track. Except we always end up hearing about her PhD – and you get rubbished if you don't agree with her point of view. She so loves those creepy guys who suck up and act like she's brilliant, just to get good grades. And if you ask about something she doesn't know, she just twists it around to something she does.

7 Aleena

We never seem to get to the heart of anything. People just say what comes into their heads, pretending they know about things when they obviously haven't understood the reading. I don't feel I'm learning a thing.

8 Callum

It's so patronising, the way they assume you want to join in their smug little world, with their deliberately obscure questions – and only the tutor's answer is ever good enough. He thinks I want his approval. I'll be earning twice as much as him in a few years and the rest of this lot. Does he really think I'm going to answer his question?

Each of the eight scenarios in Activity 7.1 represents an important issue that can arise in discussion groups. There are many ways you might have responded to them. I hope my comments make some useful connections.

1 Not understanding

Daniel: I wish I knew what they're talking about …

Daniel is feeling anxious. Not understanding is always unsettling. But why does he feel so threatened? Most of the other students are probably as confused as he is. He's bound to feel out of his depth at times. His course *should* be presenting him with lots of new words and ideas. The purpose of the discussion is to tease out what the topic is all about and familiarise him with terms. If he understood everything, there wouldn't be any point in it.

But he needs to join in. He should say that he doesn't understand. Why not ask if someone can talk him through an example to show what the topic is about. And if he still doesn't get it, he can ask again. The session belongs to him as much as anyone else. It's his education. His fees are worth the same. He should make sure he gets some sense out of each session. Anyway, clarifying things will be just as helpful for the other students. It's much better to err in the direction of over-clarifying, than have people sitting about in a fog of confusion. The discussion isn't going to be much use if half the participants don't know what they're talking about.

Daniel shouldn't worry a lot about notes. His main job is to experience the flow of dialogue. Any important information ought to be available from course texts and handouts. Nor should he pin hopes on working out the meaning of his notes later. If they don't make sense as he writes them, they certainly won't later. He might want to jot down a few reminders of things to follow up but he doesn't need a detailed record of the discussion. It's far more important to stay actively in touch with what's being said.

2 Uncertainty about rules

Caitlin: Should I just say what I think?

It's often not clear in a discussion what is expected and what is allowed and it seems brash to jump in without knowing. Some groups do talk about expectations and rules in the first meeting. But if nothing has been said Caitlin should ask, particularly if she thinks there may be an element of assessment. If she feels unsure then other students are probably feeling unsure too.

Caitlin *should* just say what she thinks. If only the most knowledgeable students speak then most of the group will get left behind. Also the tutor will get the wrong impression about the level at which to pitch things. It's even helpful to the more confident students to try to explain things to the others – it's far better than playing the game of who can say the cleverest sounding things. If Caitlin's done at least *some* of the relevant reading, she should dive in – few will have completed it *all*. On the other hand, if she hadn't done *any* of the reading, then she should keep quiet. It isn't fair to use precious discussion time making up for what some students have been unwilling to do in preparation. Pretending you've done the reading, or trying to change the topic to something you know about, undermines everyone's progress.

Yes Caitlin should ask questions, however unsure she is about what she's asking. We all have to grope our way forward when we're grappling with new ideas. If Caitlin doesn't see the relevance of Ella's point she could say 'I'm not sure how that ties in, Ella – could you explain?' Not in a critical tone, but assuming that for Ella there was a link. It's very helpful to the group if members try to pull threads together and keep the discussion focused.

3 Difficulty joining in

Harry: It's so hard to join in ...

When there is competition for speaking time it's always difficult to know when and how to join in. Generally, one or two students step in and play an active role for a while, then pull back and let others take a turn. But it's hard to jump in successfully with a single weighty contribution. For Harry's point to make sense to the others they need to know where he's coming from. If they're not ready for his point they *will* misunderstand it, but out of politeness pretend they understand; and if it sets a whole new agenda they won't want to shift so suddenly so they *will* just carry on. It would be better if Harry didn't try to say something ambitious straight off. He should make a simple point or two and ask simple questions, then, as the group gets the drift of his thinking, he may be able to come in with his more weighty point. However if he doesn't he shouldn't worry about it. Discussion is a hit and miss process. It's not so very important what exactly is said or who speaks (as long as everyone gets a reasonable share over the weeks). What is important is the process of talking together, the flow of shared ideas, the use of the language of the subject. Harry shouldn't raise his stakes too high. He should just take the discussion as it comes and join in with simple points until the moment arises for something more ambitious.

4 Feeling exposed

Maya: I shouldn't be here ...

If Maya asked around the group, she'd be amazed to find how many are thinking exactly the same as her. In any group, in any walk of life, you can't feel comfortable and confident until you have established a sense of your identity within the group. You need people to know a bit about who *you* are, and you need to know a bit about *them*. Otherwise you feel vulnerable and exposed, which makes you underestimate yourself and overestimate everyone else. You perceive *them* as threateningly capable and confident. But other students perceive *you* in just the same way.

Maya is feeling so unsure that she feels rebuffed when someone disagrees with her. But disagreement is bound to happen, she shouldn't take it personally. When she gets to know the others better, she'll realise that they don't mean harm. It would help to talk to some of the group outside class so that she doesn't feel such a stranger. She could also join in the discussion saying something about herself and how she felt about the reading, just to 'insert' a bit of herself into the group. When she knows others and feels 'known', the fantasies about how critical of her they are will evaporate and she'll stop worrying whether she's making a fool of herself. However, if she just stays home and reads books she'll never feel she belongs.

5 Frustration with other students

Jessica: If Kelly goes on about her kids any more I'm going to scream ...

Perhaps what Kelly is saying about her kids is actually relevant to the topic, perhaps it gives a practical focus to the discussion. Perhaps Jessica is just frustrated because she wants to speak but doesn't know how to join in. On the other hand, it certainly can be tedious if some students don't keep their personal concerns in check. Kelly may be nervous because she's a mature student who did modestly at school and is worried that the younger students are better educated. Perhaps she's unconsciously shifting attention to what she sees as her strengths – her life experience. Maybe, rather than 'shutting her up', Jessica could ask her how she found the set reading to deflect her onto a topic she's less authoritative on. That's the tutor's role but perhaps Paul is wary of upsetting Kelly by not seeming to value her experience. Or maybe he's just grateful when anyone speaks. Jessica is right in wanting to stay on topic and resist the commandeering of sessions by a few students. She might talk to Paul out of class to say she had been hoping to get more from the sessions. Or maybe she can take more direct action in the group by asking where they are trying to get to with the discussion.

6   Frustration with the tutor

Amir: *Why doesn't Gina take more control?*

It seems that Gina might be an inexperienced tutor, still completing her PhD and very focused on its content. Everyone has to learn sometime, and the big advantage of inexperienced tutors is that you're special to them. They haven't seen it all before, they're enthusiastic about the subject, and it's important for their self esteem that the class goes well. Perhaps Gina feels threatened by perceptive students like Amir, especially when they challenge the point of view she's spending all her research time on. Maybe it's best for both of them if Amir accepts the situation as it is and works out how to get the most out of it. He could talk to Gina out of class about his concerns, without seeming to challenge her competence. Perhaps he and one or two other students could work out how to help her gain confidence and move things along. Or he could help with keeping the discussion on track during sessions. She will know that the group should really be addressing the wider course themes, so she may be grateful for the help.

7   Frustration with the group

Aleena: *We never seem to get to the heart of anything.*

Good discussion is elusive. Some classes don't go particularly well – the chemistry only fizzles. However, there are usually things that can be done. When discussion keeps drifting around and students are 'busking' – pretending they know what they're talking about – it usually means there is a lot of uncertainty, nervousness and lack of focus. Again it would be perfectly reasonable for Aleena to mention to the tutor that she's finding the discussions disappointing. She might ask whether the group can take a short time to talk about how things are going and see whether a better way forward can be worked out. Perhaps students could commit to spending more time on preparation or the tutor could set clearer discussion topics. Perhaps the group could focus on something more concrete, like case studies. There are plenty of strategies that might help.

8   Alienation

Callum: *It's so patronising ...*

Why does Callum express such hostility? Is he reacting to the inequalities of the student-tutor relationship? Discussion groups present tutors with a powerful and satisfying role but offer weak, under-defined roles for students. They can play at being deferential, eager and grateful, but Callum looks down on students who accept such roles. Callum recognises the power that the tutor has over his immediate prospects, whether by putting him down in class, or through marking his work. And at the same time

> I want it to be always very focused ... They are a waste of time if you just sit there and everyone just talks about what they feel like talking about.

> I don't like when tutors focus all the time because I think that's wrong ... it is to me very important to understand the relationship between two things which maybe initially you don't think of relating but as you go to discussion you think, 'Oh, maybe they are'; and I think that's very important

Clearly it's difficult for a tutor to try to accommodate all the competing needs and preferences in a group. Some of the responsibility needs to be shared within the group.

The part played by the students

Generally students expect an open, democratic atmosphere within which all group members participate constructively and considerately. They disapprove of group members who fail to prepare adequately and hold the group back, and they disapprove even more strongly of group members who dominate the group, taking up an unfair share of the time (Anderson, 1997).

Ground rules

In order to make sure that all members share expectations groups sometimes start with a discussion of what everyone hopes to achieve from sessions and what 'ground rules' the group might establish. These are rules that all members agree to abide by in the interests of the group as a whole. Here are some examples of typical ground rules:

- listening attentively to others

- asking others for information

- giving examples

- giving reactions to the contributions of others

- encouraging others to take part.

(Source: Forster, 1995, p. 16)

And here is a set of ground rules with a different emphasis:

- No smoking except in coffee break.

- Do not interrupt other people.

- It is OK to opt out and opt in again.

- Anyone can suggest changing or adding to the ground rules at any time.

- Every group member is entitled to time.

- It is OK to ask other people for help.

- We start on the hour and finish at ten minutes to.

(Source: Habeshaw et al., 1992, pp. 23–4)

> ### *Key points*
>
> - The success of group learning depends both on the skills of the tutor and on willing, constructive participation by students.
>
> - Students generally want an informal, open, democratic atmosphere, but they also expect the tutor to play an active role in shaping discussion and drawing out the important points.
>
> - Students expect each other to abide by 'rules' whether they are implicit or have been drawn up as 'ground rules.'

7.2.6 Rising to the challenge of group learning

We've seen what the group can do, but what can *you* do to get the most from discussion groups?

Belonging

Your first priority is to feel part of the group. If you are to contribute effectively you need to feel liked and respected – a group member with a useful contribution to make. In short you need an 'identity' in the group. People have to know a bit about you and you need to know a bit about them. So arrive at sessions early and don't sit in silence waiting for the tutor. Chat to one or two other students about themselves – their lives, their plans, why they are taking the course, how they are feeling about things at the moment. This will make *them* feel more at home, so they will feel kindly disposed towards *you*. Usually they'll ask you similar questions. Don't worry about seeming 'forward' or pushy. People may appear reserved, but it's usually just nervousness, most people find it a relief to start talking. At the end of the session chat with other people. Over a few sessions you will be able to talk with the whole group. This will make you feel a lot less exposed when you talk in discussions.

Be sure to position yourself physically within the group. Don't sit where you can't be seen. If your chair is on the edge of things, or facing slightly away, push it right in. It's harder to feel part of a group if you're physically on the fringes. And if people can't see you when you speak they feel less sympathy with what you say. This becomes a self-fulfilling situation – you feel left out, so you join in less. Then, as others do join in and feel more comfortable, you feel even more left out.

(If you're in a group of twenty or more, then you won't often be able to contribute within the wider group, so you may not be able to establish much of a sense of 'belonging', except perhaps amongst people sitting around you. But equally the need for a sense of belonging is less intense, as it's a less personal environment. There is less pressure on you to contribute and if you do speak it's more as a 'voice from a crowd'.)

Preparing

With the exception of the very first meeting, you can't expect simply to turn up to group sessions with an open mind and sit there waiting to be 'taught'. Discussion is a *support activity* to help develop learning you have already begun on your own. Setting aside time for preparatory work is *essential* to the group learning process. A reasonable rule of thumb is to spend two hours in preparing for each one hour group session. (This may include relevant reading you are doing for other aspects of your studies.) You may not always be able to complete the set work as thoroughly as you would like, but you need to have made a decent attempt at it. Otherwise you hold the group back and let yourself down.

If, in a crisis, you have to skip preparations it is still worth attending the session so that you don't lose touch with the group. But let your tutor know so that allowances can be made in class. If the crisis extends beyond one session talk to your tutor about how best to manage the situation. Even doing a modest proportion of the preparation is a lot better than nothing; but the general rule is always prepare.

Listening

As the group discusses it's important to stay in close touch otherwise you will become confused and feel left out. But, as we saw in Daniel's case, listening can be difficult. When you are new to a subject and unfamiliar words are in use it is easy to lose the thread – especially with the focus continually shifting as different members of the group contribute. Don't just hope for the best. Nip confusion in the bud. Ask for clarification. Ask for an example to make things less abstract. Don't be anxious that you are the only one confused. Other students probably feel just the same.

Taking notes

Don't worry too much about taking notes in a discussion. You might want to write down a few points if they seem particularly important, but the purpose of discussion is to follow the flow and to participate, not to take away information.

Speaking

Don't hang back thinking that other students are cleverer, more articulate, and more knowledgeable than you. Remind yourself that *they* are thinking exactly the same about *you*. Throw caution to the winds and join in. It isn't worth worrying about what others think of you because *they* aren't concerned about the quality of what *you* say. *They* are worrying about what *they* say and what you think of *them*. Don't let yourself be intimidated. It's just as much *your* discussion, intended to help *you* learn.

BOX 7.2   SAYING THE SIMPLE THING

You may feel that you ought to wait until you have something important to say before taking up the group's time by speaking. Don't. It's better to set your sights low. Ask the simple question, make the obvious point, offer the everyday illustration. What seems ordinary to you is often more interesting to other people. And in any case the group doesn't require 'brilliant' contributions to have a good discussion. It just needs everyone's mind focused on the main theme and a steady flow of contributions.

Don't worry if you don't always say a lot. You can get plenty from a debate by participating in listening mode. As long as you try to join in some of the time don't worry if you find yourself playing a relatively minor role. Groups need support players just as much as leading lights.

Helping the group process

Try to encourage other group members to participate, particularly those who haven't contributed much. Ask for their views and take an interest in what they say. Ask follow-up questions to give them confidence that they made a point worth exploring. Refer to other students' contributions when you make your own. Try to summarise group members' points of view from time to time. Don't treat 'winning the argument' as your primary aim; use the group as a way to explore a range of different arguments. You have plenty of other times when you can think about your own particular views. While you are in the group, value the diversity of viewpoints it enables you to explore.

Arriving late, leaving early

Arrive in good time for group sessions. It disrupts the flow if there are frequent breaks and the need for recapping. However if you are unable to arrive in time for the beginning of a session, or have to leave before the end (fairly common for part-time students), don't feel you have to miss the whole thing. Just let your tutor know about your difficulty (leave a note if necessary) and arrive or leave discreetly when you have to.

Key points

- Make an effort to talk to group members before and after group sessions. It will make a big difference to your confidence in speaking within the group.

- Do the best you can to complete the relevant reading before group meetings but if you haven't been able to manage it, tell the tutor. Don't skip the session.

- If you feel confused then say so. Don't let yourself get left out of things.

- Don't wait for inspiration before you speak. Just jump in, ask the simple question, give the obvious example.

- Don't be anxious about the quality of your contributions. Other people are concerned about what they say rather than what you say.

- Share responsibility for keeping the group going. Help to make the group enjoyable for other students. You'll enjoy it more yourself.

Group learning can be one of the most stimulating and supportive elements of your course, but it can also be frustrating and tedious. It is worth reflecting on the group process so that you understand what works and what doesn't. That way you can play your part in making your experience of group working as productive as possible.

7.2.7 Self-help groups

If you want more group study opportunities than your course provides, find some like-minded students and set up a study group of your own. Just arrange a place and time to meet and work out how you are going to manage the meetings. You'll need a clear agenda and a group leader for each meeting or the group will drift into disorder and lose heart. Generally someone has to take the initiative in deciding when and where to meet, what to discuss and how to proceed. But if you can work all this out then you may find your self-help group just as useful as tutor-led sessions.

Key point

- A self-help group can be excellent, but they need organising. Work out right at the start how you will share out leadership tasks.

7.3 Giving a presentation

Many courses require students to make presentations to a group. You might be asked to do this on your own or in partnership with others. Presentations are often weekly events with a different student, or team, taking a turn each week. You might be asked to present a summary of an article or a book or to research a topic for yourself. A presentation is generally expected to take ten to fifteen minutes at the start of a session, followed by a discussion. In principle it's a very straightforward task. However delivering your own ideas and words to an audience for the first time can seem daunting, so it is worth exploring the basic principles.

7.3.1 Speaking to an audience

Why presentations?

A series of presentations by group members is an excellent way to 'democratise' the group learning experience. Instead of your tutor retaining all responsibility for knowledge, your whole group shares the work of connecting its discussions to the literature in the field. In the process you develop skills that will be valuable in your future studies and in the wider world – namely:

■ researching a topic and extracting key points relevant to a particular purpose

■ planning a short presentation and preparing visual aids

■ delivering a presentation to an audience.

What is a good presentation?

What are you trying to achieve with your presentation? What will make it go well?

Activity 7.2

Think back to a lecture or talk that you enjoyed. Then think of a lecture or talk that you didn't enjoy.

1   Jot down a few notes about what you liked about the enjoyable lecture or talk, then a few notes about what you didn't like about the other.

2   Now draw a line down the middle of a piece of paper to make two columns. Put the headings 'Good Talk' and 'Bad Talk' at the top of the columns. Using the notes you've already written and anything else that comes to mind, make a list of the features of 'good' and 'bad' talks. For each item in the 'Good' column try to think of its opposite and write it in the 'Bad' column, and vice-versa.

This is a reflective exercise (see Section 1.6 in Chapter 1). You have used your own experiences to tell yourself what works well in talks and what doesn't. As you read through the discussion that follows, see how well it corresponds to your own reflections. I'm sure you will have identified some points I haven't included but it will be interesting to see whether we have agreed on the basics.

Pitfalls of giving presentations

Let's begin by looking at some of the things that can go wrong. There are several points you can easily misjudge when you make a presentation:

■ Because you are nervous and hoping to impress you try to make *far too many* points for the time you have available.

■ You think of your presentation as being addressed to your tutor, instead of the other students, so you pitch it at *too high a level.*

■ Because you have been reading intensively about your topic you become very familiar with *specialist terms* which mean nothing to other students and you forget to explain their meaning.

■ Similarly, because you have been absorbed in pulling apart and thinking about the issues raised by your topic, you forget that the rest of the group has no idea what the issues are so you *fail to start from first principles* when you explain them.

■ Because you are aware of the time constraints you *speak much too quickly.*

■ Because you are nervous you *speak too quietly* and you *don't look at your audience* to check that points have been understood before moving on.

■ For safety's sake you decide to *read* your presentation from a prepared script, so you can't 'connect' with your audience, and the presentation is dull and uninvolving.

Basic rules of presenting

■ Keep it *simple.* Don't pack your talk with information and ideas.

■ Make it as *clear* as you can. Explain everything as though to a beginner. Give examples. Remember that clarity is much more important than quantity or 'cleverness'.

■ *Don't read* it – talk to your audience.

■ *Don't rush* it – take your time. Cut material rather than rush.

■ *Use slides* to provide the backbone of your presentation.

■ Keep reminding yourself that the other students are not concerned with how clever *you* are but with how well *they* can understand what you say.

7.3.2 Preparing your presentation

First things to find out

■ Are you supplied with any guidelines on making presentations?

■ How long is the presentation meant to last?

■ How long should you spend researching and preparing? Is the presentation meant to be the equivalent of an essay or is it intended to be prepared quite quickly?

■ What visual aids will you be able to use? Will you be using a flip-chart, an overhead projector and transparencies, or a slideshow on a digital projector? If transparencies, how do you get them made? If a slideshow then do you bring the presentation with you on a disk?

- Are you expected to produce a handout?

- How will discussion be handled after the presentation? Will you be expected to stay at the front and answer questions? Will you, another student, or the tutor be expected to chair the discussion? Will you return to being just another member of the group?

- Is the presentation assessed? If so then how are marks awarded?

Researching

Don't get carried away trying to cover a wide range of sources. Just cover the basic ones and use your time instead to make good notes. Then make notes from your notes. Focus on the parts you understand best, leave out points you don't understand. The better you understand your material the clearer your talk will be.

Planning

Broadly the same principles apply as when you write an essay. You work up an outline but instead of writing it out as an essay, you *speak* it. Your notes will be quite similar to an essay outline, but more direct and punchy. As with an essay you need:

- a title

- an introduction where you set things up so that your audience knows what you are talking about

- a sequence of main points

- a conclusion where you remind your audience of the title and say how you have addressed it.

The most important thing is to avoid being too ambitious. In ten to fifteen minutes you can only make a few main points. If you prepare a lot more you will end up gabbling everything and no one will understand a word. For example if you are introducing a book chapter indicate in a few words what is special about the book (why it's worth having a presentation on it), what the central question is that the chapter deals with and how it approaches that question.

Nobody ever complains about presentations being too easy to understand. Use examples where you can to show what you are getting at. Work up a diagram if it will make things clearer.

Preparing slides or transparencies

Using presentation software

Whether you are making transparencies for use with an overhead projector or preparing a digital slideshow the best way to prepare slides is to use presentation software (such as Microsoft PowerPoint). You *can* prepare overhead projector transparencies using your word-processor but presentation software has many useful features which will help you to design better presentations. If you haven't used such software before, this is an excellent opportunity to learn which will be useful to you in many situations during your course and beyond. The software enables you to insert charts and pictures and usually has a facility for printing handouts.

Wealth without happiness

- In West – huge wealth rise over 50 years
  - Layard (2003) The secrets of happiness
  - Many have access to cars, foreign holidays etc.

- **But**
  - No increase in proportions happy
  - Apparent rise in levels of depression
- **Why?**
  - Habituation
  - Competitiveness – keeping up with Joneses

Figure 7.1 A slide created with Microsoft PowerPoint

Presentation software can be confusing when you first try it out, so it's worth seeking out support:

■ Your university computing centre may offer training.

■ Your software probably includes 'wizards' which take you step by step through preparing a presentation.

■ You may find tutorials are supplied with your software.

■ You could get hold of one of the excellent 'teach yourself' style of software manuals.

After a session to learn the basics, you'll be away.

Design

Take time over the design of your slides or transparencies:

■ Use layout to show the structure of your argument.

■ Use a large font size for the basic text (for example 20-point), and even larger for headings. And use plain fonts rather than fancy.

- Have one main theme per slide (think of a slide as being like a paragraph in an essay). Have two or three sub-points per slide (five maximum).

- Three slides may be all you need (plus a title slide and a concluding slide) depending on how much you have put on each and how easy they are to read (graphics generally take less time to read).

Polishing

- When you have completed your slides, switch to slideshow mode and go through them talking yourself through your points using only the slides as triggers. As you come to words on the slides that don't seem quite right, make adjustments.

- Do the same again the next day, fine-tuning the wording so that it fits smoothly with the flow of what you want to say.

Think about how you will reveal the information on the slides:

- You can show all the points on the slide at once, then use a pen or cursor to point to each line as you refer to it. However, a whole slide is a lot for your audience to take in, and it may distract them from listening to you.

- If you are using an overhead projector you can cover most of the transparency with a piece of paper then pull it down to reveal points gradually.

- If you are using presentation software you can use slideshow animations so that a point appears each time you click the mouse or use the arrow keys.

- Whatever approach you choose, practise switching slides smoothly.

Spending time on the design of your slides is *not* time wasted. By thinking about exactly how to present your message you get it clear in your head. This will help you to deliver a good presentation. But more than that you will have learned a lot about the strategic skills of preparing a presentation.

7.3.3 Practising

When your slides are ready give yourself a full rehearsal.

Rehearsing the talk

- Give your presentation out loud, timing yourself to see how long it runs.

- Speak loudly and clearly, at a measured pace.

- Use only your slides. If you try to speak from more detailed notes you risk losing your thread and confusing your audience. It's very difficult to switch between talking to an audience and reading notes. As you focus on the notes you lose contact with the audience. That's why slides are excellent – you can read your notes from the screen along with your audience, staying in touch with them throughout.

■ Don't try to think ahead to what comes next. Keep your mind clear for what you are saying at the moment. When your next slide comes up it will trigger the next part of your presentation.

■ If you find you need an occasional prompt, jot down a few trigger words on a card or a single sheet of paper.

■ Speak your points as they arrive in view, using the same or very similar words. Having your words on the screen shows listeners how what you're saying fits into the overall structure of your talk. It also allows them to check back to remind themselves of what you just said.

■ Don't put up a slide then carry on talking about something other than what's on the screen. Sometimes speakers seem to think that what's onscreen doesn't need to be said. But if you appear to be giving people a choice between reading one thing and listening to something else, some will read and others will listen so you will have split the audience's attention.

■ Jot down a schedule showing the time in which you need to have completed each slide.

Putting your presentation into the appropriate format

When you are sure that you don't want to make any further adjustments to your slides you need to put them into the appropriate format for the presentation.

■ If you are going to use an overhead projector make transparencies of your slides.

■ If you are going to use a digital projector make sure you have saved your presentation in a suitable format for use with the projector.

■ If you need to produce a handout use the handout facility of the presentation software.

A beginning

Having worked out what you are going to say, think about how you will get yourself started. It isn't good to launch straight into a presentation. You need to capture your audience's attention and establish a rapport with them.

■ Will everyone in the group know you? Would it be worth opening by saying 'Hi I'm ... and I'm studying ...'?

■ Begin with one or two informal, inconsequential remarks. Comment, perhaps, on problems you ran into in getting hold of material, make a wry remark about your life during the preparations, or make a connection with the weather or something in the news. It doesn't matter what you say, the purpose is simply to get yourself talking without the pressure of trying to say something significant. You just need to get your voice working and your audience listening. As you speak look one or two people in the eye to establish contact with them. All this only takes a minute but it makes a big difference.

- If it makes you feel better sketch your opening words on paper and take them in with you. You won't read them but you'll feel reassured.

An ending

Think also about your closing words. A talk ends rather tamely if you just reach the end of the last slide and stop. Don't just look around in relief that it's over, wondering what happens next. You need to think of a way to signal that you have finished then either stay where you are for questions or go and sit down. It can be as simple as 'OK that's it – now you can ask me any questions'. It'll make you feel better and sound more confident.

Relaxing yourself

Spend time alone practising getting tuned up for speaking. You need some adrenalin flowing, but also a calm feeling that you are in control – that you have done the best you can to prepare, so you have no need to worry.

- Take some deep breaths. Feel yourself slowing down and compose yourself so that you can speak at a sure, steady pace.

- Get your voice working by clearing your throat and humming loudly with your mouth shut then wide open.

- Sing a simple song such as 'Three Blind Mice'. Sing it slowly, loudly and clearly, letting your voice flow out and using your stomach muscles to project your voice. Try making your voice deeper. See if you can make it resonate. Then raise it higher. Pronounce all the words as clearly as you can. Do this until you feel your voice is as strong, full and clear as you can get it.

Keeping a sense of proportion

Remind yourself that a presentation is not a major event. You are simply serving a routine function for the group, by 'kicking-off' a discussion. For everyone else it's just another session. They won't be bothered about how hard you worked or how clever you are. All they'll be concerned with is whether they can understand what you say.

7.3.4 On the day

Getting set up

Get to your session well ahead of time. Check the equipment you will be using. Switch it on and off. Try out your first slide. Practise switching from one slide to the next. If you are using an overhead projector work out where to put transparencies before and after you use them so that you don't get confused. Put a chair where you want to sit. Move furniture just for the sake of it to make the space around you 'your space'. Make yourself feel that you 'belong' there.

Delivery

Remember to start informally. Make contact with the audience and make yourself feel comfortable talking to them. Don't rush. Take the time you need to settle into your stride. Then go steadily through your slides, talking your audience through your points. Add in a few thoughts or stories if they come to you, but only briefly. Show that your mind is alert and in touch with the audience.

As you speak look around the audience. Pick on one or two people and look straight at them from time to time. Make sure they are still following you. If they aren't, change your tone, throw in another example, or ask a question – whatever it takes to get their attention back.

Keep an eye on the time. Stick to a measured pace so that people have time to connect fully with your line of argument. But be careful not to dwell so long that you run out of time before you get to the crunch of the argument. If you see yourself dropping behind, speed up. You can build up to a fairly high pace towards the end if the audience is with you. Skip points, if necessary, to make sure you finish on time. But don't forget to deliver your conclusion, however rushed the ending. Don't just fizzle out.

The discussion after

Don't become defensive during the discussion afterwards. Accept criticism with good grace and show an interest in alternative points of view. Ask follow-up questions to get your critics sharing the spotlight with you. Take the attitude – 'I did this to help the group. I've done the best I could. I'm not personally responsible for the views of the authors I read. Now its up to all of us to work with the topic and see what we can make of it'.

7.3.5 Group presentations

If you are asked to give a group presentation, rather than doing it solo, the same general principles apply but you share out the work. This can be an advantage in reducing pressure and allowing you to develop your presentation skills while supported by your team mates. However it can also create difficulties:

- It may not be easy to divide up the research activities or see how to coordinate them.

- Disputes can easily arise with team members working to different agendas and some, perhaps, feeling they have put in more work than others, only to be held back by them.

- Time has to be made for working out how to collate what different team members have found, how to decide what gets left out, and how to pull together a coherent presentation.

- You may also be less in control of what is on the slides that you are presenting.

- In the presentation itself you may be unlucky in following on from a weak contribution.

- If you are assessed as a team, there can be a sense of injustice in achieving a communal mark for contributions of very different quality.

Bearing all these possibilities in mind, it's clearly important to take team management seriously. You could try to establish 'ground rules' within the team, before starting out on the work. On the other hand with a willing, cheerful team, the whole experience can be very rewarding.

Key points

- When you make a presentation, keep it simple and make it as clear as you can.

- Use examples to give your audience rocks on which to anchor their thoughts.

- Make your slides do the work of presenting your main points so that your mind is free to focus on communicating with your audience.

- The day before, practise going through your slides and practise relaxing.

- Check the equipment and make yourself feel at home.

- Take your time.

- Remember: your audience doesn't care how clever you are – they just want to be able to follow what you say.

7.4 Listening to talk

Listening plays a prominent part in many university courses. Mostly it takes the form of listening to 'live' talk but increasingly it is recorded talk on CDs and DVDs, some of it accompanied by video images. We look first at learning from live talk.

7.4.1 Listening to lectures

Lectures have traditionally been the primary mode of teaching in higher education. However doubt has frequently been cast on whether they are effective. So what can you expect to learn from them?

See Chapter 4 Section 4.4.2, Listening

What lectures offer

Critics say that lectures simply 'present' knowledge instead of encouraging you to *think*, that listening is a passive and tedious mode of learning. They also claim that students can't concentrate for more than about twenty minutes and that after a lecture they can recall only a small proportion of what was said. Yet lectures continue to be a key method of teaching. And students themselves are not generally so critical of lectures (Beard and Hartley, 1984). They regard 'good' lectures as offering good value. So what can we conclude? Do students really retain very little yet continue to come back for more?

It is true that lectures are *not* a good method of delivering a lot of detailed *information*. Essential information is better presented in *print*, you can study it when you are ready to take it in and return to it as needed. But lectures do have an important part to play.

BOX 7.3   LECTURES AND LEARNING

Where lectures come into their own is in helping you to understand how the ideas in the subject work. The lecturer projects meaning into the words for you, adding emphasis by tone of voice, gestures and facial expression, so the ideas you are grappling with in the course are presented to you much more forcefully. But this is *not a passive* experience. *You too have to make the effort to follow the argument.* However, you do it with the support of the lecturer, who can talk you through from the beginning to the end of the argument. Even if you don't understand it all you can still pick up the gist of how the debate is carried on.

This makes lectures an excellent counterpart to reading. When you're reading you can stop and think over difficult points so that you really get to grips with details of the argument. But when you're listening you can take in the broad sweep of it and get a feel for what the subject is all about. With an unfamiliar subject *both* approaches are useful. Listening takes you forward into new territory, reading lets you get your bearings and take time to map out the ground around you.

So, rather than depositing information in your head, the effect of a good lecture is stir up your *thinking* on a subject and pose new *questions*. Well-delivered lectures help you to get inside the various discourses of your field of study. Their purpose is *not* to ensure that the lecturer's notes end up being your notes. What lectures offer is 'live' discourse – words which engage directly with the thoughts in your mind.

Reading around lectures

See Chapter 4 Section 4.4.1, Reading

The popular image of lectures is of students sitting in rows being *told* things. But this is highly misleading. The lecture itself is only the public part of a larger learning process. There is an equally important private component – the reading you do before and after the lecture. Your course reading lists should show what readings go with the lectures. If you aren't sure, ask.

As with group discussion allow two hours of reading for each hour of lecture (see Section 7.2.6). Reading beforehand primes you for the lecture so that it doesn't just wash over you, and reading afterwards consolidates what you have learned during the lecture. Without the reading, the flow of ideas in the lecture is too much for you to take in and most of it floats away from you as you leave the lecture theatre. *If you don't do at least some reading around your lectures you miss most of the benefit.*

Learning in lectures

Lectures present you with three challenging tasks simultaneously:

- ■ You have to *listen* to the lecturer's line of argument.

- ■ You have to *think* about it and make connections with what you already know.

- ■ You have to *take notes* of some kind.

In practice you have to keep switching your focus between these three tasks. In an odd way the struggle to cope with this mental juggling act is helpful. By putting you under pressure, lectures force you to make leaps and take short-cuts. You have to seize the initiative and make what sense you can quickly, because the scraps you jot down are all you will take away with you at the end. You have to learn to think on your feet.

Taking notes

Since your notes are made in time 'stolen' from listening and thinking your note-taking strategy matters a lot. You have to weigh up quality against speed and this means you have to think about your broad objectives:

- ■ Why are you attending the lecture – how does it fit into your studies of the topic?

- ■ Why are you making notes – how will you use them?

Then you need to develop a note-taking strategy which meets these objectives.

See Chapter 6 Section 6.2.2, Lecture notes

How many notes do you need?

If your course uses lectures as the main source of information then you will have to write down quite a lot to be sure of getting hold of what you need. But if your lectures are backed up by good handouts and readings then quite sparse notes may be fine. Similarly, if a lecture is rather monotonous, you may have to keep writing just to stay in focus, but if it's lively and absorbing you may find that you learn most by concentrating on listening and just writing down occasional key points. The most important factor, though, is you.

BOX 7.4   WHAT SORT OF LECTURE LISTENER ARE YOU?

Do you tend to daydream in lectures? Do you get anxious about whether you are understanding enough? Do you prefer to concentrate on listening in lectures and rely on the set reading for detailed note making? Do you feel confident that a few lines here and there will be enough to remind you of the main points? Or do you feel that unless you are writing you are missing something? Think about how you feel during lectures and develop a note-taking strategy which suits *you*.

Key points

The strength of lectures lies not in feeding you with information but in:

■ engaging your mind with the debates going on in the subject

■ showing you how the explanations work, and

■ letting you hear how the language of the subject is used.

To get the benefit from lectures you need to:

■ make a decent effort to read some of the prescribed texts before and after lectures, and

■ develop a note-taking strategy that suits the subject matter, the circumstances and you.

7.4.2 Learning through audiovisual 'media'

What can you learn?

Most of us learn a great deal from TV, radio and other media. However, when you watch a report on drug smuggling, a nature documentary, or a historical reconstruction, you learn in a very different way from listening to lectures or reading books. (In this final section I use the term 'video' to include all moving images and sound recordings, including TV, film, and DVD.)

BOX 7.5   LEARNING FROM VIDEO

With a book or a lecture you follow a sequence of words and try to make connections between them and the world as you know it. However with video you see pictures and hear sounds which give the sense of actually 'being there' in the world. You don't have to struggle to hold your focus on the subject matter. All your basic processes of

---

experiencing the world are brought into play. Any accompanying narrative, which discusses and explains what you see, seems to be simply elaborating on 'the truth' presented by the images and sounds.

With images, sounds and ideas synchronised, an explanation has an immediate impact. You see the starving people in the refugee camp, the bags of grain being unloaded, you hear the voice saying that Western countries are doing all they can to help – the urgency of the crisis and the scale of the relief operation hits home much harder than if you just read the story in your newspaper. You see the map with shaded areas and arrows showing where the grain is being distributed. It looks and sounds such an impressive account of the events that it is easy to forget that this is *just* an account, a *version,* of what is going on. It is easy to absorb the message about the generosity of the West without stopping to ask how famines arise in the first place and why some countries have a surplus of food while others have famine. As a medium for putting across a line of argument video is immensely powerful.

This suggests that video has great potential as a teaching medium – especially for presenting and explaining complicated subjects, where many different aspects of the world need to be considered at the same time. Instead of just examining a particular case study, or looking at a table of figures, or following a line of explanation, all three can be used together.

BOX 7.6 'DYNAMIC' KNOWLEDGE

Video is good for understanding the *dynamics* of processes. Where it takes many words to describe a hospital operation, or the way a demonstration turns into a riot, video can convey it in minutes. It can show the world in terms of 'processes' rather than 'objects' and build up a different kind of knowledge from 'book knowledge' – a more rounded and dynamic understanding.

However, in spite of all this promise, and much investment in 'multimedia' teaching, print remains the most popular teaching and learning medium. Why?

Drawbacks of video

It's almost as if the very power of audiovisual media creates a problem. With your eyes and ears busy taking in richly textured images, information and arguments, you are fully absorbed, particularly if the subject matter is unfamiliar. Independent thinking and note taking are difficult. It's easy to feel that the argument is running ahead of you, out of your control, so that you can't quite be sure what you are learning, or what you think of it. Indeed audio alone can be better than video for presenting arguments simply because you are not distracted by images. Where video demands your whole attention, audio leaves some space for you to think and take notes. However, both tend to be used to support teaching presented in print rather than as self-sufficient learning resources.

Case studies

See Chapter 3
Section 3.6,
E-learning

Where audio and video make an undoubted impact is in presenting case material, particularly in combination with activities which allow you to interact with them. This works particularly well when they are developed for use on a computer, where interactivity can be structured in. An example of this is shown in Figure 3.4 in Chapter 3.

Learning from audiovisual media

The skills you need for learning from video and audio can be quite varied. Generally it's worth asking yourself:

- Are you stopping often enough to take notes? Is it best to go right through once then go through it again taking notes?

- How many times it is worth rerunning a resource? The material will often be very rich and will repay being visited several times. But of course you need to balance this against other things you could spend time on. The pay-off for allocating time to revisit audiovisual material is that you will remember it well because of the power of the images.

- How does your next essay link to the audiovisual material? How can you make notes that will help you to extract what you need as you review it? Would it help to draw a table to help with analysing what you are looking at and listening to?

Key points

- Audiovisual media are excellent for presenting the world in all its richness and dynamism, so they work well for case studies and for small, intensive bursts of explanation.

- But they are not always easy media to follow for sustained study. They tend to leave inadequate space for thinking and writing unless activities are built in.

- Since the use of audiovisual resources is often quite structured you need to work out your study strategies as you discover what is involved.

Studying through the spoken rather than the printed word can be a very lively and 'natural'-seeming way to learn; however, it is also unpredictable and challenging. The dynamism of live talk can make new ideas come alive, but you need to be flexible and strategic in working out how to get the most from it.

References

Anderson, C. (1997) 'Enabling and shaping understanding through tutorials' in Marton, F., Hounsell, D. and Entwistle, N. (eds) *The Experience of Learning: Implications for teaching and studying in Higher Education* (2nd edn), Edinburgh, Scottish Academic Press.

Beard, R. and Hartley, J. (1984) *Teaching and Learning in Higher Education* (4th edn), London, Harper and Row.

Forster, F. (1995) 'Tutorials in arts and social sciences' in Forster, F., Hounsell, D. and Thompson, S. (eds) *Tutoring and demonstrating: a handbook*, Edinburgh, University of Edinburgh Centre for Teaching, Learning and Assessment.

Habeshaw, S., Habeshaw, T. and Gibbs, G. (1992) *53 Interesting Things to do in your Seminars and Tutorials*, Bristol, Technical and Educational Services.

Mercer, N. (1995) *The Guided Construction of Knowledge: Talk amongst teachers and learners*, Clevedon, Multilingual Matters Ltd.

Qualifications and Curriculum Authority (2002) *The Key Skills Qualifications Specifications and Guidance: Communication, Application of Number and Information Technology*, Sudbury, Suffolk, QCA Publications.

CHAPTER 8 WORKING WITH NUMBERS AND CHARTS

8.1 Numbers and studying

What do you do when you come across tables, charts and graphs as you study? Are you comfortable and confident with this kind of information, or a bit bemused? Are you inclined to skip straight past? If you do it's a shame, because numbers can give you valuable information very quickly and effectively if you take time to learn how to read them. With a bit of know-how, you are in a position to inform yourself very precisely, make your own interpretations and draw your own conclusions, rather than being reliant always on the judgement of others.

BOX 8.1   KEY SKILLS: APPLICATION OF NUMBER

Application of number is one of six 'key skills' identified by the UK government and business community as essential to successful participation in a modern society. The skill, they say, consists of 'interpreting information involving numbers, carrying out calculations, interpreting results and presenting findings'. You are expected to be able 'to interpret information presented in different graphical forms and to produce these [yourself], to present [your] own findings'. (QCA 2002, p. 42.)

This doesn't mean you have to become a wizard with numbers. You just need regular practice and a little support. This chapter gets you started with *interpreting information involving numbers*. As you study you need to make a habit of taking time to explore tables, charts and graphs whenever you meet them, to familiarise yourself with the basic principles. Working through the exercises in this chapter will help you to approach tables and charts confidently. After that your skills will continue to develop as you keep reading the tables and charts you encounter.

The other aspect of number skills involving calculations and presenting information you would expect to learn as a taught activity within a course, so you don't need to concern yourself with it till you come to it. If you do find yourself needing help with calculations and presenting numerical information, seek support from your course teachers.

Key points

■ Tables, graphs and charts give you precise information fast, once you know how to read them.

■ Don't skip! You need access to that information. Just build up your skills gradually. Reading this chapter is a good way to begin.

8.2 Living with numbers

In our daily lives we encounter a lot of information in the form of numbers. Consider, for example, the extract from a newspaper article in Box 8.2:

BOX 8.2

The Times, July 17, 2004

20m suffer as floods hit South Asia
By Catherine Philip, South Asia Correspondent

> Surging river waters fed by torrential monsoon rains have inundated huge areas across Bangladesh, Nepal and northeastern India over the past month, wiping out thousands of villages. The official death toll in India stands at 235, with 67 killed in Bangladesh and 77 in Nepal.
>
> *(Source: Philip, 2004)*

Here, numbers are used to convey to us the appalling scale of grief, misery and destruction caused by monsoon floods. Whenever a train crashes, a bomb explodes, or a natural disaster strikes, media reports give estimated numbers of casualties. It's as though we need numbers to signal to ourselves how shocked to feel. But what do the numbers in this report tell us? Twenty million is obviously a very approximate estimate. Nobody would be surprised to read a smaller or larger number in the following day's report. It is also a number too big to comprehend, unless you pause to make comparisons – saying to yourself, for example, 'That's more than a third of the population of the UK'. The much smaller numbers of the 'official' death toll are easier to comprehend, but still you might find yourself comparing with other disasters, to try to get a sense of proportion. You might also remind yourself that early official numbers are often far below the eventual numbers, when details have been formally established. So, although the numbers in the article might appear precise, you know enough to treat them as rough guides. Numbers like these are far from 'dry facts', they are part of a 'picture' that the report paints for us. We read them not as neutral 'data', but interpret them, weigh them up and generally try to 'make sense' of them, as we strive to grasp the nature of the tragedy being described.

You may have noticed that numbers are also used in this article to tell us the day of the month and year it was published. Or perhaps you didn't even register those as numbers. Laid out in this format we simply read them as 'the date'. To us they have *become* the thing they stand for. We are no longer aware that numbers in a date are abstract symbols – familiarity has made them seem 'natural'. We live our lives surrounded by numbers like this: dates, times, temperatures, weights, prices, speed limits, which we translate instantly into something meaningful. And we translate so effortlessly that we no longer think of them as numbers that have to be 'understood'. Our minds leap straight to whatever it is they stand for.

Let's look now at an example which is a shade more complicated than instant recognition – where you might have to pause for a moment to check out the meaning of the numbers. Figure 8.1 shows a table designed to give information to the general public.

Activity 8.1

■ Do all the numbers in Figure 8.1 make sense to you?

■ What meanings do the numbers convey?

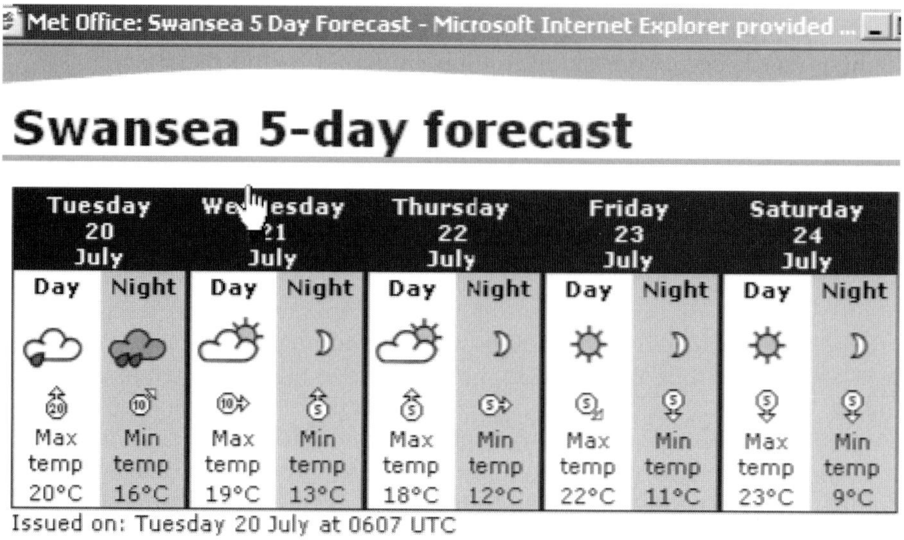

Figure 8.1 Weather forecast on the Meteorological Office website.

(Source: Met Office, 2004)

- What interpretation skills do the numbers expect of you?

- Do the images of sun, moon, clouds and rain have anything to do with numbers?

Weather forecasting is based mainly on numbers: numbers for air temperature, air pressure, wind speed, hours of sunshine and centimetres of rain. These are recorded at specific times of day, at many different locations, then all the numbers are brought together to create general summaries of how the weather has been and how it seems to be changing. From this predictions are made of how the numbers might turn out in future, as in Figure 8.1.

What do the numbers in Figure 8.1 convey to you?

- Reading from the top row, '5-day' tells you how far ahead the table forecasts.

- The date numbers, '20' through to '24', identify the days to which the forecast applies.

- The numbers in circles with arrows tell you the wind speed and direction.

- Then come temperatures in degrees Celsius.

- At the bottom is the date the forecast was issued, along with '0607' which expresses the time UTC (Coordinated Universal Time, formerly Greenwich Mean Time).

■ The images of sun, clouds, etc. do, in effect, represent numbers. The number of rain drops is a very approximate estimate of the predicted quantity of rain. The amount of sun shown is a very approximate prediction of the number of hours of sunshine, and so on.

So what did you find out about the weather on Tuesday 20 July? Did you form a mental image of a windy day, with a few showers and not particularly warm temperatures for mid summer. That is quite an impressive picture to be able to pick up from just a few numbers and symbols. But you would not be able to 'take it in' if you didn't bring your own skills to the task. For example, you have to make '20°C' mean something. Just to be able to say it as 'twenty degrees Celsius', you have to know that '°' stands for degrees and 'C' for Celsius. Then you also need experience of what a day feels like when it's 20°C – how it compares with a hot day when the temperature is 30°C, or a cool one when it's 10°C. For numbers to be meaningful you have to be able to link them to your knowledge and to your experience of life. In themselves numbers don't 'mean' anything. You have to interpret them and make them meaningful, yet with practice this happens without effort. You just glance at the clock, the speedometer, or the TV listings and take in the meaning of the numbers straight off. So, as you see, we are all highly skilled at reading numbers which are significant in our daily lives.

Notice too that, having 'taken in' the information for Tuesday, it is then easy to read the equivalent information for the other four days. Because everything is set out systematically in this table, the reading becomes straightforward. This is a key feature of tables. They build on the strengths of being systematic. You first have to adjust your mind to the way a table is arranged, but then it can communicate a lot to you quickly.

Weather information is not always presented as tables. Sometimes summaries are presented as charts, as in Figure 8.2. Here the BBC has converted numbers for wind speeds into arrows – the size of each arrow indicating the wind speed number. Apart from the time at the bottom of the picture, you might think of Figure 8.2 as not presenting numbers, yet, like all such charts, it is nothing other than a graphical representation of numbers.

It is quite normal to be expected to take in numerical information. An employer assumes you know that '4%' stands for 4 per cent, and that you know what it *means* to be offered a 4% pay rise – that for every 100 pounds you earned previously, you will now be earning 104.

BOX 8.3   RUSTY WITH PERCENTAGES?

Do you need refreshing on percentages? Here's an example. Let's say you started with thirty pupils in a class and the number was then increased by 10%: you would then have thirty-three. How does this work out?

Here's how: 10% means ten for every hundred (centum is Latin for hundred). To work out what 10% of something is, multiply it by ten, then divide by a hundred. (Similarly, to calculate 4% you multiply by four then divide by a hundred.) If you multiply your thirty pupils by ten you get 300 – then dividing by 100 you get three. So, a 10% increase means you have three new pupils to add to the original thirty, making thirty-three.

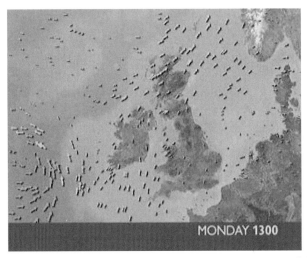

Figure 8.2 Wind speed figures represented as arrows of different sizes

(Source: BBC, 2004a)

Transport operators expect you to be able to make sense of lots of numbers set out in rows and columns in the form of a timetable as in Figure 8.3.

You *really* need to 'make sense' of these numbers or you won't be there when the ferry leaves; yet you are given very few clues. Essentially, the meaning of each number is communicated by its *position* in the table, and you are assumed to have enough experience of timetables to understand the conventions. If you do, this is an extremely convenient way to communicate some quite complicated information – convenient for both the travel operator and you. So *they* assume that you have learned the appropriate table reading skills and *you* assume that they will follow the common conventions.

A complicated society like ours involves a lot of co-ordinating of activities. Consequently, coping with life presumes an ability to inform ourselves of the details of what is happening around us. And indeed we *can* generally cope with many kinds of basic numerical information. But when you come across a *new* kind of numerical information, particularly if the layout is complicated, it conveys very little to you. Your eyes glaze over and you turn away. Why?

Summer timetables: Valid 2 APRIL 2004 TO 23 OCTOBER 2004
Page 1/2

ARRAN

🚶 🚗 R 🍴 🍷 ♿

Latest check-in before departure
Vehicles 30 minutes, passengers 10 minutes

ARDROSSAN – BRODICK						Table 5
	🚆 Glasgow Central	⛴ ARDROSSAN	⛴ BRODICK	⛴ BRODICK	⛴ ARDROSSAN	🚆 Glasgow Central
	Depart	Depart	Arrive	Depart	Arrive	Arrive
MON – SAT	–	0700	0755	0820	0915	1022
	0833	0945	1040	1105	1200	1322
	1115	1230	1325	1350	1445	1622
	1415	1515	1610	1640	1735	1852
	1650	1800	1855	1920	2015	2122
	1915 A	2030 A	2125 A	2140 A	2235 A	–
SUN	0840	0945	1040	1105	1200	1328
	1115	1230	1325	1350	1445	1550
	1405	1515	1610	1640	1735	1850
	1655	1800	1855	1920	2015	2117

Figure 8.3 Train and ferry times for the isle of Arran

(Source: Caledonian MacBrayne, 2004)

BOX 8.4   WHY NUMBERS CAN BE DIFFICULT

Numbers present information in a very condensed and abstract form. A number on its own means little. You have to learn how to read it. You have to find out both how the number is used (what the conventions are) and what the number is intended to stand for. Until you do, nothing happens when you look at it.

Perhaps you have forgotten how long it took you to learn what 'time' is and how to read it from the hands and numbers on a clock face. In fact a clock face presents an extraordinarily abstract and complicated representation of time. The numbers represent hours in relation to the small hand, but divisions of minutes in relation to the big hand. And time itself is not an easy concept. It's a marvel that children eventually do grasp how to read time from a clock. Yet years of practice make it seem 'natural' to adults.

But what if you saw a price tag saying '5/-'? Would you be able to read this? Fifty years ago it would have conveyed an instant message to British people. It says 'five shillings' (the equivalent of 25 (new) pence). The convention for writing that amount now is 25p, and it's hard for us to imagine that 5/- could ever have been the 'natural' way to write it. It no longer even looks like 'money' to us. We now divide pounds into a hundred pennies rather than into twenty shillings, so we no longer carry around the concept of 'one-twentieth of a pound' in our heads. So 'five-twentieths of a pound' seems an exceedingly odd way to express 25p (or twenty-five hundredths). It's positively confusing to us, yet our great grandparents would not have been able to see why.

Numbers, then, are just symbols. They can be used to represent all kinds of things. But they only carry meaning for people who have learned how to read them as intended.

Each time you come across a *new* kind of numerical information, the question arises: 'Is it worth making an investment in learning how to make these numbers mean something to me?' With so many numbers around us, the answer is often no. You haven't time to discover the significance of *all* the numbers on the backs of tins, in the manuals of technical equipment, or in the financial pages in newspapers. On the other hand, within any field of knowledge a *general* level of *numerical 'literacy'* tends to be taken for granted. If you want to play stocks and shares, for example, you do have to *learn* how to read the *Financial Times Share Index*. If you intend to participate regularly in *any* field, you need to take time to develop the relevant 'numeracy'.

BOX 8.5   NUMERACY

'Numeracy' is not a single ability which you either have or you don't. It is the specific skills, experience, and knowledge required to read the numbers used in a particular field of discourse. You can be 'numerate' in one field, such as betting on horses, but 'innumerate' in another, such as accountancy. We all display a wide-ranging numeracy in our daily lives, without even noticing it. But, ironically, we tend to be much more aware of numbers we don't understand than those we do, so it's easy to end up worrying about being innumerate.

Key points

You are already highly skilled at reading numbers of the kind that are relevant to your daily life. But, when you need to be able to take advantage of unfamiliar numerical information you have to invest time in learning:

■ *how* the numbers are being used in that particular context, and

■ *what* they are being used to represent.

8.3 Describing the world

But does academic study have to involve numbers? Can't words be used instead? One of the central purposes of academic inquiry is to produce convincing and reliable *descriptions* of the world around us. Say you were setting out to *describe* ways in which society now is significantly different from that of fifty years ago (and there's a number already). One very obvious feature is the impact of modern technology on the way we live our lives, in particular the impact of the enormous growth in electronic communications.

You might describe, for example, how the rapid spread of mobile phones has affected the way people keep in touch with their family, friends and workplace. You might discuss how people send each other text messages – perhaps photographs too – during lectures, in the cinema, on holiday, or anywhere – eroding longstanding boundaries of time, geography, institutions and social convention, and in the process creating new kinds of community. Alternatively you might describe the impact of the internet on the way people access information, shop, work and spend leisure time – creating many new social and commercial opportunities and dangers, and profoundly affecting the institutions through which they previously did these things. Or you might outline the impact of satellite and cable television in offering immense access to entertainment programming of all kinds while at the same time undermining previous forces of cultural and political coherence and fragmenting the financial basis of programme production itself.

However, as you pursued such themes, your reader or listener might say: 'Hold on! How do you *know* that all this communications technology is so widely used? Maybe it's a lot of hype. Perhaps just a minority of people use mobile phones, the internet, or satellite receivers. What evidence do you have? Just how many homes actually own this equipment? I want to know the scale of all these changes before accepting that they're so significant.' To answer questions like these you would need some numbers.

Key point

■ Why use numbers? Because they add a great deal to the power of your descriptions of the world. Numbers can indicate the *dimensions* of what you are talking about and serve as *evidence* to back up your claims.

8.4 Describing with tables

For information about people's use of communications technology we can look up data gathered regularly by national bodies. One very useful source is *Social Trends*, published annually by the Office for National Statistics.

Social Trends draws together social and economic data from a wide range of government departments and other organisations; it paints a broad picture of British society today, and how it has been changing.

(Office for National Statistics, 2004a)

BOX 8.6   WHAT ARE STATISTICS?

Originally the term 'statistics' meant facts about the state (or society). Then statistics came to mean facts in the form of numbers, though not necessarily about the state.

Statistics is now a branch of science concerned with techniques for gathering and working on large sets of numbers, in order to present summaries of their main features.

I looked for *Social Trends* on the internet and soon found it on the National Statistics website. I downloaded the most recent issue and found in it the highly relevant table shown in Figure 8.4. Try out your skills in table-reading by answering the questions in Activity 8.2.

Households with selected durable goods[1]

United Kingdom					Percentages
	Mobile phone	Satellite receiver	CD player	Home computer	Internet access
1996/97	17	19	59	27	0
1997/98	21	26	63	29	0
1998/99	27	28	68	33	10
1999/00	44	32	72	38	19
2000/01	47	40	77	44	33
2001/02	65	43	80	50	40
2002/03	70	46	83	55	45

1 Based on weighted data. Data from 1998/99 onwards include children's expenditure

Source: Family Expenditure Survey and Expenditure and Food Survey, Office for National Statistics

Figure 8.4   A table from *Social Trends* (2004 edition) showing ownership of electronic communications media

(Source: Office for National Statistics, 2004b)

Activity 8.2

Write down answers to the following questions, and check them against mine afterwards. It will take a little time, but if you work steadily through the activities in this chapter, by the end you will feel much more confident about reading tables and graphs. If you need help getting started, read the guidance in Box 8.7 'Finding your way round a table of numbers'.

1   In 1996, what percentage of UK households had a mobile phone?

2   What percentage of UK households had a home computer in 2000/01?

3   Do more UK households have a satellite receiver than have a home computer?

4   Which of the five items is most commonly owned by UK households?

5   Is it true to say that by 2002/03 twice as many households had computers as in 1996/97?

6   Is it true to say that home access to the internet was over four times greater in 2002/03 than four years earlier?

7   When was the biggest surge in numbers of UK households with internet access?

8   Is it true to say that UK household ownership of mobile phones quadrupled in the six years after 1996?

9   Did ownership of mobile phones rise steadily from year to year (i.e. by roughly the same amount each year)?

10 When did UK household ownership of mobile phones overtake ownership of satellite receivers?

11 By 2002/03 did the majority of UK households have a home computer?

12 By 2002/03 did the majority of UK households have internet access?

13 By 2002/03 did most UK households have a CD player?

14 Where do these numbers come from?

15 How up to date are they?

BOX 8.7   FINDING YOUR WAY ROUND A TABLE OF NUMBERS

Question 1 asks what percentage of UK households had a mobile phone in 1996. You begin by finding the column of figures under the heading 'Mobile phone'.

Now look at the row headings at the left of the table. You can see that the headings are dates in the format 1996/97. (The figures are for the 'tax year', which runs from April to the following March.) The 1996/97 figure is the closest you can get to the calendar year 1996.

If you read across from 1996/97 to the mobile phone column, you see the number 17. But is it a percentage? If you look to the top right of the table, you can see that the numbers are indeed percentages.

And is this a figure for 'UK households'? The heading at the top of the table tells us that the figures are for households and underneath is confirmation that they are for the United Kingdom.

So, although the number 17 stands alone and unadorned, its position in the table gives it a meaning. It carries the message: 'In 1996/97, 17 per cent of households in the UK had a mobile phone'. In other words, each of the numbers in this table (and any table) is much more than just a number. It is loaded with meaning by its position, by the headings to the table, rows and columns, and also by the notes accompanying the table.

If you read across the top row of figures, you can see the percentage of households owning other items of electronic communication in 1996/97. And if you read down any of the columns you can see how ownership of that goods item increased over the following six years.

(To save page turning, print off a copy of Figure 8.4 from the Good Study Guide website www.goodstudyguide.co.uk)

Answers

1 17 per cent is the best answer you can draw from the table, given the slight fuzziness over calendar years and tax years explained in the box above.

2 Find 2000/01 at the left, then follow along the row as far as the column for 'Home computer'. You might find it helpful to put a ruler across the table to keep your eye on the row you want. The answer is 44 per cent.

3 The 1996/97 figure for satellite receivers is 19 per cent. This compares with 27 per cent for home computers – so the answer is definitely 'no' for that year. The following year satellite receivers have risen to 26 per cent. This is much closer to the 29 per cent for home computers, but it's still lower, so the answer remains 'no'. The same is true for each year in the table, so the answer is clearly 'no'.

4 Looking at the top row of figures, 59 per cent for CD players is easily the highest. And in fact, the CD figure is clearly the highest in every row (although mobile phones are catching up). So a quick skim through the table tells us that the answer is: a CD player.

5 In 1996/97 the proportion of households with computers is 27 per cent. In 2002/03 it has risen to 55 per cent. If you multiply 27 by 2, you get 54. Fifty-five is just a little higher than this so, strictly speaking, there are slightly more than twice as many households with computers in 2002/03. But it's so close that the sensible answer to question 5 is 'yes'.

6 The 2002/03 internet access figure is 45 per cent. Four years earlier it was 10 per cent. Forty-five per cent is more than four times greater than 10 per cent, so the answer is 'yes'.

BOX 8.8   WHICH QUESTIONS GET INCLUDED IN THE SURVEY?

Why do you think there are zeros against internet access for 1996/97 and 1997/98? Do you think it's likely that no households had internet access in those years? Not really, it's much more likely that households weren't asked about internet access in those years. Surveys have to be kept within bounds. People won't complete questionnaires if they go on for ever. Meanwhile, researchers want, as far as possible, to keep questions identical from year to year, so that figures can be compared. However, as the world changes, questions do have to change to some extent, or the survey becomes irrelevant. It looks as if the researchers began to realise the significance of internet access and by 1998/99 decided to add a question about it.

7   If you look at the rise in internet access from one year to the next, between 1998/99 and 1999/00 it went up from 10 per cent to 19 per cent – a rise of 9 per cent. The next year it went from 19 per cent to 33 per cent – a rise of 14 per cent. In subsequent years the rises were 7 per cent and 5 per cent. So the most rapid rise was the 14 per cent between 1999/00 and 2000/01, which makes the answer 2000/01.

8   The 1996/97 figure for mobile phones was 17 per cent. Six years later in 2002/03 the figure was 70 per cent. If you multiply 17 by 4 you get 68. This is very close to 70, so the answer is 'yes', household ownership of mobile phones did quadruple in the six years after 1996.

9   To see how steadily ownership of mobile phones rose you need to run your eye down the mobile phone column. Are the gaps between the figures fairly even? It's clear that the gap between 27 and 44 is much bigger than the gap between 44 and 47. Then there is another big leap to 65, followed by another smaller rise to 75. So, although household ownership of mobile phones rose each year, it did *not* rise *steadily* (according to this table).

BOX 8.9   'BLIPS'

Picking out 'blips' is one of the 'tricks of the trade' of table-reading. You scan down columns and across rows, looking for patterns of steady rising or falling. Wherever you find a 'blip' in the pattern it is worth stopping to take a closer look and think what might have caused it.

In the case of mobile phone ownership in Figure 8.4, there are a series of blips. Why? If it were due to rising and falling family income, you would expect to see the same blips in ownership of the other items. But those all rose fairly steadily. Possibly there were changes in mobile phone tariffs, or technology, which affected buying patterns. It's also possible that there was some ambiguity in the question. (Does a 'household' have a mobile phone if one of its members has one through their work?) Or it might have been random variations in the statistics (sampling errors). Whatever the case, if patterns of mobile phone ownership were important to you, these uneven figures would need further investigation.

BOX 8.10 SAMPLING ERRORS

If you follow the political opinion polls, you will know that every now and then a freak result comes up. Most surveys study a sample from a large population. The total number of people in any particular group is known in statistics as a 'population'. Some populations are very small, such as the population of internationally ranked British tennis players. To find things out about that group you wouldn't need to 'sample' them. You could study every member of the population individually. Others, such as the population of people who own mobile phones, or the population of driving licence holders, are very large, so it would be impossible to study more than a small sample of the total population.

When researchers are picking out members of a population for a sample, they aim to pick at random. However, they can be unlucky and pick by chance more people of one kind (say, older) and fail to pick many of another kind (say, rural dwellers). The variations in results that you get from picking different samples are called sampling errors.

There are several ways to try to avoid sampling errors. One is to make the sample very large, since the effects of chance ought to even out when you select lots of people. On the other hand, big samples are expensive, so an alternative is to do small surveys on several occasions, to check whether you get the same results.

---

10 In 1996/97 household ownership of satellite receivers was slightly higher than of mobile phones. By 2002/03 ownership of phones was much higher than of satellite receivers. 1998/99 was the last year when satellite ownership was higher. Every year after that mobile phone ownership was higher. So the year household ownership of mobile phones overtook ownership of satellite receivers was 1999/00.

11 The answer is 'yes'. By 2002/03, 55 per cent of households had a home computer. Any figure higher than 50 per cent is a majority. But of course this is not the same as saying that 'most' people had a home computer: 45 per cent didn't.

12 The answer is 'no'. 45 per cent is less than 50 per cent. So by 2002/03 there was not yet a majority of households with internet access.

13 This is a slightly tricky question. At an ownership level of 83 per cent, certainly the large majority of households had a CD player – more than four in every five households. However 17 per cent did not have a CD player. If you took 'most' to mean 'nearly everyone', you would run the risk of ignoring the 17 per cent of households without a CD player. To be on the safe side, the answer to this question is 'no'. (Whereas it *is* true to say that most households have a TV because the figure is about 98 per cent.)

14 The table shown here comes from *Social Trends* but as you can see the figures come from the 'Family Expenditure Survey' (FES) and the 'Expenditure and Food Survey' (EFS). (The EFS took over from the FES in April 2001.) This is an annual survey carried out for the UK Office for National Statistics.

15 How up to date these numbers are depends on when you are reading this book. As you can see they go as far as March 2003. But they were published in the 2004 edition of *Social Trends*. Since ownership of these items was rising rapidly from year to year, particularly in the case of mobile phones and internet access, the numbers will soon be unrepresentative. So it is important to be well aware of the dates.

BOX 8.11   OUT OF DATE DATA

Social statistics are almost always 'out of date', simply because of the time it takes to collect, process and publish information. A survey has to be designed, samples chosen and questionnaires filled in. Then data have to be coded, entered, analysed, adjusted and interpreted. Finally the report has to be written, approved and published. Consequently numbers are usually several months old by the time they are published, a delay you need to take into account when you examine tables.

However, not being right up to date doesn't undermine the value of numbers. You never get exactly the figures you want. And some information is a lot better than none. The table you have been examining has provided answers to some important questions, even if you have to attach a reminder to yourself about when the data were collected. You almost always have to work with data gathered by other people, for their own purposes, some time ago. You haven't time, or resources, to gather all the data you might like to have. Research is expensive. The trick is to make intelligent use of data that other people collect.

That was quite a marathon review for just one table. However, I hope you felt you got to know it very thoroughly and that you are confident now about what all its numbers mean. By going over it so carefully we have covered a lot of useful points about reading tables in general.

8.4.1 Tips on reading tables

Take your time and be cautious

Numbers can say a lot in a very compact and efficient way, but you have to give yourself time to 'get on the inside'. You need to feel your way around the figures and the words, to get a sense of the kind of information you are looking at. It is easy to be misled by numbers, so you should approach them in a cautious and questioning frame of mind.

Finding your way in

It is often difficult to get a grip on a new table. When you look at the headings and labels they can be a bit baffling at first. A good way in is to pick a specific *number* and work out what it stands for. Check across to the headings at the left and the top of the table. Say aloud to yourself what the number means. This may make you realise that you aren't sure – is it, for example, households or individuals? Cross-check against what you know of the 'real world' to see whether the figure seems credible. (Does it seem likely that 17 per cent of households had a mobile phone in 1996 for example?) Try out a few other checks on Figure 8.4: if the proportion of households with a CD player is nearly 60 per cent in 1996 and just over 80 per cent in 2002, then in 1999, halfway between the two, you'd expect it to be about 70 per cent. It is – so that looks fine. Then run your eye across some of the rows and down some of the columns to see whether you can detect any patterns in the way the figures rise and fall. In other words, look for 'trends' in the figures. If you *can* spot patterns, think whether they seem to make sense.

Reading the words

When you have had a good look over the *numbers*, go back to the *words*. Having a feel for what the figures are about, the significance of the main table heading will be clearer to you. Check the row and column headings carefully. Make sure you are clear about what units of measurement the numbers represent. Are you dealing with numbers of people, or numbers of households, or millions of people, or percentages? Look at any notes that go with the table. Who collected and published the data and when? You may find your ideas about the numbers change once you have read the small print that goes with the table.

Extracting information

When you are satisfied that you know what the numbers in the table mean, you can start pulling out what you want to know:

■ Look for the highest figure and lowest figure in each row to see what the range is. Do the same for each column. Are any of the highs and lows surprising?

■ Can you find an interesting trend? If so, how would you summarise it in a few words?

■ Are there 'blips' in the trends? If so, can you think of reasons for them?

■ Try to summarise for yourself in a few words the main patterns which emerge from each row and column of the table.

This is the 'super de luxe' treatment. You won't want to look at *every* table you meet in such close detail. But make a point of building up your table-reading skills, by picking a table from time to time and giving it the full treatment. If you keep practising, you will become skilled at quickly extracting the essence.

Key points

■ Take your time with tables and be cautious. Remember that the figures can easily mislead.

■ Look quickly at the main headings of a table, then pick a number and check what it seems to be telling you. Does the table 'make sense'?

■ Go back to the words round the edges of the table. Read them all carefully, including any footnotes, to be sure you know what you are looking at.

■ Scan the rows and columns for interesting features and patterns. Check for high and low points, trends and blips.

■ Summarise for yourself the main conclusions that you think can be drawn.

8.5 Describing with graphs and charts

You have found out a lot from the numbers in the table in Figure 8.4. However, when there are so many numbers it's not easy to take in the overall picture. To provide that overview, the numbers can actually be turned into a picture. There are various ways of doing this, including graphs, bar charts and pie charts. We begin with graphs:

8.5.1 Showing numbers as a graph

Figure 8.5 shows exactly the same data as Figure 8.6, but this time presents it as a graph.

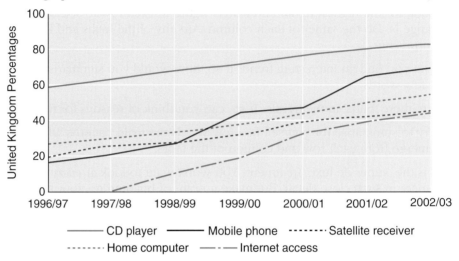

Figure 8.5 The same data as in Figure 8.4, shown in the form of a line graph

(Source: based on Office of National Statistics, 2004c)

Households with selected durable goods[1]

United Kingdom					Percentages
	Mobile phone	Satellite receiver	CD player	Home computer	Internet access
1996/97	17	19	59	27	0
1997/98	21	26	63	29	0
1998/99	27	28	68	33	10
1999/00	44	32	72	38	19
2000/01	47	40	77	44	33
2001/02	65	43	80	50	40
2002/03	70	46	83	55	45

1 Based on weighted data. Data from 1998/99 onwards include children's expenditure

Source: Family Expenditure Survey and Expenditure and Food Survey, Office for National Statistics

Figure 8.6 A repeat of Figure 8.4 so that you can cross-check the data with Figure 8.5

Activity 8.3

To check that the graph in Figure 8.5 is simply the numbers from the table in Figure 8.6 presented in a different way, try comparing the two. you will be able to do this easily with a copy of Figure 8.6 printed off from the Good Study Guide website (www.goodstudyguide.co.uk). Look at the column of numbers under 'CD player' in Figure 8.6. The number against 1996/97 is 59 per cent. Now find the line for 'CD player' in Figure 8.5 and look at the left end. It cuts the left axis at just below 60, about where you would expect 59 to be. If you look along the bottom of the graph, you can see it shows the same years as in the table. The year at the left is 1996/97. To the left of the graph it says 'Percentages'. You can see that the left axis is marked from 0 to 100, in intervals of twenty. So the 59 for CD player reads as '59 per cent' and it is directly above 1996/97. All this matches up correctly with the table.

In Figure 8.6, the 2002/03 figure for CD player is 83 per cent. In Figure 8.5, if you look to the right of the CD player line you'll see it rises to just above 80, over the 2002/03 mark. Again this is correct. Quickly check some of the other numbers in Figure 8.6 and convince yourself that they are shown correctly in the graph in Figure 8.5.

The graph in Figure 8.5 shows very clearly that ownership of the five items increases as you move from left to right. At the left is 1996/97, at the right is 2002/03. CD player ownership starts at a high level (59 per cent) and rises steadily higher. While internet access starts from nothing, but rises quickly to 45 per cent. You can also see the kinked line for mobile phones, showing clearly the unevenness of the rise in ownership that you identified in the table. And you can see how ownership of satellite receivers stays just below ownership of a home computer throughout the seven years. The information in the graph in Figure 8.6 is not as precise as in the table, because you don't have the actual numbers. However, it takes much less time to take in an understanding of the data shown. The graph *tells* the story, instead of you having to dig it out for yourself.

The graph also helps you predict ownership figures for the years following 2002/03. If you drew an extra section to the right of the graph and added a few more years, you could continue each line to see where ownership might rise to (assuming growth continues at roughly the same rate). Clearly CD player ownership can't rise beyond 100 per cent, so that line will gradually flatten off. (In general all the lines are likely to flatten off somewhat.) Of course, it isn't so easy to project the mobile phone line because of the kinks. It's all guesswork to an extent, but a graph offers much better guesses than just scratching your head. For example, you can see it is likely that by around 2003/4 half of all UK households will have internet access. However, it also looks likely to be many years before as many as 90 per cent of households do.

8.5.2 Numbers as bar charts

A bar chart is another common way of turning a table of numbers into a picture. The bar chart in Figure 8.7 shows ownership of mobile phones in different age groups, for 2001 and 2003. (Note that this time it's individual ownership, not household.) Figure 8.8 shows the table of numbers from which the bar chart was drawn.

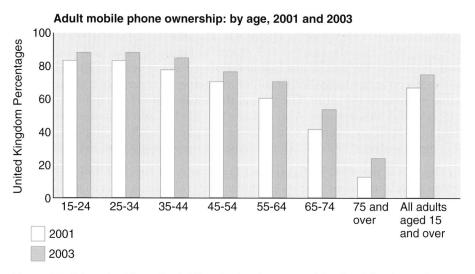

Figure 8.7 A bar chart from *Social Trends* showing ownership of mobile phones by age groups

(Source: based on Office for National Statistics, 2004d)

Adult mobile phone ownership: by age, 2001 and 2003[1]

United Kingdom	Percentages	
	2001	2003
15-24	83	88
25-34	84	88
35-44	78	85
45-54	70	76
55-64	59	70
65-74	41	53
75 and over	13	24
All adults aged 15 and over	67	75

1 At February. Source: Oftel

Figure 8.8 Data corresponding to the chart in Figure 8.7

(Source: Office for National Statistics 2004e)

Activity 8.4

Check that the numbers in the table in Figure 8.8 agree with the bars in the chart in Figure 8.7. For example, does the figure of 83 per cent for 15–24 year olds in 2001 look correct for the first bar on the left of the bar chart? Does the 88 per cent for 2003 look correct?

When you are satisfied that bar chart and table correspond, try answering these questions using just the bar chart.

1   Write down two messages that Figure 8.7 conveys to you.

2   Which two age groups have most mobile phones?

3   Is it true that by 2003 nearly 90 per cent of adults under 35 owned mobile phones, but under one-quarter of people over 75?

4   Are the older age groups catching up?

5   Above a certain age, mobile phone ownership falls below the national average. What is that age?

Finally, using the table in Figure 8.8 this time:

6   Where do these figures come from and how up to date are they?

7   Is it true that ownership of mobile phones went up from two-thirds of UK adults in 2001, to three-quarters in 2003?

Answers

1   For both years, this chart shows a beautifully smooth 'trend', curving down to the right. The key messages I took from the chart were that:

   i)   ownership of mobile phones was taken up quickly by younger adults, but more slowly the older the age group

   ii) ownership of mobile phones was still increasing steadily in 2003, in all age groups.

You may have picked out other equally strong messages.

2   The two youngest age groups own the most mobile phones. The size of their bars are almost identical.

3   It's true that for both groups aged under 35, the blue bars reach almost to 90 per cent. For the over-75 group, the blue bar falls short of 25 per cent, which is one-quarter. So the second part is true also, making the whole statement true.

4   If you look at the difference between the white and blue bars for each group, you can see that the differences get bigger for the older age groups. This means that ownership is rising more quickly for the older groups, which in turn means they *are* catching up. However, they may never catch up completely, and it looks as though it could be many years before the over-75 group closes the gap. (Of course, each year some people move out of one age group to the next, taking their mobile phones with them. So ownership in the older groups will increase anyway, as people leave higher-owning younger groups to join them.)

5   The national average is the pair of bars over to the right. (A figure for 'all adults' has to be the average, if you think about it.) The bars for the three age groups over 55 are shorter than the 'all adults' bar. So the answer is 54 years. (You might have put 55 years, which is a reasonable answer, but strictly the question says 'above a certain age'.)

6   The table tells us that the figures are from Oftel. This was the UK government's Office of Telecommunications (which was replaced, at the end of 2003, by Ofcom, the Office of Communications). It regularly surveyed phone usage. (Notice that *Social Trends* quotes from a variety of government sources.) The second set of data is labelled 2003, but the note tells us that the figures are for February 2003. These data appear in the 2004 *Social Trends* (as well as earlier Oftel reports). Again we see a gap between data gathering and publication.

BOX 8.12   PLURAL DATA

Did it read strangely when I wrote 'these data' in the answer to question 6? Strictly the word 'data' is the plural of the Latin word 'datum'. Just as 'criteria' is the plural of 'criterion', though you may hear people say 'What is your criteria?', when they mean either 'What is your criterion?' or 'What are your criteria?' However, because people seldom use the singular 'datum', you will sometimes see the word 'data' being used as though singular.

---

7   In the table you can see that the figure for all adults is 67 per cent for 2001. If you divide 100 per cent by 3, you get 33⅓ per cent. (One-third (⅓) of 100 per cent is 33.3 per cent.) Two-thirds of 100 per cent is 66.6 per cent; this is very close to 67. So it is true that two-thirds of UK adults had mobile phones in 2001. The equivalent figure for 2003 is 75. If you divide 100 per cent by 4, you get four quarters of 25 per cent each. So three-quarters (¾) are 75 per cent – making the second part true also. So, the whole statement is true.

BOX 8.13   PERCENTAGES AND FRACTIONS

You have just been converting percentages into fractions: 25% is one-quarter, 50% is one-half, 33% is one-third and so on. It is useful to be able to switch back and forth between fractions and percentages because, although percentages can be more accurate, you may begin to lose touch with their meaning. If you remind yourself occasionally that 75 per cent is the same as three-quarters, and that 20 per cent is one-fifth, and so on, it helps to fix in your mind the kinds of quantities you are dealing with. So translating between percentages and fractions is a helpful habit.

'Rounding' up or down

You also just encountered the figures 33.3 per cent and 66.7 per cent. Why have none of the other figures you've looked at had a decimal point and a number after it? The answer is that, in all the tables shown here, numbers after the decimal point have been *rounded up*, or *rounded down*. Any parts of whole numbers have been ignored. Instead, you have been given the nearest 'round number' (or whole number). The nearest round number to 4¼ (or 4.25) is 4 – so you 'round down' to 4. But the nearest round number to 4¾ (or 4.75) is 5 – so you 'round up' up to 5. Any fraction lower than ½, or 0.5, is 'rounded down'. Any fraction above 0.5 is 'rounded up'. If the fraction is exactly ½, or 0.5, then, by convention, it's rounded up. So how would 33.3 per cent and 66.7 per cent be 'rounded'? You round 33.3 per cent *down* to 33 per cent, and you round 66.7 per cent *up* to 67 per cent.

Graphs and bar charts compared

You can often use either a graph or a bar chart to represent the same data. When would you use one and when the other? Notice how each bar of the bar chart gives you a sense of the size of a group of people. For example, the size of the dark bar for mobile phone owners in the over-75 group is very clearly only about one-quarter of the size of that for the 25–34 group. The lines on a graph are more abstract, it's easier to forget that they represent quantities of something. On the other hand a graph shows trends more clearly. The bar chart in Figure 8.7 would have made two very nicely curving lines. Also a bar chart becomes confusing when several different sets of numbers are being compared. For example, a bar chart of the data in Figure 8.6 would be pretty complicated to read, and the uneven rise of mobile phone ownership would not stand out clearly. So graphs and bar charts have different strengths and weaknesses. When you are *creating* charts using a computer, it's very easy to switch between different types of chart, so you can quickly try out various ways of presenting your data to see which gets your message across most effectively.

See Chapter 8 Section 8.6.3, Creating your own tables and charts

8.5.3 Numbers as pie charts

Pie charts are also commonly used. The pie charts in Figure 8.9 link household ownership of at least one mobile phone to the level of income of households. For the years 1996/97 and 2002/03 we can see what proportion of the mobile phone owning households were in the top fifth of incomes, the next fifth, the middle fifth, the next fifth and the bottom fifth. See if you can answer the questions in Activity 8.5.

Activity 8.5

1   In 1996/97 what percentage of mobile phone owning households were from the top fifth of household incomes?

2   In 1996/97 what percentage of mobile phone owning households were from the lowest fifth of household incomes?

3   Would it be true to say that in 1996/97 nearly three-quarters of the mobile phone owning households were in the highest earning 40 per cent of households?

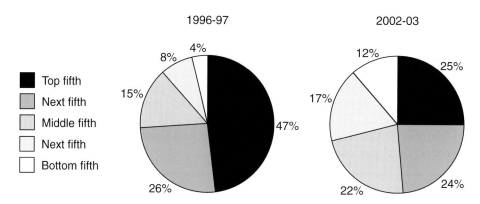

Charts created by the author using data from the Family Expenditure Survey
(Social Trends, 2002) and the Expenditure and Food Survey (ONS, 2004)

Figure 8.9   Pie charts showing ownership of mobile phones by different income bands

(Source: based on Office for National Statistics, 2002 and 2004h)

4   Would it be true to say that in 1996/97 less than one-eighth of the mobile
    phone owning households were in the lowest earning 40 per cent?

5   Did the link between household income and mobile phone ownership
    change over the next six years? Write a sentence summarising the changes.

6   What is the source of the data here?

Answers

1   Looking at the pie chart on the left, we see that 47 per cent of the
    mobile phone owning households were in the fifth of households with
    the highest income levels (or nearly half).

2   We also see that just 4 per cent of the mobile phone owning households
    were in the fifth of households with the lowest incomes.

3   The highest earning 40 per cent means the top two-fifths. Adding those
    two segments of the pie together you have 47 per cent plus 26 per cent,
    which is 73 per cent. This is very close to 75 per cent, or three-quarters.
    So the statement is true.

4   The lowest earning 40 per cent means the bottom two-fifths. Adding
    those two pie segments together you have 4 per cent plus 8 per cent,
    which is 12 per cent. To work out one-eighth as a percentage, you divide
    100 by 8, and get 12.5 per cent. Twelve per cent is less than this, so
    again the statement is true.

5   Six years later we see a marked shift in the pattern of ownership. The
    higher income households still own more of the mobile phones, but the
    lower income households have done a lot of catching up. So ownership is
    more evenly spread between income groups. (If it were exactly even, each
    group would have 20 per cent.) The lowest income households still
    account for only 12 per cent of the phones. But households in the next fifth
    and the middle fifth have substantially increased their share. To summarise,

over this six year period, we see a shift from mobile phones being owned largely by households from higher income groups, to their being fairly widely distributed across households at all income levels.

6   The data sources are the Office for National Statistics' Family Expenditure Survey and Expenditure and Food Survey.

As you see, pie charts, appropriately used, make a strong visual impact. By showing slices of pie of different sizes, they get messages across very effectively. For example, it's very striking, to see the huge slice of the 1996/97 'mobile phone pie' taken by the highest income households, next to the tiny slice for the lowest income households.

8.5.4 Summary of tips for reading graphs and charts

The advice for graphs and charts is similar to that for tables of numbers.

Take your time and be cautious

Graphs and charts *ought* to be easy to read. The whole point of turning numbers into a picture is to bring out their meaning clearly. However, they need some effort on your part to bridge the gap between the picture on the page and the 'reality' they stand for. The visual impact can make it hard to see past the pretty lines and shading, to the underlying message. Don't just *assume* you 'get' what a graph is about. Take a thorough look.

Finding your way in

As with tables, it's important to give yourself time to 'get the feel' of what you are looking at. Look quickly at the main headings, then focus on something specific to check what you are being told. With a bar chart, pick a bar and say out loud what it stands for. For example 'this bar tells me that in 2003 about 70 per cent of 55- to 64-year-olds owned a mobile phone'. With a graph pick a line and say out loud, for example, 'by 1999 household ownership of mobile phones exceeded 40 per cent and had overtaken ownership of a home computer'. Scan your way around the chart – up and down and from side to side. Check that it makes sense in terms of what you already know of the world.

Reading the words

When you feel comfortable with what the chart shows, examine in more detail the words written around it – the main headings, the axes, and any 'key' to shading. Also read the small print by the chart. Be sure you don't draw the wrong conclusions.

BOX 8.14   AXES

The 'axes' of a graph or chart are the lines at the bottom edge and the left edge. The line along the bottom edge is called the horizontal axis (or x-axis), and the line at the left is called the vertical axis (or y-axis). The *axes should always be labelled,* to tell you what units you are counting in. In Figure 8.5, for example, the horizontal axis is 'time' in years and the vertical axis is 'percentage owning'. In Figure 8.7, the vertical axis is the same as in Figure 8.5, but the horizontal axis is 'age' in bands. (Note that 'axes' is the plural of 'axis'. It is pronounced '*axees*'.)

Extracting information

When you have checked what a chart or graph is about, look for any trends it seems to suggest. Jot down a few conclusions you think can be drawn. It may take a little time before you grasp the full extent of what a chart has to tell you, but it's worth the effort. Information in the form of a graph is highly patterned and since your memory works by finding patterns in information and storing them, graphs are ready made for storage. It can be a lot easier to remember information you have taken in from a chart rather than a table, or a text.

8.5.5 Try out your skills

Here is a final chart to give you an opportunity to try out all these skills. This time it's a bar chart with the bars drawn horizontally.

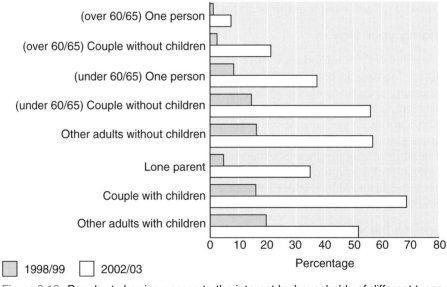

Figure 8.10 Bar chart showing access to the internet by households of different types
(Source: Based on Office for National Statistics, 2004f-g)

Activity 8.6

Is it true that by 2002/03 more than three-quarters of couples with children had internet access at home?

Write down five worthwhile conclusions you can draw from this bar chart. (Note, over 60/65 refers to 'over state pension age' (65 for men, 60–65 for women.)

Answers

The statement about couples with children is not true. Just under 70 per cent have internet access. This is a trick question, to see whether you remembered to read the percentages on the horizontal axis. As this chart only goes up to 80 per cent, the bars look bigger than they really are.

Here are five of my conclusions. You may have drawn different ones, which is fine.

1   Home internet access increased dramatically in the four years up to 2002/3, more than doubling in every household type.

2   By 2002/03 households of couples with children were the most likely to have home access to the internet. Their access quadrupled over the four years.

3   Households of people over state pension age are least likely to have home access to the internet.

4   Lone-parent families are much less likely to have internet access than two-parent families. However, over four years their access increased dramatically from a very low base.

5   Households with couples are more likely to have internet access than single households.

I hope you found reading this chart quite straightforward, after all the practice you have had. I hope too that you can see how I drew the conclusions I did, and that you were able to draw interesting conclusions of your own.

Numerical data can be presented in many different ways. Although they *look* different, tables of numbers, bar charts and graphs can all be used to present the *same* information. They are simply different ways of trying to sketch a picture using numbers. It's a matter of deciding what kind of presentation will best show up the key features

Key points

When you are reading charts or graphs:

■   Take time to get a 'feel' for what the chart is telling you.

■   Pick on one or two points and convince yourself that they make sense.

■   Read the words around the edges very carefully.

■   Look for patterns, peaks, troughs and blips.

8.6 Using numbers intelligently

In Section 8.3 'Describing the world' I raised some questions about the impact of new modes of electronic communications in reshaping our society and the lives we live. The tables and charts we have explored have taken us quite a long way in showing how rapidly the new communications media are spreading. But they have also shown that ownership is uneven. Not all income groups, age groups and household types have the same access. And while new media have spread remarkably rapidly it seems likely to be quite a while before they will be anything like universal. For example, if the internet came to be taken for granted as a key means of access to such essentials as shopping, banking, government forms, health advice and education, some groups appear to be in danger of getting left out. However, we should also recognise the limitations of the data we have explored. We would need to look at a lot of other numbers to get a satisfactorily rounded picture. And, in any case, numbers are never the whole answer.

8.6.1 Not all data are numbers

This chapter has focused on numbers to help you develop skills in making use of them. However, even in such subjects as social science, you shouldn't assume that 'science' automatically implies numbers. Don't think that:

social *science* = research = data = numbers

Science is not *all* about research. Research is important, but so is *constructing theories,* and so are *thinking, arguing* and *applying* ideas to 'real life'. Research becomes sterile and irrelevant if it loses touch with these other equally important activities.

Nor is research simply about producing *data*. Research is always about testing out *theories*. There is an infinity of possible facts to record. The only thing that makes fact-gathering manageable and worthwhile is the *theory* shaping the research. For example there wouldn't be much point in counting the insects squashed on your car number plate, unless you happened to know there was a theory that bird populations are being affected by fluctuations in the insect population and you wanted to contribute to a data-gathering project.

The RSPB's Big Bug Count is encouraging people to count the number of insects 'splatted' on their car number plates after a journey and send the results back to be analysed [...] It's hoped the data will help build a picture of insect populations across the UK [...] with some bird species [...] facing declines, conservationists are concerned the countryside is losing its buzz, as well as its birdsong.

(BBC, 2004b)

Furthermore, 'data' are not exclusively 'quantitative' (numbers). A lot of social research focuses on qualitative information. You would know very little about the significance of internet access if all you collected were quantitative data. You also need to collect qualitative data by talking to people, accessing the internet yourself, exploring what people say to each other online, and so on. The figures for internet access are only a small part of the picture.

8.6.2 Finding useful statistics

You can find lots of useful tables and charts online. A straightforward web-search may find exactly what you need. Alternatively as you have seen in this chapter, government statistics are an invaluable resource, with data kept up to date and well checked and vetted. The UK Office for National Statistics website, *National Statistics* (www.statistics.gov.uk), is an exceptionally rich source.

It's also important to find out the key sources of statistics in your field. For example, a publication like *Social Trends* is tremendously valuable for the social sciences. Check with your teachers, your department, or your university library to find out the best sources for your subject.

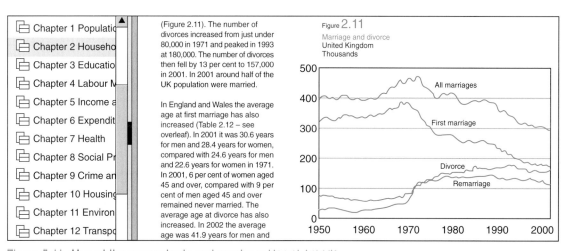

Figure 8.11 One of the many charts and graphs in Social Trends

(Source: based on Office for National Statistics, 2004a)

It is extremely valuable to spend some time dipping into the statistical sources relevant to your field. It will set you up very well for future essays and projects. You will know *where* to start looking, whenever you need numbers to back up an argument and you will know *how* to find your way around the relevant statistical sources. There are immense informational riches readily available. You need to know how to access them.

Download/View entire documents for free here (Left click to View or right click to Download)

▶**Press Release January 2004** (pdf)

▶**Social Trends 34** (4.99Mb – pdf)

▶**Social Trends 34** (Datasets)

▶**Social Trends 33** (4.48 Mb – pdf)

▶**Social Trends 33** (Datasets)

▶**Social Trends 32** (3.89 Mb – pdf)

▶**Social Trends 32** (Datasets)

Figure 8.12   Weblinks offered on the Social Trends page of the National Statistics Website

(Source: Office for National Statistics, 2004a)

8.6.3 Creating your own tables and charts

You have spent time exploring tables and charts created by other people, but how about creating your own? It's actually surprisingly easy if you use a computer. If you feel moderately confident with computing you could open the spreadsheet program on your machine, and knock up a table for yourself very quickly. You may need a bit of help to make it look nice, but you can probably get enough support from the program's Help facility, or an electronic tutorial may be supplied.

You might like to practise gathering numerical information, such as answers to a questionnaire you have made up. Even easier, you could gather some data about yourself over a week or two, such as your daily weight, hours of sleep, or time spent online. With a spreadsheet program you can create a simple table out of such data in a few minutes, once you've invested a little time in finding out how.

However, the real magic of spreadsheet software lies in their charting capabilities. When you have typed in some numbers in the form of a table, with suitable headings for columns and rows, you then 'select' the table by clicking at one corner and 'dragging' to the other corner. Then, look for a button such as 'Chart Wizard', and just click and keep clicking to see what you get. With luck the results will be stunning – a multi-coloured chart, beautifully drawn, all in immaculate proportion and superbly accurate. You may need to repeat the process a few times, trying different options – perhaps even, as a last resort, read the instructions. Anyway, just have a try. You've nothing to lose.

There is more to number work, of course, than producing dazzling charts. Statistics, as we all know, can be used to tell lies. As well as the technical skill to create tables, charts and graphs, you need insight into when and how to use them sensibly, and how to interpret them legitimately. That is why, if your course requires you to produce tables and charts, you would normally expect to be given support in learning how to do so responsibly. If you don't get support, ask.

Key points

■ Important though numbers are, qualitative data and proper scientific thinking are equally important.

■ Make time to locate the key sources of statistics for your field of study. Then explore them to see what is available. Familiarise yourself with the way data are organised and accessed.

■ Try using software to make tables and charts of your own to see how easy it is. But seek support if you need to produce them as part of your course work.

8.7 Review

If you were new to tables and charts you have done some hard work in this chapter. Perhaps you have been baffled at times. If so, don't worry about it. Any course requiring you to work with numbers ought to give you assistance. You will then be taught many other interesting and valuable things about statistics, tables and charts. This has just been a beginning. I hope you will now feel encouraged to develop the habit of stopping to look carefully at tables and charts, working out what they mean, rather than skipping over them. As you have seen they offer a lot of information in a very compact form. Following the basic steps outlined here, you will soon make yourself familiar with the common ways of presenting numerical data. Then you will be in a position to start finding out facts for yourself instead of waiting to be told.

Key points

■ Making sense of numbers is a normal part of modern life.

■ Numbers can supply a lot of information very quickly and effectively.

■ An ability to work with numbers is about building up experience, rather than being a special 'gift'.

■ Tables present numbers systematically, so that you can examine data in detail.

■ Charts and graphs help you to see the patterns in sets of numbers.

■ You should approach a table or chart in a spirit of exploration and questioning, looking for what it can tell you and summarising to yourself what you think it says.

■ You have to be prepared to invest time in learning how to read different kinds of tables and charts.

References

BBC (2004a) 'UK Weather – Wind', *BBC Weather*, www.bbc.co.uk/weather/ukweather/wind.shtml (accessed 19 July 2004).

BBC (2004b) Is the UK losing its buzz?, *Essex nature*, www.bbc.co.uk/essex/discover_essex/nature/big_bug_count.shtml (accessed 25 July 2004).

Caledonian MacBrayne (2004) 'Summer: ARRAN: Ardrossan-Brodick', *Caledonian MacBrayne Hebridean & Clyde Ferries*, www.calmac.co.uk/summer-arran-timetable2.html (accessed 20 July 2004).

Met Office (2004) *Swansea 5-day forecast*, Met Office, www.meto.gov.uk/weather/europe/uk/wales.html (accessed 20 July 2004).

Office for National Statistics (2002) 'Data for Chart 13.15, Ownership of mobile phones: by income quintile group, 1996–97 and 2000–01, Chapter 13 Lifestyles and social participation', *Social Trends* no. 32, p 218, www.statistics.gov.uk/downloads (accessed 20 July 2004).

Office for National Statistics (2004a) 'Social Trends', National Statistics Online, www.statistics.gov.uk/STATBASE/Product.asp?vlnk=5748 (accessed 20 July 2004).

Office for National Statistics (2004b) 'Chapter 13 Lifestyles and Social Participation', *Social Trends,* no. 34, National Statistics Online, www.statistics.gov.uk/downloads/theme_social/Social_Trends34/13_13.xls (accessed 20 July 2004).

Office for National Statistics (2004c) 'Chapter 13 Lifestyles and Social Participation', *Social Trends,* no. 34, p. 203, National Statistics Online, www.statistics.gov.uk/downloads/theme_social/Social_Trends34/Social_Trends34.pdf (accessed 20 July 2004).

Office for National Statistics (2004d) 'Chapter 13 Lifestyles and Social Participation', *Social Trends,* no. 34, National Statistics Online, www.statistics.gov.uk/downloads/theme_social/Social_Trends34/13_14.xls. (accessed 20 July 2004).

Office for National Statistics (2004e) *Social Trends,* no. 34, www.statistics.gov.uk/downloads/theme_social/Social_Trends34/Social_Trends34.pdf (accessed 20 July 2004).

Office for National Statistics (2004f) '13.15, Households with internet access: by household type, Chapter 13, Lifestyles and social participation', *Social Trends,* no. 34, p. 204, www.statistics.gov.uk/downloads/ (accessed 20 July 2004).

Office for National Statistics (2004g) 'Percentage of households with durable goods by income group and household composition', *Family Spending: a report on the 2002-2003 expenditure and food survey*, p. 153, www.statistics.gov.uk/downloads/ (accessed 20 July 2004).

Office for National Statistics (2004h) '9: Household characteristics & ownership of consumer durables: Table 9.4 Percentage of households with durable goods by income group and household composition', *Family Spending*, 2002–03, p. 155, www.statistics.gov.uk/downloads (accessed 20 July 2004).

Philip, C. (2004) '20m suffer as floods hit South Asia', *The Times*, 17 July, p. 17.

Qualifications and Curriculum Authority (2002) *The key skills qualifications specifications and guidance: communication, application of number and information technology*, Sudbury, Suffolk, QCA Publications.

CHAPTER 9 RESEARCHING ONLINE

9.1 A world of information at your fingertips

With a computer connected to the internet, you have access to information resources undreamt of by earlier generations. Moreover, these resources are available on demand, for twenty-four hours every day. Whether you are setting out on a sizeable research project, or just checking the weather forecast, the internet will help you find what you need. There's a whole world of information out there if you have the skills to find your way around it.

9.1.1 Information literacy

People with skills in accessing and using information are said to be 'information literate'.

> Information literate people [...] know how knowledge is organised, how to find information, and how to use information [...] They are people prepared for life long learning, because they can always find the information needed [...] To be information literate, a person must be able to recognise when information is needed and have the ability to locate, evaluate and use effectively the needed information.
>
> *(American Library Association, 1989)*

Information literacy is increasingly important in this 'information age', not just for study purposes but in all aspects of life. The Higher Education Funding Council for England (HEFCE) recognises this in its strategic plan:

> In the modern world, people increasingly need skills of evaluating and managing information, in both their personal and working lives.
>
> *(HEFCE, 2004)*

Finding up-to-date, accurate and relevant information increasingly means knowing how to search for it *online*. And managing this information means knowing how to *file* it effectively on your *computer*.

As a *student*, however, you need more than purely technical web-searching and filing skills. You need to know how to access *online libraries* and *academic databases*. You need to be able to weigh up the *academic credibility* of what you find. And you need to know how to make *appropriate use* of it within your studies. So, whether you are new to online searching, or relatively experienced, you probably need to invest time in developing your own information literacy.

9.1.2 Developing your information skills

One of the most remarkable features of online research is how easy it is to get started. Yet, your skills will develop indefinitely as the internet grows and changes, with new information resources appearing and search tools becoming ever more sophisticated. The aim of this chapter is to help you with the first steps. The rest you can learn through experience, or by seeking further advice.

In Section 9.2 'Finding information' I describe some searches and show what I found. Bear in mind that if your computer is set up differently from mine, some of the searches I describe won't work in exactly the same way for you. The details will also date quickly as the internet develops. However, the important thing is to understand the general principles. To find equivalent steps, you may need to use your software's Help facility, or perhaps ask someone with more online experience. Section 9.3 'Evaluating information' looks at how to check the academic credibility of what you find online. Section 9.4 'Misuse of online information' draws attention to some of the pitfalls of using the internet indiscriminately or unethically.

Key points

- Information literacy is a basic life-skill for modern living. It involves recognising when you need information and knowing where and how to search for it.

- All students need to develop skills in finding the key pathways to information in their field of study.

9.2 Finding information

9.2.1 A quick search

Searching online can be a serious and thoughtfully planned activity, but it can also be a quick, impulsive hunt for a fresh approach. For example, in Chapter 1 I describe Zahra struggling to read; but instead of wallowing in despair, she could have used the internet to boost her progress. In this section I describe some searches that I did on the topic Zahra was reading about – happiness and socioeconomic policy.

I didn't tell you at the time, but you won't be surprised to learn that Zahra was reading the Richard Layard article at the back of this book. One thing holding her up was that she didn't know what some of the words in the article meant, such as 'paradox' and 'habituation'. Here's how I looked them up:

1 My computer was on, so I opened a browser window. Then I opened a search engine and typed 'dictionary' in the search box. I was offered several dictionaries to choose from, so I clicked to open one and typed 'paradox' in the search box. In an instant the text shown in Figure 9.1 appeared on the screen.

par·a·dox
(click to hear the word) (păr′ə-dŏks′)
n.

1. A seemingly contradictory statement that may nonetheless be true: ***the paradox that standing is more tiring than walking.***

Figure 9.1 Search results

(Source: yourDictionary.com, 2004)

2 After reading this and clicking on the link to hear the pronunciation, I tried another dictionary, which offered me the text shown in Figure 9.2.

paradox [Show phonetics]
noun [C or U]
a situation or statement which seems impossible or is difficult to understand because it contains two opposite facts or characteristics:
[+ *that*] *It's a curious paradox* **that** *drinking a lot of water can often make you feel thirsty.*

Figure 9.2 Search results

(Source: Cambridge Dictionaries Online, 2004)

3   These two definitions gave a pretty clear idea of what 'paradox' means, so I then tried 'habituation'. Figure 9.3 shows the definition given by the first dictionary.

ha·bit·u·a·tion

(click to hear the word) (hə-bĭch'ōō-ā'shən)

n.

1. The process of habituating or the state of being habituated.
2.
    a. Physiological tolerance to a drug resulting from repeated use.
    b. Psychological dependence on a drug.
3. *Psychology* The decline of a conditioned response following repeated exposure to the conditioned stimulus.

Figure 9.3 **Search results**

(Source: yourDictionary.com, 2004)

4   This wasn't very easy to take in so I printed it out in case I might want to read it later and think about it some more. The second dictionary did not include the word 'habituation', nor did the next dictionary I tried, so I typed 'habituation' straight into the search engine's search box. This found an article called *Puppy Socialisation and Habituation* (Appleby, 2004), published by The Association of Pet Behaviour Counsellors. Surprisingly, a couple of minutes' scanning through this actually gave me a pretty good idea of how the word is used.

I then found an excellent website providing links to a range of free dictionaries. Using this I soon found more help with understanding the meaning of 'habituation'.

Don't be surprised if you follow the same steps as me but get different results. The internet is constantly changing.

A few minutes of online searching can quickly provide new leads as you grapple with a topic. Instead of being bogged down with a text which isn't working for you, you can 'step outside' and find another angle.

What did I need to know to be able to carry out this search?

See Chapter 3 Section 3.2.1, What equipment do you need?

■   I knew how to open a web browser.

■   I also knew about search engines. I used Google but I could have used Alta Vista, Excite, or others. (I actually used GoogleUK (www.google.co.uk) because it has a helpful option to search just UK pages.) Your browser may list some search engines in the 'Favorites' or 'Bookmarks' menu. You can find detailed help in choosing a search engine by visiting *Choosing a Search Tool* (TERENA, 2001).

■ I set up my browser's home page so that when I open it I am taken directly to my favourite search engine (look up 'home page' in your browser's Help to see how to do this).

■ I had enough experience to guess that typing 'dictionary' would be enough for the search engine to find me some useful results. I also guessed that by typing an unusual work like 'habituation' directly into the search engine I might find what I wanted to know.

■ I also knew about using 'links' (hyperlinks) to move from one web page to others. I knew that when the mouse pointer changed to a 'pointing finger' icon I am over a link. And, in my browser, if I click on words that are blue and underlined, I am taken to a new web page.

Perhaps some of this is new to you and you need advice from someone with more experience. Once you have done a few searches, however, it all seems very simple.

9.2.2 Filing web addresses

As soon as I found the dictionaries I saved their web addresses in case I wanted to visit them again. This is very easy: when I opened a dictionary's website, I went to my browser's menu toolbar and clicked on 'Favorites', then 'Add to Favorites'. (I was using Internet Explorer as my browser; in Netscape the equivalent menu is 'Bookmarks'.) Before you save a web address check that you are on the website's homepage so that your saved link takes you back to the right place.

You can, if you choose, accumulate an extremely long list of web addresses. However, it then becomes difficult to find an address you want. Because I use the web a lot and want to be able to find addresses quickly, I set up a filing system in Favorites. Figure 9.4 shows an example of a filing system.

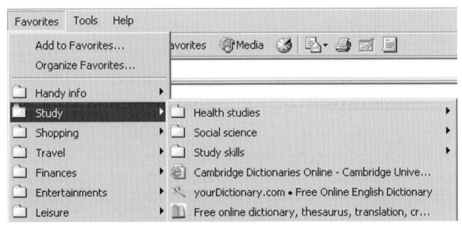

Figure 9.4 **Example of a web address filing system**

When I click on the Favorites menu a list of folders drops down. In Figure 9.4 you can see that I've opened the Study folder, revealing three more folders inside it: two for course topics and one for study skills.

See Chapter 3 Section 3.4, Organising files

It is a hierarchical filing system. I decided to store the dictionary site addresses in the main Study folder; you can see that three are listed. This enables me to click on any one of the links and be taken straight to that online dictionary.

I created the folders by clicking on 'Organize Favorites' and using the buttons available (you can see it in Figure 9.4, under 'Add to Favorites'). To store a website's address, all I had to do was click on 'Add to Favorites', and then on the folder that I wanted to add it to.

Saving useful web addresses in a well organised filing system is a key strategy for effective web searching. The worldwide web is a huge, unstructured and potentially confusing environment to work in. But if you take the time to set up your own customised system of links to the sites you visit regularly, it soon becomes familiar and extremely convenient.

9.2.3 Tracking down academic material

In Section 9.2.1 I describe carrying out a quick, informal search to see if anything useful shows up. But what if I wanted to find another article on 'happiness and socioeconomic policy' (the topic of the article Zahra was reading)? This involves searching for a specific category of academic information. Can I use an ordinary search engine for that? Figure 9.5 shows what happened when I searched for 'happiness' using Google.

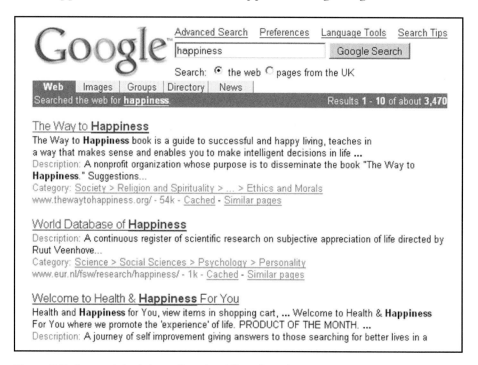

Figure 9.5 **A search for information about 'happiness'**

(Source: Google, 2004a)

The darkened bar in Figure 9.5 shows that Google is displaying the first ten of 'about 3,470' results. Should I look at all of them? If not, then how many? Usually, I would scan quickly through the text under the headings and click on a few of the most likely looking. At the same time I'd be weighing up whether I'm getting the kind of leads I want. If they seem fairly promising, I might work through the first ten results and even go to the next page to see the next ten. But, just as likely, I would try new searches instead, using different words.

Most of the links offered by my search were to websites giving advice on how to live a happier life. These were not relevant to my interest. On the other hand, the link to the *World Database of Happiness* looked promising. It claims to be a register of scientific research. If you look at the 'Category' line, you'll see it says Science > Social Sciences > Psychology > Personality. This appears to be a serious academic category.

I clicked on the *World Database of Happiness* and added it to the Social science folder in my Favorites so that I could come back to it later. Then I decided to try another Google search, putting the word 'research' before 'happiness', to see whether that would bring up more academic-related sites. Figure 9.6 shows what this produced.

Figure 9.6 **A search for 'research happiness'**

(Source: Google, 2004a)

Putting 'research' before 'happiness' gave a different flavour to the results. The total number increased from under 4,000 to 527,000. However, the sites at the top of the list were closer to what I wanted. The *World Database of Happiness* is there again, but is now at the top of the list. This time I decided to explore it.

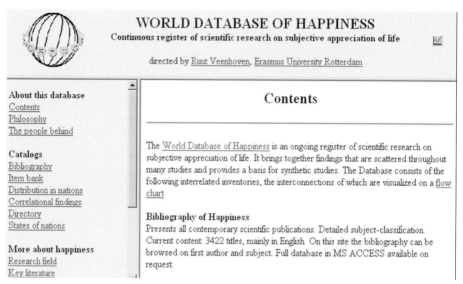

Figure 9.7 The home page of the World Database of Happiness (WDH)

(Source: Veenhoven, 2004a)

I was reassured to see 'Erasmus University' prominently displayed; this gave me confidence that the site was worth exploring. You could spend a long time browsing around a site like this, so I decided to look under the 'More about happiness' menu and clicked on 'Research field'.

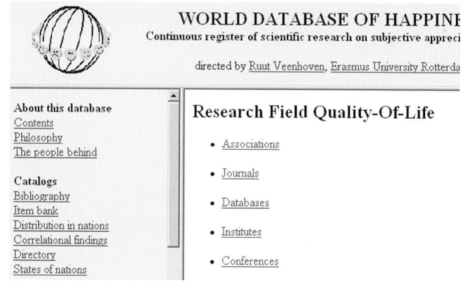

Figure 9.8 The Research Field pages of the WDH

(Source: Veenhoven, 2004b)

This looked promising. I saw that the research field was titled 'Quality-of-Life', so I noted this down as a phrase I might find useful in my searches. I then clicked on 'Journals':

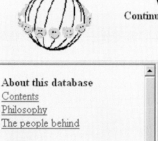

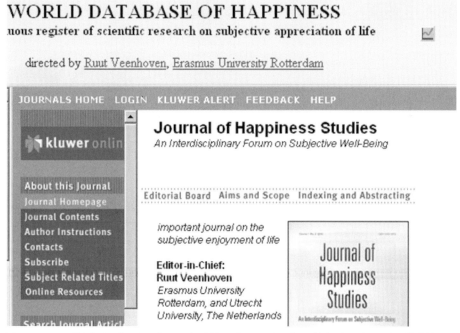

Figure 9.9 Journals listed under the research field 'Quality of Life'

(Source: Veenhoven, 2004c)

I selected the *Journal of Happiness Studies* and was taken to the journal's website:

Figure 9.10 Website for the Journal of Happiness Studies, linked to from the WDH

(Source: Kluwer, 2004)

Working my way around the journal website, I soon found some recent articles which I could download for free and print off. I felt confident that these were 'respectable' articles because I could see that the journal editors hold senior posts at universities in various countries. Also, when I clicked on the 'kluwer online' home page link I saw that the company is a large, well-established publisher of academic journals. Better still, these articles included lists of references. I scanned through these and began to build up a picture of the kind of research being done and of the names of important researchers in the field.

This search took less than fifteen minutes and delivered high quality literature straight into my hands. With a few online search skills, you can follow up all kinds of hunches and get useful results, and electronic copies of documents, almost immediately.

9.2.4 Doing an advanced search

As it happened, I struck lucky in going directly to the *World Database of Happiness* using a non-specialist search engine. But this shows that a simple search can be worth trying, as it's so quick and easy. However, when you are not so lucky, you can try using your search engine's 'advanced' search facilities.

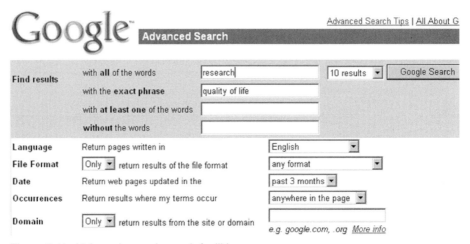

Figure 9.11 **Using advanced search facilities**

(Source: Google, 2004b)

In Figure 9.11 I have entered the text 'quality of life' (having picked up this phrase from the *World Database of Happiness*). I also added 'research' to help steer the search towards the more academic-related web pages and I specified searching for pages written in English and recently updated. Figure 9.12 shows what this produced.

Do keep in mind that you are likely to get different results, even if you follow exactly the steps I describe.

The advanced search gave me plenty to explore. But what if I wanted to take a more 'academic' route, to check that I'm not missing out important resources?

Figure 9.12 **Results from an advanced search**

(Source: Google, 2004c)

9.2.5 Academic search tools

I decided to try the library of my own university. I went to the homepage of the Open University Library and immediately added the address to my Study folder in Favorites, so that I could get back to it easily, then clicked on the 'question mark' icon at the top of the screen to get to the 'Search Open Library' page:

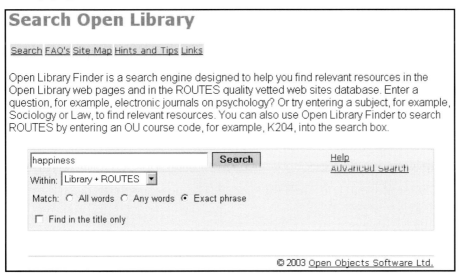

Figure 9.13 **A library search engine**

(Source: The Open University, 2003a)

As the page says, this is another search engine, but it searches only selected sources. Unfortunately, when I set it to search 'happiness' it replied 'No results were found for your search'. So I tried 'quality of life' instead and checked 'Exact phrase', to eliminate results relating to just 'quality' or just 'life'. This time I got eight results.

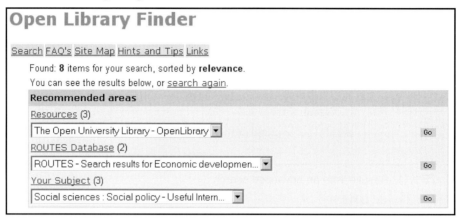

Figure 9.14 **Results using a library search engine**

(Source: The Open University, 2003b)

I was interested to see 'social policy' mentioned after Social Sciences, under 'Your Subject', as the Layard article also has social policy concerns. So I clicked the 'Go' button against it, which brought me to:

Social Sciences: Social Policy - Useful Internet Links

This page links to electronic resources chosen for the study of social policy. You can find more general information on the main General Social Sciences resource page, or there are more resources for other subjects within the social sciences which you can access from the main Social Sciences Index page.

General and Specific Gateways

ROUTES
A database of internet resources designed by the Open University Library to support students registered on Open University courses. All the links are accompanied by searchable descriptions and keywords which allow users to understand the scope of a website before connecting to it. Each link is checked regularly to maintain currency. You can go straight to Social Policy related sites or browse by course.

Academic Info
Gateway to Internet resources catering for an academic user base. Has specific subject areas for; Sociology, Environmental Studies, Political Science, Statistics.

Government Information - UK Online
Links to DfES and OFSTED ; government ministries ; official agencies and commissions ; civil and military services ; local authorities, etc.

SOSIG
The **So**cial **S**cience **I**nformation **G**ateway. The most comprehensive site of subject specific information and links.

Figure 9.15 **OU library links to Social Policy within the category Social Sciences**

(Source: The Open University, 2003c)

After scanning through this page I selected SOSIG, the Social Science Information Gateway, bringing me to:

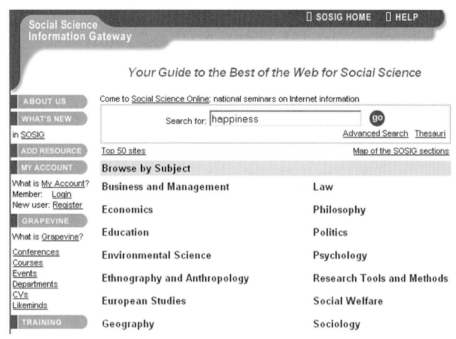

Figure 9.16 **The Social Science Information Gateway**

(Source: Social Science Information Gateway, 2004)

This clearly is an immensely useful 'gateway' from which to begin any research in the social sciences, so I quickly added it to the Social Sciences folder within my Study Folder in Favorites. I was now accumulating some useful links for future searches.

There are many ways you can search for publications through a gateway as powerful as the SOSIG. I tried a quick search for 'happiness' and the first two results were old friends: the *World Database of Happiness* and 'Happiness: Has Social Science a Clue?' by Richard Layard, from which the article at the end of this book is derived. This is a reassuring sign. When you research completely separate avenues and end up at the same place, it suggests that you have located some of the key sources.

9.2.6 Searching reference databases

Finally, I tried one more search, starting from yet another point. This time I used OCLC FirstSearch (shown in Figure 9.17), one of the key search facilities provided through my university library. This gives me access to many specialist reference databases, if I use my password supplied by the library.

I selected 'Social Sciences' databases and typed in 'happiness'. This returned a list of relevant databases, as shown in Figure 9.18.

Figure 9.17 **OCLC FirstSearch search screen**

(Source: OCLC Online Computer Library Center, 2004)

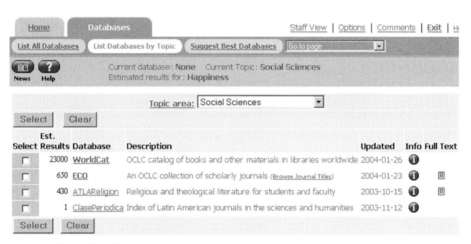

Figure 9.18 **OCLC FirstSearch search results**

(Source: OCLC Online Computer Library Center, 2004)

WorldCat showed 23,000 hits – and the first author listed was Layard. Having used a very powerful database search this time, this was another reassuring sign that I was connecting up with the right networks of research and publication.

The purpose of these examples has been to show how quickly and straightforwardly you can track down research data, articles and books that are relevant to your studies. With powerful search tools at my command, I was able to do all this searching in under an hour, without moving from my desk.

Of course, tracking down information is not always easy. You can get yourself started by following the kind of steps I took, but you will need to develop a basic knowledge of the major gateways and databases in your own field of study. You also need to know about your own university library's electronic access facilities. It is well worth taking advantage of any training in information searching that you can find. You could try the Open University Library's SAFARI website (The Open University Library, 2001a) for example, and your own university's library will offer its own training and support programme. Investing time in developing information skills early in your studies will pay dividends many times over.

Key points

- For a quick information search, just type a well chosen word or two into a search engine. If you don't find what you want, try different words, or other search engines. For more specific enquiries use the advanced search facilities.

- Make a shortcut to your favourite search engine(s), so that you can use it whenever the need strikes. For example, save the address in your Favorites folder or set it as your home page.

- Set up a web address filing system, so that you can keep track of all the useful addresses you save.

- Invest some time exploring the sources in your field. Practise finding relevant articles and journals, so that when you are under pressure with assignment deadlines you can find what you need quickly.

- Find out from your university library how its catalogue works and what access it offers to wider information sources. Take advantage of any training offered on information searching; it will pay big dividends.

- When you need to do a serious search for literature, start by finding the major gateways and databases in your field.

- Take a flexible approach to searching. Start from different points and pursue different avenues of enquiry. Gradually you will begin to recognise the main features of the network of knowledge in your field.

9.3 Evaluating information

The internet holds unimaginable quantities of information and is continually growing and changing. It is largely unregulated however. 'Bad' information can be posted as easily as 'good', so how can you judge the reliability of the information you find? The Open University Library's SAFARI website offers a useful checklist called PROMPT (presentation, relevance, objectivity, method, provenance and timeliness) (The Open University Library, 2001b). It's helpful to look at each of these six criteria in turn.

9.3.1 The PROMPT checklist

1 Presentation

You can tell a lot about sites by their appearance. Many of the sites I found when I searched for 'happiness' in Google displayed pictures of smiling faces and used big headlines. They offered such prospects as:

> LIVE IN A WORLD WITH NO PROBLEMS Using the Impossibility Transformer [...] Confidently dissolve "problems" with: Money, Relationships, Time pressures, Goals, Weight, and more!
>
> *(Copsey, 2004)*

The style was clearly intended to attract attention and arouse hope and enthusiasm. This contrasted with sites such as that of the *World Database of Happiness*, which specialise in academic writing and research. These tend to have a formal, sober style; they are not trying to persuade, or to attract custom. They aim to give an impression of soundness and dependability.

2 Relevance

Although the sites found by Google all related in some way to the topic of 'happiness', most were not relevant to my interests. They were mainly about achieving personal happiness in life rather than happiness as a goal of social policy, and so it was easy to see their lack of relevance. It would be more challenging to judge the relevance of different articles from the *Journal of Happiness Studies*. I would have to look at their titles and skim through the abstract at the start of each one.

Finding a lot of high quality information brings its own problems. You have to think about what exactly you are looking for, so that you can weigh up the relevance of what you find.

3 Objectivity

See Chapter 4 Section 4.3.2, Key features of academic discourse

Academic research and writing aims to be objective. It is impersonal, using logical argument rather than appealing to emotions. If I had explored the websites which offered pathways to personal happiness, I might have encountered some interesting and valuable ideas. However, it seemed unlikely that they would be academically compelling, because they were presented from extremely committed standpoints. The writers showed little interest in achieving a balanced and fair presentation. There was no effort to take a detached stance and leave me to draw my own reasoned conclusions.

4 Method

Academic writers provide a list of references to show how what they say connects with what others in their field have said. They also back their argument up with evidence and make clear how this evidence was gathered. When you see references and discussion of evidence, you know you have found the right kind of website. You can then examine the evidence in detail: for example, if you want to check how large the research samples were, or the quality of questionnaires used.

By contrast, many of the commercial 'happiness' websites made bold claims without offering evidence or indicating who is being quoted. One I found (Sedona Training Associates, 2004) opened with the quotation: 'the fastest, easiest, and most powerful self-improvement technique available today', but gave no obvious indication of who said this. Was it just a claim by the sponsor of the site? There was a section of the site devoted to testimonials, but you would have to do some searching to find out whether the quotation is attributed to anyone.

Another announced, 'Think The Same Thoughts As The Most Effective, Successful & Happy People, And You'll Get Exactly The Same Results In Your Life' (Think Right Now! International, 2004). This is a very difficult claim to verify. What are 'same thoughts', or 'same results'? Interestingly, neither of these websites made mention of the 'Impossibility Transformer', for which so much was claimed in the *Live In A World With No Problems* website (see '1 Presentation' above). How can all these competing claims be reconciled? Within this genre of website there is little effort to connect with what other websites say. Indeed, each stresses its uniqueness.

5 Provenance

Provenance is to do with origin and authenticity; it is a bit like 'respectability'. Who knows you? What is your reputation and status in the world? Many people tend to trust websites presented by government departments, the BBC, or large commercial organisations. Is this justified? It always pays to be cautious, but on the other hand, you have to take your information from somewhere. At least large, well-established institutions have reputations to preserve and could be damaged by being exposed as unreliable. On first sight, I did wonder how respectable the *World Database of Happiness* was, but when I saw the name of a famous university on it I was reassured. Then, as I explored the site, I came across more links to well-established universities.

By contrast, most of the commercial websites offering happiness confidently presented people and organisations I had never heard of as 'world leading', and made no reference to institutions that I had heard of. It might seem unfair to hold doubts about sources just because you haven't heard of them, but trust has to be based on something.

6 Timeliness

Finally, if you use information on the internet it is important to know when it was produced. An academic publication will always give the date it was published, and 'serious' websites tend to display the date when they were last updated (some websites can sit untended for years). At the foot of the contents page of the *World Database of Happiness*, which I accessed in January 2004, it said it had been updated on October 4, 2003. In any case, the links to the journal websites brought me right up to date.

Summary

This PROMPT checklist is an excellent aid when you find information on the web. Not all of the six criteria are equally important in every case but using the checklist will help you to develop your ability to evaluate what you find.

> ### Key points
>
> ■ You need to be able to distinguish 'good' information from 'bad'.
>
> ■ Practise using criteria such as those in the PROMPT checklist to evaluate the information you find.

9.4 Misuse of online information

Having stressed the immense benefits of the internet as a source of information, it is important to sound a note of caution.

9.4.1 The myth of infinite access to knowledge

See Chapter 4, Understanding how you learn

Access to the internet will not turn you into a wise and knowledgeable person. A mountain of information does not amount to 'knowledge'. A telephone book is packed with information, but you will learn little from reading it. Information is of value only if it is put into context. It is the *understanding* within which information is framed which constitutes knowledge; and understanding takes time and thought. It is not produced by a series of quick 'hits' on relevant websites.

Websites which are carefully structured and lead you through a well organised sequence of ideas will help you to acquire knowledge. You can also develop your knowledge by undertaking searches provided that you start out with a well-formed idea of what it is you are looking for. The internet is invaluable when your thoughts have reached a point where you need more information, but meandering across cyberspace at the whim of a search engine will leave your knowledge untouched.

9.4.2 Substituting a search engine for your brain

It is easy to produce dreadful assignments by using a search engine to do a quick, undiscriminating trawl. Searching for a few words from your assignment task, copying results from websites you come across, then pasting together disconnected bits and pieces to present as your assignment will get you a very low grade.

It is *not* the purpose of assignments to show that you can use a search engine, or that you can copy and paste text. Anyone can do those things. It is an insult to your teachers' intelligence to expect them to waste time looking at your 'What I found on the web' scrapbook. The point of an assignment is to show that your mind is developing – that you can grapple with new ideas and put them to work.

It is an excellent use of the internet to conduct a careful search, using relevant catalogues and databases, evaluate what you find using the PROMPT criteria, then work carefully selected elements into your line of argument. However, using your search engine as a substitute for your brain is simply a waste of everyone's time, including your own.

9.4.3 Plagiarising assignments

A variation on the last theme is to substitute a search engine plus someone else's brain for your own. If you hunt for other people's assignments online, then submit them, whole or in part, as your own work this is plagiarism. Together, word-processing and the internet have opened up huge opportunities for cheating. However, not all the technology is on the cheats' side. Plagiarism detectors are increasingly sophisticated, making it quite likely that you will be caught if you substitute the words of others for your own. Just as it takes moments for a search engine to trawl the internet, it takes little time to scan your assignment searching for matches with other work. Universities tend to come down hard on plagiarism as it threatens the integrity of assessment and awards systems. Plagiarising other people's assignments is not an intelligent risk to take.

9.4.4 Theft of intellectual property

The ICT age has placed new emphasis on the concept of intellectual property. Now that most texts are produced in electronic form and many are accessible on the internet it is extremely easy, with a little copying and pasting, to 'capture' other people's words and images and reuse them. You might easily do this without ill will. You see a well-expressed idea and grab it for your electronic files, so that you can think about it some more. So far so good. You are allowed to take a copy for private study purposes, and it's fine to quote from these sources, provided you make clear which words are quoted and give a reference. However, when you are writing something of your own if you incorporate borrowed words without any acknowledgement, this becomes plagiarism. If you then publish what you write, whether conventionally or on the internet, it also becomes theft of intellectual property and an infringement of copyright laws.

> ## BOX 9.1 GOVERNMENT ADVICE ON INTELLECTUAL PROPERTY
>
> [T]here are a number of exceptions to copyright that allow limited use of copyright works without the permission of the copyright owner. For example, limited use of works may be possible for non-commercial research and private study, criticism or review [...] teaching in schools and other educational establishments [...] But if you are copying large amounts of material and/or making multiple copies then you may still need permission. Also [...] it is generally necessary to include an acknowledgement.
>
> *(UK Patent Office, 2002a)*
>
> Under UK law copyright material sent over the Internet or stored on web servers will generally be protected in the same way as material in other media. Anyone wishing to [...] download material that others have placed on the Internet, should ensure that they have the permission of the owners of rights in the material unless copyright exceptions apply.
>
> *(UK Patent Office, 2004b)*

Key points

The accessibility of online information is open to a number of abuses:

■ It is easy to be seduced by the immense availability of information into a kind of 'beachcombing'. Confusing information with knowledge, you can wander from website to website collecting mental flotsam, instead of working seriously and coherently with new ideas.

■ It can be tempting to duck the mental challenge of an assignment by assembling your accumulated flotsam and presenting it as your finished assignment. This leads to very poor academic work.

■ A further temptation is to plagiarise – to trawl the web for an assignment on the same topic to present as your own. This is an increasingly risky strategy that can bring harsh penalties.

■ The texts you find online are the intellectual property of the person who published them. It is important to be aware of intellectual property rights and to avoid breaking copyright law.

9.5 Conclusion

The internet has transformed access to information of all kinds, as well as communications between teachers, students and universities. In a sense it has torn down the walls of academia and opened up access, both *into* university knowledge systems, and *out from* university departments to other universities and the wider world. But, transformations create new challenges. To be information literate in your field, it is now necessary to be skilled in online searching, in finding your way round the main online gateways and databases in your field, and in evaluating and making appropriate use of what you find. Indeed, skills in working with online information have become vital not only to success as a student, but to competence as a member of a 'knowledge society'.

> ### Key points
>
> - Information literacy is a basic life-skill for modern living. It involves recognising when you need information and knowing where and how to search for it.
>
> - The technical side of online searching can be picked up very quickly. The skill lies in your search strategy – choosing words shrewdly and excluding what you don't want.
>
> - It is important to set up a web address filing system, so that you can quickly find your way back to key sites.
>
> - To find academic articles and electronic journals you need to know the key gateways and academic databases in your field.
>
> - Being able to find information is not enough: you have to be able to evaluate its quality. Anyone can put information on a website. Critical-analytical skills are as important for online information as for print.
>
> - Access to online information has been an inestimable boon to students, but it is open to abuse. It can lead to very poor study habits and low marks. It is important to be aware of the pitfalls and to learn how to avoid them.

References

American Library Association (1989) *Presidential Committee on Information Literacy: Final Report*, Chicago, American Library Association.

Appleby, D. (2004) *Puppy Socialisation and Habituation*, The Association of Pet Behaviour Counsellors, www.apbc.org.uk/article5.htm (accessed 27 January 2004).

Cambridge Dictionaries Online (2004) *Cambridge Dictionaries Online*, Cambridge University Press, http://dictionary.cambridge.org/, s.v. 'paradox' (accessed 27 January 2004).

Copsey, G. (2004) *Live in a world with no problems: Using The Impossibility Transformer*, Live In A World With No Problems, www.live-in-a-world-with-no-problems.com/ (accessed 30 January 2004).

Google (2004a) *GoogleUK*, www.google.co.uk/, s.v. 'happiness' and 'research happiness' (accessed 27 January 2004).

Google (2004b) 'Google: Advanced Search', *GoogleUK*, www.google.co.uk/advanced_search?hl=en (accessed January 27 2004).

Google (2004c) 'Google: Advanced Search', *GoogleUK*, www.google.co.uk/advanced_search?hl=en, s.v. 'quality of life' 'research' (accessed 27 January 2004).

HEFCE (2004) 'Enhancing excellence in learning and teaching', *HEFCE strategic plan 2003-08*, www.hefce.ac.uk/Pubs/hefce/2004/04_17/ (accessed 28 January 2004).

Kluwer (2004) *Journal of Happiness Studies*, Kluwer Online, www.kluweronline.com/issn/1389-4978 (accessed 27 January 2004).

OCLC Online Computer Library Center (2004) *OCLC FirstSearch*, http://firstsearch.oclc.org/ (accessed 27 January 2004).

Sedona Training Associates (2004) *The Sedona Method*, www.sedona.com (accessed 30 January 2004).

Social Science Information Gateway (2004) *Your Guide to the Best of the Web for Social Science*, SOSIG, www.sosig.ac.uk/ (accessed 27 January 2004).

TERENA (2001) 'Choosing a Search Tool', *Guide to Network Resource Tools*, www.hgmp.mrc.ac.uk/Documentation/gnrt/websearch/choosing.html (accessed January 2004).

The Open University Library (2001a) *SAFARI*, www.open.ac.uk/safari/ (accessed 27 January 2004)

The Open University Library (2001b) 'Section 5 Evaluating Information', *SAFARI*, www.open.ac.uk/safari/ (accessed 27 January 2004).

The Open University Library (2003a) *Search Open Library*, http://library12.open.ac.uk:8080/kbroker/search.jsp, s.v. 'happiness' (accessed 2 September 2004).

The Open University Library (2003b) *Open Library Finder*, http://library12.open.ac.uk:8080/kbroker/search.jsp, s.v. 'quality of life' (accessed 2 September 2004).

The Open University Library (2003c) *Social Sciences: Social Policy - Useful Internet Links*, http://library.open.ac.uk/bysubject/socialscience/socialpolicy/socsci_socialpolicy_websites.html (accessed 2 September 2004).

Think Right Now! International (2004) *Thinkright now!*, www.thinkrightnow.com/ (accessed 30 January 2004).

UK Patent Office (2002a) *FAQ: Copyright: Are there any exceptions to copyright?*, Intellectual-property.gov.uk, www.intellectual-property. gov.uk/std/faq/copyright/exceptions.htm (accessed 30 January 2004).

UK Patent Office (2002b) *FAQ: Copyright: Is material on the Internet protected by copyright?*, Intellectual-property.gov.uk, www.intellectual-property.gov.uk/std/faq/copyright/internet.htm (accessed 30 January 2004).

Veenhoven, R. (2004a) *World Database of Happiness*, www.eur.nl/fsw/research/happiness (accessed 27 January 2004).

Veenhoven, R. (2004b) 'Research Field Quality of Life', *World Database of Happiness*, www.eur.nl/fsw/research/happiness (accessed 27 January 2004).

Veenhoven, R. (2004c) 'Research Field Quality of Life', s.v. 'Journals', *World Database of Happiness*, www.eur.nl/fsw/research/happiness (accessed 27 January 2004).

yourDictionary.com (2004) *Quick*Lookup*, yourDictionary.com, www.yourdictionary.com/, s.v. 'paradox' and 'habituation' (accessed 27 January 2004).

CHAPTER 10 WRITING THE WAY 'THEY' WANT

> In my experience the most important thing is to write the way they want. You can write all kinds of stuff you know about, but you don't get good marks unless you write it the proper way.

10.1 Getting to grips with writing

Of all aspects of studying, writing is perhaps the most challenging. It's also the most rewarding, at least in retrospect. This is no accident.

10.1.1 The importance of writing

Writing is not simply a chore that you endure for the purposes of *assessment*. It's an essential part of the learning process. When you look back over a course, you will find that those subjects on which you have written assignments are the ones that you remember best and understand most clearly.

Deepening your learning

See Chapter 4 Section 4.4.3, Speaking

One reason why assignment writing is especially demanding is that it forces you into a deep and powerful kind of learning. In earlier chapters I have talked about how you absorb ideas from books and lectures. However, until you are able to *use* the ideas of a subject to *say* things for yourself, you haven't really *learned* them. Ideas only become a properly functioning part of your thought processes when you can call on them in *expressing* yourself to other people. One way of doing this is through talking about new ideas with others. But the most effective way is to argue a case in writing.

Developing your writing skills

Writing assignments significantly develops your powers of self-expression, and in our society, being able to write clearly and persuasively is an extremely valuable skill. You may eventually discover that the most significant thing you have gained from your studies is the ability to write much more effectively. This is as likely whether you start with a relatively weak writing style or with a well-developed one. Wherever you start from, there is valuable progress to be made.

Doing yourself justice

On many higher level courses, the bulk of assessment is done through writing. Consequently, your results are affected throughout by your ability to write the kinds of answers required. So, investing time in developing your writing skills can be critically important. *You may find that it pays to spend a little less time on mainstream coursework in order to allow more time for developing writing skills; otherwise you risk getting less credit than you deserve for your learning.*

Key points

Writing is a key part of studying for three reasons:

- It deepens your *learning* of the subject that you are studying.

- It strengthens your powers of *self-expression*.

- It is the major medium through which your progress is *assessed*.

10.1.2 Different kinds of writing

There are various kinds of writing which you might do on a course – some 'academic' and some more 'professionally' oriented. The more *academic* types of writing focus on ideas, research and debates between theoretical perspectives. They involve skills in developing a clear and forceful line of analysis and argument. Different subject areas have their own styles and emphases, but they share what we can call the critical–analytical mode of writing. For such courses, the essay is the most common form of writing, whether in coursework or in exams. And although a growing emphasis is placed on other forms of assessment, the essay retains its central role. Styles of essay vary to some extent between subject areas; but basic techniques can be applied, with a bit of adjustment, in most subjects. So, although developing an effective essay-writing style is a fairly long learning process, you can continue with it from course to course through your studies.

See Chapter 4 Section 4.3, Why do they write that way?

The more *professionally* oriented types of writing emphasise your ability to understand real-life situations, pick out salient features and write about the issues they raise, as well as possible courses of action. They involve, for example, reports, diaries, problem analyses and reflective accounts of work experience. These more 'practical' modes of writing tend to address the needs of particular areas of professional training and may involve links to specific work situations.

This chapter focuses on *essays*, the more 'academic' type of writing. Because developing writing skills tends to be a long haul, you may want to find out what type of writing your course involves before going any further, particularly if you are taking a more professionally-oriented programme of studies. You may find it frustrating having developed skills for one kind of writing to find yourself criticised for using them in a different context. On the other hand, the various modes of writing are not utterly different and many higher level courses do require essays at some stage. So, working on your essay writing skills may be a good investment anyway. If in doubt, ask your course department for advice.

10.1.3 Writing essays

What is an essay?

The original meaning of the word 'essay' was a *first attempt* or a *practice*, but it now has the more general meaning of *a short piece of writing on a set topic*.

- An essay begins with a *title* which sets out the issues that it will address.

- It takes the form of an *argument* which leads the reader from the title at the beginning to a conclusion at the end.

The challenge of essay writing

The nature of the challenge of essay writing depends, to an extent, on your cultural background and your personal language history. Essays can be a big leap from the language environment of your normal life. If you have had little contact with the kind of formal, controlled language used in essays, you may need to focus more time on your writing skills. (You can find an interesting exercise in exploring your language history on the Open University's Learner's Guide website (Open University, 2004).) It's a good idea to do this early on in your studies, as you are more likely to get advice and support at this stage. Don't hold back, thinking you have more important priorities to attend to in your studies, your writing may be the most important. Everyone can develop a serviceable essay technique eventually, but how long it takes will depend on where you are starting from. If you have further to travel, you need to invest more time.

Writing is not an extra you can tack on to the end of your other study activities. It requires serious effort and plenty of time. Because it is challenging it's always tempting to put off writing until the very last minute, but this is a big mistake. You risk missing out on learning the course content in depth and on developing your writing potential to the full.

Getting help

In developing your writing it is extremely helpful to have support from teachers. Your teachers will be able to give you feedback through your assignment work, and your university support services may offer general help with essay writing skills.

It is also an excellent idea to swap essay plans and marked essays with other students and share writing strategies and tips. This is *not* cheating, as long as you then write your own essays. By comparing your approach with that of others you can gain insight into your own writing. Letting people see your work is daunting at first, but once you have broken the barriers, other students are often as useful as teachers in giving you feedback and new ideas.

Developing your essay writing skills

To develop your essay writing skills you need to address two basic questions:

1   What is a good essay?

2   How can I set about producing one?

We shall consider the first question in this chapter and the second in Chapter 11. Much of the discussion in this chapter is based around short sample essays. The two main essays are in Section 10.2. You will need to work on this first to get the full force of Sections 10.3 to 10.6 and 10.8.1. Sections 10.7 and 10.8.2 can be read separately.

> ### Key points
>
> ■ This chapter focuses on essay writing. If you are studying a professionally oriented course you may want to get advice on the relevance of essay writing skills before going further.

- Developing your essay writing can be a significant challenge if you are unfamiliar with more formal writing. Make sure you give it the time it requires.

- Don't keep worries to yourself. Seek help from teachers and from other students.

10.2 What are you meant to write?

A perplexing thing about essay writing is that it can be difficult to get a clear idea of what is wanted. Writing seems to be treated as a private activity. You know what *your* essays look like and what your teachers say about *them*, but you have very little idea what *other people's* essays are like and what comments *they* receive back. You might be told that your essays ought to be more structured, or less subjective, but you don't really know what a *more structured* or *more objective* essay would look like. It's unnerving. You are left sailing in the dark, without landmarks to steer by, so it's not much help being advised to head for the harbour and avoid the rocks.

One of the best ways to find out about what is expected in an essay is to see what other students write. This is not so that you can *copy* someone else's style, it's to broaden your vision of the possible ways you might approach an essay. In this chapter we explore two short essays about the Richard Layard article discussed in Chapters 5 and 6. The writers were mature students on an access course (you met them in Chapter 5). This is the task they were set:

Write a short essay of 300 to 400 words on the following:

As our society gets wealthier, are we doomed to become ever more unhappy? Discuss in the light of the Richard Layard article.

The word limit here is unusually low, simply to keep this chapter manageable. A target of somewhere between 1,000 to 2,000 words would be more usual – allowing more space for you to develop your ideas and bring in relevant material. Nevertheless, these short pieces help to reveal the essential principles of essay writing.

BOX 10.1   RECOMMENDED PREPARATION

You are recommended to read the rest of this chapter *after* you have worked on Chapter 5 Section 5.2, which guides you through reading Richard Layard's article. You will also find it useful to have at least glanced at the notes on Layard's article in Chapter 6 Section 6.2.1. Knowing what the article is about will enable you to understand the writing challenge the students faced and judge how well they succeeded. It will also help a lot when following my discussion of their essays throughout this chapter.

Making copies of the essays

Although the essays are printed here in this chapter it will be easier to work with copies since you will be 'marking' and improving them. You can download these from the Good Study Guide website at www.goodstudyguide.co.uk. Then you can print off several copies and write on them without inhibition.

Activity 10.1

Read the essays by Lewis and Erin on the pages that follow (or your downloaded copies of them).

1 As you read:

(a) mark any places where you find it hard to get the point

(b) jot any questions in the margins, along with other points that come to you

(c) write in alterations you think could usefully be made.

2 When you have finished reading both essays, take a sheet of paper and write two headings: 'Strengths' and 'Weaknesses'. Note down the best and the weakest things about Lewis's essay.

Do the same for Erin's essay.

3 Try to weigh up the quality of the two essays:

■ Do you think one of the essays is better than the other?

■ Are they good in different ways?

■ Overall, do you think that they are good essays?

■ Are you judging mainly in terms of the *ideas* in the essays, or on how the essays are *written*?

4 Imagine you are Lewis's and Erin's teacher. Write a few sentences to each of them to help with their future writing.

5 Finally, look back over:

■ your lists of strengths and weaknesses

■ your advice to the two students, and

■ your conclusions regarding the overall quality of the essays.

Can you draw any general conclusions about the qualities a good essay should have? Write the heading 'Qualities of a good essay' and see what you can jot down under it.

BOX 10.2 DEVELOPING YOUR JUDGEMENT OF WRITING

Activity 10.1 is demanding. You may find that you can't complete all parts of it at this stage in your skills development, however *try to do as much as you can*. It's time well invested, because you need to develop your ability to judge what works well in writing. You don't become a good writer by learning *formal 'rules'*. Instead, you become a *reasonably good judge* of pieces of writing, including your own. 'Marking' other people's work is an excellent way of deepening your grasp of what it is you are aiming for in your own writing.

Here are the two essays I received. The first, from Lewis, came with a note saying 'Sorry Andy, I had no time to do the essay the way I would of liked to. I thought something was better than nothing. Lewis.'

Lewis's essay

As our society gets wealthier, are we doomed to become ever more unhappy? Discuss in the light of the Richard Layard article.

I will discuss in the light of Richard Layards article whether as the nation gets richer we are doomed to become ever more unhappy?

You would think women would be hapier because there pay and job opportunities has improved. Women can do the same job as men with the same demands and responsibilities and they still get less pay, this might be one reason why women are less happy than men within the work environment.

Richard Layard looked at all different surveys taken in US, Japan, Continental Europe and Britain to look for evidence to see if we are doomed to become ever more unhappy.

The past fifty years are society has become richer because of this we have better health and quality of life but does this mean as a society we will be a happier one?

He looked at a study showing on average rich people are happier than poorer. People earning more money was 41 per cent 'very happy' compared with people on a lower scale of income which shows 29 per cent.

It was revealed in 2000 that as many as 29 per cent of women aged 30 suffered with nerves or feeling low, depressed or sad, compared with a similar survey among those aged 36 in 1982 which was just 16 per cent. But perhaps it is because as a society we are more aware of depression there is less stigma attached to it. This could be why reports of depression have increased. Living life in the fast lane could also contribute to the depression level.

It seems the more other people have, the more we want. We all want to large it. We cant be happy with the fact that we have free NHS, because a rich man can afford Private Care we want the same and we do not want to wait for Health Care. The class gap is so big.

(315 words)

Erin's essay

As our society gets wealthier, are we doomed to become ever more unhappy? Discuss in the light of the Richard Layard article.

People go to great lengths to gain happiness, and many assume that money is an automatic route to achieving it. However, evidence presented by Richard Layard suggests that this is not the case. Over the past 50 years society has changed dramatically. People have many more material possessions and higher quality services, yet there are no signs of increasing happiness. Instead there seems to be rising dissatisfaction and depression.

As we might expect, wealthier people are generally happier than poorer. According to Layard 41% of the richest quarter of the population say they are very happy, but just 26% of the poorest quarter. Yet, surprisingly, overall levels of happiness have not risen as wealth has risen. Meanwhile, serious unhappiness seems to be increasing. For example, studies found that for women in their thirties clinical depression almost doubled over two decades (Layard, 2003, p. 25).

Layard argues that one reason rising wealth has not brought happiness is that we live in a highly competitive society and we are all aware of people within our 'reference groups' better off than us. It is as if we are 'polluted' by their wealth. Just as someone enjoying loud music creates noise pollution for people in their neighbourhood, so someone enjoying a rising income pollutes the happiness of other people in their family or workplace. We even pollute our own happiness, because we get 'habituated' to high standards of living.

'On the principle that the polluter should pay', says Layard, we should tax the extra income which causes the pollution. If this money is then spent in the community, it will make society feel less competitive. 'The electorate now understands that the scramble to spend more is partially self defeating [...] [and is] more favourable to public expenditure.' (Layard, 2003, p. 26).

From this point of view, it seems that, unless we reduce the competitiveness of our society, for example by using taxes to repair the 'pollution' caused by wealth, then we really are doomed to increasing unhappiness in a world of increasing plenty.

References

Layard, R. (2003) The Secrets of Happiness, *New Statesman*, 3 March 2003.

(338 words)

In Sections 10.3–10.6 I discuss the points that struck me as I read these two essays. I expect you will find that you have picked out many of the same points. There's no great mystery about what is good writing and what is not. Good writing is easy to read and makes sense. Poor writing is unclear and confusing; it keeps making you stop to try to work out what it's saying and where it's going.

10.3 Argument and structure

Which essay did you find easiest to read? For me it was definitely Erin's. As I read Lewis's essay I was uncertain where it was going. There were interesting points, but no real sense of direction. Erin's on the other hand flows as an 'argument'.

10.3.1 Presenting an argument

It's clear that Erin has worked out a sequence of points for her essay, with links from one to the next. Look carefully at how the logic flows in her first paragraph:

People go to great lengths to gain happiness, and many assume that money is an automatic route to achieving it. However, evidence presented by Richard Layard suggests that this is not the case. Over the past 50 years society has changed dramatically. People have many more material possessions and higher quality services, yet there are no signs of increasing happiness. Instead there seems to be rising dissatisfaction and depression.

Erin's sentences pass on the logical flow from one to the next, as shown in Table 10.1 (the numbers refer to sentences):

Table 10.1 The logical flow of Erin's sentences	
Erin's sentences	**Contribution to the argument**
1(a) People go to great lengths to gain happiness	Takes up the theme from the essay title, which connects wealth to unhappiness: notes that happiness is a fundamental goal of human action.
1(b) and many assume that money is an automatic route to achieving it.	then points to the common assumption that happiness can be pursued through money.
2 However, evidence presented by Richard Layard suggests that this is not the case.	Connects with the reference to Layard in the essay title: signals that his article will provide evidence casting doubt on the assumption just mentioned.

3	Over the past 50 years society has changed dramatically.	Sets a context for the evidence by specifying a time frame and the theme of large-scale social change.
4(a)	People have many more material possessions and higher quality services	Gives more detail on the social change theme and ties it in with the theme of wealth.
4(b)	yet there are no signs of increasing happiness.	Signals the key line of argument: that levels of happiness do not run in parallel with levels of wealth.
5	Instead there seems to be rising dissatisfaction and depression.	Amplifies the point by linking rising unhappiness to rising wealth.

I am not suggesting that Erin thought it all out in the same detailed way. I would guess that she worked intuitively and wrote what made sense to her. However, this analysis shows that she has a strong sense of purpose in the way she writes. What she says links back to the title and forward to her unfolding argument. Consequently, as readers, we have a clear sense of direction. We are carried along by the flow and the sense of purpose.

With Lewis's essay the flow of his argument isn't nearly so clear:

I will discuss in the light of Richard Layards article whether as the nation gets richer we are doomed to become ever more unhappy?

You would think women would be hapier because there pay and job opportunities has improved. Women can do the same job as men with the same demands and responsibilities and they still get less pay, this might be one reason why women are less happy than men within the work environment.

It isn't obvious why he moves from talking about 'the nation' in his opening sentence, to 'women' in the next. Nor is it clear how the third sentence follows on from the second. When you have read it a couple of times, you can see that he means something like 'However, although women can often get the same jobs as men, they do not yet get the same pay, which makes them more dissatisfied, rather than happier'. If he followed on with 'This illustrates Layard's argument that we are more concerned with how our incomes compare with other people's than the actual size of our incomes.' this could then lead him into explaining Layard's basic argument – and we would be able to follow the flow. Instead he leaps to talking about the different countries of the world which Layard refers to.

You can tell that in Lewis's head there were probably links between all the points he makes in his essay, but they are not set out clearly so that we can see them. Consequently, we can't properly follow what he's trying to get across. He has not succeeded in presenting a line of argument that we can follow.

BOX 10.3   ARGUMENT

An essay should read as a logical argument, with each point following on clearly from the preceding one. Ideally:

1   The argument in an essay should run from the *title* through to the *conclusion*, without breaks.

2   *Everything* in the essay should contribute in some way to the argument.

3   Anything which *doesn't* contribute should be *left out*.

This isn't easy to achieve, but it's what you aim for.

10.3.2 Answering the question

As well as finding Erin's essay *easier* to read, I also found it more *satisfying*, because it ends up answering the question raised in the title. Her final paragraph gives an answer in the form: 'Yes – unless X happens'. In other words, a conditional 'Yes'.

From this point of view, it seems that, unless we reduce the competitiveness of our society, for example by using taxes to repair the 'pollution' caused by wealth, then we really are doomed to increasing unhappiness in a world of increasing plenty.

Erin signals that this answer depends on accepting Layard's point of view, as sketched out in her preceding paragraphs, so we know how she has arrived at her answer. It is not suddenly sprung upon us, it flows from the line of argument that runs through her essay.

Lewis's ending, on the other hand, leaves us hanging in the air.

It seems the more other people have, the more we want. We all want to large it. We cant be happy with the fact that we have free NHS, because a rich man can afford Private Care we want the same and we do not want to wait for Health Care. The class gap is so big.

He ends with a remark about the class gap, but this seems to come out of the blue and is not linked in any obvious way to the question in the title. The first sentence of the paragraph does imply that we won't get happier, but nowhere does he offer a view on whether we are 'doomed to become ever more *unhappy*'. So, regardless of how good or bad his points here are, they don't achieve the primary aim of a concluding paragraph, which is to offer some kind of answer to the question asked. This is bound to affect his mark.

BOX 10.4   MAKE IT CLEAR THAT YOU HAVE ANSWERED THE QUESTION

Your *primary purpose* in an essay is to arrive, in the final paragraph, at an *answer* to the question posed in the title. (Not all titles contain a 'question' as such, but always there is some issue to be resolved.) The answer doesn't have to be a 'yes' or a 'no'. It can be a 'maybe', 'it depends', 'partly yes and partly no', or, like Erin's, 'yes, unless', or a variety of other responses. The key thing is to show that your essay has addressed the specific challenge you were set.

10.3.3 Showing what you mean

Another thing that Erin does well is to explain what she means. For example, when she says:

Over the past 50 years society has changed dramatically.

she doesn't leave us to guess what she is talking about. Her next sentence begins by telling us:

People have many more material possessions and higher quality services.

And when she writes about the unusual and rather challenging idea that wealth has a 'polluting' effect, she introduces the example of noise pollution to illustrate how the idea works:

It is as if we are 'polluted' by their wealth. Just as someone enjoying loud music creates noise pollution for people in their neighbourhood, so someone enjoying a rising income pollutes the happiness of other people in their family or workplace.

We can see that Erin isn't just bluffing when she talks about society changing, or about pollution by wealth. She shows that she can explain herself. Lewis also uses a helpful example when he refers to our attitudes towards the National Health Service, to illustrate his point that we always want more than we have:

It seems the more other people have, the more we want. [...] We cant be happy with the fact that we have free NHS, because a rich man can afford Private Care we want the same and we do not want to wait for Health Care.

Illustrations and explanations help your reader to see the force of your argument. But they also demonstrate to your teacher that you understand what you are talking about.

BOX 10.5   SPELL IT OUT

Things you write can seem perfectly obvious to *you*, but be utterly obscure to a *reader*. Indeed, if you come back after several months to something you've written yourself, you can often find your *own words* mystifying. It is important to remind yourself that your reader cannot see into your mind. *Your points often need more explanation than you think.* It's always a good policy to take the time to spell things out clearly.

I try to be clear and develop points. I don't assume that my reader knows what the topic is about. Explain, explain, explain.

Yes, I do tend to take too much for granted in the reader and forget to give the really basic info that would give my essays a solid basis.

Definitely. I just assumed I was being clear, but when I got my essay back (and had forgotten some of the topic) I couldn't follow some of my own points!

10.3.4 Backing up your argument

As well as enabling readers to follow your argument, you also need to convince them of it. You can't just make a point and expect a reader to take your word for it. For example, at the end of his sixth paragraph Lewis says:

Living life in the fast lane could also contribute to the depression level.

But what exactly does he mean by this? And why should we take him seriously? He has not offered any *evidence*. He has not suggested that any recognised *expert* believes this to be the case. Perhaps it's a valuable insight – but perhaps not. To make us take any notice of it, Lewis needs to back it up. He should give us grounds to take it seriously. Otherwise, the point is worth very little; a reader will just ignore it.

When Erin makes a point she generally backs it up. For example, when she claims that:

wealthier people are generally happier than poorer

She provides evidence of this in the very next sentence:

According to Layard 41% of the richest quarter of the population say they are very happy, but just 26% of the poorest quarter.

Because she backs her points up, her argument is much more compelling.

BOX 10.6   CONVINCE YOUR READER

Give your reader grounds for taking a point seriously. Offer evidence, or quote an authority.

10.3.5 Bringing in concepts, cases and authors from the course

The point of writing essays is to give yourself the opportunity to take hold of ideas and information presented in the course and practise using them. Your teacher is primarily interested in how well you rise to this challenge. An essay is not the place to show off your general knowledge.

Erin shows her careful reading of Layard's article by taking some of Layard's terms such as 'reference groups', 'polluted', and 'habituated', and using them correctly. She also brings in some of the research Layard discusses, such as the surveys of happiness and depression. And she frequently refers to Layard. It is very clear that Erin is not answering off the top of her head, but on the basis of her reading of Layard's article. Lewis likewise draws in some of the survey material, but he doesn't keep Layard as clearly in the frame, nor use Layard's terms and concepts as much as Erin does. This means he isn't able to demonstrate such a thorough grasp of Layard's ideas and arguments.

BOX 10.7   DISPLAY YOUR KNOWLEDGE OF THE COURSE

The main substance of an essay should come directly from your studies. Construct your arguments using what you've read and heard within the course (unless you are specifically instructed to do otherwise). Don't be tempted to bring in lots of extraneous knowledge. It's very hard for teachers to judge material they are unfamiliar with. And they are usually working with a marking guide based on what is taught within the course.

 I find you have to relate everything back to the course work – it's what you get out of the books that counts.

10.3.6 Structuring the argument

One more difference that struck me as I compared Lewis's and Erin's essays, is the way that they are structured. In Section 10.3.1 we saw how in Erin's essay the argument flows continuously from sentence to sentence, but in Lewis's the flow often gets lost.

The same is true if we step back and take a broader look at how the argument flows from paragraph to paragraph through the essay as a whole. Erin's essay runs like this:

Paragraph 1: Introduction *explains the issue* presented in the *title question*, from Layard's point of view.

Paragraph 2: Presents *a selection* of Layard's *evidence* to back up his basic proposition.

Paragraph 3: Summarises Layard's *explanation* for our not getting happier.

Paragraph 4: Outlines Layard's *proposed action*, following from his explanation.

Paragraph 5: Conclusion *answers the question* in the light of Layard's evidence and arguments.

I can see a clear logic to this sequence of paragraphs. Each takes the argument a step forward, from the title question towards the conclusion. With Lewis's essay I found it harder to see a logic. Lewis's essay runs like this:

Paragraph 1: Introduction repeats the essay *title* with the words slightly reorganised.

Paragraph 2: Considers why *women* are not happier, in spite of advances in pay and opportunities.

Paragraph 3: Indicates the nature of Layard's review of *research*.

Paragraph 4: Re-states the *title question*.

Paragraph 5: Outlines some of Layard's *evidence*.

Paragraph 6: Outlines more of Layard's *evidence*.

Paragraph 7: Conclusion begins to *summarise* but then adds some *new points*.

Can *you* see a logic to this sequence? Or, perhaps more to the point, can you see a way to *reorganise* Lewis's paragraph sequence to make things flow better?

Activity 10.2

If you have downloaded a copy of Lewis's essay from the Good Study Guide website, save a copy with a new name, such as 'Lewis reorganised'. (If you haven't downloaded the essay, do it now.)

Now open the new copy in your word-processor, as shown in Figure 10.1.

You can see that I've selected paragraph 4 of Lewis's essay in Figure 10.1. This is because I think this paragraph would make a better opening for his essay than paragraph 1.

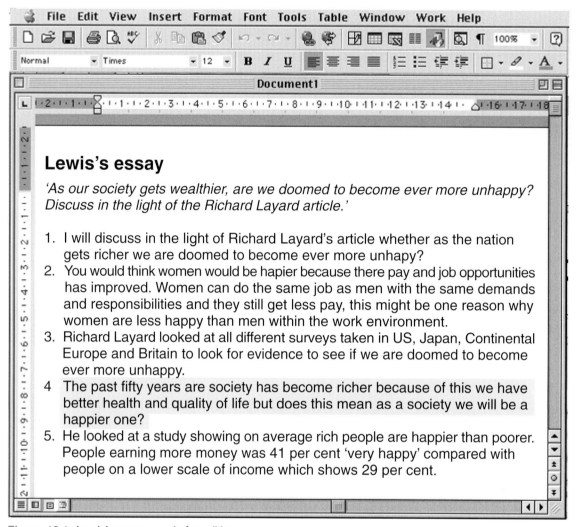

Figure 10.1 Lewis's essay, ready for editing

Lewis's essay

'As our society gets wealthier, are we doomed to become ever more unhappy? Discuss in the light of the Richard Layard article.'

1. I will discuss in the light of Richard Layard's article whether as the nation gets richer we are doomed to become ever more unhapy?
2. You would think women would be hapier because there pay and job opportunities has improved. Women can do the same job as men with the same demands and responsibilities and they still get less pay, this might be one reason why women are less happy than men within the work environment.
3. Richard Layard looked at all different surveys taken in US, Japan, Continental Europe and Britain to look for evidence to see if we are doomed to become ever more unhappy.
4 The past fifty years are society has become richer because of this we have better health and quality of life but does this mean as a society we will be a happier one?
5. He looked at a study showing on average rich people are happier than poorer. People earning more money was 41 per cent 'very happy' compared with people on a lower scale of income which shows 29 per cent.

Activity 10.3

In your open copy of Lewis's essay:

1 Select paragraph 4, then drag and drop it in front of the existing first paragraph. (Use the 'Undo' facility if anything goes wrong, then try again.)

2 Select the original introductory paragraph (paragraph 1) and delete it. It doesn't add anything to the essay, it simply repeats the title.

3 Then spend a while moving the other paragraphs around, to see if you can find a sequence which seems to flow better. You may want to run some of the paragraphs together. The paragraph numbers will change as you work, so you may lose track of what you've done. But remember

you can always start again by making another copy of the original essay or by using 'Undo'.

4   When you've finished, save your file and print it off.

There isn't a correct answer to this activity. You could make Lewis's argument flow in various ways. I didn't actually reorganise very much, I just moved the paragraph focusing on women near to the end, because it was more specific. I felt it would be better to start with the general and move towards the specific. I also ran two paragraphs together.

My revised sequence of paragraphs for Lewis's essay ended up like this:

Paragraph 1: Comments on the *title question* (old paragraph 4).

Paragraph 2: Indicates the nature of Layard's review of *research,* then outlines some of Layard's *evidence* (old paragraphs 3 and 5).

Paragraph 3: Outlines more of Layard's *evidence* (old paragraph 6).

Paragraph 4: Considers why *women* are not happier, in spite of advances in pay and opportunities (old paragraph 2).

Paragraph 5: Conclusion (old paragraph 7).

Can you see the logic to this new sequence? How does it compare with yours? It's not the product of blinding insight, just a pragmatic untangling and straightening out the sequence of points.

Activity 10.4

Make another copy of Lewis's essay and try reorganising into the sequence I've suggested. Then print it off and read it to see whether it works any better.

Even reorganised into the new sequence, Lewis's essay remains fairly difficult to read, because of its other weaknesses. However, it does have a bit more of a flow to it and could now be worked up into a stronger piece of writing. (You can find a reworked version on the Good Study Guide website.)

The way in which paragraphs are organised gives an essay its structure. The most basic level of structure is to have an opening paragraph, some middle paragraphs and a concluding paragraph. Both Erin and Lewis knew about this. But then there is the more thought-provoking task of working out a sequence for the 'middle' paragraphs. Generally you need to group related points into clusters, so that they can be discussed together. You then make a paragraph for each cluster. A straightforward structure like Erin's: introduction, evidence, explanation, implications, and conclusion can be very effective. Sections 11.2.6 and 11.4 in Chapter 11 discuss how to do this. For now, the main point is to recognise the importance of structure in making Erin's essay clear and powerful, and the extent to which poor structure weakens Lewis's essay.

> ## BOX 10.8 GIVE YOUR ESSAY A STRUCTURE
>
> When people say writing 'lacks structure' they mean that it moves along without any obvious sequence or direction. The reader has to struggle from point to point and try to guess what it's all meant to be about.
>
> To write a good essay, you have to think about the order in which you want to cover things, then sketch out a plan for yourself. It doesn't have to be 'clever', a simple structure is generally fine.

Exploring the strengths and weaknesses of Erin's and Lewis's essays has revealed how important it is for an essay to have an *argument* which *answers the question* in the title. This is important because working out your argument tests your *understanding* of the ideas and information you have been studying. And developing it into a *well organised* and *convincing* argument helps you to take control of your new knowledge and learn how to *use* it for yourself.

Key points

- An essay should have an argument running through it, from the title to the conclusion.

- In the conclusion of your essay, show that you have answered the question asked in the title. (If the title doesn't contain a question, make it clear that you have completed whatever task it sets.)

- In presenting your argument, take the time to explain to your reader what you mean. Where helpful, use examples to illustrate your point.

- Don't expect your reader to take your word for things. Back up your points up with evidence, or by referring to the views of other writers on the subject.

- Make use of your new knowledge by bringing in concepts, names and case material from the course.

- Give your essay structure by organising it into a sequence of paragraphs with a logical flow.

10.4 'Proper English'

Another difference you may have noticed between Lewis's and Erin's essays, is that Lewis's written English is less polished than Erin's. On the whole it works reasonably well, but at times it reads awkwardly.

10.4.1 Sentences

Lewis has a sense of what a sentence is, because he writes perfectly good ones, such as: 'This could be why reports of depression have increased'. Some of his sentences are shaky however. Take this example:

Women can do the same job as men with the same demands and responsibilities and they still get less pay, this might be one reason why women are less happy than men within the work environment.

This is punctuated as one sentence, with a capital letter at the beginning and a full stop at the end. But it would work much better as two sentences. Lewis probably sensed this, because he has put a comma where the break should come. If the comma is changed to a full stop and 'this' given a capital 'T', then it reads more comfortably. Try making this change to your copy of his essay, then read the second sentence aloud. You'll 'hear' that it works fine on its own. The first sentence is still a bit rambling, but it's better.

Activity 10.5

Here is another example for you to try. Make a copy of the fourth paragraph from your original copy of Lewis's essay and paste it into a new document:

The past fifty years are society has become richer because of this we have better health and quality of life but does this mean as a society we will be a happier one?

1   Type in 'Over' at the beginning of the paragraph and change the capital letter in 'The' to lower case.

2   Then change 'are' to 'our'.

3   Now insert one or more full stops with capital letters where you think they should be.

4   Make more copies of the original paragraph and play around with other ways of breaking it down into sentences.

I put full stops after 'richer' and after 'life' (and a couple of other small changes) to make it read like this:

Over the past fifty years our society has become richer. Because of this we have better health and quality of life. But does this mean that as a society we are happier?

I now have three short sentences, each of which packs its own punch. The first is a general statement. The second is a conclusion drawn from the first. And the third is a question following on from the second. Again, try reading the passage out loud. When it was all one sentence it began as a statement but meandered off into a question, making it confusing to read. It feels more like a paragraph now (though rather short for a paragraph).

Making three sentences is not the only solution here. I produced another version where I changed 'because of this' to 'because of which', and could then make just two sentences.

Over the past fifty years our society has become richer, because of which we have better health and quality of life. But does this mean that as a society we are happier?

Did you break the paragraph down into similar sentences or did you find a different solution? There's plenty of scope for creativity in playing around with sentences. Incidentally can you see why adding 'over' to the first sentence makes it read better? The phrase 'the past fifty years' was just loitering next to 'our society'. The word 'over' works as a link between 'the past fifty years' and 'society has become richer'.

BOX 10.9   WHAT IS A SENTENCE?

A sentence starts with a capital letter and ends with a full stop, question mark, or exclamation mark. It is a self-contained unit of meaning. In other words, it can stand by itself. 'She rang the bell.' is a sentence, as are the sentences in this paragraph. Try reading each aloud, to check that it works standing on its own.

- Every sentence needs a *verb* – a 'doing' word.

- And virtually every sentence needs a *subject* – the person or thing that is carrying out the 'doing'.

In 'Chloe rang the bell.', 'Chloe' is the subject (because she is 'doing' the ringing) and 'rang' is the verb (because that is what she was 'doing'). A simple test you can apply if you are not sure whether you have written a sentence is to ask, 'Does it have a verb and a subject?' ('does have' is the verb in that sentence and 'it' is the subject).

Many people can 'hear' when a string of words is a sentence, because it 'sounds' complete. They don't have to stop to think whether there is a verb or a subject. But if you find it *isn't* obvious to you, get advice. Look online, get a book, or attend a class. Until you have a reasonable 'feel' for what works as a sentence, you will find it very difficult to develop your writing.

See Chapter 3 Section 3.3.3, Getting help with your writing skills

One way of being able to tell that Lewis's original sentence is too long is to count the verbs. I found 'has become', 'have', 'does mean' and 'will be'. A sentence usually has just one main verb, though it can also have subordinate verbs. Having three main verbs means that too much is going on. Each verb is generating its own momentum. You just can't hold the whole thing in your head.

You will find *websites* offering support with sentence structure if you search for 'grammar'; your own *university* may offer one. Also, your word-processor's *grammar checking* facility should offer some support. It won't be infallible, but it can be useful to have the prompt, to help you double-check what you have written. Make sure you know how the grammar checker works (look under Help if necessary), and when you see a 'mistake' picked out, take the time to find out what might be wrong. In this way you will gradually build up your ability to get things right without needing help. Alternatively, buy a book on grammar, or if you feel in need of more direct help, ask your local library for information about classes.

Grammar can be fiddly and technical, but fortunately you can use it effectively without knowing its rules in a formal way (just as you can live within the laws of the land without knowing them in detail). It can be helpful to read aloud what you write, or get someone else to read it aloud to you. By listening to a sentence on its own (i.e. from one full stop to the next), you may be able to 'hear' where something is missing, or where there are complications. A practical ability to judge what works is more important than detailed knowledge of the technical terms and rules of grammar.

10.4.2 Punctuation

Erin uses punctuation well and, on the whole, so does Lewis. But there are a few slips in Lewis's essay which you might have noticed. I've picked out four mistakes in punctuation in the following extracts. See how many you spot:

It seems the more other people have, the more we want. We all want to large it. We cant be happy with the fact that we have free NHS, because a rich man can afford Private Care we want the same.

I will discuss in the light of Richard Layards article whether as the nation gets richer we are doomed to become ever more unhappy?

Apostrophes

It's common to be confused about apostrophes (') and, in the first extract, Lewis hasn't used any. Although there *is* a word '*cant*' (which means 'insincere moral talk'), Lewis actually means '*can't*', short for '*can not*', or '*cannot*'. Putting in an apostrophe signals that you have left letters out. The same happens when you shorten '*it is*' to '*it's*', or '*rock and roll*' to '*rock n' roll*'. (However, in the phrase 'standing on *its* own' there is no apostrophe. Here 'its' is not shortened. 'Its' is one of seven possessive pronouns along with 'mine', 'his', 'hers', 'ours', 'yours' and 'theirs' that don't require an apostrophe.) Generally you *don't* use shortened forms ('don't', 'can't', etc.) in *essays*, because they are too informal for this mode of writing. I am using them in this book because it's a friendly and helpful guide, not a formal text book.

Lewis has also left out an apostrophe in *'Layard's article'*. When an 's' is put on the end of a word to signal *ownership* or possession of something, then there should be an apostrophe before the 's'. An exception arises when the word already ends in 's' because it is plural. In this case you add an apostrophe for possession, but not another 's', for example you write 'students' bar', not 'students's bar'.

Another common mistake is to use an apostrophe when adding 's' to make a word plural. *'I have three cat's'* is wrong; it should simply be *'I have three cats'*.

Capital letters

Lewis correctly uses capital letters in *'Richard Layard'* and *'NHS'*. Proper names require capital letters as do acronyms like NHS and BBC, in which each letter stands for a whole word. However, *'private care'* does not need capitals, because it isn't a proper name. If it were a company called Private Care, then it would be a proper name and would need capitals.
(I counted these two capitals as one mistake.)

Punctuation marks

At the end of the second extract Lewis has put a question mark, possibly because he copied 'doomed to become ever more unhappy?' from the title, where it *is* part of a question. But Lewis's sentence is *not* a question. It's a statement of what he is going to do. However, he has used punctuation marks quite well elsewhere. I was particularly impressed by his use of a comma part-way through the sentence 'It seems the more other people have, the more we want'. Lewis has sensed that there is a slight pause or shift in the flow of meaning at that point.

Activity 10.6

There are no commas in the following sentences taken from Lewis's essay. Can you see where commas might help?

Women can do the same job as men with the same demands and responsibilities and they still get less pay.

I'd put a comma after 'men', and probably also after 'responsibilities'. This makes the main part of the sentence read 'Women can do the same job as men – and they still get less pay'. The commas mark off 'with same demands and responsibilities' as an extra bit of explanation, adding to the main flow. Without the commas you could mis-read the sentence as 'Women can do the same job – as men with the same demands and responsibilities'. This doesn't make sense, so it will be momentarily confusing.

All this is simply to help you think about how you use punctuation and to check whether you have a reasonable working grasp of what's required. If your punctuation is shaky, you can improve by paying attention to the grammar checker on your word-processor. There are also helpful books, websites and even interactive guides, such as the one illustrated in Chapter 3 Figure 3.4. However, you don't have to be an expert at punctuation to write essays. Reasonable use of full stops, commas and capitals will get you a long way. On the other hand, all your efforts to become confident and consistent with your punctuation will be good news for your readers.

BOX 10.10   PUNCTUATION

Punctuation is a system of signals that you give to your reader to show how the grammar of a sentence is supposed to work. Done well, it makes reading much easier. The basics are the capital letter at the start of a sentence and the full stop at the end. You then use commas to mark off any sub-segments of a sentence, to divide up lists, and so on.

10.4.3 Consistency

Another common problem is having different parts of a sentence that don't match up. Can you see what doesn't match in these extracts from Lewis's essay?

pay and job opportunities has improved

People earning more money was 41 per cent 'very happy' compared with people on a lower scale of income which shows 29 per cent.

Single or plural?

You have to make up your mind whether you are talking about one thing or lots of things. It would be correct to say 'pay *has* improved', because 'pay' is singular. But you would say 'job opportunities *have* improved', because 'job opportunities' are plural. So if you are talking about 'pay *and* job opportunities', you definitely need the *plural* version of the verb 'to have'. Similarly, the word 'people' is plural, so the second sentence should be 'People [...] *were* 'very happy', not 'was'.

Tense

There is another 'glitch' in the second extract from Lewis's essay. 'Was' is in the *past*, whereas 'shows' is *now*. Are we in the past, or the present? We can be in either but not both at the same time.

> ### BOX 10.11 TENSE
>
> The tense of a verb is its setting in time. For example, 'I shout' is set in the present, 'I shouted' is set in the past, and 'I will shout' is set in the future. There are other possibilities, but you don't need to worry about them right now. The main point is to be *consistent* in using tense. Decide whether you are talking about the past, the present, or the future, then stay there, unless you have a good reason for shifting.

We have already looked at this next example. Lewis again seems uncertain about his use of tense.

The past fifty years [our] society has become richer because of this we have better health and quality of life but does this mean as a society we will be a happier one?

As we noted earlier, there are four verbs used here: 'has become' which is set in the past, 'we have' and 'does this mean', which are in the present, and 'we will be' which is in the future. If you divide this passage into three sentences as we did earlier, the shift of tense just about works. But as a single sentence, it's difficult to hold onto a sense of what is happening when.

And while we're on verbs and tense, did you notice the mistake in Lewis's note to me?

I had no time to do the essay the way I would of liked to.

Lewis should have written 'would *have* liked'. Some people think '*would've*' is short for '*would of*'. But actually it's short for '*would have*'. It's quite a common mistake. For example you might say 'I have finished', or, if you were making an excuse, you might say 'I would have finished'. But putting in 'would' does not change '*have* finished' to '*of* finished'. 'Would of' is always wrong.

Broken connections

In the following extract, *what* is it exactly that was 16 per cent?

compared with a similar survey among those aged 36 in 1982 which was just 16 per cent.

'Which' appears to refer back to 'survey'. But the *survey* wasn't 16 per cent. The *figure* for women reporting depression was 16 per cent. In Lewis's mind he's connecting back to an earlier part of the sentence, but he hasn't made that clear. It's easy for your reader to get lost if you don't make the connections obvious. Instead of 'which', it would have been better for Lewis to write 'in which the figure'. This would have made things clear.

These may seem like small points. However, I am not picking them out just for the sake of it. Errors and inconsistencies blur meaning. They slow your reader down and distract them from picking up your meaning. Reading is hard enough, without constantly stumbling over distractions along the way.

BOX 10.12   BREAKING RULES

You may have noticed that I have persistently broken a rule myself. In the fourth sentence in the previous paragraph I referred to 'your reader' as 'them', although the first is singular and the second plural, so breaking the rules of consistency. However, this is a difficult case. I could have said 'him or her' but this is cumbersome. Thirty years ago the convention was to say 'him', and leave the reader to 'understand' that 'her' was also included. But this meant that many texts appeared to refer to an all-male world. In child-care books, for example, the child was always 'he'. This is now unacceptable, but no elegant alternative has been established for 'he or she' and 'him or her'. Some people write s/he, but how is this to be pronounced? I have adopted the alternative convention of using the 'ungendered' plural: 'they' and 'them', even though it reads awkwardly. This is an example of how rules of grammar can legitimately be broken, where other considerations require them to be.

10.4.4 Everyday language

What did you think when Lewis used such phrasing as:

We all want to large it

Living life in the fast lane

Terms such as 'large it' emerge in popular speech and take on a richness of meaning as people pass them around. But vibrant and useful though 'living' language is, it tends to be too loosely defined and changeable for the job of making crisp, precise points in a written argument. Even the phrase 'life in the fast lane', which has been around longer, doesn't really have a precise enough meaning for analytical writing. Do we all live in the fast lane, or just some people? What aspects of our lives is Lewis referring to here? It's a vivid image, but not a well-defined concept. If, for some reason, you *deliberately* choose to use an expression like this, then put quotation marks ('...') around it, to show that you are conscious of your departure from form.

Everyday phrases can look weak and out of place in an essay. It isn't that they are 'bad' language, rather, that they carry a lot of associations and local meanings, and so are not exact enough for the purposes of arguing a case in an essay.

10.4.5 Spelling

Did you see any mistakes in Lewis's spelling? There weren't many. Using his word-processor's spell-checker, he should have been able to intercept most mistakes before handing the essay in. For some reason he hasn't noticed 'unhapy', or 'hapier', which his spell-checker will almost certainly have picked up. However there was another mistake it wouldn't pick up. Did you spot it?

there pay and job opportunities have improved.

It should be '*their* pay and job opportunities'. Because '*there*' is a properly spelt word the spell-checker has left it. But this is the spelling for 'over there', or 'there are'. It's a completely different word. Similarly, when Lewis wrote 'are society', meaning 'our society', the spell-checker left the mistake alone.

Do you lose marks for bad spelling? In principle, no. However, your essay marker is bound to be influenced by work with lots of mistakes in it, whether in spelling, grammar, or punctuation. They detract from the general effect of your essay, as well as making it harder to read. If you want your writing to make its full impact, you really need to make time to read through your work carefully before sending it off to be marked.

If you are very poor at spelling, don't worry that it will hold back your progress, but don't be entirely blasé about it either. There are websites that offer spelling tests and general advice. And when you are not sure about a word it's worth checking it in a dictionary. It would also be useful to start making a list of words that you regularly spell wrongly, so that you can test yourself from time to time. However, it isn't worth setting out on a major campaign to memorise dozens of words. In general, the more you read and write, the more you develop a sense of the broad, though rather idiosyncratic, rules of English spelling.

Having given Lewis's use of English a very thorough going over in this section, it's important to emphasise that it is really quite serviceable. He will certainly benefit from improving on some aspects, but overall it is not difficult to pick up what he's trying to say. While Erin's use of English is already good enough to enable her to express complicated and subtle arguments, Lewis's is more patchy and will make it a bit tougher for him to write clearly about complex subjects. However, if he works at his writing and has good ideas to express, he will still make good progress with his studies.

Key points

■ Good writing for higher level study is primarily to do with the quality of your ideas and arguments. Nevertheless it is important to work at making your written language as technically correct as you can, simply to be able to get your ideas across effectively.

■ Improvement takes time, but regular practice and attention to detail will gradually make a difference. As you begin to gain greater control over your use of language, you will also get more pleasure out of writing.

10.5 Strong, clear writing

While it helps to write 'properly', what really counts is being able to write clearly and forcefully. So how did you rate Lewis and Erin in this regard?

10.5.1 A taut, spare style

A strong feature of both essays is that they don't carry much excess baggage. There are few unnecessary words and no efforts to impress with complicated language. An essay should get straight to the point. You don't need to say things in elaborate ways; just say enough to make yourself clear. Then, when you have finished, check back over what you have written to make sure that your words say what you intended. And cut away whatever you can do without.

Activity 10.7

Here is a sentence containing fifty-five words. Try to reduce its length, without losing the essential meaning. To give you a target, I got it down to eleven words: an 80 per cent reduction.

Since the long-heralded and eagerly anticipated unification of East Germany with West Germany, those living in the Eastern part of the combined nation have gained considerably in income, prosperity and general standard of living, but over the very same period their levels of happiness and overall wellbeing have gone into a marked downward spiral.

Erin is good at writing short, direct sentences. She generally delivers one main point in each sentence, so that the meaning moves along in clear cut steps. Some of Lewis's sentences, by contrast, are rather rambling. If a sentence delivers two points, consider splitting it in two. Your reader can then examine the logic of each before committing to the whole package.

It isn't easy to achieve simplicity and clarity in your writing at first draft. As you write, you have to use the words that come to you. If you stop to worry about every word, your writing loses all fluency and direction. So, it's best to go with the flow of sentences as they form in your mind, then return later to cast a more critical eye over what you have written and edit as necessary. As an example of editing down, here is my shortened version of the sentence in Activity 10.7:

Since unification, East Germans have become more prosperous but less happy.

Finding the right words

At one point in his essay Lewis has chosen not quite the *right* word. When he writes 'It was revealed in 2000', he really means 'reported'. Revealed sounds as though something had been concealed and was then uncovered. On the other hand he hits on exactly the word he wants when he talks of the 'stigma' attached to depression. In essay writing it is important to try to use words that mean exactly what you intend. If you have difficulty finding the words you want, you could try using a thesaurus.

 I have a thesaurus program which I downloaded. I'd be lost without it.

Creating a flow

Another reason why Erin's writing is strong is that she knows how to use words and phrases to link her points together and to 'signpost' the direction in which the argument is flowing. For instance, in her first paragraph she uses 'however', partly to connect two sentences together, but also to signal that the second sentence runs counter to the first.

Activity 10.8

Try highlighting words in the second paragraph of Erin's essay which do the job of directing the flow of her argument:

As we might expect, wealthier people are generally happier than poorer. According to Layard 41% of the richest quarter of the population say they are very happy, but just 26% of the poorest quarter. Yet, surprisingly, overall levels of happiness have not risen as wealth has risen. Meanwhile, serious unhappiness seems to be increasing. For example, studies found that for women in their thirties clinical depression almost doubled over two decades (Layard, 2003, p. 25).

These are the words I highlighted:

As we might expect – Sets us up to hear something uncontroversial.

According to – Links Layard's evidence into the argument.

But – Signals a shift of tack.

Yet – Signals another shift.

Surprisingly – Sets us up to hear something that contrasts with the earlier 'expected' point.

Meanwhile – Brings in another related theme.

For example – Brings in Erin's example.

It is 'signposting' words like these which give Erin's writing its thrust and help her argument to sweep us along.

BOX 10.13   SIGNPOSTING

Readers easily get lost as they follow your journey across a range of ideas. Signposting words and phrases are a necessary guide to the way the meaning of your writing is meant to work.

I think it's important to make writing flow and not be jumpy. I put all the related information in the same paragraph and try to have linking sentences, so the essay isn't disjointed.

Beginnings and endings

It's particularly important to pay attention to the flow of meaning at the beginning and at the end of your essay. In your introduction you need to set the flow going. Back in Section 10.3.1 we saw how effectively Erin did this.

BOX 10.14   PUNCHY OPENINGS

There is a lot to be said for brisk and direct openings to essays. You need some kind of scene-setting to launch your reader's thoughts in the right direction, to be able to follow your argument. But there is no virtue in a lot of formal 'throat clearing' and 'beating about the bush'. The first sentence should grab your reader's attention. It should bear some obvious relation to the title of the essay and be doing useful work for your argument. It doesn't have to be flamboyant or fancy. It should just get down to business quickly.

At the end of the essay you need to draw the flow of ideas to a conclusion. We looked at how Erin did this in Section 10.3.2 – in just a few words she brings us back to the title question and summarises what it is she considers Layard's arguments say on the question.

BOX 10.15   CRISP CONCLUSIONS

Your essay should end with a concluding paragraph which sweeps briefly back over the arguments you have presented and pulls them

---

together. This overview should show how the discussion in your essay has answered the question in the title. A conclusion doesn't have to be particularly grand. It just needs to be crisp and direct and give a clear sense of having arrived at a worthwhile response to the challenge in the title.

10.5.2 Speaking to a reader

One of the reasons why Erin's essay works well is that she shows a confident sense of whom she is speaking *as*, whom she is speaking *to* and *why*.

Activity 10.9

To give an idea of what I mean by 'speaking to a reader', here is a very different kind of writing.

> WHEN Busted told us they were popping into Sun Online for a webchat, we couldn't wait to catch up with all the gossip from Matt, James and Charlie.
>
> *(Sinead O'Neill, 2004).*

How does Sinead O'Neill present herself here? What does she assume about us, her readers? And what does she imply is the context and purpose of our relationship to her?

From her opening words, we find ourselves in a buzzing media world of pop groups casually 'popping in' on magazines for a chat. All friends together. 'Catch up with all the gossip' implies that there's plenty to tell, and that normally Sinead and her set keep well abreast of it. Who is the 'us' whom Busted told? Do we imagine a group of half a dozen fashionable young journalists lounging on sofas, sipping cocktails, waiting eagerly for stars to call by for a gossip? They 'couldn't wait' to catch up, so it's an exciting world of juicy stories. And we the readers are lucky enough to be included in this glamorous but at the same time intimate world. How could we be anything but enthusiastic to hear what Matt, James and Charlie have to say?

No hint here that this could have been a routine promotional interview arranged by the group's agent, or that Sinead might be hammering away at her keyboard in a noisy office, rushing to file her copy by the deadline. In just a few words, she has very cleverly created a much more attractive scene, which she is inviting us to join. Now we are in the right frame of mind for what she has to tell.

Writing is a very special form of 'conversation'. You talk to someone you cannot see and who never answers. You just have to assume that they are 'listening' and reacting to what you say. Moreover, *you* have to shoulder responsibility for deciding *what* is to be discussed and *how*, and for sustaining the other person's *interest*. And *you* are responsible for establishing the *relationship* between you and your 'listener'.

This is one of the trickiest things about writing. You have to convey a sense of *who* you assume your *reader* to be, and the *frame of mind* in which they will be approaching your words. This is known as '*sense of audience*'. You also have to convey a sense of who *you* are claiming to be and from what *position* you are 'speaking'. Are you speaking as an expert on the subject, as a witty entertainer, or as a friend? This is known as your '*writing voice*'.

As you can see, a professional journalist, such as Sinead O'Neill, is very aware of the importance of these subtle signals about context and about the nature and purpose of the relationship between writer and reader. Such signals are important in all writing, including essays (although you don't have to worry that your teacher might skip off to read something else because you haven't captured their attention). Of course, an essay is a very different kind of dialogue – sober, reflective and purposeful. Essay writers present themselves as serious, thoughtful people and 'construct' their readers to be the same.

Lewis signals this very directly, opening with the words 'I will discuss in the light of Layard's article...'. He presents himself as the kind of person who discusses academic articles and constructs his reader as a person who would be interested in Layard's views. Erin manages to achieve the same effect less directly. By striding straight into the topic, speaking confidently and purposefully about the issues and Layard's views on them, she positions herself as competent to talk on the subject and us as willing to accept her competence and interested in her views. She does, though, make one explicitly inclusive gesture towards her reader, when she says 'As *we* might expect'. But who is this 'we'? Is it just Erin and her reader? The tone suggests not. This 'we' is the wider audience of people who read articles such as Layard's. She is positioning herself and us, her readers, within the '*academic community*'.

See Chapter 4 Section 4.3.1, Accessing academic knowledge

Where Erin's writing is particularly effective is in positioning her in a three-way relationship involving herself, Layard and us. Phrases like 'According to Layard', 'Layard argues', 'says Layard' create an inclusive relationship, where she is a confident intermediary between Layard and ourselves.

Sense of audience

Who then do you to assume your audience to be when you write an essay? Is it someone very learned and critical, or someone who knows nothing and couldn't care less about the subject? One standard approach is to say '*Write for the intelligent person in the street*'. In other words, assume that your reader has *not* read the books you have been studying, but that he or she is *interested* in the question posed by the title of the essay and is *capable* of picking up your arguments quickly, provided you spell them out clearly. This is helpful, but slightly puzzling, as the average person in the street is unlikely to want to know about Layard's views, or to be interested in an academic style of debate. Perhaps writing for another beginner in your subject is a more realistic formulation – someone who needs things explained, but who is basically interested and ready for a well argued case.

Your writing 'voice'

And who are you to present yourself as? Basically you are a calm, detached observer, pointing out to an equal (who happens not to be informed on the subject) some arguments which are relevant to a question you are both interested in (i.e. the question in the essay title). It is not easy to find a comfortable writing voice. It may take several essays before you can settle satisfactorily into one. One of the key reasons you get stuck at the start of an essay is the difficulty of trying to work out where you are 'coming from'. Sometimes you have to take several shots at your opening before you can find a voice with which you can proceed.

Key points

- To write goods essays aim for a clear, direct, unfussy style and simple sentences.

- Check that your words say what you want them to.

- Use signposting words to signal the flow of meaning from sentence to sentence.

- Try to create momentum at the start of your essay with a punchy opening, and draw your arguments together at the end with a crisply sketched conclusion.

- One of the key challenges of writing is to develop a sense of your 'audience' and also a 'voice' in which to speak to your reader. Both take time and practice, but as they develop, you become much more confident in your writing.

10.6 Using your own and other people's words

I was struck by the difference in tone of the opening sentences of the two essays. Here is Lewis's followed by Erin's:

I will discuss in the light of Richard Layard's article whether as the nation gets richer we are doomed to become ever more unhappy?

People go to great lengths to gain happiness, and many assume that money is an automatic route to achieving it.

Lewis stays so close to the words of the title that we get very little sense of either him or his ideas. His style feels cramped and awkward, as if he is hedged in by constraints. With Erin on the other hand, we immediately have the sense of her speaking to us confidently and clearly. One of the pleasures of reading her essay is that it seems as if she is talking directly to us, forming her thoughts in her own words as she writes. This is of course an illusion. Well-structured writing has to be carefully composed. But it is a valuable illusion, because it makes for powerful writing and interesting reading.

Yet there is also, paradoxically, a strong sense in Erin's writing that she is putting forward *Layard's* ideas to us, using *his* terms ('reference groups', 'polluted', 'habituated') and *his* evidence. *Both Erin and Layard are 'present' at the same time in the writing.* It is a three-way dialogue between Erin, Layard, and us her readers.

Lewis's writing tends to go in the opposite direction. He stays *too* close to specific sequences of words which appear in Layard's article, as though he hasn't the nerve to say things differently, in case he gets it wrong. Yet he doesn't use Layard's key terms, and he doesn't keep us closely in touch with Layard's ideas. Take for example this passage:

He looked at a study showing on average rich people are happier than poorer. People earning more money was 41 per cent 'very happy' compared with people on a lower scale of income which shows 29 per cent.

Layard himself writes:

rich people are on average happier than poorer ones. For example, 41 per cent of people in the top quarter of incomes are 'very happy', compared with only 26 per cent of those in the bottom quarter of incomes.

You can see how Lewis's version relies strongly not just on Layard's concepts but on his actual sequences of words, with the order rearranged. (Ironically, one thing Lewis *has* changed is the evidence itself, with 26 per cent becoming 29 per cent.) Yet Lewis does *not* go on to deliver Layard's *main point*, which is that *these percentages have not changed over the years*. So Lewis has stuck too closely to Layard's words, but not closely enough to the meaning behind the words.

When Erin presents Layard's evidence, she is not afraid to summarise it in her own words. For example where Layard says:

A survey from London University's Institute of Education, out this month, shows that as many as 29 per cent of women aged 30 in 2000 reported suffering trouble with nerves or feeling low, depressed or sad; the comparable figure in a similar survey, among those aged 36 in 1982, was just 16 per cent.

Erin summarises this as:

For example, studies found that for women in their thirties clinical depression almost doubled over two decades.

Similarly, when Erin uses Layard's concept of pollution by wealth, she explains it her own way, using her own words. Erin has mastered one of the most important yet trickiest skills of essay writing – *finding a way to work with the language and ideas of the study text, while at the same time using her own words and ideas.* Where Lewis tends to be shackled by Layard's words, Erin uses them as a springboard.

10.6.1 The significance of writing in your own words

It is tremendously important to write in your own words, even if you feel your writing is weak. It is also a big challenge. You are trying to write in a subject area where the terms are unfamiliar and your ideas are still forming. If it is also the case that you don't do much writing in your everyday life (true for most people) and you are unused to writing about ideas (true for almost everyone returning to study after a break), it's hard to know where to begin. That's why it feels safer to stay close to the wording in the textbooks; it seems less likely that you will embarrass yourself by writing nonsense. Yet, as you see in Lewis's case, you are just as likely to write weakly if you rely too closely on the study texts. Worse still, you will not improve. Just as you don't make progress in learning to swim while you still have a foot on the bottom of the pool, *you don't begin to develop as a thinker and writer in your subject area while you are still relying on the words in the study texts.*

See Chapter 4 Section 4.2.3, What do you have to do to learn something?

The main purpose of writing essays is to practice *using* the ideas you have been reading about in the course. This comes across very clearly from the students talking about the nature of the learning process in Section 4.2 of Chapter 4.

Often the things I learn most about are essay topics, because the process of structuring and writing an essay helps me to understand the main points of the argument.

This means you have to write about ideas in words that makes sense to *you*. They may come out badly to begin with, but like a learner in any field you have to be prepared to make simple mistakes. It is through exposing your weaknesses that you learn how to do something about them. Also, by using your own words, you show your teacher the progress you are making, so that you can get due credit for it. And, having seen where you have reached in your understanding, your teacher can enter into fruitful dialogue with you to help move your ideas along.

A further reason to write in your own words is that you will get more satisfaction out of it. It may have embarrassing moments, but with practice you will build up respect for yourself and your own ideas. This is the most powerful of incentives to carry on studying. If essays feel like a chore, because you are simply making a selection from other people's words and rearranging them on the page, then you are much more likely to give up your studies. You need to allow yourself to experience the deep satisfaction of expressing your own arguments and seeing your powers of writing develop.

10.16 WRITING IN YOUR OWN WORDS

There are four important reasons why it is important to write in your own words:

1 It enables you to learn the ideas in the course in depth, by using them to say things for yourself.

2 It enables your teacher to give you credit for your learning.

3 It make possible a genuine dialogue with your teacher.

4 It makes studying much more stimulating and develops your powers of self expression.

10.6.2 Plagiarism

We have seen that Lewis tends to rely too heavily on using the words from Layard's article. At times this spills over into 'plagiarism'. That is to say, he is presenting Layard's words as though they are his own. In his article, Layard writes:

> A survey [...] shows that as many as 29 per cent of women aged 30 in 2000 reported suffering trouble with nerves or feeling low, depressed or sad; the comparable figure in a similar survey, among those aged 36 in 1982, was just 16 per cent.

While Lewis writes:

It was revealed in 2000 that as many as 29 per cent of women aged 30 suffered with nerves or feeling low, depressed or sad, compared with a similar survey among those aged 36 in 1982 which was just 16 per cent.

I have underlined Lewis's wording where it's identical to Layard's. It's quite obvious that Lewis has simply 'lifted' a section out of the article and switched around a word or two. The bit about 'with nerves or feeling low, depressed or sad' immediately struck me as being unlike Lewis's writing elsewhere in the essay; it is much more detailed and specific. I could tell straight away that it came directly from Layard's article. There are very obvious differences between the way students write and the way experienced authors write, so it is quite easy to spot when an essay is lurching between an 'expert' style and a 'beginner' style. A particular 'giveaway' is where smoothly flowing sections are interspersed with short stuttering link phrases. In fact, most people write particularly badly when they are cobbling together somebody else's words. Instead of having control over 'making sense' as you write, you cling desperately to the coat tails of someone else's thoughts and get pulled all over the place.

Plagiarism is regarded as cheating, and it can be a lot more serious than in Lewis's case. Whole paragraphs are copied unchanged, or even whole essays. When such practices are detected, students can find themselves in serious difficulties, suffering heavy cuts in marks, or even being thrown off their course. In Lewis's case it doesn't look like deliberate cheating. It's mainly his lack of experience in finding the right balance between using his own words and those of Layard. If his whole essay was cobbled together this way, it would be more worrying, but there are clear signs elsewhere that he is presenting his own ideas and using his own words. At this stage his teacher might deduct a few marks and warn him to avoid over-dependence on the source texts. But if he persists, his marks are likely to drop significantly.

BOX 10.17   PLAGIARISM

Plagiarism is using other people's words without acknowledgement. It is seen as a form of cheating. If detected it can seriously affect your course result. But it is also cheating yourself of the opportunity to learn.

10.6.3 Quotes

Erin too makes direct use of Layard's words, so why did I not include her in my discussion of plagiarism? Here is a case in point. What is the difference between this and the last example from Lewis's essay?

'The electorate now understands that the scramble to spend more is partially self defeating ... [and is] more favourable to public expenditure.' (Layard, 2003, p 26).

Erin is quite open here about the fact that she is using Layard's words. Indeed, she is 'quoting' from him. The essential differences from Lewis's case are that:

- She signals to us that it is a quotation by using *quotation marks*.

- She tells us where the quotation is from in brackets at the end. This source information is known as a 'reference'. She follows it up at the end of her essay by giving full details of the source in a 'reference list'.

- She quotes *exactly*, word for word, what Layard says.

- She inserts '...' when she leaves words out; and when she inserts her own words into Layard's quote '[and is]', she puts square brackets around them.

This means we know exactly what Erin is claiming that Layard said. And I can go straight back to the source if I sense that she is distorting Layard's views, or quoting him out of context. There is no hint of cheating.

There are two other important features about this quotation:

1 **It is not too long** – there is seldom good reason in an essay to use a quotation of more than a sentence or two.

2 **It fits into the flow** of what Erin is saying. It isn't left standing on its own.

Long quotations can have a flavour of plagiarism in disguise. It looks as though you are simply saving yourself the trouble of working out how to say something. This impression is strengthened if you don't discuss your quotations, or comment on them. It is important to *show* that you *understand* what your quotation is saying and to make clear *why* you thought it worth including. In Erin's case she has been attempting to summarise Layard's argument about taxing pollution and his controversial view that voters are actually prepared to be taxed more to enable social spending. The quotation is clearly intended to demonstrate that she has accurately represented his views; it is part of her effort to maintain a three-way dialogue between herself, Layard and her reader.

BOX 10.18   SHORT, RELEVANT QUOTATIONS

Quoting is an excellent way of bringing the views of an author into your essay. But quotations should be fairly short and infrequent and they should always be accurate and accompanied by a reference. They should also be tied into the flow of your argument to show that they have a purpose and that you understand them.

Essays require you to tread a fine line between using your own words and those of other people. You can easily find that your work is criticised because you don't make enough use of the language and ideas of the course texts, then criticised next time because you have followed the texts too closely. It takes experience to find the right balance between the two. Erin has found the balance nicely.

Key points

■ You are expected to write in your own words in an essay, except where you deliberately choose to include a quotation.

■ At the same time you are expected to make use of the language and ideas of the texts you have been reading.

■ Copying text from other sources into your essay without acknowledgement is known as 'plagiarism'. It is strongly discouraged and can lead to serious consequences.

- When you do quote from other sources you are expected to use quotation marks and give a reference.

- Quotations should always be exactly in the words of the original text, with any omissions or additions clearly marked.

10.7 The academic way of writing

We have talked about writing in your own words. However, you could hardly say that Lewis and Erin have written in the way they would talk in their day-to-day lives. So in a sense they *didn't* write in their own *habitual* words. They deliberately set out to write in a way that they assumed was expected when you write essays. This section is about that 'academic' way of writing. And we begin by looking at another essay, this time written by their classmate Kate.

Activity 10.10

Read the essay by Kate that follows (you can download a copy from the Good Study Guide website at www.goodstudyguide.co.uk, if you want to write on it). Then answer these questions:

1   Is Kate's essay stronger or weaker than Lewis's or Erin's?

2   Do you think that Kate writes in 'the academic way'?

Kate's essay

As our society gets wealthier, are we doomed to become ever more unhappy? Discuss in the light of the Richard Layard article.

In the light of Richard Layard's article, I do not agree that we are 'doomed to become ever more unhappy'.

Firstly, in my view, Richard Layard's article is not representative of the population as a whole. Richard Layard says 'society has got richer but people have not become happier', but what does he know, living his privileged London life?

In any case it's well known that money cannot buy happiness and having a high income just puts more pressure on any individual. People have expectations and sometimes reaching them such as owning a very expensive car does not bring happiness.

It is the quality of any person's life that leads to contentment, and also how you live your life? Money is able to buy materialistic possessions but it does nothing to improve genuine feelings such as a sense of well-being, a sense of giving, raising self-esteem, a sense of worth, and so on and so forth.

The old saying 'money is the root of all evil' speaks for itself.

Perhaps if Richard Layard looked around him a bit more and conducted more surveys amongst people who do voluntary work for example he would reach a different conclusion.

So in conclusion, I do not believe that we are doomed to become ever more unhappy.

To me, Kate's essay is a lot weaker than the other two. She writes fluently enough, in reasonably tidy sentences (which could do with a bit more punctuation), and she has clearly made an effort to bring some points together and to argue in response to the essay question. But although the essay clearly presents Kate's strongly held views, it doesn't make any attempt to present Layard's arguments and evidence. And though she *does* answer the title question, both at the beginning and the end, she simply presents her answer as a personal opinion. There *is* some argument, but it is based entirely on what Kate regards as 'common sense'. Essentially, Kate has not written in 'the academic way' and, as a result, it's difficult to assess her essay, other than to give it a low mark.

10.7.1 How academic debate works

Take nothing for granted

Kate has not grasped the way in which academic debate works. One of its core purposes is to go beyond folk-wisdom and common sense. Whatever is 'taken for granted' is to be challenged. Truth is meant to be established through logical analysis and by seeking evidence. So when Kate says things like: 'In any case it's well known that money cannot buy happiness' and 'The old saying 'money is the root of all evil' speaks for itself', she is not strengthening her argument. Instead, she is undermining it by showing an unwillingness to challenge everyday wisdom. When she says 'In any case it's well known', she seems to be implying that Layard's views are scarcely worth presenting, because everyone already know them. Yet, within academic debate there is often a very good reason for arguing that something is the case, however 'obvious' it might seem. What you can't do is *assume* common sayings to be the truth.

The status of the published word

Within academic debate, books and journal articles have a special status. They are reviewed before publication and, once published, they are assumed to meet high standards of logical argument and sound evidence. So Kate is taking on a lot when she says:

in my view, Richard Layard's article is not representative of the population as a whole.

She seems to be suggesting that Layard, a senior figure in his field, with many publications to his name, is prepared to give a public lecture and publish an article (though, in this case, in a non-academic journal) which contains very basic flaws in its approach. She is entitled to suggest this; after all, nothing is to be taken for granted. However, it's a big undertaking. She would need to present a pretty powerful analysis of his arguments, or some very convincing counter-evidence, to make the charge stick. Just saying 'in my view' doesn't do it. Her view is no more relevant than anyone else's.

Assumptions about others in the debate

The fact that Richard Layard works in London has nothing to do with the case. People's personal details and backgrounds are assumed to be irrelevant in academic debate. In most cases, this information is not available anyway. Everyone is treated as having an equal right to present a case, so long as they can get their voice heard (i.e. their work published). Arguments are meant to be treated on their own merits, regardless of who presents them. Consequently, personal comments about authors are not made. When Kate writes:

what does he know, living his privileged London life?

and:

Perhaps if Richard Layard looked around him a bit more

her remarks are entirely out of place. Casting doubt on his personal experience of life has no more bearing on the quality of his argument, than if Kate's teacher made remarks about Kate's personal circumstances when commenting on her essay.

Relating to published work

Kate seems to assume that she is arguing with Layard's personal opinions and research. But little, if any, of the evidence Layard presents is his own research and his arguments takes into account what many before him have argued. He has done what is expected within academic debate – before speaking, or publishing, he has 'reviewed the literature'. In other words, his arguments are based on his reading of a wide range of research from different countries and time periods. So it is quite implausible when Kate, as a beginner in the field, dismisses his approach out of hand. She needs to develop a clearer sense of the 'background' of published work that lies behind the debates she engages with. And to mount arguments of her own, she needs to quote published evidence and arguments, along with citations and references.

Objectivity

With her appeals to folk wisdom and common sense and her suggestions about Richard Layard's lifestyle, Kate tries to get us to 'sympathise' with her point of view rather than his. In everyday arguments we try to get people 'on our side' in the hope that, out of loyalty, they will agree with us. However, academic arguments are meant to work in quite the opposite way. You are supposed to present them *objectively* – that is without any emotion, or personal strings attached. You present your points neutrally, then leave them to stand on their own merits. In an essay you have to be wary of using phrases like: 'I do not agree', 'In my view', 'It's well known that', and 'I do not believe'.

You have to ask yourself 'Am I trying to sway my reader with my own personal beliefs? Am I being completely neutral?' (In some subjects, the use of 'I' is discouraged altogether. You will have to find out about that from your teachers.) It's fine for Kate to hold strong views, but they are irrelevant to our response to her arguments. She should keep them hidden and leave us to draw our own conclusions. On the other hand it's alright for Lewis to use 'I' when he says 'I will discuss', because he is not presenting an opinion.

There are various ways you can present a viewpoint in a neutral way. For example, you can say 'I will argue', 'it can be argued that', 'McKay (2004) proposes that', 'Kelly notes the widespread belief that (Kelly, 2005, p. 23)'. But, as you can see, these all keep the argument or viewpoint 'at arms length'. It isn't presented as *your* opinion. They are all ways of maintaining your *detached* position 'outside' the argument.

Disciplined argument

Arguing in an essay is not at all the same as having an argument in daily life. When people argue vigorously in everyday life, there tends to be a hint of confrontation in the air, and stubbornness – even irrationality, wild generalisation and emotion. In an essay, you should try to make your argument the opposite of this. You should aim to be objective, precise, logical, ready to back your case with good evidence, and open to doubt and criticism. Kate's essay shows few signs of this. When she makes sweeping points such as: 'having a high income just puts more pressure on any individual', and 'It is the quality of any person's life that leads to contentment', she makes no effort to back them up. Why does having a high income create pressures? What does she mean by quality of life? Can she give any examples to show what she is talking about? Does she have any evidence or expert opinion to support these propositions? Without support, the points are hardly worth reading, because she has offered us no grounds for taking them seriously.

Critical analysis

As I noted in Chapter 5, Kate may have a legitimate criticism to make of Layard's article. She seemed to feel that the research he was quoting made unjustified assumptions about the nature of happiness and was insensitive to the life experience of people on low incomes. However, to make her criticism work, she would have to spell out those parts of Layard's argument that she felt were faulty and show exactly what the faults were. General criticisms are ineffective in academic argument; you have to home in on specifics. In fact, Lewis made rather an impressive criticism of one of Layard's points when he said:

But perhaps it is because as a society we are more aware of depression [and] there is less stigma attached to it. This could be why reports of depression have increased.

See Chapter 4 Section 4.3.2, Key features of academic discourse

This is a well thought out and well presented criticism. And it is impressive because it shows that Lewis is not simply accepting everything Layard says as true. He is probing Layard's logic and questioning it. That is exactly what *critical analysis* involves. (For more about critical analysis, see Chapter 4 Section 4.3.2). Unfortunately Kate offers no analysis to go with her criticism.

Precision and accuracy

One further feature of academic debate is the high value placed on writing precisely and accurately. For example when Kate quotes Layard (without giving a reference) she writes:

'society has got richer but people have not become happier.'

This is almost an exact quotation but actually she should have written:

'society has got richer, [but] people have not become happier.'

leaving in Layard's comma and showing that she has added the word 'but', or alternatively:

'… as society has got richer, people have not become happier.'

to show that the quotation follows on from something else, making it unnecessary to add 'but'. These are tiny variations, but quotations really are meant to be *exactly* right, because sometimes a single word can make a big difference to the meaning.

There are no further examples in Kate's essay because she made no other reference to Layard's article, so here are some examples from Lewis's essay:

Richard Layard looked at all different surveys taken in US, Japan, Continental Europe and Britain to look for evidence to see if we are doomed to become ever more unhappy.

Lewis says that Layard looked at *all* different surveys. But you could never be sure to have covered *all* possible sources and Layard does not make that claim. Nor did he say that he was looking 'to see if we are doomed to become ever more unhappy'. That phrase comes from the essay title. These may seem small points, but to understand the nature of Layard's research, it is important that we are not given the wrong impression about his purpose, or the scale of his studies. Another example from Lewis's essay:

People earning more money was 41 per cent 'very happy' compared with people on a lower scale of income which shows 29 per cent.

What Layard actually says is '41 per cent of people in the top quarter of incomes are 'very happy''. Lewis could simply have said 'a higher proportion of people with high incomes are 'very happy' than of people with low incomes'. However, if he's going to quote the *41 per cent*, then we *also* need to know that it's *of people in the top quarter of incomes*, otherwise we don't know what it's 41 per cent of. The way he writes it could be read as meaning wealthier people were 'very happy' *41 per cent of the time.* (Also, as we noted earlier, the '29' should be '26'.) This may seem to be nit-picking, but accuracy is what you are meant to aim for.

10.7.2 Developing an academic style

Having read all this – DON'T PANIC!

This talk about the demands of academic writing may make it seem daunting. So it is *very* important to add that:

- you are *not* expected to write beautifully crafted academic arguments straight away, and

- *everybody* takes time to pick up the general approach and the finer points.

It is not a way of writing that flows easily when you first come to it. But, *as you've seen from Lewis's and Erin's essays,* you can begin at quite a basic level. That is all that's expected. It's more of a concern when someone like Kate pretty much misses the point. For her this is an issue that needs to be addressed and worked on. Otherwise, so long as you get into the basic mindset of *arguing a case* in response *both* to the essay *title* and to your *course texts,* then you can forge ahead. You will pick up details of technique as you go. The point of sketching the whole thing out here is to give you an overall picture of what you are aiming at. If you are new to academic writing, then a year or two is a reasonable time frame for working up all aspects of the approach.

What you have read here is enough to be going on with. However, when you have made some progress with your academic style and you are ready to think some more about it, there is further discussion in Chapter 4 Section 4.3. The key points below deliberately run parallel to those in Chapter 4.

See Chapter 4 Section 4.3, Why do they write that way?

> ## *Key points*
>
> The academic way of writing takes a year or two to acquire. The main features are:
>
> - **Debate** Write in the spirit of joining in a debate – responding to arguments, evidence and points of view that you have read, by offering arguments of your own.
>
> - **Scholarship** Link your arguments to 'the literature' on the subject, by including citations and references.
>
> - **Argument** Organise an essay so that it reads as a coherent argument, running from the essay title to your concluding paragraph.

- **Critical analysis** Don't simply 'present' other writers' arguments and points of view, focus in to see where their strengths and weakness lie. (This may not be expected if you are a first-year student.)

- **Evidence** Present evidence to back up your arguments.

- **Objectivity** Write in a detached, unemotional way, leaving your arguments to stand on their own merits.

- **Precision** Try to say exactly what you mean, and pay attention to getting details correct.

10.8 What is a good essay?

In this chapter we have given a lot of detailed attention to three very short essays, using them as a springboard for discussing what is expected in academic essays generally. However, we shouldn't leave the essays yet without commenting on their overall quality.

10.8.1 How good are the essays we have reviewed?

The significance of context

'How good' depends enormously on the context. In one sense, any essay is excellent if it is genuinely the best you can write at that particular point in your understanding of the subject matter and given your particular level of experience of essay writing. It's like asking 'How well has my day's walk gone, now that I've reached Bradford Town Hall?' It very much depends whether you started from Low Moor on the outskirts of Bradford, Halifax eight miles away, or Manchester nearly sixty miles away over the Pennines. We all have to start writing from where we are, and one measure of the quality of our work is the progress we make from that starting point.

In this case we have three people returning to study after a long gap and not having thrived in their previous studies at school. I was not their teacher but, by arrangement, I asked them to read the Layard article as an extra item alongside their access course work. It's on a topic completely new to them and presents some quite subtle and technically challenging arguments. There was no classroom discussion of the article. Nor were they given guidance on how to tackle the essay title, or opportunity to share ideas about how to approach it. In short, they faced a tough challenge. To produce an essay at all was a considerable achievement.

Levels of performance

On the other hand, it would be misleading to say that we can't make comparisons between these essays, or judge them against any general standards. Erin's essay is clearly more accomplished than the other two and

Kate's is clearly the weakest, since she didn't engage with the basic task of discussing Layard's article. Bearing in mind that this was set up as an unusually short essay, work like Erin's on an access course would be outstanding. In its current form I would certainly give it a high mark. Lewis's strikes me as a fair piece of work at this level. There are plenty of points that need working on, but also some promising features, such as the criticism he makes of Layard's interpretation of rising figures for depression. I would give his essay a mark a little below the middle of the range. Kate's essay, I would say, is on the borderline. If this were her first essay, I would give a pass, because she had not been given guidelines and she has certainly made an effort to put some points together and argue them. However, if this were the second or third time she had avoided discussing the set reading, I would give a fail.

Feedback

Essay writing is the nub of the teaching/learning relationship between students and their teachers. It is where the teacher gets to see how ideas are developing in the student's mind and where the student gets feedback on the progress they are making. The dialogue that develops in the form of the teacher's comments on the essay and the student's response to those comments in writing the next essay is of critical significance.

So what did I say to these students? Here is the note I wrote to Lewis:

Dear Lewis

Thanks very much for writing this under such pressure.

I realise that this was quite a tough article and so quite a tough essay to tackle at such short notice. However, you got well stuck in and put together some good points, even though you didn't feel you had time to do the task justice.

You have a strong clear underlying style, though there are a few points to work on. And you have a good sense of how to make a forceful point, though at times you need to go a bit further to make your argument clearer to your reader. This was particularly true of your final paragraph, where there were a number of important points crammed up against each other, so that it was difficult to get the full force of them.

In fact, I didn't think this really worked as a final paragraph, which is where you should be pulling together what you've already said and offering an answer to the title question. If you wanted to pursue those points, it would have been better to move them earlier and spell them out more, to show what you mean.

Similarly with your paragraph about women's pay, I would have added at least a sentence to put across your point and I would have moved it to later in the essay. In fact, you could have made your argument flow better through the essay with a general rearranging of the order of your paragraphs (see the note written on the essay).

I have made a few other detailed suggestions on the essay. But overall this was a good effort at tackling some subtle arguments. With the directness and force of your writing and your drive to get to the nub of the argument, you have an excellent base on which to build for future studies. I hope they go very well.

Best wishes, Andy

If you are interested in seeing a reworked version of Lewis's essay, taking into account the points made in this chapter, you can find it on the Good Study Guide website at www.goodstudyguide.co.uk.

To Kate, who had been extremely vocal in her hostility towards Layard in a classroom discussion after handing in her essay, I wrote somewhat gingerly:

Dear Kate

Thanks very much for sending me this. You clearly have a good general writing style and you know how to get your points across in writing. This will stand you in good stead for future work. But your essay isn't as strong as it could have been, because you haven't really done what is asked for in the title. You haven't discussed Layard's article. You have focused only on your own views. This make it appear as if you've already decided what you think on this topic and you are not interested in what anyone else has to say. It also means I can't tell whether you've understood Layard's view. I know what your views are, but I can't really comment on how well you have worked on this topic.

Obviously it's fine for any of us to think what we like. But when you are studying, the point of reading is to try to get on the inside of what an author is saying to see whether there is something useful to learn from it. Then in your essay you are meant to show that you have understood the force of the argument that an author presents, before weighing up whether the argument convinces you. Here are some points to think about for your next essay:

1   Try to make sure you've explained the arguments you've been reading about. (Then I can see you've understood them.)

2   Assume your reader has not read the course texts. This will help you strike the right tone in explaining ideas.

3   If you don't agree with an argument, don't just present your opinion. Back up your points with evidence, or with the views of other authors.

You'll see some more detailed points on the essay itself. Don't be put off by anything I've said. It always takes a while to get into the swing of writing the way a course like this requires. The important thing is to have a go and then build from there. As I say, it's obvious from your writing that you will do well once you start bringing the course ideas more directly into your essays. So just keep up the momentum now. I hope you enjoy your next reading much better. Do get back to me if you want to talk over anything I've said.

Best wishes, Andy

I won't show you my note to Erin, as I have not shown you her original essay (I make some improvements to it, to help me make points in this chapter). And in case you are wondering what happened to Salim, I didn't have space to discuss another essay here; however, you can find his essay on the Good Study Guide website if you want to read it.

We have looked at three very different pieces of writing in response to the same essay title. Each shows a student's mind at work, grappling with challenging new ideas. And each shows particular strengths and weaknesses in both approach and writing style. From all this we have drawn out many important pointers to what you are trying to achieve when you write your own essays. All that remains is to pull the threads together.

10.8.2 The key ingredients

I think what they're asking us to do is write a clear concise answer to the question, using a balanced argument and reaching a conclusion, backed by references.

It's hard to improve on this student's summary, but here are the basics of what you should be aiming to do in your essays.

Answer the question

An essay can be good in every other way yet be judged poor because it ignores the question posed in the title. You are never asked to 'write all you know' about a subject. You are set a specific *problem* to think about in the light of what you have been studying. Your task is to argue a case in relation to that problem and everything you say in your essay should be relevant to that task. It isn't enough that a point is interesting to *you*. You have to work to convince your reader that it has some bearing on the title. Life is too short to read every interesting point. Each sentence has to be relevant to the issue the reader is expecting to read about.

BOX 10.19   WHAT IF THERE IS NO QUESTION IN THE TITLE?

Not every essay title contains a *question*, as such. However, there is always an issue of some kind to be resolved, or a task to be carried out. You could say 'Have I done what the title asks?' It just seems more direct to ask yourself 'Have I remembered to answer the question?'

You should always write the title of the essay across the top of your opening page. It reminds you where your reader is starting from as they launch into reading your essay. And you must always stick *exactly* to the title you are given, not devise a modified version of your own. Your marker faces a demanding job in assessing and commenting on your essay. It is made possible by framing it tightly, so that it's quite clear what has to be done.

This is the purpose of the title and the reason you have to pay attention to it at all times. Your marker will get impatient if you insist on displaying a whole lot of knowledge other than what has been asked for.

Draw on the course material

An essay is an exercise to help you consolidate what you have been studying. You are not being asked to respond to the title 'off the top of your head', or on the basis of your prior knowledge. You use the essay as an opportunity to scan back over what you have been reading and extract relevant material. Your marker will already have in mind a range of course material that could be brought into an answer. If you miss out *some* of the important ideas and information it may not matter, provided you have made good use of *other* material from the relevant part of the course. If, however, you answer entirely on the basis of knowledge drawn from outside the course, you will run into trouble. It is very difficult for your marker to evaluate your account of material they are not familiar with, and they won't have time to read your sources. By answering in this way, you focus attention on what you *haven't* done with the relevant material in the course.

I got my worst mark on a subject I know all about from work, and my best on a subject I know nothing about.

See Chapter 4, Understanding how you learn

This is a common tale of woe. You are not just learning 'stuff' about a subject – you are learning to think and write the way members of the academic community do, using their ideas and language. Until you are comfortable with this specialised way of arguing, it may be a challenge too far to try to integrate the knowledge you bring from other parts of your life. In the context of a course, a *lot* of knowledge can be a dangerous thing. It can distort your view of the knowledge presented by the course and over-complicate your thinking.

Give full, accurate references

At any point in your essay where you draw directly on ideas you read in a printed text, it is important to give a *brief reference* there and then. It is particularly important whenever you include a quotation. This allows your reader to go back to the original words if they have doubts about the way you have quoted or interpreted them, or if they want to follow points up more fully. You also need a *list of references* at the end of your essay, giving the full details for *every* brief reference in the main text.

Erin's essay shows examples of appropriate referencing and these were discussed in Section 10.6.3, 'Quotes', there is also a further short discussion of references in Chapter 11 Section 11.2.8. But, for more detail, the Good Study Guide website at www.goodstudyguide.co.uk.

Show a good grasp of the ideas in the course

Your marker will be looking out for signs that you have grasped key points in the course. You show this in the way you select relevant terms, cases, names, evidence and ideas from the course to use in your answer, and in the way you tie them in to your answer. Don't just 'litter' your essay with items from the course. Select them carefully and explain them well. Erin made a point of explaining concepts such as 'pollution' by wealth, whereas Lewis tended to quote evidence without giving necessary detail and without fully explaining what it meant. It's not so much the quantity of course material you bring in, more how you make use of it. Your marker has to be able to see your thought processes at work.

Write in your own words

To demonstrate your grasp of the ideas you have been studying you have to use them for yourself *in your own words*. But at the same time you have to use the language you are picking up from the course. This is a tricky balance to strike. You just have to keep trying, and looking at any feedback you get. Don't be tempted to hide behind wording 'lifted' from the course texts. This will very seriously slow down your learning, and may also get you into trouble for plagiarising. You have to be bold and risk writing badly, in order to learn to write well. Gradually the language of the course will become your own.

Present a coherent argument

The essence of essay writing is argument. Even with much of the right material in your essay, it will not score highly unless the material is organised so that it hangs together. To develop an argument implies two things:

1   that you *sort out* your points into groups, so that they can be presented in a *structured* way, giving the essay a *beginning*, a *middle* and an *end*, and

2   you keep a *thread of meaning* running through your essay. By including *signposting* words and phrases you make each sentence flow on from the previous one.

Anyone can copy material from books. The point of an essay is to make you *think*. When you present a coherent argument you are showing that you can *take hold of the ideas* and *organise* them to do some work for you.

Write in an objective, analytical style

An essay argues by force of reason. If you want to dispute someone's claim, you use argument and evidence, rather than setting out to cast doubts on their character. Because, in daily life, we often prefer to rely on emotional force, it takes practice to develop an objective style – cool, detached and fair to all sides. You show *respect* to other writers, assuming you are writing as a member of a community of equals, all of whom are intelligent, open-minded and fair. You take your reader to be also one of this community and assume that they will be interested in your *reasons* for holding the ideas you do. You don't expect them to be interested in ideas *because* they are *your* ideas.

Avoid sweeping generalisations and vague assertions. Instead, analyse issues carefully as Erin did in her opening paragraph, and take a questioning, critical stance, as Lewis did in questioning Layard's figures on depression. Recognise that your reader needs evidence to be convinced of your point. Don't just hope that your reader picks up the general gist and goes with the flow. Take time to set points out calmly and carefully with all the necessary explanation and supporting evidence.

Write clearly

What we have seen from the three essays in this chapter is that a good essay is easy to read. *Clarity* and *succinctness* are what win a reader over. Use simple, direct language and short, tidy sentences, especially while you are building up a basic essay-writing style. (You can play with elaborate words and grammar later, when you have established a good basic technique.) Don't beat about the bush. Pitch straight into answering the question in a direct and purposeful way.

But remember to think from your reader's point of view. They cannot see into your head, so you have to explain points carefully, giving examples to illustrate what you are talking about. You don't want the reader wondering, 'What's this all about?' With a clearly written essay it's obvious.

Finally, do the best you can with spelling, punctuation and grammar. Always read through your essay at least once, preferably a day or two after completing it, to give yourself a chance to spot mistakes your eyes may have skimmed over when you were deep in the writing.

Key points: Criteria for writing a good essay

As your marker works through your essays they will ask the following questions:

- Have you *answered the question* in the title?

- Have you drawn on the *relevant parts of the course* for your main content?

- Have you given a *reference* for each of your sources in the main body of your essay and provided a *list of references* at the end?

- Do you show a *good grasp of the ideas* you have been studying *in the course*?

- Have you written in your *own words*?

- Have you presented a coherent *argument*?

- Is the essay written in an *objective analytical* style, with appropriate use of *evidence*?

- Is the essay *well written*? (i.e. is it easy to read?)

10.9 Review

Let me highlight a few key messages to take from this chapter. One is that there is no great mystery about *what* good writing is. You were able to spot it yourself, just by reading the sample essays. The mystery is how to produce it. On the other hand, it's not so easy to judge the quality of your own writing as you progress through your studies, so you will find it useful to return to the above *criteria for writing a good essay* when you are about to submit an essay. Alternatively, after you get it back with comments on it, check through the list and see what progress you are making. Of all the chapters in the book this and the next are the most likely to be worth revisiting over your study years.

You might also like to think over the fact that as you read the essays in this chapter, you briefly took on your teacher's role. This will have given you insight into what your teacher looks for as they mark your essays. As you saw, it isn't easy to read and make sense of other people's writing. Nor is it easy to pinpoint strengths and weaknesses and work out how to give appropriate advice. This suggests two lessons:

1   Be sympathetic to your teacher and present your work as clearly as you can.

2   Don't be too upset if your teacher misses your point, or if they offer advice you think is inappropriate or unfair. It's almost impossible to get these things right all the time.

Finally, take reassurance that *you don't have to worry about getting your writing 'perfect' before submitting* it. The essays you have been looking at were not 'perfect', but two, at least, were fine as early essays. These students were doing exactly the right thing in getting stuck in and having a go. Just assume that your first attempts will not be particularly wonderful and get on with it. A good learner in any field is prepared to make mistakes. The task of the next chapter is to look at how to develop your skills as a writer.

References

O'Neill, S. (2004) 'Bustin' into our office', *SunOnline*, 6 August 2004, www.thesun.co.uk/article/0,,7-2004350656,00.html (accessed 6 August 2004).

The Open University (2004) 'Language History', *Learner's Guide to the OU*, www3.open.ac.uk/learners-guide/learning-skills/english/pages/reflect_index.asp (accessed 12 August 2004).

COVENTRY UNIVERSITY LONDON CAMPUS
East India House,
109-117 Middlesex Street, London, E1 7JF
Tel: 020 7247 3666 | Fax: 020 7375 3048
www.coventry.ac.uk/londoncampus

CHAPTER 11 MANAGING THE WRITING PROCESS

This chapter is the second of a pair concerned with writing. While Chapter 10 explores *what* it is that you are trying to produce when you write an essay, this chapter looks at *how* to set about the task of writing.

11.1 The challenge of writing

Managing the process of writing assignments is critically important to your progress as a student. It is, potentially, a deeply satisfying activity, but also a very challenging one. Writing is never a simple or straightforward process. You can't expect to sit down at a keyboard and just type out a good piece of work. Writing essays is a multilayered activity. It interweaves your studies of the course, your emerging understanding of the subject matter and your developing powers of self-expression. You need to approach it with cunning, self-insight and a strategic understanding of the writing process. You have to be able to manage set backs, changes to your plans and sharp mood swings. Good writing emerges out of a resourceful response to constraints and challenges (many of which you impose on yourself). It is an intense experience.

As an essay deadline approaches, many students find it all-consuming:

I take ages to write an essay. And I can't get it out of my head until I finally send it off. Do you find it gets easier? I don't! I keep thinking I'll get faster but I don't.

It's funny how each essay is dreadful and the next topic always looks so much more interesting than the current one. That is until you're on the next topic and the essay is due and then it suddenly becomes really dull and the hardest one yet.

I panic because I have read it over so much and I know it off by heart. Then I start thinking I have picked the wrong option – ha ha. What madness! Then I finally get the courage to send it off – and the whole thing starts again.

To gain a measure of control over the writing experience, you need a basic strategy. Section 11.2, 'Stages in the writing process', sketches out an approach which breaks writing into stages, so that you can tackle it one step at a time. However, writing is a highly individual activity and people succeed in very different ways. So the stages outlined are not meant as a 'recipe' to be followed slavishly. Take what suits you and develop a strategy of your own. Then keep developing it. Your approach to writing will evolve as you become more skilled at some aspects and switch your focus to others. If ever the Kolb reflective cycle (see Figure 1.1 in Chapter 1) is relevant to studying, writing has to be the prime instance. It is essential to plan your approach, write, reflect and plan again for next time.

I find I'm thinking loads about how I do the writing – what I should do when and what to leave to later – and I get incredibly useful ideas from this online chatting.

Perhaps the most challenging aspect of writing is to turn ideas in your head into eloquent and purposeful sentences, rather than dry, stilted ones. Section 11.3, 'Expressing ideas in writing', outlines some suggestions for tapping into the flow of your thoughts and trying to emulate the flow of the spoken word.

You can learn a great deal about writing from other students. But what can *you* learn from *experienced* writers? Having looked in Chapter 10 at three short essays by students starting out on their studies, we switch to the other end of the scale in Section 11.4, 'Making your essay flow', by taking a close look at how a published author makes writing flow. Once again we use the article by Richard Layard at the end of this book. But instead of focusing on the content, we examine it as a piece of writing. Then finally we review the *experience* of writing – exploring why it is so intense, how to survive its challenges and how to focus on its pleasurable and satisfying aspects.

11.2 Stages in the writing process

Writing an essay does not simply 'happen' on a particular day. Effectively, you start the writing process as soon as you begin to study the topic of your next essay. Imagine if you had an essay due in two or three weeks' time, how would you set about it? Here are my eight stages in the writing process:

1   thinking about the essay title

2   planning the writing process

3   studying the course content

4   taking stock before you start writing

5   getting ideas written down

6   organising your material

7   drafting an answer

8   reviewing and polishing.

Key points

- Taking a close look at the title is a vital part of producing a good essay.

- It is very important to look carefully at each of the main words or phrases in turn, otherwise you can waste a lot of time writing about things for which you won't get marks.

- Writing down a few notes helps to set your thoughts rolling, so when you come back to the title later you will have begun to develop ideas about how to tackle it.

11.2.2 Planning the writing process

An essay is a major commitment within your study schedule. It represents a substantial investment of your study time and energy, and from it you can reap significant benefits. If you handle the process effectively, writing the essay will deepen your understanding of the subject matter and advance your writing skills. So it's important to think ahead a bit and plan how you will tackle it.

Planning your study of the topic

First make a list of the set reading and any other studies relevant to the essay topic. What will you need to cover, in order to answer the question effectively? You may not have time for all that's recommended, so plan to cover enough to write a well rounded answer. If you've been asked, for example, to compare two points of view, don't spend so long studying one that you don't have time for the other. Or if you've been asked to focus on a CD-ROM-based case study, make sure to give it a prominent place in your study schedule. And if you need to spend time tracking down online information, or consulting specific library resources, put this on your list. Use the essay task to think strategically about how you want to use your time.

Planning time

Review your commitments over the coming days and work out how you will make time for studying the essay topic. What date is the essay due by? Do you have other work to submit during the period? What other commitments do you have in your study and non-study life? Will you be able to spread the writing over two or three days? How much time will you allow for studying the topic, before you switch to writing? Set yourself a target date for starting work on the essay itself. With your writing timetable sketched and your notes on the essay title, you can now set these to one side and move on with your studies.

Key point

- Producing an essay is too time-consuming and too valuable to leave your preparations and timing to chance. You need to plan strategically, so that you stay in control.

11.2.3 Studying the course content

It's helpful to think ahead about a forthcoming essay before pitching into reading, researching, attending seminars and other study activities relevant to the topic. But it would be a great shame to let the essay dominate your agenda. Different course elements will generate their own themes and you should feel free to pursue what interests you. There are bound to be intriguing and important aspects of any topic that happen not to be linked to the essay titles. You would end up with a very narrow and lopsided view of your subject if your whole attention were focused on essays.

On the other hand, if you keep a separate note-pad handy, you can note down useful points for your essay whenever you come across them. Write the essay title at the top of the page, then jot down case studies, authors' names, sources, references – whatever seems likely to help. And, if a thought strikes, about a possible line of argument for the essay, sketch it out. Untidy scraps of notes, which look like nothing much, can turn into your best ideas.

Use highlighter pens and yellow stickies to mark relevant places in course texts (you could reserve one highlighter colour for essay material). And, of course, keep an eye on progress with your plan for covering the ground required for the essay. Indeed, as the target date for writing nears, you may need to adjust your plans, to ensure that you cover the essentials.

Do you plan your essay as you read, or wait until you've read everything and then start?

While doing the reading I'm always thinking about what I'll put in my essay.

Key points

- Keep a note-pad, highlighters and yellow stickies handy as you study, so that you can accumulate information and ideas as they arise, but don't let the essay dominate and distort your studies.

- Adjust your reading plans if necessary as the time for essay writing approaches.

11.2.4 Taking stock before you start writing

When you arrive at your target day for starting the essay, you need to take stock and get yourself organised.

Reviewing your strategy

You will need to revisit your plans, review your progress and make adjustments.

■ What studying have you managed to complete? If you haven't covered all that you'd intended, *don't* be tempted to carry on reading. Better to go with what you've done, than use up vital writing time. It's *always* tempting to put off writing – don't. Get started in good time, so that you can give the essay your best shot.

■ Do you still have the time available that you had intended for writing? If not, adjust your writing plans. Keep in mind that writing is a long, drawn-out process. Don't assume that the later stages will be quick and easy.

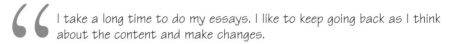

> I take a long time to do my essays. I like to keep going back as I think about the content and make changes.

Another thing you might take stock of is whether you have any specific goals for this essay. For example, is there an aspect of your writing skills that you want to work on?

> Before I start I read my tutor's remarks on my last essay, so I can try to make sure I am applying what has been suggested to improve my writing.

Organising your sources

You also need to gather around you all the relevant books, notes and anything else. Then sort it all into piles, folders, or whatever. This organising can be time consuming, but it is a vital process of 'loading up' into your head a picture of all the resources you have accumulated, and where everything is. Your work space may look a mess for some days.

> I usually have all the course material surrounding me as I'm going through – open at various pages to make sure I'm keeping the essay relevant.

Identifying material for the essay

With all your source material gathered together and organised, you now need to work through, reminding yourself of what is relevant to the essay. Again keep a pad handy, so that you can make a list of your sources, with notes alongside reminding yourself what you might use them for.

Williams article: defn. of depression – recent figures – supports Layard

Look out for relevant arguments, concepts, authors, evidence and theories. A lot should already be marked up, from when you did your reading. The point of this run through is to give yourself an overview of what you have gathered together, and to add a few notes reminding yourself of how ideas link to each other.

> I read the question, break down the points I am going to write about, then go through my notes to identify which bits relate to the points I am writing about. By the time I start writing, my books have yellow stickies poking out everywhere.

Key points

As you are about to start the main writing of an essay, take stock as follows:

- Review your overall writing strategy in the light of the time now available for writing the essay.

- Assemble all your source material and organise it so that you can find things.

- Skim through your sources marking up what you hope to use in your essay.

11.2.5 Getting ideas written down

You've already begun the process of writing ideas down, in the notes you've made. However, the emphasis has been on grasping what *other* writers have to say. Now you need to focus on what *you* are going to say. You don't want your essay to be just a rehash of what you've read. That would be boring for you and wouldn't get you a good mark. And it wouldn't help you to understand the subject, or develop your writing skills. So, put your notes and books to one side and work at developing your *own* thoughts on how to approach the essay title.

> After a few days I usually write down all the things I think should be included in my essay, usually far too much, but I prefer this as I spend a lot of time editing it.

Revisiting the title

Having had the title in your head for a few days, your ideas will have moved on. Look again at the words you highlighted and your notes about them. Do you want to highlight other words now, or revise your thinking about their implications? Try sketching some notes in answer to the title question, without stopping to think about what you've read. Or try breaking the question into sub-questions? For example:

Is the UK getting wealthier? What is the evidence?

Can we really measure happiness?

Why doesn't prosperity make us happier?

Can anything be done to change levels of happiness?

Then just *write lots of thoughts relating to the title*, without worrying about what comes out. Write down points *for* and *against* – perhaps a whole sentence if one comes to you – and any *extra questions* that the essay title throws up. My notes in Figure 11.1 are a sample of 'off the cuff' ideas I might want to explore in writing the essay on Layard. I just typed them out as they came to me – they may not make much sense to you but no matter – I would only use them for a day or so, then throw them out.

> First I write down key words or phrases that spring to mind when reading the question, these include case study material, theories, models, etc. I then elaborate on them and write paragraphs based on a rough plan of what topic should be where.

NOTES FOR LAYARD ESSAY
As soc gets wealthier are we doomed to be unhappier? Discuss re Layard article.
1) Why is this an issue at all?
    a) General belief - wealth = success = happiness
        i) Underlies personal striving in life - also government policy
2) NO answer: i.e. we're NOT doomed to unhappiness
    a) Because we're not getting unhappier
        i) Happiness figures aren't getting worse - just staying the same
            Perhaps happiness just stays the same whatever
                i.e. not down to economy, or society, but human psychology
        ii) Questionnaire relies don't tell us much anyway
            We rely how happy we are by how happy we think we ought to be
                - looking around us in society
    b) Because we can do something about it
        i) Layard - tax 'excess' income + social spending
3) YES answer: i.e. we ARE doomed
    a) E.g. Happier in Denmark/Iceland - compared with richer USA
    b) Increasing competitiveness of society
        i) Layard says - more aware of 'reference groups'
        ii) E.g. EGermans/women in work

Figure 11.1 Sample of quick thoughts related to the essay title

Pen and pad or computer?

As you can see I made my notes using my word processor's outlining facility. Some people prefer to jot notes on a pad instead, perhaps organising it as a mind map. I tend to use both, note-pad and computer. Sometimes ideas seem to flow more creatively on paper. In fact I like to work with two or three note-pads, so that I can start on a different one if another approach strikes me, then I don't get confused. I cross things out, scribble extra points slantwise to get them in, draw arrows to show where things could be moved to and generally create a chaotic looking page, but one which contains lots of germs of ideas I can work up. The advantage of the outliner is being able to get ideas down as you think of them, then move them around. Also, it forces you to organise points into a linear sequence, which is how you are going to have to write in the end. In fact, with a messy page of handwritten notes, I often type them into the outliner, so that I can sort out the mess before starting to write. It might seem a lot of extra work, but it's much less time consuming than getting completely stuck later, or going off on the wrong tack.

Brainstorming

Sketching out ideas quickly is known as brainstorming. You write fragments of thoughts as fast as you can, flitting from point to point, trying to avoid losing new thoughts while you are writing other ones out. The aim is to create a store of possible ideas.

At the beginning of an essay I do brainstorming on the title of the essay to come up with ideas of what to write about. Then I do a sort of structural plan, of what, why and how — trying to answer all these questions. Don't know if it's the correct way but it works for me.

After I've finished my reading I find that certain things tend to stick in my mind. I then have a brainstorming session where I write down absolutely every thing that I can.

By working fast and uncritically you get access to ideas you'd never reach through more logical thinking. Your studies of the course texts will have set all kinds of thoughts churning away half-formed in your mind. Brainstorming aims to *trap* some of these ideas and *fix* them in writing, *outside* your head. There you can examine them, move them around, tidy them up, and improve wording. But get plenty of words on paper before you start the tidying up. Thinking analytically and critically may dry up the flow of ideas. You want to start out with more ideas than you actually need, so that you can throw some away and be left with just the best.

I try looking at things completely differently, taking the essay question and breaking it into as tiny bits as possible, and writing sentences and paragraphs relevant to them. Once I have all this down on paper I can sort out what I need in the essay and what I don't need.

The point of jotting notes before starting on the writing is to avoid that depressing experience of sitting in front of a blank screen with nothing to say.

Why is it that I do all the reading, study the other materials, join in the online chat and when it comes to putting pen to paper, or fingers to keyboard, NOTHING happens?

Most of us, if we sit down and try to start typing an opening paragraph, soon run out of words. It's best not to begin with whole sentences. By busying yourself with jotting down notes, you can get your thoughts flowing; then sometimes you will find that whole sentences come out fully formed, perhaps even running on into a paragraph, which you can set aside to use later. But don't force it – wait for it to happen. In the meantime just concentrate on getting down notes. It's much easier to come up with interesting ideas in this informal way than to achieve inspiration while you are writing out a full draft.

I write it all in note form then change it round, I do this sometimes days apart as I seem to be able to keep it in my head and think about it when I am gardening or even when I am relaxing (ha ha!). I don't think I will ever be able to sit down and write an essay just like that, but you seem to learn more doing it in stages, well I do, it can take me two weeks to get it ok.

BOX 11.1   DO YOUR ESSAYS TEND TO BE TOO SHORT?

If you keep finding yourself falling short of the word requirements for essays, focus more effort on this note-jotting stage. Just keep writing ideas down, trying to come at the essay title from different angles, and making links to different authors, theories or case studies. And remember that you have to *explain* your points, so that your reader understands. Write down ideas for this too.

Key points

■ 'Brainstorm' in a free and uninhibited way to get together some ideas you can work up. Generate more than you need, then throw some away.

■ The quality of the essay you eventually produce will reflect the richness of your informal, scrappy notes at this preliminary stage.

11.2.6 Organising your material

See Chapter 10
Section 10.3.6,
Structuring the
argument

Now you are ready to start thinking about *structure*. As you saw with the essays written by Lewis and Erin in Chapter 10, structure makes a big difference. Basically it involves:

■ going over your notes and grouping ideas together in clusters, then

■ working out a sequence for those clusters.

Any kind of crude dividing up is useful to begin with. For example, you might start by separating your notes into points *for* the proposition in the title and points *against*. Then you decide which of these to take first in your essay and which second. Then you could break each of these two clusters into two or three sub-sections, and again decide in what order to take them.

Using an outliner

This is where working onscreen with an outline view comes into its own. Outliners are designed specifically for creating outline plans for your writing. They give complete freedom to move points around into different clusters. You can drag your points up or down the page to cluster them with other points. And you can 'promote' points by dragging them to the left, or 'demote' them under other points by dragging them to the right. You can see the general idea in Figure 11.2.

```
□  ESSAY PLAN
□  As soc gets wealthier are we doomed to be unhappier? Discuss re Layard
   article.
1) Intro: what are consequences of pursuit of increasing wealth?
2) Backdrop of long growth in wealth - quote figures from National Statistics
3) Are we getting unhappier?
     □  a) Layard's evidence
     □  b) Objections to his evidence - e.g. a high proportion are 'very happy'
4) Why people don't get happier through wealth - the psychology of prosperity
□  a) Examples of habituation
□  b) Examples of rivalry
5) Are we doomed to continue the way we are?
□  a) Can't do much about habituation, but can try to temper competitiveness
□  b) Doubts: isn't rising competitiveness inevitable? globalisation. mass media
   etc.
          □  i) Seems to be trying to hold back the tide
6) Conclusion:
     □  a) Not everyone would be growing unhappier anyway, some will be 'very
        happy'
     □  b) Summarise points re happiness trends
     □  c) Summarise possible courses of action
     □  d) Draw conclusions which answer the question.
```

Figure 11.2 Sample essay plan, made using Outline view in Microsoft Word

This flexibility is a tremendous asset in trying out different ways of structuring your points. And you can keep saving your outline with a new name, then printing it off, so that you can compare different structures without worrying that you are messing up what you've already done.

Working on paper

If, on the other hand, you prefer to work on paper, you could cut your notes into strips and sort these into clusters. Then you can look at each of the clusters and work out a sequence to take the points within it – perhaps separating them into sub-clusters. You will then be in a position to sketch a rough outline plan. Number the headings and subheadings, to help you keep track as you work on the essay.

Simple but purposeful

Simpler is generally better where essay plans are concerned. Your essay will be *easier to write* if it has a simple structure and, equally important, your reader will find it *easier to read*. My plan in Figure 11.2 is for an essay of about 1,200 words (about four times as long as Lewis's and Erin's). I would expect to write a paragraph on each of points 1, 2 and 6. Then at least two paragraphs on each of 3, 4 and 5. Notice how the plan leads towards a conclusion. (See also the examples in Section 10.3.6 of Chapter 10.) A key weakness with Lewis's essay is that it doesn't flow towards a conclusion. Lewis needed to spend more time on this stage of organising his points. It's important to remind yourself that the purpose behind an essay plan is to lead from the title to your conclusion.

See Chapter 10 Section 10.3.6, Structuring the argument

For a 1,500 word essay I aim for a 100-150 word introduction then six paragraphs of similar lengths then a final conclusion of approx 100 words.

BOX 11.2   GROPING TOWARDS AN ESSAY PLAN

The period when you are groping towards a workable essay plan can be unsettling. The shape may take quite a time to emerge, as your thoughts slowly resolve themselves. When it does, it may be so simple that you wonder why it took you so long. However, simplicity is a sign that your thoughts *have* resolved themselves. Everything seems simple *after* you've thought of it.

Marking up your notes

Once you have sketched out a plan, you go back through your notes, labelling points according to where in the plan you think they fit.

I try to plan my essay into paragraphs and next to every idea I write which para I think it should go into. I then have to leave it for a day to think it over in my head.

Leaving things out

As you plan an essay, you have to make hard choices. Which points will you put at the centre of your argument and which ones will you chop? You make your essay worse, not better, if you try to cram everything in.

It's not a matter of how *much* you say, but how well it reads *as an argument*. So if points don't fit, let them go. Don't worry about showing that you've read everything. You are simply presenting a sample of what you can do. In fact, however far you progress with your writing, you will *never* be able to include *everything* you want to say. All readers have limited time and patience. One of the highest skills of writing lies in choosing what to say and what to leave out.

I'm finding it really hard with this topic, choosing what to include and what to exclude. There are so many things I could say.

Well I was surprised last time to find I got a very good result by restricting myself to one area and exploring it thoroughly.

BOX 11.3   DO YOUR ESSAYS TEND TO BE OVER-LONG?

If you always write too many words, you need to be more ruthless in scaling down your ambitions at the planning stage. If your plans are too broad and complicated, your essay becomes very difficult to follow. And if you rush your points because of the word constraints, you don't provide enough explanation and back up for your points, so your writing becomes cramped and impenetrable. Generally, a measured, well delivered explanation of a limited range of points makes a better essay and is more enjoyable to write.

On the other hand, writing too much, then editing down can also produce good results. By trimming away all the excess, you can end up with a nice taut line of argument, so long as you don't grieve too much at all those butchered words.

Key points

■ The planning stage is essential. It is at this point that your essay begins to acquire some coherence and force.

■ Planning simply means sorting your point into clusters and then into a sensible sequence.

■ Your plan should lead you to a point where you can draw a conclusion which addresses the task in the essay title.

11.2.7 Drafting an answer

With your notes roughly sorted and labelled according to your sketched plan, you are ready to start turning your notes into sentences. You have decided *what* to try to say. Now you have to concentrate on *how* to say it so that a reader will be able to understand.

Where to start?

You might start straight into your introduction to the essay. But sometimes it's easier to start somewhere else. The introduction can be easier to write when you've seen what you're actually going to say.

 I used to get completely lost trying to start my essays with my introduction because I didn't know what to put in it. So I often start by writing the middle bits, or towards the end, and expand it from there – finally organising it all into the right place and adding an introduction and a conclusion.

However, it can be useful to write a quick sketch of an introduction just to get yourself into the right frame of mind for the first main section. Then you can come back later and work it up properly. Try out different approaches, to see what works for you.

 I usually finish by writing the introduction then conclusion, though I may have done a dummy intro first.

A fluid approach

Try to work in a fluid, open-ended way, turning your notes into more fully explained points, then fleshing out a point a bit more if it seems to need it, or adding a word or two of explanation leading up to it, to show where it's coming from. If you plod forward in a rigid, 'linear' fashion, progress tends to be slow and you easily get stuck. You need to be able to see beyond the sentence, to where it is leading.

 I expand my ideas into sentences, then split them into paragraphs if the ideas get complicated. I worry later about what it's doing to the essay structure. Once I have some ideas in sentences, I can look at whether I've answered the question.

Build up from what you've already sketched out in your notes. Most people find it difficult to compose sentences straight out of their heads.

Reviewing as you go

You may prefer to work to the end of your essay before stopping, so that you don't get bogged down with the first few paragraphs. Or you may find it helpful to stop at the end of a section, to print off what you've done and see how it's going. This helps you to switch to the role of your reader, to see whether you've said what you meant to say and whether your writing flows along reasonably and the tone seems right. Could you make a few tweaks to improve things? Have you done enough explaining to get your points across? Would an example help? Are you remembering to make your points relevant to the title question? Stopping regularly to review progress can be a good way to develop your writing style, allowing you to 'craft' your line of argument. However, if it discourages you, or slows you down too much because you keep refining the same few sentences, then get to the end before stopping to review.

BOX 11.4   DO YOUR ESSAYS TEND TO BE TOO SHORT?

Once again, if you are a person who tends to write *too little* in your essays, you may not be giving enough attention to how much *explaining* you need to do to get your points across to someone else. You probably need to discuss more examples and show more carefully how your points link up with each other and to the essay title.

Shut yourself away

Expressing newly learned ideas to your reader requires full concentration. You have to get yourself into the right frame of thinking. Then once you are into a flow of argument, you want to be able to push along until it runs out. If you keep having to stop and start, you can end up doing a lot of mental work without having much to show for it. Do your best to cut yourself off from distractions whenever you are drafting an essay. And try not to make up distractions of your own.

 It's amazing how tidy my house suddenly gets when the essay deadline is closing in.

Taking breaks

On the other hand, do allow yourself breaks. It's very hard to stay productively focused for long spells. You need time to clear your mind, then re-gather your thoughts. Just make sure you achieve a reasonable amount between breaks. It's also good to spread the writing over several sessions. You can usually arrive at a more balanced perspective.

 I type up a bit then go out or watch a bit of telly or do stuff around the house and then come back and have another go.

I go to the pub, gym, a friends house or just downstairs for a cup of tea or something ... just to relax my mind and reflect on the point I am trying to put across.

I usually have to leave it for a day at a time to think things through and then I come back and rearrange things or take them out or put new things in.

Key points

- Start drafting by working from your essay plan and turning your notes into sentences.

- Don't start with the introduction, if you find it easier to start elsewhere.

- Work fluidly, going back over what you've written and reshaping as you go. But also keep moving on. Don't stay obsessively on the early sections.

- Cut yourself off from distractions, but take breaks from time to time.

11.2.8 Reviewing and polishing

When you finally reach the end of your draft essay, print it off, put it to one side and take a break. Then, when you are ready for another session, come back to it and read it through. Even if you have been reviewing and editing as you've gone along, you need to take a look at the whole essay and check that the essentials are there. If you have time, leave the reviewing to another day, when you can look from a greater distance, more as your reader will see it.

Reviewing

It's generally easier to work on a printed copy, marking up changes in pen. As you read through, check the following:

- Do your sentences 'work'? Does the 'sense' move along reasonably smoothly? A good check is to read out loud. If you find you stumble, or have to pause over the meaning, then probably you have a sentence which is too long or has something important missing (such as a verb, or a link to the previous sentence).

 I always look at the drafts of my essays to see where points can be clarified by use of more concise or appropriate language.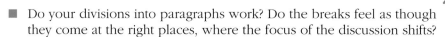

- Do your divisions into paragraphs work? Do the breaks feel as though they come at the right places, where the focus of the discussion shifts?

- Have you given enough explanation and illustration to enable your reader to understand what your argument is all about?

- Does your argument make sense as you move from point to point? Have you signalled the main moves clearly to your reader? Is it obvious, as you start each new paragraph, why it's relevant to the question?

- Does your introduction set things rolling effectively? Does it lead your reader from the title to the next paragraph?

■ And, most important of all, does your conclusion *answer the question in the title?* Look back at the words you highlighted in the title. Have you addressed the implications of each of them?

As you read through and mark up changes, think about whether you want to reorganise parts of the essay. As you saw with Lewis's essay in Chapter 10, moving a couple of paragraphs to different places made quite an improvement to the flow of his argument. Reviewing can be a highly creative process, through which you come to understand your own argument more clearly and get new insights into how to make your writing work better. You learn a lot about the way ideas work in your subject area as you think about different ways to say things.

It is amazing how an essay can develop as you write, so that final editing is so important.

Revising and polishing

Now you need to go through the essay making all the changes you have marked up. It's a good idea to save a back-up copy, so that you can make changes freely without worrying that you will mess things up. You will then be able to go back to your earlier version if you don't feel happy with a change. Entering your marked up changes can be surprisingly time consuming, especially if you think of new improvements while you are making the changes. But it is also very satisfying, working your writing up into a more polished form. Again it's an excellent learning process, which helps with your long term writing development.

References

You also need to go through your essay checking that you have put *references* in the text in all the appropriate places: that is, whenever you have *referred* to an author's work and whenever you have included a *quotation*. And as you come to each reference in the text, make sure there is a corresponding *entry* in your *list of references* at the end. (You can see examples of references in Erin's essay in Chapter 10 Section 10.2.)

Make sure that you have written the references in the way required. The rules vary a little from one subject area to another and from one institution to another. So make sure you find out what is required. Check your university or department website, or ask at your department or the student support services. It can be a finicky business getting them right, but it improves the presentation of your essay a lot. And it's worth finding out early on, because once you get into the habit, it becomes quite routine. If you would like detailed guidance on one of the common systems of referencing, go to Chapter 10 downloads on the Good Study Guide website at www.goodstudyguide.co.uk.

Layout

Take a look at how your essay is laid out on the page. Is it clear and easy to read? Does your university or department issue guidelines on layout?

In the absence of other guidance go for plain, simple and clear. Don't use fancy fonts. Use a font size of 10 point or 12 point for the main text, unless you have a reason to do otherwise. Stick to black print on a white background. Only use italics where useful, or required, and use bold formatting very sparingly. Use single line-spacing, unless you are asked to do otherwise.

Make sure the title is written at the top of the first page, and that it is the same, word for word, as the one you were given. Put your name and the course title or code in a header, so that they appear on every page. You could also put the date in a footer. Number the pages and set generous margins.

If you have to submit the essay on paper, print on just one side of the sheet.

Spelling and grammar

Be sure to run your word processor's spelling and grammar checks, to see whether there are things you need to tidy up.

Submit it and forget about it

Print the essay off one more time and take a last look through. Make any required tweaks. Then put your essay in an envelope and seal it, ready to hand in, or send it off electronically. There comes a point when you need to get on with the rest of your course and the rest of your life. If you've given an essay a decent shot in the time you have available that's all that is required. Now give yourself a treat.

I always panic after sending off my essay, wishing I had gone over it one more time. I just have to remember that it's the same for everybody else. You could go on forever.

Key points

- The final stage of reviewing and revising your essay makes a vital contribution to producing a readable, coherent, well argued and well presented piece of work.

- Although time consuming, this is an important part of the learning process, because you really get to grips with working out how to express an argument in your subject area.

- You also need to check your references, page layout, spelling and grammar, to make your essay look as good as it really is.

- But don't keep revising for too long. Do a reasonable job, then move on.

11.2.9 An overview of the eight stages

Having considered this eight stage approach to writing in such detail, you can get an overview of the whole sequence in Table 11.1. The second column summarises what you do to complete each stage. Then the third outlines the mental processes involved and indicates how these contribute towards producing a high quality essay. So the table both reminds you what to do and explains how the writing process works.

Table 11.1   The eight stages of essay writing

Stage		What you do	What it contributes
1	Thinking about the essay title	Highlight key words and make notes about them.	Focuses your attention on what you are being asked to do.
2	Planning the writing process	Plan how you will cover the reading and make the time.	Keeps you in control of the writing process, so you cover all aspects.
3	Studying the course content	Highlight and take notes of essay-relevant material.	Gives your studies a creative edge, as you make links between the essay title and your course studies.
4	Taking stock before you start writing	Update plans, gather together essay material and get an overview of it all.	Gets your mind sharply task focused and loaded up with all the relevant ideas.
5	Getting ideas written down	Refocus on the title, then 'brainstorm' to get lots of ideas in writing.	Gets ideas out of your head and onto the page where you can examine them and work them up.
6	Organising your material	Group your notes, then sequence them to create an essay plan.	Helps you to arrive at a line of argument for your essay and a structure to deliver it.
7	Drafting an answer	Turn your notes into sentences and paragraphs: a dialogue with your reader.	Translates your notes from 'private' into 'public' language, and from vague links to explicit argument.
8	Reviewing and polishing	Read through, revise and add finishing touches.	Turns raw potential into an attractive read.

The value of breaking writing down into stages

As everyone who has tried knows, it's easy to get stuck when you are writing. You sit and wonder what you are trying to say and how to get yourself moving again. So, it is enormously helpful to think of the challenge of writing as a set of smaller, more manageable tasks, which you can tackle one at a time. Writing becomes less of a mystery and more of an ordinary activity, in which you make a finished product by following a sequence of practical steps. Approaching writing in stages also helps you to think about it more *strategically*, because the process has a clearer shape to it. You can *plan* each stage and try to make sensible use of your time. And should you become stuck, you can switch to a different stage then come back later.

Overlap between the stages

Although it's helpful to be able to think about the stages of writing separately, it's important to recognise that they are not completely separate or rigidly sequenced. Indeed, they overlap and are best tackled flexibly:

- As you plan, you may suddenly think of another source book to look at, or some notes you made that you could use after all.

- When you are writing the first draft, you may become aware that your essay plan needs to be altered.

- When you are reviewing your draft essay, you may remember a question you jotted in your notes which could be worked up to use as an introduction to your essay.

Since the stages of writing impact on each other, you need to move back and forth between them. No stage is entirely complete until the whole is complete.

Becoming a more powerful writer

If you are to fulfil your potential as a writer you need to give careful thought to each of these stage of writing. You need to experiment with different approaches to them, reflect on your successes and failures and refine your strategy. Your writing becomes more powerful as you learn how to blend this sequence of activities together – how much time to give to each stage, which ones you are particularly good at, and where you need to work at developing your skills. You don't worry about whether you have genius, or verbal flair. You simply think of writing in practical workaday terms and 'get stuck in', gradually building up your control over the whole process. Powerful and original writing is achieved not through communing with a muse, but by working to a realistic plan, within well defined constraints. Originality is something you happen upon, rather than achieve by seeking it. What you need is a framework within which you can see a way to take the next step forward. The control this gives enables your writing power to develop.

Key points

- Being aware of distinct stages of essay writing greatly increases the options open to you and gives you more control over the writing process.

- Treat essay writing as a practical task not as a mysterious search for inspiration.

- It is not a one-session job. Ideally it should be spread over several days.

- Don't simply sit at your keyboard and begin to type, do a lot of your work before you start the writing proper.

- Break writing into stages, so that you can tackle it a bit at a time rather than face the whole thing at once.

- Work flexibly, moving back and forth between the stages as necessary and moving on if you get stuck.

- Build up your writing ability by developing your strategies and skills within each of the stages.

11.3 Expressing ideas in writing

Writing is a very special kind of *conversation* which requires skill and practice. If you've already made notes of what you want to say, it might seem that the writing ought to be straightforward. Not so. You have to take the scraps of ideas in your notes and *speak* them as whole sentences. You have to give examples to illustrate to your reader what you are talking about along with supporting evidence. And you have to lead your reader carefully step by step from the question in the title, through the points you want to make, showing how they all follow on from one another. So it's quite a formal, task-driven conversation, but it's also one in which meaning has to flow, otherwise your reader will be lost. Somehow you have to get yourself into a 'conversational' frame of mind, where your focus is not only on the ideas you want to put across, but also on whether your reader will be able to follow you.

Yet so much is undefined at the outset. Where are you going to start from? What will your opening words be? They set the tone for what follows, but you don't yet know what follows. It's a tough challenge. In this short section I outline some approaches I have found helpful in turning half-formed ideas into readable sentences.

11.3.1 Finding your voice

It's hard to get meanings across to an absent reader with the clarity and force you can achieve in conversation with people you know. You sense what you *want* to say but, when the words come out on paper and you read through them, you can see that you haven't conveyed what you intended. The words are there to be read, but they come across as dull and dead. There seems to be no 'voice' speaking them.

One approach to developing a writing voice is simply to make yourself write on a regular basis, in order to build up practice in occupying the role of writer. Peter Elbow, who has led writing programmes at a number of American universities and colleges, advocates a technique he calls 'freewriting' – see Box 11.5.

BOX 11.5   FREEWRITING

 To do a freewriting exercise, simply force yourself to write without stopping for ten minutes. Sometimes you will produce good writing, but that's not the goal. Sometimes you will produce garbage, but that's not the goal either. You may stay on one topic, you may flip repeatedly from one to another: it doesn't matter [...] Speed is not the goal, though sometimes the process revs you up. If you can't think of anything to write, write about how that feels or repeat over and over 'I have nothing to write' [...] if you get stuck in the middle of a sentence or thought, just repeat the last word or phrase till something comes along. The only point is to keep writing [...] There are lots of goals of freewriting, but they are best served if, while you are doing it, you accept this single, simple, mechanical goal of simply not stopping.

(Elbow, 1998, p. 13)

Elbow's idea is that you write continuously for a short burst, about *anything* that comes into your head, without concern about quality or being read by others (a bit like brainstorming except that you concentrate on keeping a flow of words going rather than on producing ideas). When you have finished the writing you put it away and on subsequent days you do some more. Then a few days later you come back and read over your work looking for places where you feel that your 'voice' breaks through – where your writing achieves some force – possibly a phrase, a sentence, or a whole paragraph. (You might exchange samples of freewriting with another student, so that you can search for each other's voice.) Over a period of time, says Elbow, a number of changes will come about:

■ Sheer accumulation of practice at 'being in the writing situation' will make you more comfortable with writing to an audience and will take the awkwardness and formality out of your writing style.

■ The freedom to write 'anything' will release you from the constraints which normally cramp your style, and make your writing more open and creative.

■ The repeated searching through your words to find your 'voice' sharpens your perception of when you are writing powerfully and when you are not.

■ You become more aware of how to set yourself up to break through to an authentic writing voice.

11.3.2 Recognising the openness of writing

Sometimes it feels as though you are searching for the 'right' way to say something. But, actually, there is no perfect way to make your points. One way will work well for one reader and another for another.

BOX 11.6   AN 'EXPERIMENTAL' APPROACH TO COMPOSITION

I once took an art class. Drawing my first picture, I put the main subject right in the centre, taking up most of the space. The art teacher pointed out that this was dull to look at. And since I didn't seem to get his point, he drew a credit card sized rectangle in which he asked me to sketch the figure and background in a different relation to each other. Then he told me to draw another dozen rectangles and sketch a different version of the picture in each. When I had finished we went over them and I began to see that some of them were much more interesting as compositions than others. And what surprised me was that *I* had been able to draw them, when at the outset I'd only been able to see one way to draw the picture. Afterwards, I began to notice that famous painters often did numerous sketches of the same scene, each with its own special qualities. In other words, having worked intently on a representation of some subject, they started all over again and produced a different version. No particular version was 'correct'. Each achieved a different effect.

Writing is like this. Every piece you compose could be written in many other ways, some, perhaps, more interesting and clear, and others confusing, or dull. Yet, at the moment you start to write, your imagination tends to be restricted to seeing only one way ahead. So it can help to sketch different outline plans, or to try out two or more versions of a particular paragraph, or several ways of opening or closing your essay. Don't feel you are looking for the 'right' way to say things. Work in an open, 'experimental' way, trying out different approaches. And be content that whichever you choose to go with it is just one of many approaches, none of which is the 'correct' one. Thinking this way helps you to feel less imprisoned inside a particular style of writing. It emphasises your powers of expression and the wealth of possibilities that lie in front of you.

What you need is an open attitude to your writing, which allows you to be *critical* in judging what has worked and what has not, but also *comfortable* in knowing, after you've made your choices, that though there are other ways you could have said things, it's not worth tinkering for too long. Don't hover in anguish over what you might possibly write better. There are so many other interesting things to write about. Just play around with some possibilities, make your choices and move on.

11.3.3 Finding fluency

If you begin at the beginning of your essay and try to compose formal sentences one after another, you are asking a lot of yourself. You will find yourself struggling to get started and when you do, your words may seem empty and ungainly. And though you go back over and over, changing your words, each new version may seem no better. To avoid such frustrating and morale-crushing experiences, and also to find a less stilted style, you need to take the pressure off yourself. You need a more free-flowing way to sketch out some 'dialogue' with your reader. In Box 11.7 I describe what I do.

BOX 11.7   GENERATING A FLOW

When I get stuck I leave my keyboard, go and sit in my 'reading and ideas' armchair, with a board to rest on, and sketch scraps of ideas on paper. I write freely, knowing that I'm going to revise later and I don't bother at all how it looks. I write quickly and restlessly – starting on different ideas, switching things around, moving on – until something starts to flow. Then I go with the flow, though I'm always ready to branch off when another thought strikes. I just draw a line out from wherever I am, to a space on the page and carry on sketching out the new idea. Then I go back and see whether I want to carry on from where I was. In a way, it's more like the loose-knit, unpredictable process of having an informal conversation. It's a bit like freewriting, but more focused and task-oriented.

When I feel I have enough ideas to work with, or just feel ready for a change, I go back to the keyboard and switch into my more formal 'composing' mode, working up the scraps, pulling them into shape and making them flow in an orderly and controlled way. (This box started out as half a page of scrawled ideas, with spidery lines coming off to notes written sideways up the margins and lots of crossing out. It looked a complete mess and much of it never made it as far as my computer screen, let alone the page you are reading.)

Trying to write polished prose straight-off cranks up the pressure, stifles your creativity, and blocks the flow of your words. Those mental blocks use up time far less productively than giving yourself time to play around with ideas and forms of words. You need to create space to think and get a written dialogue going with yourself.

11.3.4 Reading aloud

Since writing is a form of speaking (though a constrained and lop-sided one), it can be helpful to hear what your words sound like when you read them out loud. You get a new angle on how well the sense flows through your sentences. In fact, if you know someone (a student, friend, or family member) who is prepared to listen, reading to another person can help you develop your *sense of audience* and your writing *voice*. It doesn't necessarily matter whether the listener fully understands, or is able to comment on what you have written. In the process of speaking the words to someone else you will *hear for yourself* which passages work best and which don't come across as you intended.

We all tend to feel reticent about exposing our writing to other people, particularly when we're writing about a subject that's new to us. However, you are writing to be read by somebody, somewhere. If you can summon up the nerve to 'be there' as your message is received by someone, you gain fresh insight into the nature of communicating through writing.

See Chapter 11 Section 11.2.5, Getting ideas written down

11.3.5 Onscreen or on paper?

I find that writing on a pad and composing to a computer screen work in quite different ways, so I do both. For more routine writing I find word processing fine on its own. But if it's challenging and creative writing, I need to switch to more informal sketching on a pad. Then after a while, I go back to the word processor and use the outliner to tidy up. I make a lot of use of the outliner in the early stages of writing, but later I stick mainly to the print layout view. For longer pieces with subheadings, I always have the 'document map' open at the left of the screen, so that I can see the whole structure and go straight to specific sections when I need to check things. However, having asked others, I know that people work differently. We all have to find out what works for us. The point is to experiment. If you want your writing to develop, you have to take a reflective, creative approach. Try using the facilities your word processor offers, but also try different ways of working with pen and paper.

11.3.6 Separating note making from writing

To be able to write fluently and convincingly you need to be able to give all your attention to 'talking' to your reader. That is why you need to have made notes of what you want to say before you start drafting whole sentences and paragraphs. If you try to think up *content* at the same time as *addressing* yourself to your reader, you will almost certainly do one or the other badly. Either your points will be weak and disconnected, or your language will be insufficiently clear and expressive. Worst of all, you will grind to a halt. Separating the stage of generating ideas from that of composing sentences is a key way of avoiding these problems.

Key points

- As you work to develop your writing voice, it can be helpful to make yourself write regularly, using a technique such as 'freewriting'.

- It's important to relax about trying to say things the 'right' way – and to recognise, instead, that you can say things perfectly well in any number of ways.

- You need to develop ways of getting your ideas and words flowing together, by working informally and creatively, rather than trying to compose high quality sentences straight off.

- You can help to develop your sense of audience by reading your work aloud.

- Work flexibly. Try out different places and different writing aids to keep your writing flowing.

- 'Talking' in writing takes all your powers of concentration. You need to have worked out the ideas of the essay, before you tackle this challenge.

11.4 Making your essay flow

In Chapter 10 we looked at how a student, Erin, made a very brief essay flow. We saw how she successfully used 'link words' and 'signposting' phrases to carry the meaning forward from sentence to sentence and paragraph to paragraph. Now we look for further tricks of the writing trade by examining how Richard Layard, an experienced writer, carries a more complex argument through a somewhat longer piece of writing. Again we return to his article on wealth and happiness, at the end of this book, but this time focusing on his writing technique rather than the content. (You may want to download another copy of the article from the Good Study Guide website at www.goodstudyguide.co.uk).

11.4.1 Link words

The first thing I want to focus on is how Layard carries the flow of his sentences along.

Activity 11.2

Read through the first two paragraphs of Layard's article and think about how he creates a flow of meaning. How does the sense get carried along from sentence to sentence? Highlight the words you think are significant in achieving this.

As usual, there are no right answers to this kind of exercise. You could argue it in different ways. However, I highlighted 'There is a paradox', 'Yet' (twice), 'happiness', 'By happiness I mean', and 'And by unhappiness I mean'.

Layard's four opening words tell us that he's is going to present us with a paradox. So we are all set up for the second sentence, where he gives us one side of the paradox. '*Yet*' at the start of the third sentence lets us know we are about to be given the other side of the paradox. However, Layard doesn't directly signal the next sentence. He expects us to have picked up the rhythm of the 'A yet B' format, and simply repeats it, so that the fourth sentence returns to the first side of the paradox, and the fifth starts with '*Yet*' and gives the other side. So, we see that linking up the meaning of sentences is more than just a matter of inserting 'link words'. It can be done by subtle devices like repeating the rhythm of the sentences.

The link to the first sentence of the *second paragraph* is again done without a direct 'link word', but in a different way. Layard simply picks up the word '*happiness*' from the previous sentence. This also links us back to the title, where 'happiness' is the leading word. '*By happiness I mean*' tells us that he is going to elaborate on this significant word. The word '*And*' then ties the second sentence very closely to the first. However, '*by unhappiness I mean*' then flips the coin over. In fact, the whole rhythm and wording of the second sentence echoes the first, but with the meanings inverted. This securely nails down how Layard wants this key term to be understood. At the risk of sounding slightly pedantic, he's defined both ends of this, potentially nebulous, dimension of human experience. And he's reinforced his point with mirror-image sentences. The third sentence reinforces his point again, by saying that 'most people' find the concept easy to apply to themselves. I wasn't sure whether to highlight the phrase 'Most people', as it didn't seem quite to be a 'link phrase'. The meaning follows through rather more subtly than that.

Already you can see that there isn't a simple formula for passing on meaning. Yet I hope you agree that Layard is paying a lot of attention to ensuring that we follow his flow.

Activity 11.3

I suggest you try going through the rest of the article underlining words and phrases that seem to do a significant job in passing on meaning. Don't spend too long, just pick out the obvious examples. Look particularly at the openings of paragraphs. In each case think how Layard lets us know the way the meaning follows on. (Note that I made a cut between paragraphs 2 and 3, so there isn't a direct link there.)

It's helpful to pick out words and phrases for yourself first, but when you are ready to see what I picked out, visit the Good Study Guide website. See whether we picked similar words and whether my selections make sense to you.

I'll now take you through some features I found interesting in Layard's use of link words.

In paragraphs 3 to 7, Layard is presenting evidence to back up his main argument in paragraph 1. As I highlighted links, I noticed him using a repeated device:

It is true that [...] The problem is that [...] This is true of [...] We also know that [...] These show that [...]

With slight variations, Layard is signalling, in a regular and rhythmical way, that he is presenting evidence to us. With a lot of information to present, it helps to set up a rhythm. The reader can then 'tune in' to the rhythm and pick the information up quickly and easily, sorting it mentally as they go. It's not like following an argument, where you have to twist and turn with the logical manoeuvres. You are just taking delivery of necessary goods.

'Further evidence' at the start of paragraph 5 does a similar job, but has the additional effect of reminding us explicitly that we are working through a list of evidence.

There are also some standard link words and phrases, such as *for example*, *this*, *also*, and *but*. However, the links are fairly scattered because these paragraphs are doing a routine job that doesn't require a lot of signalling.

Then, in paragraph 6, Layard switches to analysis and now there are lots of linking words and phrases, steering us through the argument:

Why is this? [...] Clearly [...] Thus [...] It turns out that [...], as (X) so (Y) [...] and in fact [...] likewise [...]

BOX 11.8   LINK WORDS FOR ARGUING

Wherever you see phrases like 'thus', 'therefore', 'because', 'in fact', 'indeed', or 'on the other hand', you know that an argument is being spelled out. Words like these enable you to set up the *relationship* between two points. They tell you, for example, that the next point is an extension of the previous point, or a contradiction of it, or a qualification of it. An argument weaves a sequence of points together in an intricate set of relationships. Words like these show how the relationships are meant to work.

By contrast the short paragraph 7, which is dense with explanation, has only 'And' as a conventional link word. Instead, Layard uses *structure* to manage the flow of meaning. He starts by telling us that there are 'Two things' for us to focus on. The next sentence tells us the first of these things, and the following sentence tells us the second. Consequently, we don't require link words. He also does another subtle thing. He starts to use *concepts* to provide his links. The link between paragraphs 6 and 7 is the concept '*norm*', which appears in the first sentence of each paragraph. Then, towards the end of paragraph 8 he introduces the phrase 'adjust their requirements'. And at the start of paragraph 9 'adjust their requirements' appears again as a link. Similarly, paragraph 9 introduces 'reference group' and at the start of paragraph 10 'reference group' appears again. Later, 'pollution' provides a link between paragraphs 11, 12 and 13.

As well as these 'conceptual' linkages, Layard uses standard link words and phrases such as: 'Typically', 'also', 'When' and 'For example'. There are also one or two other standard linkages using words like 'this' and 'it' to refer back to what has been discussed in the previous sentence.

BOX 11.9   BREAKING RULES?

It used to be a 'rule' that you should never start a sentence with 'and' or 'but', let alone a paragraph. So, is Layard breaking rules at the start of paragraph 11? The rule can actually be a useful one when you are not very confident about sentence structures. You may be tempted to leave half-formed sentences lying around, hoping that an 'and' or 'but' will connect them up to something.

In formal terms these two words are 'conjunctions', which are placed between equal items within a sentence, to link them together. Because a sentence is supposed, in principle, to be an independent unit of meaning, starting with 'and' or 'but' throws its status as a sentence into doubt by making it dependent on what has gone before. However, in reality, sentences *cannot* be fully independent. Reading only works because sentences pick up the meaning of their predecessors. After all that is what all our talk of 'link words' is about. So in practice, the rule is widely broken, if it is a rule at all.

Key point

■ A writer weaves a *thread of meaning* through a piece of writing by using link words and phrases and other devices which carry you along from one sentence to the next. These signal how to approach each new sentence, given what has been said in the previous one.

11.4.2 Signposting

Some of the links Layard uses also serve an important signposting function. For example, he signals the start of his presentation of evidence with 'It is true that' in paragraph 3. Then he signals that paragraphs 4 to 5 are continuing the evidence by putting 'also' and 'further' at their openings. Layard's most striking use of signposting, however, comes at the start of paragraph 6, where he puts the short, direct and dramatic question 'Why is this?'. Here we have a pivotal point in his article. He has sketched his evidence, now he is switching to analysis and explanation. He signals this loud and clear, so that we switch mind set and prepare to pay close attention to his argument. Then in paragraph 7, when he names his 'two things' as *habituation* and *rivalry*, he sets us up for paragraphs 8 and 9, which are about habituation and rivalry respectively (though rivalry is translated to 'keeping up with the Joneses'). In this way, he guides us through the structure of his treatment of his two main explanations.

Layard's next highly visible signpost comes at the start of paragraph 12: 'So now we can see why'. This signals that he is going to summarise his answer to his earlier question: 'Why is this?'. Then in paragraph 13 he signals his next move by starting with 'The policy implications are dramatic'. This launches a series of paragraphs discussing policy implications (of which I cut all but one). Finally, in his concluding paragraph, Layard uses another device similar to his 'two things' in paragraph 7. He recommends 'four principles' then lists them. This works as a kind of retrospective signpost. He is reminding us of his discussion of four policy implications.

BOX 11.10   THE NEED FOR SIGNPOSTS

In an essay you are talking your reader through an argument. In order to follow your train of thought the reader has to know what direction you are heading in and why and what questions and issues to hold in mind. Readers have their own inclinations of thought, and they will follow these in preference to yours, unless you keep them in close touch with what you are doing. To maintain the thread of argument for the reader you have to keep signalling what is going on.

One means of doing this is to use link words and phrases to pass meaning from one sentence to another. The other is to use signposting devices which explain where you have reached in the development of your argument.

Some phrases perform both these functions at the same time. An important essay-writing skill is to have a good repertoire of words and phrases which you can call on to do these jobs for you.

Key point

■ Signposting is reminding your reader from time to time where you have reached in the argument and pointing the way you are going next.

11.4.3 Sentence and paragraph lengths

A further device a writer can use to signal the unfolding of their argument is to play around with the structures of sentences and paragraphs. Again, Layard offers valuable insights.

Activity 11.4

If you have access to the internet you can see how Layard varies his use of sentences and paragraphs by downloading a marked up version of his essay from the Good Study Guide website: 'Layard Sentences and Paragraphs'.

I've put red dividers between sentences, so that you can see clearly where each starts and ends. Also, as the key explains, I've highlighted short sentences in yellow and long sentences in blue.

1   Scan through the article looking at the blue sentences (over 25 words). What kind of job do these longer sentences do in the article, especially the extra long ones, which also have blue text (over 35 words).

2   Where do the short, yellow sentences (under fifteen words) come and what do they seem to be used for? What about the very short ones (red text) and the extra short ones (red bold text)?

3   Can you detect any overall pattern in the use of long and short sentences?

Here are some statistics on Layard's use of sentences.

Table 11.2 Length of Layard's sentences		
	No. of words	**Percentage**
Very short	1–10	22%
Shortish	11–15	21%
Middling	16–20	19%
A bit longer	21–25	18%
Long	Over 26	21%

So the lengths of Layard's sentences are remarkably evenly distributed. Roughly one-fifth (20 per cent) of his sentences fall into each category from 'Very short' to 'Long'.

■ Layard's sentences vary from one word to fifty-four words, the average being eighteen words.

■ His paragraphs vary from three sentences to nine sentences, the average being five sentences.

The long sentences seem to have two jobs. Some, especially those in the first half, tend to be presenting information (i.e. evidence from research). But in paragraphs 9, 10, 13 and 14 the longer sentences appear where Layard is explaining his arguments.

The short sentences tend to come at the start or end of paragraphs, where they are setting things up, or summarising. Or they come just before or after long sentences, again setting up for the longer delivery, and summarising afterwards. They also come at the start and end of the article – yet again setting up and summarising.

Paragraph 11 is particularly interesting. It takes the form of two extra-long sentences, sandwiched between some very short sentences:

- An initial short sentence prepares the ground.

- A long sentence then spells out the first part of the Harvard study.

- A very short sentence gives the result then a fairly short sentence summarises its meaning.

- Another long sentence then spells out the second part of the Harvard study.

- Two short sentences give the result and summarise its meaning.

- A middling sentence summarises the overall implication of the two parts of the Harvard study which is then encapsulated in another very short sentence.

This is a very sensitive way of helping us to take in the study. The long sentences are necessary in order to explain the two quite tricky propositions the students were presented with. Layard supports us in coping with the demands of these sentences by wrapping them in some very compact units of meaning, to help us keep our bearings. Paragraph 13 works in a similar way. It has two successive highly demanding long sentences, sandwiched between short, bite-sized sentences.

Paragraphs 7 and 12 are at turning points in the article and both present Layard's key arguments in a very direct and succinct way. Both are short three-sentence paragraphs, with sentences of modest length. Meanwhile in the mainstream explanatory section, from paragraphs 8 to 10, Layard strikes a steady, comfortable rhythm with a run of mainly 'middling' sentences of just over twenty words. By contrast, the final paragraph (15) begins with three nine-word sentences, creating a quick and remarkably consistent rhythm. Then the last sentence is almost like four staccato mini-sentences. The points come like bullets and the article builds up to a rhythmic crescendo.

BOX 11.11   PLAYING WITH SENTENCES AND PARAGRAPHS

The way sentences and paragraphs are used can do a lot to carry readers through your argument and bring out its force. Each paragraph does its own job within the argument of the essay and each sentence makes a specific contribution to its paragraph. As a writer you have a lot of scope in choosing *how* to make them achieve their functions. You can make sentences or paragraphs long, you can make them short, or you can vary them deliberately.

Having done this analysis of Layard's writing, you could now look at one or two of your own past essays to find patterns in your own use of sentences and paragraphs. How long are your sentences? Do the variations in length show a different pattern from Layard's?

> ### *Key point*
>
> ■ Developing an effective writing style is partly a matter of playing around with effects you can achieve with sentences and paragraphs of varying length and structure. By changing the tempo you can keep the focus of your reader's attention right where you want it.

11.4.4 Summary of practical tips

In this section we have been looking at how to guide your reader through your essay. You pick them up in your introduction, by getting hold of their attention and starting a train of thought. Then, in the main body of the essay, you divide what you want to say into segments and lead your reader from section to section. Finally, you draw together the ideas you have been presenting and try to show the reader what has been accomplished.

■ **Linking** Use *link* words and phrases to *carry the meaning forward* from one paragraph to the next, such as: 'however', 'on the other hand', 'nevertheless', 'not only ... but also', 'whereas', and 'conversely'.

■ **Signposting** Periodically remind your reader *where you have got to* and show them *where you are going*. Use words and phrases like: 'in short', 'as we have seen', 'to summarise', and 'having dealt with X we must now consider Y'.

■ **Sentences** To make an impact with your opening or your conclusion, consider using shorter sentences. However, when you are developing an argument, you will tend to need longer sentences; it may help to sandwich these between shorter ones. And sometimes you may want to change the sentence length simply to vary the texture of your writing and maintain your reader's interest.

■ **Paragraphs** You should have *one* main theme per paragraph. The paragraphs signal the natural breaks in your argument when the focus of attention shifts. Avoid excessively long paragraphs. The first sentence of each paragraph should link it in some way to the previous paragraph. It should also have a fairly obvious relevance to the essay title.

11.5 The experience of writing

Few people feel blasé about writing. Producing a carefully composed piece tends to be an intense experience and not one everyone can talk comfortably about. Why should writing evoke strong feelings? And why is it difficult, sometimes, to discuss those feelings with others who also experience them?

11.5.1 Revealing yourself

As skills go, writing is a special case. It isn't like juggling or line dancing, which are 'take it or leave it' skills. Communicating with others is fundamental to our lives. What is more, an ability to communicate well tends to be associated with perceptions of how intelligent you are. Revealing in public a lack of prowess at juggling would pose no great threat, whereas revealing a lack of ability to express yourself in writing is a much more 'personal' thing. But how would you know whether you have the ability to learn to write well? How much practice do you get? Have you had any training in it? And how much honest, reliable, helpful feedback have you had?

11.5.2 By what standards do you judge yourself?

We are surrounded in modern life by the printed word. The impression is created of a world full of people who find writing easy. It seems almost shameful to be weak at it. It's a bit like those first driving lessons when you are surrounded by drivers speeding confidently about, breezing through roundabouts, parking with inches to spare. Unskilled driving is such a 'public' display of incompetence, as you crunch through the gears in the middle of the road with a queue of people behind. It's almost impossible to imagine that all those other people went through the same humiliation themselves once. In a similar way, if your inexperienced writing is about to be exposed in the 'public' of a classroom, you can't imagine that others around you have been through the same struggle to find adequate words and string them together coherently.

With writing the situation is made worse by the fact that what you see in print is generally *published* writing. In other words, most of what you read is written by *experienced* writers, *selected* for their skills in writing. You seldom read the words of ordinary writers who muddle along as best they can. You see mainly the output of writers who are the equivalent of rally drivers. So when, as an inexperienced writer, you read back over your own words, what are you comparing them with? Almost inevitably your writing looks weak in the light of the comparisons you are in a position to make. This is one reason for feeling shy about your writing and for doubting that you have talent. If you compare yourself only with professionals, you are bound to feel inadequate. Try sprinting after a trained athlete.

11.5.3 Writing: private or public?

Although writing can feel like a very private activity, it is also, paradoxically, intrinsically public. It's private in that you do it alone, locked in your own thoughts, guided by your own personal beliefs and rituals and with very little idea of how other people cope with its challenges; yet it is public in that you write to be read by others, perhaps strangers. Indeed, writing can become a kind of public property, discussed by all and sundry, with very little reference back to the writer. Critics feel able to pronounce on what words 'really' mean, without needing to ask the author who spent hours struggling to string them together. There is a wide gulf between the very private world where writing is done and the public world of reading and discussing. So *is* writing private or public?

It seems almost indecent to hand over your words to the gaze of others, who know nothing of what went into writing them. The thoughts which floated in your mind brimmed with potential. Their possibilities lay ahead. Then the act of putting them on paper 'fixed' a particular formulation and destroyed all other possibilities. Putting ideas in print is a fateful act. Can words on a page ever live up to your hopes for them? And what of the brazen act of showing them to others, who know nothing of the great intentions behind them, only what they see? Surely this is a step too far?

And yet you *do* want the words to be read. What would be the point otherwise? That is the great contradiction in writing. You *want* 'the world' to read what you write – but at the same time you don't want *anyone at all* to read it *yet* because it is so personal and might not be understood as you meant it.

Obviously you don't write an *essay* with 'the world' in mind as your audience. Yet these contradictory impulses arise: an impulse to express your insights, accompanied by a desire to keep them to yourself – a feeling of vulnerability, and yet an urge to go on. Writing is a process which gives rise to intensely ambivalent feelings – surges of enthusiasm and feelings of satisfaction, accompanied by waves of doubt and self-criticism.

11.5.4 Coping with criticism

One particularly ambivalent moment is when you get your essay back with comments from your teacher. Many students take a quick look at the *grade*, then shut the essay away in a drawer to 'look at later'. Some find it difficult *ever* to get round to taking the essay out again, to see what the teacher wrote. Comments patiently thought out and written down are left unread – too personal and discomforting to face. This rare and costly 'feedback' is left for a future day, when it will have lost all relevance. Why?

It is easy to take comments on your writing 'personally', as though you are being told you are stupid, ill informed, or inarticulate. It is difficult to 'stand back' and see essay writing as a routine process of skill development, in which you benefit from doing tightly defined exercises, followed by detailed commentary on your performance. Each piece you write feels like a personal statement on an issue of importance – not just a process of going through your paces in front of a 'coach'. A teacher will be looking out for quite specific signs of the extent of your progress, so as to assist your development – not seeking enlightenment on the subject of the essay. The relationship between the two of you breaks the usual conventions of politeness between adults. But by sidestepping convention and entering into very direct communications you get the chance to try out new ideas and new techniques and find out whether they work. Teachers may 'sound' critical, even rude, in the frankness of their comments, but that is simply the way this special kind of relationship works. It allows them to 'tell you straight' when your point doesn't come across, when your sequencing of ideas is confusing, or when your logic is unconvincing. You are then in a position to work out how to overcome these weaknesses.

Receiving direct and detailed comments on your writing is a privilege, but not an easy one to appreciate. Intensely personal feelings about your writing and the unusually direct nature of your relationship with your teacher make it sensitive. However, it is important to put the relationship into perspective: to learn to live with the irritation caused by criticisms which seem to miss your point, to be glad of the detailed crossing out of your words and substitution of others, and to be able to pay close attention to subtle nuances in the alterations suggested.

Would you want a teacher who was like an indulgent parent, admiring everything you wrote? To learn how to cope with the 'big world' you have to leave parent figures behind and 'go to school'. You have to brace yourself for whatever comes from teachers, recognising the special nature of the relationship. Most do their best to be civilised and considerate in their remarks, but that will not protect you from feeling annoyed and misunderstood. These are feelings you have to come to terms with in a teaching-learning relationship.

11.5.5 Routine hardships

The other key reason why writing is an intense experience is that it is just plain difficult.

Open-endedness

For one thing, the outcome you are aiming for is *ill defined*. When you paint a door, you know pretty well what you want to achieve and how to set about it. But when you write an essay, perhaps the only thing you can be certain of is that the end product will be different from what you had in mind.

Because of this open-endedness, it takes hard thinking at the outset to establish a 'frame of reference' within which to tackle the question. Then you have to continue thinking hard as you develop a line of argument within that frame. This continuing struggle to forge a way ahead gives rise to feelings of frustration and exhaustion at one end of the scale and satisfaction and elation at the other. So your mood can swing quite sharply as you write.

Then there is the general feeling of uncertainty – an absence of solid meanings to hold on to. Since we all depend on being able to make sense of our surroundings, it's intensely uncomfortable to be faced with sustained uncertainty. That is why the writing experience has a restless quality. You keep wanting to get up and do something else – something more solid and routine. In fact, it may help to switch back and forth between writing and routine chores, to give yourself a break from the pressures of uncertainty.

The mysterious 'reader'

Writing is also uncomfortable because of the uncertainty of your relationship with your reader. On *your* side, this relationship is a very personal thing, because it involves the way you project yourself. Meanwhile on the other side the relationship is shrouded in mystery. Your 'audience' is a mythical entity. The teacher who *actually* reads your essay will take on the role of 'the intelligent person in the street' to read it. This hypothetical audience is one you can never meet, to check whether you are getting your tone of voice right. You can only guess, from the remarks your teacher makes, whether you are anywhere near the target. As a result you can go through a lot of self-doubt as you re-read what you have written. Thinking of your audience in *one* way, it reads like a nursery book, but then thinking of them in *another* way, it reads like cryptic code.

Being too close to see

When you are in the thick of wrestling with a line of argument and trying to construct intelligible sentences, your attention is so focused that it is very difficult to judge what your words will convey to someone approaching them fresh and without emotional involvement. All you can do is press on and hope for the best. It is, perhaps, only after weeks, or even months, that you can come back and read your work from sufficient 'distance' to experience it from the point of view of others.

Nausea

According to Peter Elbow (1998, pp. 173–5) 'nausea' will always hit you at some point in your writing – a feeling of revulsion as you read your own words. It may come right at the start as the words leave your pen, or some time later when you come back to re-read your work, or at any time in between. He says it's a reaction endemic to the process of writing. If you escape it earlier, expect it later.

Keeping going

Finally, essay writing is a long, drawn-out process. With so many stages to it, you have to develop a certain stamina to write regularly. It is tedious at some times and disappointing at others. Consequently it draws on your inner resources of will power and determination, as well as the courage to face possible disappointment. Writing is great when it 'comes right', but that moment can be a long time coming.

Putting the whole picture together it's clear that writing essays is a particularly challenging experience. In the course of it you may feel:

■ frustrated when stuck

■ uncertain when you can't see where you are heading

- bored when it goes on and on

- despairing when you never seem to have enough time

- repelled when you read what you have written

- disheartened when you come up against the limitations of your abilities

- irritated when you read your teacher's comments.

However, don't let any of this put you off! These feelings *will* come to you at some time or other and, since writing is so private, *you need to know* that you are not alone in experiencing them. But if you are ready to cope, then you will still be around when good experiences eventually arrive.

Why do sane people write essays at all? For the same reason they willingly choose to do other fairly gruelling things – because it is also *intensely rewarding*. No other experience in your studies is likely to be more satisfying than having completed an essay and handed it in, nor more elating than finding that you have done better than you expected when your essay is returned.

11.6 Taking control of writing

Here is a summary of principles and practices drawn from all that we've explored in Chapters 10 and 11. And remember, there is more about the nature of academic writing in Chapter 4, when you feel ready for it.

Key points

Some basic principles

- Your ability to express yourself is fundamental to being a member of our society. Developing that ability is one of the most profoundly worthwhile activities you can undertake.

- You won't become a good writer by learning a set of formal rules. Essentially, you are learning to communicate ideas and your style will develop through practice at explaining things to a reader in your own words.

- Think of writing as a craft in which you are an apprentice. You learn by practising a range of different skills. You get this practice by regularly churning out one piece after another and getting feedback from a skilled craftsperson.

Some useful thoughts

- Don't worry about writing well straight away. Just pitch in and write. You have to risk writing badly in order to learn how to write well.

- Remember that most of what you read is written by professionals. If you are a beginner, then compare yourself with other beginners.

- You cannot judge your own writing until some time after the event.

- You have to learn to 'let go' and allow others to see your writing, however far it may fall short of your ideals.

- Think of your teacher as a 'coach' who is working on your technique. You won't agree with everything they say, but you will make much more progress with the coaching than without.

Practical hints and tips for essay writing

- Work to the essay title at all times.

- Use material drawn from the course.

- Present an argument – i.e. cluster points together in paragraphs organised around a simple essay plan, with a beginning, a middle and an end.

- Write clearly and simply.

- Write for the intelligent 'person in the street'.

- Read your work aloud to yourself (or to someone else, if you can) so that you can 'listen' for sentences that don't work.

- When you get an essay back from a teacher, read aloud any suggested alterations to your wording or punctuation, then read your original to 'hear' the differences.

- Keep practising. Write short pieces regularly (get comments from other students if you can't get them from a teacher), this will:

  (a) help you to establish a sense of audience and a writing voice

  (b) help you to adapt to the objective, critical-analytical academic style of writing

  (c) extend your repertoire of ways of making your writing flow

  (d) increase your sensitivity to the processes of structuring and signposting.

References

Elbow, P. (1998) *Writing with Power: Techniques for Mastering the Writing Process*, New York, Galaxy Books, Oxford University Press.

Pauk, W. (2001) *How to Study in College*, Boston, Houghton Mifflin Company, pp. 236–46.

CHAPTER 12 PREPARING FOR EXAMINATIONS

12.1 The positive side of exams

Are you looking forward eagerly to your exam? I guess not. An exam is not most people's favourite course activity; yet it isn't simply an unpleasant ordeal *en route* to getting a qualification. In spite of the stress and the disruption to your life, an exam can make an extremely valuable contribution to your learning. In fact, *because* of the stress, an exam can help you to find the will-power and energy to take matters in hand and finally pull your understanding of a course together into the best shape you are capable of. During the rest of your studies there is always something new to be getting on with, so you keep leaving behind what you have learned. Whereas when an exam approaches you take stock and ask yourself 'What is this course all about? How can I bring all my new knowledge under control?'

An exam brings a *performance* element into your studies. With an essay you can work for as long as you choose before submitting it, but in an exam you have to *perform* at a specified time and place. You have to 'think on your feet' and try to get things as right as you can first time. This puts pressure on you, but the pressure can be a creative force. The exam is a kind of 'ritual' that helps you to draw a peak performance out of yourself. If you can channel all your nervous energy into sensible preparations for the exam, you will come to understand the course far better than you ever would otherwise. Similarly, once you are in the exam, the pressure to write 'off the top of your head' can help you take command of your new knowledge, saying things as they come to you in ways that makes sense to *you*. No longer are you reliant on checking what it says in the books. You present the knowledge as your own.

The stress exams create is a powerful fuel – very useful but dangerous to handle. It can help you to achieve a great deal, but you need techniques for *managing* and *using* it. These are what this chapter aims to provide:

- Section 12.2 helps keep your anxiety levels down by poking holes in some common myths about exams.

- Section 12.3 switches from myth to reality by outlining some common pitfalls you should avoid.

Then come three sections looking at how you can take a positive approach to the exam:

- Section 12.4 explores strategies for tackling exam *revision*.

- Section 12.5 discusses how to make *final preparations* prior to the exam.

- Section 12.6 considers how to manage your performance *during the exam* itself.

If you use these sections to plan a strategy of your own you will be able to approach your exam confident of doing the best you are capable of. You sign up for courses because you want to learn. If you approach exams properly, they can help you achieve that learning.

BOX 12.1   THE EXAM MODEL ASSUMED IN THIS CHAPTER

Exams vary in the time allowed and the number of questions you have to answer. Some include multiple choice questions and some are divided into sections with different weightings for the marks.

For the sake of simplicity, however, I'm going to write in terms of:

- a three-hour exam, in which you are asked to answer

- four questions, requiring

- essay-type answers

- each carrying 25 per cent of the marks.

When you have found out the details of your exam, you will have to make appropriate adjustments to what I say in this chapter.

Key Points

- Exams may not be the most wonderful of experiences, but they can make a major contribution to your learning.

- You can use the stress created by exams as a positive force, if you harness it to help you pull the course together and strengthen your grasp on it.

To control and channel this stress:

- You need to keep your anxieties in perspective.

- Make sure you know what is expected of you.

- Work out sensible plans for preparing for the exam.

12.2 Myths about exams

The tensions around exams create warped perceptions. And the effect of generations of students sharing their warped perceptions has given rise to some unhelpful myths. If you want to take a constructive approach to exams, a good first step is to take these myths apart, then cast them aside.

12.2.1 To fail would ruin your life

The stress of having to 'perform' in an exam can help you to focus a lot of energy on efforts to do well. But the other side of that coin is becoming preoccupied by fears of failure. You begin to feel that a bad result is the worst thing that could happen to you. And, of course, it *is* disappointing not to do well, after you have put a lot of time and energy into something. But exams are *not* a life-or-death matter. Most people get results similar to their marks during the course, but if you *did* fail – so what? Taking a course of study is a worthy undertaking, and you will gain a great deal from it, whether or not you do well in the exam. Life will go on. Usually you can resit, if you want to. Many students go on to great success in spite of exam set backs. Albert Einstein, Winston Churchill and Sigmund Freud are just a few of the high achievers who failed exams. Recognise that you can survive the worst the exam can throw at you – failure – then shrug your shoulders and hope for the best.

Remember, most of us did this course for ourselves. Some will go on to complete degrees, some may go no further – but it doesn't mean we're failures. It just means we prioritise our lives differently. I don't have many qualifications, but I have two fantastic kids, who are the biggest credit to me and I intend to spend more time with them when this is over. Does that make me a failure? Me thinks not!

12.2.2 The exam will expose you as a fool and a fraud

I'm having restless nights. I can't get the exam out of my head.

It's quite common to dream of being in an exam where you are unable to answer a single question. Exams seem to bring lurking fears that you will be revealed as an imposter – as though you've only been pretending to understand and now the exam will expose the truth. Dreams of abject inadequacy show the intensity of our hopes and fears. Our fantasy examiners sternly probe for any signs of weakness and mercilessly reject anyone with less than comprehensive knowledge of the course. Yet real exams are not at all like that. Examiners are delighted when students pass and usually go out of their way to find what is good in the answers they read. Nobody will think you stupid if you don't do well. Nobody will accuse you of wasting their time. People will just be sorry if you don't do well and hope that you do better next time. If you have made a genuine effort to understand the course and you have made progress with your assignments, then there is something wrong with the exam if you fail.

12.2.3 You have to know the whole course in detail

Most students (especially part-time adult students) have to miss out some sections of a course. Even the best students tend to specialise in those areas which interest them. You have done well to make it as far as the exam. It's no use at this stage worrying about what you've left out. It is far better to consolidate what you *have* done than attempt any desperate catching up on what you haven't. It's too late for studying from first principles.

BOX 12.2   CUTTING EXAMS DOWN TO SIZE

To put things in perspective, think about the practical constraints of exams. How much can you write in a three-hour exam? Not a lot! So you don't need to know 'everything'. If you have to answer four questions you need to know enough to write about three sides on each (depending on your handwriting). And bear in mind that your marker isn't going to pore over your script in fine detail to see whether it's worth publishing. Markers spend between five and ten minutes on an answer, seeing whether the general gist seems right, whether a reasonable number of key points are there, and whether the argument flows tolerably well. That's how exams are! Your essays during the course are your opportunity to put together detailed and carefully thought out arguments for close reading by your teacher. The exam is a much more rough and ready exercise, both in the writing and in the marking.

So *don't* worry about having left parts of the course out. You just need to be able to pull enough together from what you *have* studied to write for around 40 minutes on your chosen topics.

12.2.4 If you haven't understood everything it isn't worth taking the exam

If you fully understand everything then you are studying a course which is too easy for you. It is 'normal' to feel confused by new knowledge. Any decent course sets all kinds of ideas turning over in your mind, some of which you will still be sorting out months later. If you have *tried* to make sense as you studied, you have probably made more progress with understanding than you realise. But on any challenging course you can't expect to achieve a full grasp of every issue by the time of the exam. The point is to use your preparation for the exam to pull things together, to make *the best sense you can.*

12.2.5 Exam questions are impossible to understand

Your first look at a past exam paper for your course may give you a fright. Exam questions often look tremendously broad and demanding on first sight. They tend to be abstract in form and often seem oblique in their wording. However, the obliqueness is not malicious. It is usually the examiners trying to *point* you towards a *specific topic* in the course *without* answering the question *for* you. They try to be helpful, without giving the game away. Always keep in mind that the exam is a test of your *understanding* of the *course* you have been studying, not your general knowledge. So the answer to each question on the paper lies somewhere within what you've studied. Don't panic, instead, carefully match what you know of the *course* against what the *questions* seem to be asking. There is no mystery, the examiners want you to display knowledge of specific parts of the course. It's just a question of working out which parts.

12.2.6 An exam shows up the gaps in your education

Some people worry that their whole educational background is somehow inadequate for tackling an exam, that failings and omissions in the past will come home to roost. This is a misleading trick played by anxiety. An exam is *not* a test of general knowledge (it would be impossible to mark in a standardised way if it were). It is a test of your grasp of the course. In fact, it's a big mistake to try to answer an exam question using only your general knowledge, your script marker is unlikely to be impressed. The marking guide will list some quite specific points from the course for which marks can be given. Going off on your own tack, however well-informed you may be, is a high-risk strategy. If general educational background does show through, it's in the 'roundedness' of answers and the refinements of writing style which might push a 'good' answer up to 'excellent'. In other words, educational background may help with the finishing gloss, but it is not part of the basics of getting the job done.

> I was not a gifted student at school – did an access course, convinced I would fail. Passed! (Shock.) Tutor encouraged me to enrol for a degree, though I was convinced I wouldn't pass a single essay, let alone the exam. Another patient tutor – passed first essay and by mid course started to believe I had a chance. By exam time, I thought what the hell, give it a shot! – nothing to lose. I passed with a distinction and am now proud owner of a posh certificate.

12.2.7 Exams are for people with a good memory

Most university level exams are *not* 'memory' tests. The purpose of your course is to develop your *ideas*. And the purpose of the exam is to give you an opportunity to show how well you have grasped the course ideas. You will be asked to *use* the ideas in *arguing a case*. If you revise constructively before the exams, the role of 'pure memory' will be fairly small. Human beings have immense memory capabilities. You just need to give yours a reasonable chance. Concentrate on *organising* your notes during your revision. Let your memory take care of itself.

12.2.8 Exams are for quick thinkers and writers

Can you think quickly enough and write quickly enough to pass an exam? Probably! You should, in any case, do most of your *thinking* in advance of the exam itself, so sheer speed of thought is not a key factor. What *does* matter is how well you *organise* your ideas and how well you *plan* your exam strategy. Working to a good plan, you can use time in an exam extremely efficiently.

See Chapter 12 Section 12.5.1, Get your thinking in before the exam

On the other hand, speed of *handwriting may* be a significant factor if it seriously restricts the amount you can get down. If you can write 500–700 words in 40 minutes that should be sufficient to get a high mark, although it is impossible to give hard and fast rules. Some students write short pithy answers which are very good, while others write pages without saying much. The fact that you have a lot of adrenaline pumping in an exam will help you to write much more quickly than usual, but if you have doubts, practise writing at speed to limber your hand up. If you are seriously worried about being a slow writer, talk to your teacher, or a counsellor. You may be able to arrange special support in the exam, or extra time. In general, though, it is far more important to focus on the quality of your answer rather than the speed at which you can write it down.

12.2.9 You have to revise till you drop

Exam folklore abounds with stories of heroic last-ditch spurts of work, done deep into the night. There may be some truth in them, we *are* capable of extraordinary feats when the pressure is on, but the telling of the stories is more do with the intensity of peoples' hopes and fears than with accurate reporting of reality. It is *not* the case that all preparations can be effectively accomplished at the very last moment, particularly as you get older, and especially if you are studying part-time and have to keep another life going at the same time.

BOX 12.3   HOW YOUR MIND WORKS UNDER PRESSURE

Your mind works differently under pressure, and you need to understand those differences in order to 'manage' yourself in the build up to the exam. In the days just before the exam the tension builds up, providing you with lots of nervous energy. You can get lots done, but it is harder to keep yourself under control and channel energy in helpful directions. Being highly charged makes you good at focusing attention on concrete matters in hand, but less good at thinking through broad, abstract issues. So do your broad planning well in

---

advance so that when the exam arrives, you have clear-cut strategies already worked out: for tackling revision, for allocating time in the exam, for taking the exam questions apart, for structuring your answers, and so on. You need to become an efficient exam-crunching machine. If you have well-developed plans, you will find you can think surprisingly clearly once the exam has started. Whereas if you leave all thought about the exam to the last couple of days you'll just be in a flap.

Key points

- Failing an exam is *not* the end of the world; keep your anxieties in perspective.

- Everyone *wants* you to pass, including the examiner.

- Don't worry about what you *haven't* done during the course. Work out how to make the best use of what you *have* done.

- You aren't expected to understand 'everything'. There are bound to be areas of the course where you feel confused and under-prepared.

- Don't panic when you look at past papers. Exam questions usually link directly to things you have covered on the course. You just have to work out the link.

- Don't worry about what you didn't know when you started the course. Build on what you have learned *during* the course.

- University exams are more about what you *understand* than *memory* for details. Getting your course notes organised will sort your memory out.

- Speed in an exam is mainly to do with having very clear plans and sticking to them.

- Don't turn your life into a complete misery by working all hours just before an exam. You probably *will* work intensively in the last days. But do it in a planned way. Use your time efficiently, conserve your energies and keep yourself calm.

In the realm of myth, exams are monstrous ordeals, survived only by superhuman effort. They are devised by sadists to expose the weaknesses of ordinary mortals. They bring life-shattering consequences. And so on – myths with a nightmare quality. Whereas, the reality is quite mundane. Exams do bring stress, but they are just another part of the education process which countless people routinely cope with, mostly successfully. To experience the least pain and achieve the results you deserve take a practical approach. Be *realistic* about *yourself* and about *what the exam requires of you.* Prepare yourself carefully and sensibly to build up to a 'peak performance'. *Don't* waste your energies dithering about in a panic. Just think calmly and clearly about the tasks in hand.

12.3 What to avoid

Having disposed of some myths, what about the reality? What mistakes might you actually make? We can get an idea of this from what boards of examiners say in reports on exams. While their reports frequently stress how *well* many students tackle exams, they also identify some common faults.

12.3.1 Not answering the question

It isn't just *what* you know but *how* you say it. You are expected to *use* what you know to *argue a case* in answer to the *specific question* that has been set. If you don't, your script marker sighs, writes 'Doesn't answer the question' below your answer and marks you down accordingly. Examiners point to several ways you can fail to answer the question:

■ Not recognising what one of the *key terms* in the question means. (For example, in a question about *institutional* racism, discussing only *individual* racism.) If there is a term you don't know, avoid the question. Your marks will be badly affected if you guess and get it wrong.

■ Not recognising *which issues* from the course are being raised. Every question tries to point you towards specific issues discussed in the course. You have to spot which.

■ Not offering *critical analysis* and argument. However the question is posed, it is generally expected that you will be presenting arguments *for* and *against a point of view* (or points of view) implied in the question. Your first job, as you read a question closely, is to *identify the point of view* it presents. Your next job is to remind yourself of some *other point(s)* of view from which you can criticise the first position. Your answer can then be constructed as a *debate* between two (or more) sides.

See Chapter 10 Section 10.7.1, How academic debate works

■ Not taking an *objective* stance. You are not supposed to 'harangue' your reader with personal opinions and flamboyant rhetoric. You should observe the same principles of cool, impartial objectivity as in essays.

■ Not arriving at any *conclusions* regarding the question. Your answer looks much more purposeful and relevant if you *refer back to the question* at the *end of your answer* and briefly explain how what you have said helps to answer it.

These are all familiar requirements. They apply equally to writing essays. You simply need to note that although exam answers are much shorter and scrappier, they are judged in roughly the same way as essays, though at lower levels of expectation, in recognition of the constraints.

See Chapter 10 Section 10.8.2, The key ingredients

12.3.2 Not using material from the course

Examiners complain that with some scripts it's hard to tell whether the student has actually *studied the course*. In other words, the student has overlooked one of the basic principles of an end-of-course exam: it is meant as an opportunity to *demonstrate* that you have worked on and thought about the content of the course. You should treat every answer as an excuse to bring in *terms* and *ideas* presented in the course. And when you are arguing a point, back up your case by using *evidence* and *examples* from the course. For example, if you say 'Rising levels of income make us no happier', it sounds like a personal opinion. If you add 'according to Layard', it shows your argument is based on some knowledge of the subject. If you put in a few important names, facts and figures, it shows that you are not making your answer up as you go along.

I found that, looking at a question, names and information would spring to mind. As the exam is all about showing you have studied the course, the examiner only knows this if you put in details from the course – even if it's only someone's surname, it proves you know something.

However, avoid giving the impression that you are desperately rummaging around in the rag-bag of your general knowledge for anything vaguely relevant. And never base your answers primarily on your own experience, or on views of people you happen to know. It looks as though you haven't bothered to study the course and brings your marks right down. *Anything* relevant that you can remember from the course will look better than an answer made up off the top of your head.

12.3.3 Stuffing answers full of names and facts

You have to use course material discriminatingly. You are *never* asked 'Write *all* you know about ...'. Exam markers are not interested in whether you can *memorise* a section of a book and *repeat* it. They want to know whether you can *put* the ideas and information in the book *to work*: whether you can *select* useful material from all that you have come across in the course and *use* it to answer a specific question. If you cram an answer full of facts and names without *selecting* them for relevance, or placing them in the *context* of an argument, it looks as though you don't understand the subject and are hoping that sheer memory will get you by. It won't.

12.3.4 Using time badly

A *very* common mistake is to write a very long first answer but leave just a few sentences and some scrappy notes for the last. This is sad, since marking schemes are usually very straightforward. Each question carries a certain number of marks and good work on one answer cannot be taken into account when marking another. It is very difficult to push a high mark up even higher by spending more time on your answer. Let's say that you are taking a four-answer exam, with all answers equally weighted, and you manage to get a 90 per cent score on your first answer but follow up with 45 per cent, 30 per cent and 15 per cent because you had not left enough time to complete your answers. Your overall score would be 45 per cent. Whereas, if you spent less time on the first answer and got only 75 per cent, but used the time gained to pull your other answers up, you might end up with 60 per cent, 55 per cent and 50 per cent. This would give you an overall score of 60 per cent – a much better result. It is far easier to pick up marks at the lower end of the scale than at the upper end, so it *always* makes sense to spend *roughly the same amount of time on each question*, however weak you feel on some of them.

12.3.5 Poor presentation

Finally, examiners also complain about answers which are:

- unstructured (i.e. no sense of a beginning, a middle and an end)
- lacking any division into paragraphs
- written in note form, rather than sentences
- in illegible handwriting.

Again these are familiar requirements from your essay writing. Obviously, it's harder to pay attention to presentation under exam pressures. But, equally, an exam marker's job is harder than your teacher's, as they grapple with a mountain of scripts. With the best will in the world, it is difficult to do justice to judging an answer which is very difficult to follow. You can't help the relative scrappiness and untidiness of your exam answers when compared with your essays. But neither can the exam marker help being influenced to some extent by excessive difficulty in working out what you are trying to say.

These then are the things examiners complain about in their examiners' reports (alongside the very pleasant and encouraging things they also say). We now turn to what you can do to make sure they say nice things about *your* answers. There are three areas in which you can tune up your performance, by careful planning and sensible preparation. These are revision (Section 12.4), 'gearing up' (Section 12.5) and tactics (Section 12.6).

Key points

- Read the question carefully and make sure you answer all parts of it exactly as asked.
- Always be sure to include ideas, terms, names, examples and cases from the course.

- Don't try to cram in everything that might possibly be relevant. Select what fits your answer.

- Always spread your time fairly evenly across questions that carry equal weighting.

- Try to present your answers in a way that doesn't require a cryptographer to read them.

12.4 Revising for exams

12.4.1 What is the point of revision?

The primary purpose of revision is to pull together all that you have learned during the course. Grappling with new knowledge will have thrown your ideas into disarray. Revision is the process of tidying up the mess, and getting your thoughts back into useable order. Without a revision period the content of a course tends to drift away from you, incoherent and unresolved. Revising provides an opportunity to *reconstruct* the course, so that the knowledge you have encountered becomes more securely your own. Consequently, revision is *not* a mammoth *memorising* task but a much more *constructive* activity. It should *not* be a dull process of scanning endlessly through pages, hoping something will stick. It is purposeful, creative, thought provoking and potentially very satisfying.

12.4.2 When should you start revising?

There is no 'right' answer to this question. Some students make a start two or three months before an exam, others leave it to the last fortnight. The right time for *you* depends on:

- the amount of time you can spare for revision outside other study and life commitments

- your personal style of studying – whether you are better at short intensive bursts of effort, or longer sustained periods

- the kind of course it is and what you are trying to get out of it.

It would be a shame to panic too early and spoil the later parts of the course through being obsessed with revision. On the other hand, it's a serious mistake to avoid thinking about the exam until the very last moment. You won't do yourself justice if you leave too little time for revision.

Don't think of exam preparation as a single, huge task, or you will find it hard to get started. There are various activities which make an important contribution, as you will see from the rest of this section. Some of these activities, such as drawing up a timetable, can be done fairly quickly. Start early on with some of the smaller tasks, just to get yourself going, so that your focus gradually shifts towards the exam.

What you should definitely do a couple of months before the exam, is start thinking about your strategy, even if you don't actually begin revising till later. The final weeks of a course are often busy, with essays to hand in and other course work still continuing. Your personal life will also make its demands. Finding time for revision isn't easy. You need to start making estimates of how much time you hope to find and thinking about how you will find it, otherwise you will be overtaken by events.

 I feel at the moment like what's the point and 'no I don't wanna bloomin well pick those books up so nah nah' – but will I feel that in another few months when its all over and those results drop on my mat?

12.4.3 Get hold of past exam papers

One task to undertake well before the end of the course is to get a clear picture of what is expected from you in the exam. The most effective way to do this is to look at papers from previous years, or specimen papers if yours is a new course. There may also be printed notes about the exam. Look on your course website, or ask university staff.

Get hold of whatever information you can then take the time to go very carefully over the exam papers and notes. It isn't easy. Your first glance at a paper may make you wince. Until you've done some serious revision, the questions may look impossible. But it is better to get the fright over with well ahead of the exam, while you still have time to do something about it (you certainly don't want to see a paper for the first time in the exam itself). Read the instructions on the paper and make sure you understand them. Take a careful note of the way the paper is organised:

- How many questions are there?
- How many do you have to answer?
- Is the paper divided into sections?
- Do you have to select questions from different sections?
- Do all the sections carry the same marks?

Then explore how the paper connects to the course content:

- Is it obvious which questions match up with particular parts of the course?
- Is there a question on each major course section?
- Can you tell which topics are likely to come up in particular parts of the paper?

Compare papers from different years:

- Do you get a sense of the kind of questions you can expect?
- Can you see patterns? If so, are they predictable enough to allow you to focus your revision on just a few course topics?

Past exam papers are essential viewing. You can see patterns and trends – the good old favourites that keep appearing.

When you have found out all you can by examining the papers, talk with other students and compare your conclusions. Ask how they plan to tackle the paper. Get what advice you can from university staff and make sure there is nothing about the paper you don't understand. You need to have a very clear understanding of the exam paper before working out your revision strategy. You don't want to waste time covering more topics than necessary, and you certainly don't want to be caught out by the real paper in the exam room.

12.4.4 Gather together your notes and books

One of your key tasks is to get yourself organised. Unless you have a superbly efficient filing system, you will have accumulated mounds of assorted bits of paper, notes, handouts, photocopies of articles and half-read books. Set aside a session to do nothing other than sort everything out. This is more than just 'housekeeping', the act of tidying everything into neater piles reminds you of what material you have and pushes you into thinking about the overall shape of the course, and how things can be grouped together. When you can look around and see *what* you have got and *where*, you will be in a much better position to get a clear perspective on the revision process.

12.4.5 Work out a revision strategy

Having studied the structure of the exam paper and gathered together and organised your course materials, you are in a position to think about how to manage your revision.

- Draw up a list of the main topics of the course and decide which of them you are going to revise for the exam.

- Look at your piles of course material and think about which items are going to be the most important to focus on in your revision.

In choosing what to focus on, don't assume that you are going to do any new reading. By revision time it's too late for learning from first principles; you need to consolidate what you have already learned. Play to your strengths and interests.

I chose parts of the course because a) I enjoyed them most, so it wasn't a big chore to revise them b) I got my best essay marks for them.

■ Make a list of your chosen topics, with the relevant sources alongside (books, notes, essays).

■ Think about priorities. If time runs short, which are the items you will definitely revise? What might you leave out? Mark the priorities on your list.

■ Read the rest of this chapter, or just look through the subheadings, to get an idea of activities you might want to include in your revision strategy.

All this will take quite a lot of thought, but go ahead and write something down even if you are undecided. Making a first attempt at a strategy will set you thinking. You can modify it later as you have further thoughts and talk with other students. Once you get into the thick of revision and run into life's complications, you are likely to have to modify your strategy several times. The point is, having sketched a plan, you can keep reviewing your situation and making intelligent adjustments.

12.4.6 Make a revision timetable

Having sketched a strategy, you need to work out how you are going to fit it in to your busy life. Drawing up a revision timetable is essential. It's the only way to make life manageable in the run-up to the exam. It will also make you feel better and more in control of events.

■ Get a blank calendar for the weeks ahead (you could use your computer's calendar feature to print off a couple of months). Write in the date of the exam and due dates of your remaining course work. Then write in all your major work and social commitments.

■ Highlight the main places on the calendar where you might be able to make time for revision.

 I've been revising the first part of the course this week. I'm averaging about 2 hrs a day about 5 days a week. Tend to do most on Wednesday which is my day off.

■ Tot up a rough estimate of the total time you think you can set aside. Then think about how to share it out between the items on your revision plan. Jot down estimates of hours against each item, this will start to bring a flavour of reality to your strategy. You will see just how limited your time is for each activity and how important it is to know where to cut corners and be practical in your ambitions.

■ Finally, starting with your highest priority revision activities, write them into your timetable.

Remember to allow time for studying the last part of the course and set aside some time for practising exam questions, and for the final stages of pulling things together. Divide the remaining revision time into equal parts for each section of the course you have decided to revise. It is tempting to allow more time for course topics where you feel particularly strong and to try to squeeze the weak topics in at the end. However, it is best to assume equal time for each revision area if all questions carry the same number of marks. You don't want to end up with too little time for the topics which most need sorting out, or to leave no time at all for brushing up the very topic you hoped to do best in.

Don't worry about getting your whole timetable worked out straight away. Just sketch a general picture and write down some specific tasks to start on in your first couple of sessions. Fill out the rest of the timetable as you get properly into the swing of revision, and modify it as events change your plans.

12.4.7 Don't try to re-read the course

Revision is not a rerun through the whole course. You haven't time and your mind would turn to jelly. You need to take a much more active and more selective approach. Many exams are designed to allow you to be selective in your preparation. Assuming you have studied the logic of the exam paper carefully and understand the choices open to you, you can be ruthless in ignoring whole sections of the course. It isn't worth just dipping into course topics, doing a bit here and another bit there, you won't end up with enough to write a good exam answer. You need to spend long enough to pull together the big picture for the topics you have chosen to revise, so that you can answer questions from whatever angle they come. Your review of these topics needs to be systematic.

12.4.8 Don't try to memorise your course notes

Don't gather up your course notes and try to read through them all to memorise them, your mind will switch off in protest. You need to be able to *think* in the exam, not *recite* back your notes. You need *ideas* in your head, not strings of words. To do something more constructive, highlight key points, or try to work out what questions you might be asked. Always work with a pen in your hand, *creating* something as you go – your mind will stay in gear for much longer! Any 'memorising' should come in the last day or two and be based on 'summary' notes.

12.4.9 Make summary notes

An excellent way to identify the main themes of your chosen course topics and anticipate the kind of questions you might be asked is to make summary notes and then make summaries of your summaries.

I decided which topics I was going to revise, then I broke each into sections and made bullet points. These I then condensed and condensed until I managed a mind map of each topic. I also did key words for each 'important' person, or concept – e.g. Goffman and institutionalisation, formal/informal care, Beveridge, etc., until I had my own 'study bible'.

The idea is to 'boil down' your chosen revision topics until you have just the concentrated essence. Exam answers are short, so you don't need mountains of detail in your mind. You want to create a rapid access version of what you learned during the course. This is how it works:

1   Make *condensed notes* from the various books, notes, etc., that you have gathered together for a particular topic.

2   For each sub-topic, extract the main points from your condensed notes to create a *sub-topic summary sheet* showing headings, key points, names, etc.

3   Finally, take the main headings from the various sub-topic summary sheets and produce one *topic summary sheet*.

The diagram in Figure 12.1 shows the basic principles for creating summary notes.

If your notes are connected hierarchically as shown in Figure 12.1 then when you are in the exam you can remind yourself of the relevant topic summary sheet as you start to answer a question. You then work out which sub-topics are relevant to the question and remind yourself of the relevant sub-topic summary sheets. You scan mentally through the main items on a given sub-topic sheet and select whichever are relevant. This then leads you back to the condensed notes which 'lie behind' the summaries.

So, in your revision, you construct pathways *up* from the basic sources, through condensed notes and sub-topic summary sheets, to a single topic summary sheet. Then, in the exam, you can quickly trace your way back *down* these pathways, to locate exactly the details relevant to the question. You may not find that your subject matter breaks down quite as neatly as this – perhaps topics and sub-topics isn't the right terminology for your course, however, the general principle is to create a systematic overview and retrieval system.

See Chapter 6 Section 6.3.2, How memory works

There are various ways of putting this summary notes strategy into practice. Some people find mind maps (see Chapter 6 Figure 6.11) very helpful.

I worked from my highlighting in the course books – picking out the key points. I wrote all these into notes – then made mind maps. It was time consuming, but the repeated writing of the sections, key words and ideas etc. made them stick. Then I spent 2–3 weeks reading them over and over again. The mind maps helped me focus. As soon as I went into the exam I was able to recall the points relevant to each exam question and draw the mind map onto the exam paper as my plan.

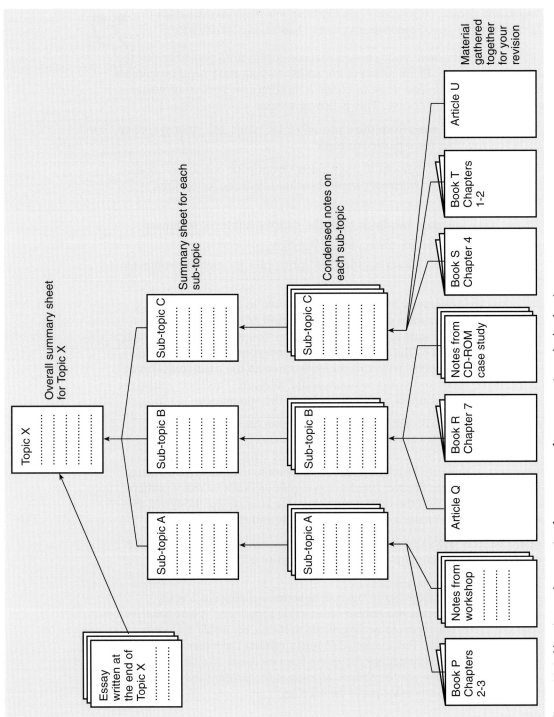

Figure 12.1 How to condense notes from a range of sources onto a single sheet

Other people value the discipline of getting ideas down to index card brevity (See Chapter 6 Figure 6.1).

> I'm trying to condense as much information as possible onto index cards – one or two for each topic. I have brief notes on main people we came across, relevant legislation/policies, pros and cons for key issues. I take the cards wherever I go (read them on the bus, at work, in bed etc.) in the hope the info will sink in.

A summary note strategy gives you a well-focused, absorbing task to get on with, rather than aimlessly scanning back over old material, sending yourself to sleep. It's a substantial time investment, but it pays off.

> I had about 30 cards, double sided, just key words on each card. This helped me focus and also I had a ready made plan for most of the exam questions. I know it looks like hard work but believe me once done it is much easier to revise from. I got a distinction, so I was well pleased.

12.4.10 Take full advantage of electronic notes

If you made course notes using an outliner you can take great advantage of them at revision time. You can very easily cut and paste from different sets of notes to create a 'master document' for each topic. Then you can view this document with different levels of headings showing, so that you can see an overview of the topic at different levels of detail (see Chapter 6 Figure 6.2). You can take stock of how the main topics and sub-topics fit together but then quickly dive down to more detail if you need to remind yourself what a topic is about. You can also move sections of notes around very easily, reorganising them under new headings. This flexibility allows you to keep working at reshaping your understanding of the topic and of how it all fits together. Finally, when you have worked your notes into a satisfactory shape, you can print them off with different levels of headings showing: an overview showing just two levels, another version showing three or four levels for a more thorough topic review, and perhaps one showing all levels, so that you can get down to the details when you need to.

See Chapter 6 Section 6.2.1, Notes from reading

You can also use your computer to create tables with headings to help organise your knowledge of the course. For example, you could list your chosen topics down the left hand side of the table and put column headings such as 'theories', 'concepts', 'names' and 'cases', then fill in examples for each topic. Or, if there are broad themes running through the course, you could put the themes as column headings, list the course sections down the left hand side and fill in examples of how the themes emerge in each section of the course.

See Chapter 6 Section 6.4.1, Getting things straight

12.4.11 Seek out the questions at the heart of the course

This is a very powerful strategy. Try to identify two or three core questions in each section of the course that you are revising, then try to write notes that answer those questions. In other words, what is this part of the course all about? What is the *point* of it? Sometimes an author will have identified core questions for you. At other times you have to tease them out for yourself. Similarly, the author will sometimes have made a point of drawing conclusions on the main issues for you, while at other times you will have to summarise and draw conclusions for yourself. The process of seeking out key questions and answers to them gets your mind working in the way that it needs to work during the exam. It alerts you to the kinds of questions that *could* be asked on the course content you have been studying. And it helps you to think in terms of pulling together ideas in the way that's needed to answer an exam question.

12.4.12 Try answering past exam questions

Perhaps the most useful revision activity of all is to attempt past exam questions. You don't need to write out a full answer every time, though the occasional practice at that may be useful. A quick exercise you can do frequently is to rehearse the vital first few minutes of working on a question; in other words, those minutes when you examine what the question means and sketch out rough notes for an answer.

> I bought past exam papers and wrote the questions onto index cards along with the course essay questions. The cards I carried with me ALWAYS. When I had 10 mins spare, I shuffled the index cards, pulled a question out at random and did a quick mind map of an answer to it. It meant I didn't panic when I turned over the real paper – and I got a good pass.

Give yourself ten minutes to produce an outline answer to a question you haven't looked at before, then look back at the course material to see what you have left out. Ask yourself:

See Chapter 11 Section 11.2.1, Thinking about the essay title

- What is this question getting at? (Underline the key words in the same way as for essays.)

- Which section of the course and which topic in that section does the question relate to?

- What themes, examples, evidence and ideas can I draw in from the course? (Jot down notes.)

- In what sequence should I take the points? (Sketch an outline plan.)

This is worth doing many times, because it helps you develop the intellectual agility get to the heart of questions quickly and answer precisely, drawing on relevant parts of the course. It helps you to organise your knowledge in the right sort of way for the job in hand. You'll soon get used to being able to quickly:

- **sift** through what you know of the course material
- **select** the most relevant items for the question, and
- **arrange** them in a suitable order for a coherent answer.

Practising writing out answers in full is not quite so urgent because, once you have an outline, the writing process is fairly similar to writing an essay (though with less time), which is a skill you have practised during the course. What you have not practised is 'thinking on your feet'. The way you think about an essay question is too reflective and lumbering for an exam. You need to develop a nimbler style for the exam.

One of the key benefits of regularly sketching out quick outline answers is that you begin to discover that topics covered early in the course, that had seemed very hazy, come back into focus. Soon you find that you have learned much more than you had realised.

12.4.13 Thinking up exam questions of your own

It is an excellent exercise to think up questions of your own. Apart from stretching your mind, it makes you step into the examiners' shoes, giving you an insight into the way they think. It helps you to take a broad view of the course, looking for the big issues and the underlying themes. On the other hand, you *might* guess badly, so don't pin *all* your hopes on your own hunches.

12.4.14 Try writing 'against the clock'

If you haven't taken exams for a long time, it's obviously useful to get in some practice at working 'against the clock'. You may not find the time and energy for a full-length practice, but it could be useful to write a single timed answer now and again. However, I have two notes of caution: first, you will have the benefit of a lot more nervous energy on the exam day, so your informal try-out may underestimate your true capabilities; second, don't be discouraged if your answers look unimpressive compared with your essays. Timed answers are always pretty flawed.

12.4.15 Keep in touch with other students

Make time to stay in touch with other students (whether in the classroom, by phone, or online). It's very easy to develop a warped perspective on exams during the stress of revision. You begin to think your problems are much worse than they really are, or you bias your revision too sharply in one particular direction. The best way to keep a sense of proportion is to talk to other people about what you are doing. This is a time when attending classes, or dropping into online chatrooms, is particularly useful. Sharing ideas makes revision a lot easier and more pleasant. Don't think of time spent 'chatting' as simply time lost from revising. Group revision can be extremely efficient. It throws up all sorts of insights into hidden problems and misunderstandings. It helps you to knock your ideas into shape and gives you many valuable clues and tips.

 We did a lot of essay plans, brainstorming topics and questions. I felt reassured that I could do it. It's amazing how much info you retain that appears again under pressure.

Key points

Elements of exam revision strategy:

- Study *old exam papers* and specimen papers thoroughly.
- *Organise* all your course materials, so that you know what you have and where.
- Carefully *select* the parts of the course you intend to revise.
- Make a *timetable* for revising.
- Condense the content of your chosen topics into very brief *summary notes.*
- Make use of whatever *techniques* appeal to you – mind maps, index cards, grids, or outliner notes.
- Seek out the central *questions* in each of the parts of the course you have chosen to revise.
- Practise jotting down *outlines* for answers to questions.
- Think up *questions* you might be asked.
- Practise *writing* out one or two answers in full against the clock.
- *Keep in touch* with other students and with your teacher to maintain your grip on reality.

12.5 Getting 'geared-up' just before the exam

Some people recommend relaxation, plenty of sleep, and outdoor exercise in the final days before an exam. Should you get away for a short holiday? Sounds great – but scarcely realistic. Even if you had the time, it's not at all obvious that it would be good for your exam performance. That last day or so is when you are gradually building yourself up to a peak of preparation.

You can concentrate remarkably well when it's too late to worry about the frills. You forget your plans for re-reading that book, or making sense of that theory you never really understood. You leave those possibilities behind and concentrate all your energies on marshalling what you do know. 'Relaxed' is the last thing you want to be when you enter the exam. Calm and unruffled, possibly (if you can manage it), but you should be keyed-up like a tennis star at a tournament, or a stage performer on the first night, ready to give your big performance of the year, transcending your normal limits by force of all that nervous energy and your single-minded concentration.

12.5.1 Get your thinking in before the exam

How will you do justice to everything you've learned, when you have only three hours in the exam? How long do you spend on an essay? Six hours, ten hours, a week? How can you condense that writing process into four 45-minute bursts? Clearly you can't. As a result exam answers don't look like essays. They are shorter, more disjointed, and much less polished; luckily they are thrown away when the marking is over. Yet, it is surprising how much you *can* get into an exam answer in spite of the time constraints. Although you can't work out a carefully considered response, as you do for essays, you can get pretty close, *provided you get a lot of your thinking done before the exam itself*. In the course of your revision you will have decided *which parts of the course* you are going to answer on. You will have identified the *key issues* and rehearsed them in your mind. And you will have practised *working up arguments* in response to a question. You should also have decided exactly how you are going to use your *time* in the exam. Then all that remains in the exam is to:

See Chapter 12 Section 12.6, Working out your tactics for the exam

- pick your question

- quickly settle on a plan for using what you know to answer the question, and

- stick to this plan, for better or worse.

You need to be in a highly organised, efficient and pragmatic frame of mind for the exam. Having stopped worrying and wondering, you can then focus intently on doing your best with the immediate tasks in hand, cutting every corner you can and generally using your native cunning.

12.5.2 Draw up a time plan for the exam

Using time effectively is one of the most important factors in doing justice to yourself in an exam. You can't afford to leave this to chance, and you certainly don't want to take up precious time working out a time plan *in* the exam. So you need to think carefully about how you can get the best out of yourself. It is very worthwhile drawing up a plan of how, ideally, you might use your time in the exam. Figure 12.2 shows one possible version.

Time

10:00   Turn over the paper and glance through it, marking the questions you think you might attempt. (5 mins)

10:05   Start planning your first answer. Underline key words in the question. Jot down relevant course material. Return to the question and work out a plan. (10 mins)

10:15   Start writing out your first answer. (35 mins)

10.50   Finish the first answer and plan out the other three. (25 mins, i.e. 3 x 8.3 mins)

11.15   Write out the second answer. (35 mins)

11.50   Write out the third answer. (35 mins)

12.25   Write out the fourth answer. (35 mins)

13:00   Finish

Figure 12.2   Sample time plan for a three-hour exam

You won't be able to stick to your plan exactly, but it will serve as a guide. (Read Section 12.6 'Working out your tactics for the exam' before drawing up your plan.)

12.5.3 Changes to your mental powers

During the last couple of days before the exam, load your plans and strategies into your head, keep going back over your summary note sheets and generally wind yourself up for action. Because the pressure builds up in these final days, your mental powers will change. You will be *less good* at *deep thinking* tasks, such as sorting out the underlying meaning of a difficult course text. But you will be *better* at working at more *routine* things like checking over your notes, practising answering questions, or reminding yourself of your strategy for the exam. Because of this, you should not leave *basic revision* to the last few days; you will only depress yourself and get into a panic. Deliberately switch your work mode and use these days as your 'polishing-up' period. As with an actor at a dress rehearsal, it's too late to learn new lines or decide on a different interpretation. You just have to 'go with it' the way it is and keep running over your lines in your head, to make sure everything is in place.

12.5.4 Anxiety

As the exam draws closer, you may find the tension starts to get on top of you. There are several types of anxiety that can develop at exam time. You may experience a general uneasiness that builds up gradually over a long period, until (very usefully) it provides the spur to a really intensive burst of work. This is a normal precursor to any kind of performance. You need to make sure you *use* the tension productively. Set yourself practical tasks to keep yourself busy. Remind yourself that this is *your* exam; you are doing it because *you* have chosen to. Remind yourself too that the tension you are feeling can be a very *productive* force, *helping* you to achieve some difficult learning. Ideally, you learn to live with exam stress and use it to achieve things for yourself.

Your anxiousness may however develop into a pall of gloom which spoils the last part of the course. You may find all your thoughts becoming centered on the exam. In this case, keep talking to other students and to your teacher about your doubt and fears and your plans for tackling them. Talking releases tension and helps you to keep things in perspective.

You may, though, be one of those few students for whom this is not enough. In the period immediately before the exam your anxiety may build up to a point where you can't sleep and your health begins to suffer, or where work, or family and friends begin to be affected. If you find this happening, then go to your doctor for advice. Some people find breathing exercises helpful, or meditation, or some other way of focusing intensively on reducing the physical manifestations of tension. If you feel bad, don't suffer in isolation. Look for help. You will find plenty of suggestions and advice on the internet, particularly on university websites.

Lay awake much of the night trying to remember the name of the guy who did the research on institutions. Of course when I came down at 6:30 on the bottom stair it came back – arrrgggh! Why oh why do I suffer with nerves? Is it the end of the world if I fail? Yes it bloomin' is cos this cost me money!! 'Don't worry mum, you'll be fine', say the kids. 'Thanks' I say, wanting to scream 'how do you know'. There are hundreds of us today, falling apart. But in a few weeks there'll be hundreds saying yippee! Got my pens, got my exam ID, gonna buy some mints – did you know they stimulate the brain?

12.5.5 Checking the arrangements

Because you get so 'geared-up' in the last day or two, you can become quite inattentive to the ordinary details of life. People sometimes make odd mistakes, like turning up for the exam on the wrong day, or at the wrong place. So, it is a good idea to get all the details of the exam sorted out well in advance. You don't want to be worrying about anything trivial on the day. Mark the exam time very clearly on your calendar. You might even consider making a practice journey to the exam centre and finding the room, then you won't have a last-minute panic about which bus to catch, where you left the address of the exam centre, or where the entrance to the building is.

I made myself feel a lot calmer by reminding myself that I'd looked at past papers, and by visiting the exam centre a couple of days before to check out parking/travel timing etc.... all to ensure that I wouldn't be panicking on the day.

12.5.6 On the great day

I was dreaming that I got to the exam centre and had forgotten my ID and had to go all the way back home to get it.

Your dream almost became my reality. My partner gave me a lift into town. Just as we were leaving he said 'have you got everything'. 'Yep, I've got it all, but I'll just check my ID'. I'd only picked up the wrong thing!

On the day itself, try to approach the exam calmly. Go about your normal business of getting up and starting the day. Take a short stroll perhaps, or do a few exercises, to get yourself tuned up and functioning properly. Don't attempt any last-minute revision. Don't even glance over your notes; it will only disturb your carefully stored ideas. Get to the exam centre in good time and keep walking around if you have to wait to get in. Don't let the other candidates disturb you. Remain apart if you need to. When you are in the exam room find your desk and calmly settle yourself in your seat. Set out whatever you have brought with you on the desk and check that you have everything you need. The exam room always seems a strange place, full of people you don't know, all locked obsessively in their own thoughts. Don't let the strangeness distract you, just keep your mind 'ticking over in neutral', ready to slip into gear when the lights change. If you have prepared yourself sensibly there is no point in worrying. In fact, once the exam has started you may find it surprisingly exhilarating and challenging. It's astonishing how much you can do in only three hours when you have keyed yourself up to a peak of mental fitness.

Key points

- In the last day or two, stop trying to revise and concentrate on pulling together what you've already done.

- Get your thinking in before the exam. Work out exactly how you intend to tackle all aspects of the paper, and sketch a plan of how you will use your time in the exam.

- Talk with others if you are getting overstressed.

- Check the practical arrangements for the exam, including travel.

- Keep calm on the exam day. Stop thinking about revision. Let fate take its course.

12.6 Working out your tactics for the exam

It is important to work out in detail what you are going to do in the exam itself. Don't drift towards the exam like a leaf caught in a whirlpool, circling round passively for ages until you are sucked down the hole in a rush. You can't afford to leave everything to chance. You need to work out exactly what has to be done and exactly how you think you will tackle it. If you do this you will improve your performance enormously.

12.6.1 The nature of the task ahead of you

When you enter the exam you have to be ready to work at peak efficiency. You have three hours to make the best show you can of all the work you have done during the course and during the final revision stages. You can't afford to waste time dithering, moping, or staring at the ceiling. You have to have a clear plan of attack on the task in front of you. You may not be able to stick to it, and in the end that may not matter. What is important is that you are clear at all times about what you intend to do next.

In order to give a very practical aspect to this discussion I will assume (as in Box 12.1) a three-hour exam in which you are asked to answer four questions. I will also assume that you can take the questions in any order you like, that you can write any notes and jottings in the exam book, as long as you cross them out afterwards, and that you are allowed only a dictionary in the way of books. If your exam is different, you need to find out *how* it differs, and make the necessary adjustments to what follows.

BOX 12.4 BOOKS IN THE EXAM: A DOUBTFUL PRIVILEGE

Some exams allow you to take in course books or even notes. This is a doubtful privilege. It isn't really consistent with the high speed writing you do in an exam to be thumbing through books and notes and reading them. In some subjects it may be reassuring to know that you can look up a particular formula if you need it. But in essay-based exams you need the ideas in your head, where you can think with them, not scattered around you in books. Moreover, if you tend to be anxious, you may spend far too much time desperately trying to find things, to be sure you have them right. Far better to take the plunge and say 'This is it! I'll press on with what is in my head and hope for the best. If I get some things wrong, so what! It's the argument that's important not details from books.'

12.6.2 Reading the question paper

The exam starts when the invigilator tells you to turn the exam paper over. If you have done your work on past papers, the general appearance of the paper should not be a surprise to you. However, you may find it difficult at first to take in the words, because you are so keyed up. So, although it might seem sensible to read carefully through the whole paper first, you may not be capable of doing that effectively. It may be better to do something more active to get yourself moving.

Certainly it is no bad idea to scan quickly through the questions, putting ticks against 'possibles' and crosses against 'definitely nots'. This will give you a first impression of what is on offer. But don't ponder over every question in detail. Search out the questions you have prepared for. It is desperately risky to let yourself be deflected from a prepared subject on to an unprepared one, just because of the wording of the questions. Your prepared topic may look more difficult to you *because* you know so much about it. Other questions may look easier *because* you aren't clued-up enough to realise their full implications. Don't attempt to 'flannel' your way through an unrevised area. You are much more likely to produce a solid answer on one of your prepared topics, even if you feel unhappy with the question.

12.6.3 How soon to start writing

It may be a good idea to find a question you *know* you are going to attempt and pitch straight into it. If you are inclined to freeze up under pressure, or if your mind tends to go blank, then starting to write can be a good way to get yourself past the opening tensions and into the action. There is no reason to worry about starting your first question before reading the rest of the paper, if you are confident it is on a topic you've revised. Some people prefer to scan through the whole paper first, but if it suits you better to jump straight in, do it. However, you *do* need to think a bit about the wording of the question and jot down some notes before starting to write your answer.

12.6.4 The order in which to take the questions

If you are allowed to tackle questions in any order you like, you may as well follow your own best interests. Some people recommend starting on your very best question, to build up your confidence. Others say take your best question second, when you are nicely warmed up and not so likely to be tempted to run wildly over your time allowance. In any case, it is a good idea to take your best questions earlier rather than later, to make sure that you have enough time to score well. It will also give you confidence and help you to relax into your stride.

12.6.5 Examining the question

See Chapter 11 Section 11.2.1, Thinking about the essay title

As with essays, make a point of underlining the key words in the questions you intend to do. This makes you take a positive approach from the outset, and it focuses your attention on answering the precise question set, rather than producing a string of vaguely relevant information. The words you underline are the ones you will have to think about carefully in deciding what material you can use and how to organise it. If you rush into the question and make mistakes about the issues it addresses you will seriously damage your marks.

12.6.6 Drawing together material to put into your answer

As soon as you have underlined the key words in the question, jot down very quickly those sections of the course you think are intended to be used in answering it. Don't worry at first about *how* to use them. Just write down concepts, theories, examples and names, to reassure yourself that you have plenty of material to work with. (This is where you think back to the summary sheets you produced.) When you have a preliminary list (it may be just five to ten words), you can begin to sort out what to use and what to leave out. Keep in mind that exam questions *always* ask for material from the course. Note plenty down at this stage, because once you start to construct an answer to the question, your mind will be fully occupied and you may then find that an important part of your argument has completely slipped from your mind. A single word is usually enough to trigger your memory and enable you to retrieve the point. Work fast and uncritically to get a good list of potential material and don't hesitate to make a mess of your exam booklet. You can cross out all of your jottings later.

12.6.7 Strike a balance between what you know and what the question asks for

As you answer a question, you have to steer a course between two equally dangerous traps. One is that you become so mesmerised by the question that you lose confidence in the fact that the answer to it lies in the course material. Then you may stop believing that if you search properly you will find the material you need amongst all that you have stored in your head. If that happens you may be tempted to bluster your way through, trying to answer 'off the top of your head'. The opposite trap is that your mind becomes so fixed on all the material you have recently stored in it that you spill your knowledge all over the pages of the exam booklet, regardless of relevance to the question you are answering. Both are very easy traps to fall into. The approach I set out below sets out to play these two temptations off against each other.

My suggestion is that you move quickly back and forth between the question and the knowledge stored in your mind. In this way you can make sure that each has due influence. Choose the question and do a quick 'first take' on what it is about. Then leave the question and go to your knowledge of the course to jot down some possible content. Return to the question to get it more sharply in focus. Then go back to your list of course material to knock it into the shape you need. Finally, with a quick look back at the question, you start answering it in a way which brings the question and the knowledge together (see Figure 12.3).

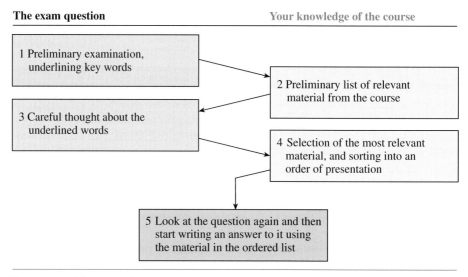

Figure 12.3 Five steps in preparing an answer to an exam question

12.6.8 Taking time to plan your answer

See Chapter 12 Section 12.3, What to avoid

But will you have time to spare for all of these preparations? It takes a lot of nerve to spend precious exam time preparing your answers. Bearing in mind the comments of examiners on 'undisciplined' answers earlier in this chapter it is time well spent, but how long should you spend? You will have to judge this for yourself, but between five and ten minutes is a reasonable target. If you don't sketch out a plan, you will run the risk of 'going blank' in the middle of an answer. Writing tends to absorb the whole of your attention, so when you get to the end of a paragraph you can find that the next point has gone. Your argument jerks to a halt and you are too keyed up to retrace your plans. At this point you will waste far more time than writing a plan would have done. And your answer will be poor into the bargain.

After my previous exam I realised how important sketching answer plans is. Today I spent time on mind maps etc. Much better first essay, passable second, third fair too. Just wish I'd practised handwriting. I'm so used to cutting and pasting text on the computer.

12.6.9 Sticking to the point

In your enthusiasm to show your knowledge of the course, don't forget to keep to the question. Exam markers are searching for points which relate directly to the question; they are not pleased by having to wade through paragraphs of unsorted and uncensored material. You begin to *lose* marks rather than *gain* them if you give the impression that you are uncritically throwing course material before the examiners' eyes in the hope that you will fool them into thinking you know what you are talking about. Of course, you must be sure to draw in plenty of material from the course, but you must always do it with a clear purpose, so you don't appear to be padding-out your answers, or 'busking' to conceal your ignorance. Anything you write that is not relevant to the question is just wasting your time.

12.6.10 Sticking to your plan

Keep the time plan you prepared before the exam (see Figure 12.2) in front of you at all times, and keep checking your watch. You can afford to slip five or even ten minutes off schedule, but be very wary of getting further out of line. If you find yourself falling behind time with an answer, draw it to a close as quickly as you can. Don't leave the question half finished in the hope that you will have time to come back to it. Most likely you won't, since you are running late, but more importantly, by then you will have lost your train of thought. Make the best of what you've achieved thus far and write out whatever conclusions you can manage to draw while the question is still hot in your mind.

12.6.11 When to plan your later questions

In the past I've got panicky and while I'm answering one question, I'm wondering what I can write for the next, which ISN'T GOOD. So I cover up the other questions.

When you have your first question under your belt, it is a good idea to 'rough out' plans for all your other answers, before writing out the next. The reason for this is that you need time on your side when you are planning. It is very hard to think straight in the final stages of the exam, as you become mesmerised by the approaching deadline. All too often the last answer represents the desperate casting about of a mind which has long passed beyond the stage of thinking coherently. *You will probably be able to write at your fastest during the last hour of the exam provided you have planned* what to say. So do the thinking which requires calmer analysis in the second quarter of the exam, when you have passed through the initial tension and have settled into a steady working mode. Then you will be ready to take advantage of your 'manic' energy in the final stages, when you may be able to get reams of useful material down.

12.6.12 What to do if your time runs out

If, in spite of all your plans, you do end up with too little time for your last question, it helps to write out notes showing how your answer would have developed if you had time. If you present an answer *entirely* in note form, you are unlikely to scrape a pass. However, if you have *part* of an answer already written out, some clear notes for the rest of your answer might convince the marker that you are worthy of a reasonable mark. However it would scarcely be fair on the other candidates to allow you the benefit of the extra time you spent on the earlier questions *and* a generous benefit of the doubt on an uncompleted question. The marker will probably give you *some* credit for good notes, but basically you need to write out an answer in full to be in the running for a reasonable mark. Make sure you *don't* run out of time!

12.6.13 Presentation

Most people write less tidily and legibly than their best in exams. But do try to do what you can to make your work legible. Start each question on a new page and number the questions clearly. Draw a line across the page between your jottings and the essay itself. If your handwriting or your written English is shaky, it is too late to worry, you can only work to improve them gradually over your years of study. In any case do try to remember your script marker a little as you write and avoid being so overwhelmed by the need for speed that your writing descends to a desperate scrawl.

Key points

- Scan through the paper finding the questions you have prepared for.

- Start writing soon, if it helps to 'unfreeze' you.

- Take your best question first (or second).

- As you tackle a question:
  1. examine the wording carefully
  2. very quickly list some relevant points from the course
  3. move back and forth between the question and your list as you sketch an outline plan for your answer
  4. take the time to plan your answer before you start writing
  5. remember that everything you write should be relevant to the specific question asked.

- Consider planning later questions in advance.

- Stick to your time plan for the exam.

- Don't run wildly over your deadlines.

- Do your best to write legibly

12.7 Will you do yourself justice in the exam?

Of *course* you ought to pass the exam (assuming you have been getting on all right with the course itself). Really you should do about as well in the exam as you have been doing with the course itself. In principle, the exam is just another way of confirming what your coursework has already shown. But although this is more or less how things turn out for most people, it is not so in every case. There are at least four possibilities:

1   Some people do better in exams than in their coursework. Exams actually bring out the best in them. Perhaps you are one of these (or could become one with a good exam technique).

2   Many people do just about as well in the exam as in their coursework. This is obviously fine and as it should be.

3   Some people tend to perform rather less well than in their coursework (scoring say 10 to 20 per cent lower). They pass, but at a lower level than they had reasonably hoped for. If you are one of these people, then this chapter is especially for you. Every time you have an exam read it to remind yourself of all the practical ways in which you can get a better performance out of yourself.

4   A few people have a tendency to come crashing down, way below their potential. If you are one of them, then I hope this chapter has been helpful, but I strongly recommend that you also seek support and advice. There is no point in struggling away on your own if you persistently ruin your good work when it comes to exams.

Whichever of these categories you think you fall into, you have nothing to lose by thinking positively. *Of course* you deserve to pass. You will forget important things in the exam, but so will everyone else. Your exam answers won't look as impressive as your essays, but the same is true for everyone else. Your scrambled efforts are only going to be compared with other scrappy efforts. So don't let the exam intimidate you. *Be realistic!* You are *likely* to pass. Yes it *is* a chore. Yes you *will* have to focus a lot of attention and energy on it. But you *will* also learn a lot in the process. And if you follow all the suggestions in this chapter, you *can* make yourself into a well tuned exam *performer*, achieving feats way beyond your normal everyday powers. Who knows, perhaps the exam might turn out to be the highlight of your course after all.

Postscript

You've reached the end of the book. But of course you haven't reached the end of becoming a better student. That process never ends. When you think you have your note-taking technique honed to a smoothly functioning routine, you find it has become too mechanical – you take too many notes, or the wrong notes; or you encounter a book that defeats your routine. Or you begin to think that you've cracked it with writing, but you come to an essay that somehow won't come right, or a tutor who criticises the very things you thought you were good at. At times like these, when your studies knock you back, you'll find it useful to return to this book and revisit basic principles. What's more, many things which you've taken in at one level will acquire fresh significance as you advance to further stages in your studies. Coming back to the book afresh you will be able to extract another set of meanings built upon your greater experience as a student. So don't set this book aside for ever. Keep it where you'll be able to find it. Learning to study is a lifelong process.

COVENTRY UNIVERSITY LONDON CAMPUS
East India House,
109-117 Middlesex Street, London, E1 7JF
Tel: 020 7247 3666 | Fax: 020 7375 3048
www.coventry.ac.uk/londoncampus

APPENDIX THE SECRETS OF HAPPINESS

By RICHARD LAYARD

1   There is a paradox at the heart of our civilisation. Individuals want more income. Yet as society has got richer, people have not become happier. Over the past 50 years we have got better homes, more clothes, longer holidays and, above all, better health. Yet surveys show clearly that happiness has not increased in the US, Japan, Continental Europe or Britain.

2   By happiness I mean feeling good – enjoying life and feeling it is wonderful. And by unhappiness I mean feeling bad and wishing things were different. Most people find it easy to say how good they are feeling, and in social surveys such questions get 99 per cent response rates – much higher than the average.

[...]

3   It is true that, within any particular society at any particular moment, rich people are on average happier than poorer ones. For example, 41 per cent of people in the top quarter of incomes are 'very happy', compared with only 26 per cent of those in the bottom quarter of incomes. The problem is that, over the years, the proportions in each group who are very happy have not changed at all although the real incomes in each group have risen hugely. This is true of all the main western countries.

4   We also know that clinical depression, assessed professionally through population surveys, has risen in most countries. A survey from London University's Institute of Education, out this month, shows that as many as 29 per cent of women aged 30 in 2000 reported suffering trouble with nerves or feeling low, depressed or sad; the comparable figure in a similar survey, among those aged 36 in 1982, was just 16 per cent. Researchers disagree over the size of the increase, but nobody believes depression has diminished, despite the much greater ease of our material life.

5   Further evidence comes from comparisons between different countries. These show that, where average income per person is less than $15,000 a year – in other words, where many people are near the breadline – extra money really does make people happier. But comparing countries where average income is above that level, happiness seems to be independent of income. For example, the average American is much richer than the average Icelander or Dane, but also less happy.

6   Why is this? Clearly people are comparing their income with some norm and this norm is rising all the time. Thus from 1946–86, the US Gallup poll asked people, 'What is the smallest amount of money that a family of four needs to get along in this community?' It turns out that, as actual average incomes rose, so did the income that people felt was needed – and in fact this 'needed' income grew in direct proportion to actual income. Likewise, when people were asked 'Are you satisfied with your financial position?', the proportion who said they were 'pretty well satisfied' fell, despite enormous economic growth.

7   Two things drive up the norm with which people compare their incomes. One is the income that they themselves have experienced – which habituates them to higher standards of living. And the other is the income that others get, and which they try to rival or outdo.

8   Habituation is a basic psychological phenomenon. It works both up and down: you adjust to good things and to bad. The clearest evidence that you adjust to income comes from asking people with different levels of actual income what income they would consider satisfactory. Typically, the income that people say is satisfactory rises by almost 50p for every extra pound that they have actually acquired. A whole range of studies shows that people adjust their requirements to their recent experience and that they are constantly surprised by this. People overestimate the extent to which the new house or new car will, once they have got used to it, make them happier.

9   People also adjust their requirements in response to what other people have: keeping up with (or trying to outdo) the Joneses. [...] When people compare their wages, it is generally with people close to themselves, rather than with film stars or paupers. What matters is what happens to your 'reference group' because what your reference group gets might have been feasible for you, while what David Beckham gets is not. Much of the most intense rivalry, therefore, is within organisations and within families. In organisations, calm can often be maintained only by keeping people's salaries secret. In families, it has been found that the more your spouse earns, the less satisfied you are with your own job. And among women, if your sister's husband is earning more than your own husband earns, you are more likely to go out to work.

10 Change the reference group and you may well change levels of happiness. In the eastern part of Germany, the living standards of those in work have soared since 1990, but their level of happiness has plummeted. Why? Because the east Germans now compare themselves with west Germans rather than with other countries in the old Soviet bloc. Again, women's happiness in the US has fallen relative to men's as their pay and opportunities have improved. The most likely explanation is that women now compare themselves more directly with men than they used to, and therefore focus more on the gaps that still exist.

11 But we do not find the same effects when we ask people about non-monetary benefits. A sample of Harvard graduate students was

asked which of two worlds they would prefer: one where they got $50,000 a year and others got $25,000, or one where they got $100,000 and others got $250,000. The majority preferred the first world. They were happier with lower income, provided their relative position improved. Then the students were asked to choose between a world where they got two weeks holiday while others got half that and a world where they got four weeks holiday while others got twice that. Most preferred the second world. In other words, people are much less rivalrous when it comes to leisure. The rat race is for income and when each of us works more and earns more, this imposes a genuine loss of happiness on others. It is a form of pollution.

12 So now we can see why happiness increases so little when countries get richer. People get hurt as their needs rise in ways they did not foresee – a form of self-pollution. And they get hurt by the extra income that others are earning – pollution by others.

13 The policy implications are dramatic. For example, if much of the extra income (say 60p in the pound) brings no overall increase in happiness, we should reduce the incentive to acquire it. It would therefore be efficient to have a marginal tax rate of say 60p in the pound – corresponding (on the principle that the polluter should pay) to the 60p worth of pollution caused by the extra pound that is earned. Up to now we have apologised for taxation. The standard economic analysis says that taxation reduces work effort, which is true. But it also says that it is inefficient to reduce work effort, and our analysis shows that, if the aim is to increase human happiness, this is false.

14 Indeed taxation is one of the most important institutions we have for preserving a sensible balance between work and leisure. We should be proud of it and stand up for it. As it happens, 60 per cent is the typical level of marginal taxation in Europe if you allow for direct and indirect taxes. I suspect that, in some almost unconscious way, the electorate now understands that the scramble to spend more is partially self-defeating and that this explains why people are more favourable to public expenditure. But the time is ripe to make the argument explicit [...]

[The article goes on to discuss other implications of treating happiness as an important policy goal, then concludes with this paragraph.]

15 The scientific study of happiness is only just beginning. It should become a central topic in social science. But for the moment I would recommend four principles. Don't apologise for taxes; foster security; fight glaring evils such as depression; and discourage social comparison.

[Professor Lord Layard is co-director of the Centre for Economic Performance at the London School of Economics. This extract, from an article in *The New Statesman* of 3 March 2003, is based on his Lionel Robbins Lectures, given at the LSE on 3, 4 and 5 March 2003. The full text is now available from http://cep.lse.ac.uk/layard/RL362.pdf.]

Acknowledgements

Grateful acknowledgement is made to the following sources for permission to reproduce material within this product.

Text

Appendix 1: Taken from an article which first appeared in the *New Statesman*, 3rd March 2003, by permission of New Statesman Limited.

Figures

Various figures from the Office for National Statistics. Crown copyright material is reproduced under Class Licence Number C01W0000065 with the permission of the Controller of HMSO and the Queen's Printer for Scotland; Figure 1.1: Smith, M. K., (2001) 'David A Kolb on experiential learning', *the encyclopedia of informal education*, http://www.infed.org/b-explrn.htm; Figure 8.1: Swansea 5 day forecast. Copyright © Met Office, 2004; Figure 8.3: Caledonian MacBrayne Ltd, www.calmac.co.uk

INDEX

visualisation, in memorisation 146
vocabulary, using thesauri 61
'voice'
    academic 95, 162
    essay writing 276, 317–18

W
weather forecast, numbers in 194–5
web addresses, filing of 227–8
websites 43
    value checklist 238–40
    see also databases; online
      information
word processing 55
    basics of 57–8
    in essay writing 321
    grammar checking 265
    labelling your work 59
    layout of documents 60
    more advanced 62–3
    outliners 132–3, 304–5, 307, 353
    protecting your work 59
    spell-checker 60–1, 270
    using shortcuts 61–2
words
    choosing 272
    counting 61
    link 322–5
    looking up 106–7
    singular and plural 212, 267

unfamiliar 83, 106–8
writing your own 96, 278–9, 293
your own and other people's
    276–9, 282
work habits 34–5, 36–7
workshops 161
World Database of Happiness 229–31
writing
    challenges of 96–7, 108–10,
      296–7
    clarity of 270–1, 294
    different kinds of 247
    experience of 329–34
    expressing ideas 317–21
    getting help with 248
    importance of 246
    judging of 251, 330
    learning through 96
    numbers in 193
    open attitude to 319
    popular 274–5
    professional style of 82–9,
      108–10, 247, 282–8
    for readers 257, 258, 274–6, 333
    self-revelation 278–9, 330–1
    taking control 334–5
    thinking process 63
    'voice' 276, 317–18
    see also academic style of
      writing; essays